W9-DIU-229

A LEGISLATURE COMES OF AGE

A Legislature
Comes of Age:
Hong Kong's Search for Influence
and Identity

Kathleen Cheek-Milby

HONG KONG, OXFORD, AND NEW YORK
OXFORD UNIVERSITY PRESS
1995

Oxford University Press

Oxford New York
Athens Auckland Bangkok Bombay
Calcutta Cape Town Dar es Salaam Delhi
Florence Hong Kong Istanbul Karachi
Kuala Lumpur Madras Madrid Melbourne
Mexico City Nairobi Paris Singapore
Taipei Tokyo Toronto

and associated companies in
Berlin Ibadan

Oxford is a trade mark of Oxford University Press

First published 1995

Published in the United States
by Oxford University Press, New York

© *Oxford University Press 1995*

British Library Cataloguing in Publication Data
available

Library of Congress Cataloging-in-Publication Data

Cheek-Milby, Kathleen.
A legislature comes of age: Hong Kong's search for influence and
identity/Kathleen Cheek-Milby.
p. cm.
Includes bibliographical references and index.
ISBN 0–19–585955–3
1. Hong Kong. Legislative Council—History. 2. Hong Kong.
Legislative Council. 3. Legislators—Hong Kong—Interviews.
I. Title.
JQ677.C54 1995 328.5125'07—dc20 95–6465 CIP

Printed in Hong Kong
Published by Oxford University Press (China) Ltd
18/F Warwick House, Taikoo Place, 979 King's Road, Quarry Bay,
Hong Kong

To Jim, J.D., and Nicholas

Acknowledgements

During my years of research into Hong Kong's Legislative Council, I have accumulated nearly as many debts as I have data. This study was originally conceived in 1984 when the Council's proceedings were formal, polite, and fairly ritualistic. I was interested at that point in understanding why Hong Kong's Legislative Council had not evolved according to the familiar pattern of colonial legislative development. I also determined that the best way to study an institution which had so few behavioural records, such as votes on legislation or even open deliberations in panels and committees, would be to interview its members about their role concepts. The research design, therefore, owes much to the pioneer work of John C. Wahlke, Heinz Eulau, William Buchanan, and LeRoy C. Ferguson, authors of *The Legislative System*. Special tribute also goes to Chong Lim Kim, Joel D. Barkan, Ilter Turan, and Malcolm E. Jewell, authors of *The Legislative Connection: The Politics of Representation in Kenya, Korea, and Turkey*, who allowed access to their questionnaire design.

As events unfolded during that year, it soon became apparent that the Legislative Council would be the locus of evolutionary, if not revolutionary, changes as it was transformed into a more representative institution to ensure accountability in the post-1997 government. The tremendous alterations that followed, in terms of both its membership composition and, consequently, its function made the legislature a challenging institution in which to conduct research. Even as its proceedings became more open, and its voting record more divisive, the original design to investigate the Council according to its members' role concepts was retained as the best way in which to provide information about the motivation behind all of the new legislative activities. Further, I believed that in light of the rapidity of the transformations, only a longitudinal study would enable a more accurate study of role trends.

Since the bulk of the 173 interviews with legislators, staff, constituents, and informed observers were held under the conditions of promised anonymity, the people who did the most to write this book will have to accept my thanks in the impersonal form of this research. In the process of conducting the research, however, there are several who must receive special thanks. I would like to thank the editors of Oxford University Press for their long-standing encouragement. I am indebted to the University of Hong Kong, which provided a Strategic Research Grant enabling me to employ research assistants: Carmen Yip, Glendy Lee Yuk Kit, and Fong Yiu Chak. I would like especially to thank Andrew Lin, who so patiently assisted in the data analysis. The Centre of Asian Studies, under the direction of Professor Edward Chen, provided invaluable assistance in securing interviews through its endorsement of this project. For their willingness to provide material and insights into their work, I would like to especially thank the staff at OMELCO. I am deeply indebted to friends and colleagues who have read the manuscript: Diane D'Jaen, Ann Pierson, Joanne Fallon, Professor David Clark, Dr Miron Mushkat, Professor Ian Scott, and Dr Norman Miners. The latter two, Professor Scott and Dr Miners of the University of Hong Kong, deserve special tribute: Professor Scott for allowing me the use of the facilities of the Department of Political Science during the second phase of interviewing, which was undertaken by commuting from Tokyo to Hong Kong, but especially Dr Miners for allowing me access to his volume of materials on the Legislative Council and sharing with me his unrivalled knowledge and insights into the workings of the Hong Kong government. Finally, this book is dedicated to my husband and sons for their steadfast encouragement and support.

Preface

The last decade of the twentieth century will best be remembered for a series of political transformations resulting from a globalization of political values. This globalization has been characterized by an emerging consensus on values.[1] In terms of political faith, something like the Reformation has occurred. The Cold War era saw the upholders of the values of capitalist democracy and communist totalitarianism at odds with one another. But a new unity, indifferent to country, race, or religion, is now evolving. With it comes the prospect of a world society of peoples with order resting as much on shared values as on alliances of states.[2] At the heart of this change is a unified political format rooted in the liberal-democratic order, but based as much on the value of glasnost as equality and social justice. Moreover, the tide of democratic change sweeping the world has not occurred in the aftermath of a destructive war, but rather during an unprecedented half-century of global peace.[3]

The most powerful impetus for this transformation has been the intensification of global communication and economic integration.[4] Whereas democracies have thrived amid the advent of the 'global village' through mediums such as Cable Network News (CNN), dictatorships have found it increasingly difficult to remain isolated and deny their citizens knowledge of world events,[5] and the prosperity of individual nations has to a large degree become dependent on the prosperity of others. The combination of easy communication, unprecedented prosperity, and peace has allowed ideas to flow more freely through the world than ever before. This has had a revolutionary effect on certain countries where authoritarian governments have found they have to educate their populations in order to compete in the global economy, only to discover this eventually has led their people to question their legitimacy. Democracy can be seen as a process of communication itself, an instrument of choice offering alternative solutions to a myriad of developmental problems.[6]

While the most dramatic examples of these late-twentieth century transformations are seen in Eastern Europe and the former Soviet Union, Asia has also seen remarkable, albeit more incremental, political change. Many of the region's fledging democracies are striving to move beyond the rule of men to the rule of law. Countries such as Japan and India first embraced democratic ideals shortly after the Second World War. More recent examples of liberalization and democratization are the Philippines, South Korea, and Taiwan, where electoral reform has widened peoples' power.[7]

Yet this transformation has not, as some have proclaimed, led to an 'end of history'.[8] There remain examples of intransigence in this sea of change, most noteworthily a monolithic communist state, China, and a relic of British colonial rule, Hong Kong.[9] China proved a critical exception to this political trend, embarking on a course of political repression graphically demonstrated in the Tiananmen Square massacre of June 1989. Moreover, without the need for a global survey, many of the contentious political issues at the end of the twentieth century are being aired in the debate over the political future of Hong Kong.

Hong Kong has been a British Crown Colony since 1843. From the outset of its development, Hong Kong has been characterized by sharp contrasts. Home to 6 million people, the territory is only 404 square miles, most of that being mountainous and unsuitable for development. Although it is the world's tenth largest economy, almost half of its inhabitants live in public housing. A barren rock taken over by the British to promote their interests in the Far East, its people are now on average almost as rich as the British and 30 to 40 times richer than the people of China. While for years it retained the world's highest sustained rate of economic growth, Hong Kong's prosperity is, nonetheless, extremely vulnerable: no other country in the world is as dependent on overseas trade; the territory has to import over 80 percent of its food, practically all of the raw materials for its industries, and 100 percent of its fuel. With only 12 percent of its land arable, it is dependent on China for the bulk of its water supply. In sum, Hong Kong, while extremely prosperous, is critically dependent on sustained demand from its major markets as well as support from China.

It is ironic that one of the world's most rapidly growing, free-

wheeling capitalistic economies has also had one of the world's
most stagnant political systems. Up to 1985 its colonial government, a nineteenth-century relic, had a royal governor, appointed
by Britain, who possessed such pervasive power that he appointed
all of the members of his executive and legislative councils, controlled their agenda, and if need be, ignored their advice. While
many scholars have argued that a capitalistic economy and political
democracy are not only mutually compatible, but mutually dependent, Hong Kong provides a critical exception to this rule.

In 1984 Hong Kong's political paralysis ended. In that year, the
British and Chinese governments signed the Joint Declaration on
the Future of Hong Kong. The agreement provided that from 30
June 1997, Hong Kong would become a special administrative
region of China. It would be governed by its own inhabitants and
would retain its capitalistic lifestyle. The form and extent of its
actual autonomy are being determined by a series of initiatives by
both the British and Chinese governments during the transitional
period. The centre of these initiatives has been the territory's legislature, the Legislative Council. This transformation has proved to
be unique, not only because Hong Kong is a capitalist, colonial
enclave soon to be incorporated into an authoritarian, communist
state, but also because of the speed with which the reforms have
been undertaken. Changes that have normally taken decades to
occur in other colonies were condensed into 13 years. That the
Legislative Council should become the locus for democratic transformation is not surprising, since the political values that are being
globalized, such as equality, the rule of law, civil liberty, and justice,
are typically promoted as well as promulgated in legislative institutions. Indeed, the extent to which a country is democratic is often
measured by how it selects members of its legislature. For it is
the legislature, more than any other institution of modern government, which best maximizes representation, accountability, and
responsiveness.

This book investigates the rapid metamorphosis of Hong Kong's
Legislative Council, and in so doing attempts to evaluate its progress in the context of the globalization of political values. To
reveal the focus of the study, Chapter 1 introduces legislative functions and roles and, in so doing, provides a basis from which to
evaluate the research design for the study. While this overview
emphasizes what the Legislative Council has in common with other
legislative bodies, we then move on to consider its uniqueness

by looking at the development of the British colonial legislative council.

Chapter 2 reveals that while most of Britain's colonial legislatures followed a similar evolutionary path, it was clear from the outset that Hong Kong's Legislative Council was not going to deviate much from its original nineteenth-century design. Determining why this was so yields a clearer understanding of its current restraints and affords a keener appreciation of its recent dramatic evolution.

Although the Legislative Council did not undergo the typical decolonization process, incremental but noteworthy changes have occurred. Chapter 3 explores the development of the Council from its conception in 1844 to the eve of the Sino-British agreement in 1984. This survey highlights one of the many ironies of Hong Kong politics, namely that the centre of tremendous change in the coming thirteen years was to be an institution noteworthy for its stability and durability.

Chapter 4 traces the dramatic evolution of the legislature since the signing of the Sino-British agreement and considers the Joint Declaration, internal governmental reports, and the future constitution of Hong Kong, the Basic Law. The chapter presents the reader with a description of the political context within which the legislature is currently operating.

The effect of these reforms is explored in the next three chapters, which investigate the contemporary operation of the legislature. The survey commences with a look at the staff support of the Legislative Council. Chapter 5 investigates the evolution of the legislative staff agency, the Office of the (non-governmental) Members of the Executive and Legislative Councils (OMELCO), which has been transformed from a simple complaint-processing bureau to a complex staff agency.

Chapter 6 reviews how the Legislative Council has performed the traditional legislative functions of policy making, representation, and systems maintenance. Analysis of these functions is divided into two periods, pre-1984 and 1985 to the present, to demonstrate how the changes in legislative membership since the Sino-British agreement have had a dramatic impact on how the legislature functions.

Chapter 7 explores these changes from a more personal perspective by investigating the role perceptions of members of the legislature. The measurement of legislative roles has become the most popular method to ascertain the functions of legislatures, the degree of consensus held by the members over various legislative features, and hence the institutionalization and durability of the legislature over time. The roles of Hong Kong's legislators were identified by extensive interviews with the members in 1987–8 and 1992–3. They reveal a body of legislators both constrained and creatively challenged by Hong Kong's political future.

Finally, Chapter 8 summarizes the findings and provides a prognosis for the legislature to 1997 and beyond as the Legislative Council attempts to define Hong Kong's autonomy within communist China.

KATHLEEN CHEEK-MILBY
Institute of Pacific Rim Studies
Temple University Japan
Tokyo, Japan
June 1993

Contents

Tables

Figures

A LEGISLATURE COMES OF AGE: HONG KONG'S SEARCH FOR INFLUENCE AND IDENTITY

1 Introduction: The Study of Hong Kong's Legislative Council

On 1 July 1997, Hong Kong, the largest and most important of the remaining British colonies, will revert to the People's Republic of China. According to the Joint Declaration on the Future of Hong Kong,[1] signed in Beijing on 19 December 1984, the territory will become a special administrative region of China.[2] The accord not only provided for a transfer of sovereignty, it also promised a large measure of local autonomy in governmental affairs and a 50-year guarantee that Hong Kong's capitalist system and lifestyle would remain unchanged. The future special administrative region is the ultimate political paradox: a place where 'Hong Kong people will rule Hong Kong' even though they do not possess sovereignty,[3] with a subordinate political structure completely distinct from, as well as ideologically incompatible with, its super-ordinate structure. This is the 'one country–two systems' concept:[4] an experiment unique in contemporary political evolution.

The extent of Hong Kong's autonomy within China's orbit will depend primarily upon the representativeness, responsiveness, and power of the Hong Kong legislature. For while the Joint Declaration provides that the Hong Kong special administrative region will be vested with executive, legislative, and independent judicial power, China will exercise pervasive power in deciding who will occupy positions in the executive and judicial branches. China will appoint the Chief Executive, who will appoint members of the judiciary, and the principal officers of his government.[5] Composition of the legislature, however, will be decided solely by the result of 'elections'. Thus, it is commonly assumed that the most effective check on Chinese influence will be the legislature.

When the Joint Declaration was signed in 1984, however, there was no strong legislative tradition in the colony. Typical of past British Crown Colonies,[6] the legislature was an executive-dominated body, both in form and function. It was composed of members who were appointed by the Governor rather than elected by the people. Moreover, for most of the Colony's history, the number of official (civil servant) members was greater than the number of unofficial (non-civil servant) members, which ensured that all executive initiatives could be enacted.[7] In addition, the power of the legislature to serve as a counterbalance to the executive was weakened by the stipulations that no bill could become law without the Governor's assent and that any measure involving public revenues required the Governor's approval before it could be considered by the legislature. Yet these constraints were exercised within a political domain dominated by British democratic values. So, although structurally the government was autocratic, in practice it worked through a process of 'consultation' and 'consensus'.[8] With the agreement to transfer sovereignty to China, a country not noted for its democratic practices, it quickly became clear that dramatic changes in the Legislative Council were necessary to guarantee some measure of local autonomy in the future. As one commentator noted, 'For there to be no change for fifty years after 1997, there must be change before it'.[9]

The composition rather than power of the legislature has proved to be the key political issue during the transitional years. It has been the main subject of two government reviews[10] as well as the key issue during the drafting of the future constitution, the Basic Law.[11] Moreover, the associated public debate has been the most extensive in Hong Kong's history.

Reforms first undertaken in 1985 created four types of legislative councillors: officials (civil servants), appointed, electoral college (selected by members of the District Boards, and the Urban and Regional Councils), and functional (representing members of various occupational groups). The first elected members of the Council were chosen from a narrow electorate; 24,803 votes were cast in the functional constituencies and only 403 in the electoral college, representing less than 1 per cent of the Hong Kong population. A 1988 review led to the abolition of the electoral college and the creation of nine double-seat geographical constituencies that directly elected eighteen members to the legislature in 1991.[12] In that election, a total of 750,467 voters cast ballots in the electoral districts and 22,919 individuals voted in the functional constituencies, reflecting less than 13 per cent of the public.

The Basic Law, promulgated in 1990, establishes the future constitutional framework for the territory's government after 1997. It provides that the first Legislative Council be composed of sixty members. Of these, twenty will be directly elected, thirty will be returned from functional constituencies, and ten will be selected by a newly formed election committee.[13] By the year 2003, the legislature will be composed of thirty functionally based members and thirty elected from geographic districts. Ultimately, the Basic Law promises that all members will be elected by universal suffrage, although a date is not specified.[14]

In October 1992, Governor Chris Patten, working within the confines of the Basic Law, proposed to broaden substantially the electoral basis for future legislators by creating nine new functional constituencies for the 1995 election. These constituencies would represent broad sectors such as manufacturing and 'import/export' and thereby provide a vote for every one of Hong Kong's 2.7 million workers. Furthermore, he proposed that directly elected members of the local district boards make up the electoral committee that would select an additional ten members of the Legislative Council. All these initiatives are reflected in Table 1.1.

With the creation of new types of legislative councillors, the debate has intensified over what is the best composition of the legislature. Implicit in the debate is the assumption that the method of selection determines the type of legislator. In other words, the legislator's conception of legislative responsibilities and view of the function of the legislature—his or her role concepts—is assumed to

Table 1.1 Composition of the Legislative Council, 1984–2003

	1984	1985	1988	1991	1995	1999	2003
Officials	29	11	11	3	—	—	—
Appointed members	29	22	20	18	—	—	—
Functional constituency members	—	12	14	21	30	30	30
Electoral college members	—	12	12	—	—	—	—
Directly elected members	—	—	—	18	20	24	30
Electoral Comittee members	—	—	—	—	10	6	—
TOTAL	59[a]	57[a]	57[a]	60[b]	60	60	60

Notes: Figures for 1995, 1999, and 2003 are drawn from the Patten proposals of 1992. [a] Total includes the Governor, who served as president. [b] Appointed member who was deputy president was eventually elected president in 1993.

determine subsequent legislative behaviour, which in turn has a crucial impact upon Hong Kong's future stability and prosperity. The aim of this study is to build upon this assumption by investigating the current composition of Hong Kong's Legislative Council.[15] It examines who is in the legislature and employs role analysis to reveal the beliefs and behaviour of legislators during a period of rapid development and challenge. In so doing, it is hoped that the findings will provide guidance to those who must determine the optimal functioning and framework of the future special administrative region. In addition, the study also seeks to add data to the growing body of comparative literature on legislatures, their functions, and the roles of their members. A brief literature review of some previous legislative research provides the context for this study. This review first takes a macroscopic perspective of the functions of legislatures, then narrows the focus to the microscopic by looking at the roles of individual legislators.

The Functions of Legislatures

The study of legislatures has been noted to pose the most 'fascinating problem of all structures of government' as they are the most 'decried and revered' of all institutions of government.[16] The form and function of the legislature have been among the oldest and most important concerns of political philosophy. Aristotle suggested that a nation should be ruled by laws, not men. It was upon this basic concept that ideas about the functions of government developed. A precursor of legislatures as deliberative bodies was first seen in pre-Christian Greece and Rome where special assemblies were chosen to make law for the entire community. The most dramatic evolution of the legislative institution occurred in thirteenth-century England, where a parliament, in the form of an assembly of knights and burgesses, was summoned by the monarch so that he could consult them on taxation issues.[17] By the end of the seventeenth century, the English parliament had evolved to the point that the monarch was dependent upon it for funds of revenue and appropriation. It essentially won the right 'to exercise exclusive power to enact legislation'.[18] The first function of legislatures, then, was to make law.

The idea of an autonomous legislative power is dependent on the idea that law could be made by human agency, and that there was a real power to make law, or to legislate. To legislate evolved from declaratory law (clarifying the laws of God and nature, not creating them) to the notion, recognized by the seventeenth century, that new law could be made by Parliament. The subsequent requirement that the monarch be limited to the execution of law was the beginning of the notion of separate functions of government. It was only when 'law' was understood as something that was man-made, conceived to solve contemporary problems, that the power to legislate was recognized as a vital function requiring the creation of an autonomous legislative body. The growth of positive law came at the expense of divine and natural law. It promoted the idea that human will working through legislative councils could amend the foundations of society. This, then, was the beginning of the sovereignty of the legislature.[19]

The subsequent structuring of the legislature in Britain and its colonies developed under the influence of philosophers such as John Locke and Baron de Montesquieu. Locke emphasized the 'supremacy' of the legislative power relative to the executive: 'There can be but one supream [sic] power, which is the legislative, to which all the rest are and must be subordinate'.[20] He concluded that the executive branch must be subordinate to the legislature, 'for what can give Laws to another, must needs be superior to him'.[21] Montesquieu, on the other hand, argued that an additional function of the legislature was to serve as a check on the powers of the executive.[22]

But the era of the legislature's supremacy over the executive in seventeenth-century England, as in other Western democracies in the nineteenth century, was short-lived. From the exaltation of legislatures as the basis of liberalism and democracy, analysts began to talk of the 'decline of legislatures' when studies revealed their general ineffectiveness. Among the first to identify this functional decline was Lord Bryce, who noted with respect to the United States Congress that 'legislation on public matters is scanty in quantity and generally mediocre in quality'.[23] Lowell found similar problems with legislatures in France, Italy, Germany, and Switzerland.[24] Ironically, at the same time that this ineffectiveness was being revealed, new legislative institutions were spreading throughout Europe and Latin America. Yet their growth 'seemed to be coupled with disillusionment about their political effectiveness'.[25] The decline thesis took on a new meaning by the mid-twentieth century as a number of 'rubber stamp' assemblies developed in communist countries, which became mere parodies of deliberative bodies.[26] Further, after the Second World War the newly emergent Third World countries created legislatures, but they often appeared to be 'decorative' rather than functional in nature.[27] In sum, during the past century, Western scholars have been asking if legislatures can survive, suggesting that legislatures have lost their ability to make law to the executive, party organizations, and to the bureaucracy.[28] It has also been argued that the organization and procedures of legislatures are unsuited to a world in which rapidly advancing technology requires 'specialists' rather than 'generalists' to make informed choices.[29]

The traditional notion that a legislature's primary function was to make laws takes no account of the tremendous complexity of government that evolved in the twentieth century. For instance, the function of lawmaking assumes heightened importance when the legislature's ability to refuse rather than just initiate is considered. There is a need for a much broader definition of the traditional lawmaking function to adequately assess the importance of twentieth-century legislatures. Blondel has therefore developed the concept of 'viscosity' to take into account the various gradations of legislative influence, including the capacity of the legislature to resist legislation initiated by the executive.[30] Furthermore, Blondel has shown that a legislature's involvement varies with the types of issues it considers. For instance, there might be less legislative influence on broad policy questions and greater influence on more narrowly defined issues. Boynton and Kim broadened the scope by dissecting the lawmaking function of legislatures in two ways: first, by measuring which branch actually initiates and drafts the legislation; and second, by ascertaining the legislature's ability to amend and change legislation.[31] An even more encompassing approach was adopted by Mezey. He looked at the constraints legislatures were capable of placing on the policy-related activities of the executive,[32] including the ability of the legislature to promote compromise or modification or ultimately veto the executive's policy proposals. Mezey suggested that the nature of the constraints imposed could vary with the policy-making stage (formulation, deliberation, and oversight) and the nature of the policy-making arena (parliamentary: chamber, committee; or extraparliamentary: cabinet, bureaucracy, political parties). The new functional emphasis, therefore, is on the policy-making authority of the legislature. What these and other studies uncovered is that 'legislatures which do not possess the power to initiate or even to compel changes in policy proposals may have a more subtle power of informally setting the parameters within which those policy-making powers actually operate'.[33]

Yet even with this broad base, it is clear that many legislatures in both Western and non-Western countries play a minor role in public policy making. In the industrial democracies of the West, the decline of the legislature as a policy-making institution can be partly explained by the emergence of the administrative state and the resultant growth of quasi-legislative rule making by the bureaucracy. But these explanations do not apply to developing countries, where such conditions rarely exist. In the developed countries, legislatures repeatedly delegated their authority to make public policy to the executive branch,[34] but in many developing countries legislatures never exercised any decision-making authority, and hence had none to give or delegate away.

As a result, more recent legislative studies,[35] particularly those based in the Third World, have identified other legislative functions. These include serving as agencies of political recruitment,[36] assisting in the managing of societal conflict,[37] fostering integration of the political system,[38] providing mobilization by linking citizens with the central government,[39] and ensuring government legitimization.[40] All these activities relate to the broader function of *systems maintenance*.

Systems-maintenance activities are those legislative activities that contribute to the stability and survival of the political system.[41] The activities are often directed, however, to the current government in power, or the individuals occupying positions of power, rather than the structure of government itself. The most fundamental system-maintenance activity performed by a parliamentary legislature is when it acts as an electoral body for positions in the executive branch. In these instances, a legislature's key responsibility involves the creation and maintenance of support for the government in power. Even in non-parliamentary systems, legislatures perform crucial maintenance activities. By recruiting and socializing political elites, legislatures create a political class of future leaders.[42] The creation of this class contributes to another systems-maintenance activity: conflict management. By early socialization to the 'rules of the game', disputes are kept within the boundaries of the system, and political participants do not become embroiled in damaging conflict. This allows for a minimum of disruption and disruption and a maximum of public support for the political system. To the extent that legislatures successfully manage conflict, they promote integration of the system, the 'process leading to political cohesion and sentiments of loyalty toward central political institutions'.[43] In sum, legislatures play a crucial role in promoting support and fostering stability for a country's political system. These maintenance activities are particularly crucial during times of rapid change; they ensure that evolution rather than revolution takes place.

But it is critical to these maintenance activities that all factions or interests in society are represented within the legislature. If some are excluded, they pose a grave threat to the system from the outside. Hence it is *representation*, perhaps the best known function of the legislature, which enables the newer maintenance functions to be successful. The term 'representation' came into the English language through French derivatives from the Latin *repraesentare*, meaning 'to bring before one, to bring back, to exhibit, to show, to manifest, to display'. Thomas Hobbes, in *The Leviathan*, was one of the first theorists to analyse the concept of representation. He saw the act of representation in terms of the authorization of one individual (the representative) to act for another.[44]

Representation has been heralded as the 'grand discovery of modern times' by the Scottish philosopher James Mill. A major challenge is to determine the governmental structure which best promotes representation of all the people: 'The problem seems to be either how to select the right representatives or how to control those selected, so that they respond effectively to the people's needs and interests. If the problem is finding a way to assure that people's affairs are well looked after, then representation is a powerful answer'.[45]

The philosophical history of the legislature is essentially rooted in popular choice—not government by the people, but of and for the people. Of the three branches of government, the legislative branch is the most representative and responsive to the views of the public. Linking the legislature with representation is viewing it in a different way than as a lawmaking body. For the difference between representation and deliberation of legislation is the difference between a body that expresses the demands of the people, a 'will organization', and a body that deliberates the public interest, a 'thought organization'.[46]

In sum, from a functional perspective, legislatures perform a variety of activities, which can be broadly categorized into representation, policy making or lawmaking, and systems maintenance. A key objective of this study is to uncover what functions Hong Kong's Legislative Council currently performs and suggest which of these will predominate into the future. Questions to be considered include: Has the Legislative Council historically been more active in performing one of these functions? Has this priority changed over time? What of its future functions? And ultimately, what impact will the legislature have on the development of the Hong Kong polity?

While the functions identified, particularly those of lawmaking and representation, are fairly traditional, the ways of assessing them have undergone a dramatic transformation. For instance, older studies of representation in Western legislatures have been closely tied to policy responsiveness, or lawmaking, with major works analysing the relationship between constituency views and the voting behaviour of legislators.[47] But until recently Hong Kong's Legislative Council has rarely had any divisions or votes, as it has prided itself on the unanimity of its decisions. So, it is necessary to ask: Did independent policy making nonetheless occur? Was representation present even if it was not apparent? How can representation be analysed when roll-call voting has seldom occurred, and when it has, has usually been unanimous? Further, how can the measurement of other legislative functions—those relating to systems maintenance and the broader representative functions other than voting—be evaluated? Clearly a more extensive and rigorous analysis of the functions of the legislature is needed, one which includes not only the actual behaviour of the legislature in terms of output, but also the orientation and behaviour of its individual members. To carry out such an analysis this study employs role theory.

Role Theory

To study the role of legislators is to study the norms that underlie their legislative behaviour.[48] Roles consist of clusters of norms allowing for a division of labour or specialization of functions among members of a group. The role concept links personality to social structure, and role expectations form the normative structure for system behaviour. In a political system, role expectations contain the rules that regulate members' political actions. In a legislative setting, these actions may involve the traditional functions of the legislature—representation, lawmaking, or performing various systems-maintenance functions. Role analysis is not only a useful concept for distinguishing between members of a legislature, but it also has great potential value for comparing legislatures, particularly along cross-national lines. One of the best ways of understanding how the functions of legislatures differ is to study the priorities that their members give to various aspects of their job.[49]

In the study of political systems in transitional or newly emergent states, such as Hong Kong, examining role orientations provides an indication of the relative institutionalization of the system, that is to say the degree to which members accept and are committed to a set of norms that orient and guide their political acts.[50] Role orientations among legislators may be complementary and harmonious or may evidence dissension and conflict. The degree of consensus among role expectations and the extent of their congruence with actual role behaviour provide indicators of system stability. Finally, the degree of role consensus will affect the extent of the legislature's autonomy. Without roles specific to itself, the legislature cannot be distinguished from other organizations of government.

Thus, investigation into the roles of Hong Kong's legislators will not only enable us to determine if there are crucial differences between types of legislators, but also help to evaluate the degree of institutionalization of the legislature itself and to provide a prognosis for its future. A brief explanation of the research design will show how role theory has been employed in this study.

Research Design

To determine the roles of Legislative Council members, interviews were undertaken between May 1987 and June 1988 and repeated from May 1992 to April 1993. During both periods, fifty-two legislators were surveyed. The two periods allow analysis of trends within groups of members as well as between them. The schedule of questions was a formidable one, requiring an average of one hour to complete, though the interview times actually ranged from thirty-five minutes to four-and-a-half hours. A total of eighty-nine questions were asked, which encompassed 167 variables. More specific information concerning the research design appears in the Appendix.

To summarize, this is the first comprehensive study of Hong Kong's Legislative Council. It can be distinguished from previous studies of Hong Kong government in that it provides not only an historical and institutional summary of its parameters, but affords a new focus of analysis by deriving much of its insight from the views of the legislators themselves. Hence, while the research provides both an historical and contemporary description of the Legislative Council's evolution, emphasis is upon discovering the role perceptions of its members. By determining what Hong Kong legislators do and why, we may be better able to uncover the actual functions performed by the legislature. We will attempt to put these findings to use: first and foremost, by offering some suggestions about the future functioning of the legislature; and second, by comparing Hong Kong's legislators with legislators in other countries. Before concentrating on the Legislative Council's similarities with other legislative institutions, Chapter 2 highlights its uniqueness by exploring the history and development of British colonial legislative councils.

THE LEGISLATIVE COUNCIL:
HISTORICAL AND POLITICAL CONTEXT

2 A Unique Legislature: The British Colonial Legislative Council

It has been said that 'to the students of politics, history can offer no richer collection of constitutional situations and devices than are to be found in the British Empire'.[1] The aim of this chapter is to consider one of those devices, the British colonial legislative council. Its development will be traced from the First to the Second British Empire, with an emphasis on its members, powers, and functions. An examination of these features will provide the basis upon which to understand the genesis of Hong Kong's Legislative Council and to appreciate how it has deviated from the normal path of colonial constitutional development.

The First British Empire

When the British settled overseas they sought to recreate the political institutions with which they were already familiar. As a result, all stages of overseas expansion saw a close relationship between the British Parliament, soon to be known as the 'Mother of Parliaments', and colonial legislative councils.

The early colonial legislatures have been called 'colonial facsimiles',[2] but in reality, there were important distinctions between the legislative tradition of the various colonies as well as between them and the mother country. The distinctions between colonies depended upon how they had been founded, that is to say, upon whether they were settled, ceded, or conquered. For what a colony could do depended upon the powers granted to it and these in turn depended upon how and when the territory was acquired by Britain.[3]

Settled Colonies

Most of the early colonies[4] were settled, as 'the First British Empire was built, not by conquest, but by pacific acquisition'.[5] Hence, early colonial law was 'dominated by the conception that Englishmen carried with them the law of England, and that, if they settled anywhere, the only constitution that the Crown had the right to grant was one based on the English model of a representative legislature'.[6] For instance, the charter of England's earliest North American colony stated that all settlers and their descendants 'shall have and enjoy all Liberties, Franchises, Immunities, within any of our other Dominions, to all Intents and Purposes, as if they had been abiding and born, within this our realm of England, or any other said Dominions'. [7]

In the seventeenth century, a series of largely commercial initiatives resulted in the settlement of tracts of land in North America. All of these ventures were granted authority by the king, via a charter or a proprietary grant, to acquire the land in the name of the government. When land was acquired under a proprietary grant, the 'grant of authority to the proprietors was so extensive as to preclude the development of local self-government', but when it was acquired under a charter 'self-government appeared early in its establishment', as was seen in the colonial prototype, Virginia.[8]

The colony of Virginia was chartered in 1606. The Virginia Charter originally centred authority in a council in London. This council in turn appointed a council of thirteen, which was given substantial legislative powers. The council of thirteen elected its own president and by majority vote passed laws 'for the better order, government and peace of the people'. It is with this body 'that the history of the colonial legislative council may be said to begin'.[9]

This arrangement was revised in 1619 when a general assembly was comprised a governor-in-council and a lower house of 22 burgesses, elected from each town and by groups of 100 planters. From then on most of the early colonies tended to assume 'a popularly based self-governing direction which removed them from the orbit of royal power'.[10] They generally had a royal governor and a two-house legislature consisting of a nominated council and an elected assembly. The governor was appointed by the Crown or proprietor (except in Rhode Island and Connecticut, where he was elected by the legislature) and in theory possessed more sweeping executive powers than even the king. He was the king's representative, head of government, chief magistrate, and commander of the armed forces; he could summon and dissolve assemblies, veto their laws, and appoint lesser officials. In reality though, his authority was increasingly limited.

The first house of the legislature was the governor's council. In origin, the council was a replica of the Privy Council,[11] and in the early colonial days its functions were as wide as the governor's: 'it assisted him in the executive administration, it sat with him as the chief judiciary, it advised him in the making of law'.[12] Members of the council 'were chosen, not for their representativeness, but for their conservatism and the likelihood of their supporting the governor'.[13] Typically, the members were local magnates and individuals from the great colonial families. The governor controlled the council through his power to nominate and suspend its members. The council had three distinct functions: it advised the governor on administrative matters; it was the highest court of appeal in the colony; and it was a chamber of the legislature. It never obtained the power and legitimacy, however, of its prototype, the British House of Lords, as the assemblies soon deprived the council of the right to initiate or amend money bills.

It was the second house of the legislature, the popularly elected assembly, which became the most powerful. The friction and hostility that developed between the governor and the assembly can be attributed in part to their being no linkage between the executive and the legislature, such as that provided by the cabinet system in Britain. The governor was appointed by the Crown or the proprietors, and the assembly was elected; although the governor was responsible to the assembly, he could not control it. In turn, the assembly could not become a cabinet because assemblymen could not be appointed as part of the administration without losing their seats in the lower house. Hence, the problem became one of 'an immovable executive confronted [with] a potentially irresistible legislature'.[14] What made the American colonies distinguishable from contemporary European colonies (such as those of Spain and Portugal) was the self-governing basis in the lower house of the legislature, investing the colonists, if freemen, with the liberties of English subjects.

Typically, the growth of colonial legislative power evolved through several stages: 'the establishment of an administrative authority in the colony, the addition of elected representatives, the transfer of the main legislative control from London to the colony itself, and lastly the separation of the legislature into two parts, the nominated council and the elected assembly'.[15] This form of government was soon adopted by other colonies: 'By the middle of the seventeenth century, governments in the colonies, having within the institutions granted in their charters the germ of growth, had developed for themselves the triptych of governor, council and assembly, whether they were corporations or proprietaries'.[16] Eventually, the assemblies' quest for power became the 'single most important feature of colonial political and constitutional development,' and a significant element in the revolutionary movement that produced the dismemberment of the First British Empire.[17]

In summary, the settled colonies were populated by British subjects who occupied lands that were previously uninhabited or not governed by any 'civilized power'. They carried with them the laws of England so far as they were applicable to the conditions of the colony, and they continued to enjoy all of their rights as subjects of the British Crown. This conception of the transference of British civil rights led the British Crown to establish legislative assemblies analogous to the British Parliament, having one wholly elected chamber. Such bodies legislated on all domestic matters and asserted the right to impose taxation.

Ceded and Conquered Territories

Whereas most settled colonies were established before the middle of the seventeenth century, the ceded and conquered colonies were primarily acquired through international conflict from the middle of the seventeenth century.[18] An important distinction between the settled and the ceded and conquered colonies was that the settled colonies were peopled by British emigrants who took with them the laws and institutions of England,[19] whereas the conquered and ceded colonies were peopled by non-British natives who were dependent upon the Crown regarding their form of government, being 'rightless' against the Crown.[20]

The empire in the mid-eighteenth century was thus comprised of colonies with different types of constitutional format. There were conquered and ceded royal provinces, with or without elective legislatures and councils. Interspersed with these were settled proprietary and chartered governments.[21] While in the former, Crown authority was retained to some degree (for example, in approving of the royal governors nominated by the proprietors and in the disallowance of legislation), in the latter, royal control was almost totally eliminated. The chartered colonies elected their own governors and often refused to submit their electoral choice for royal approval. They enacted laws repugnant to English law, refused to recognize Admiralty jurisdiction or the right to appeal from their own courts, and neglected their quotas for defense.[22] The executive power of the Crown in these colonies became 'something of a figment'.[23] They were to become significant to their more tightly constrained neighbours as examples of legislative independence.

Where there existed a strong royal government without an elected assembly, imperial control was supreme and unchallenged, but where there was an elected assembly, imperial relations were characterized by friction and hostility. The disallowance of legislation created grievances, and colonial assemblies countered it by passing a temporary act and constantly renewing it when it lapsed.[24] Similarly, executive control, as exercised by royal governors, proved problematic as the governors were typically dependent on the local assemblies for finance. The governors found that their powers to supervise administration, appoint officers, and enforce trade laws were deficient since the local assemblies often enacted devices that enabled legislative rather than executive will to be carried out.[25] Because the royal governors were dependent upon the assemblies for money, they were seen as 'constitutional hostages to the colonists'.[26] In general, the constitutional format of the colonies began to merge into a common type, based on the English government at that time. The governor represented the king, and his council was a pale imitation of the House of Lords. The assembly, more or less popularly elected, such as was the House of Commons, had rights of legislation subject to a veto. Yet these similarities were only superficial: 'Governors had little power of initiating legislation, and not much more of withholding assents. As a constituent part of the legislature, they tended to lose significance, as also did their councils, which in no way achieved the constitutional status of the Lords in the British Parliament'.[27]

By the end of the eighteenth century the defects of colonial government were becoming apparent: they included 'the lack of effective imperial control, disunion between the colonies themselves, the weakness of the colonial executive, [and] the means of aggression possessed by colonial elective assemblies'.[28]

The American Revolution

The central issue in the American Revolution was legislative rights. While its concern with individual rights—to choose the form of government and to hold that government accountable—has been repeatedly emphasized, it has perhaps been overlooked that the conflict pertained to these rights as they were represented in a legislative body.[29] The colonial legislatures' quest for power evolved through three distinct phases. During the first phase, comprising most of the seventeenth century, the lower house remained subordinated to the governor and his council, slowly grasping the power of taxation and the right to sit separately from the council, and ultimately to initiate its own laws. The second phase, following the English Restoration and especially after the Glorious Revolution, saw the assemblies dealing with the governors and councils on equal terms, and beginning to challenge London as well. By the end of the Seven Years War in 1763, and in some instances earlier, the assemblies reached their final phase of evolution, becoming involved in executive affairs to the extent of determining executive personnel, which prepared them for their dominant role during the revolution.

In these phases of evolution the legislatures gained four types of power. First, in an attempt to imitate the seventeenth-century House of Commons, they asserted their right to be sole authority over all matters of taxation and expenditure, beginning with the right to initiate and amend money bills, progressing to auditing executive accounts, and culminating in the power to appropriate public monies. Second, they began to control the civil list, or the salaries of royal officials. Third, they attempted to formally separate their powers from the executive by issuing rules governing their electoral system and regulating their internal proceedings. Fourth, they exceeded the powers of the House of Commons by becoming involved in executive affairs, especially the appointment of executive officials.[30]

The extension of their powers was first at the expense of the royal governors and their nominated council, but later, the assemblies were to realize their fight was not so much with the governors as with the colonial proprietors and Crown officials in London. What eventually emerged were two incompatible interpretations of the British constitution which took the form of a contest between two legislative bodies: Parliament and the colonial assemblies.[31] The central issue became the question of Parliament's jurisdiction over the colonies.[32] As James Madison was to write after the American Revolution:

The fundamental principle of the Revolution was that the Colonies were coordinate members with each other and with Great Britain, of an empire united by a common executive sovereign, but not united by any common legislative sovereign. The legislative power was maintained as complete in each American Parliament, as in the British Parliament. . . . [A] denial of these principles by Great Britain, and the assertion of them by America, produced the Revolution.[33]

When the British Parliament passed the Declaratory Act of 1766,[34] asserting the supremacy of Parliament over the American legislatures, and followed that declaration with a series of laws designed to raise revenue from the colonies to pay for defense and other arrangements, the rallying cry of 'no taxation without representation' united the colonies in a common rebellion against Britain.[35]

In terms of colonial policy, perhaps the chief result of the American Revolution was the 'eclipse of Locke's doctrine of a legislature limited by fundamental law, to which the Americans appealed . . . by Blackstone's doctrine of sovereignty of the imperial Parliament'.[36] The American Revolution

seemed to instil into English statesmen only the lesson that, if it was unwise to tax the colonies through the Imperial Parliament and the practice must be abandoned, it was nevertheless equally unwise to permit in the colonies the growth of democratic institutions which would inevitably follow the same course as those of the thirteen lost colonies.[37]

Many British leaders were convinced that the American secession had occurred because colonial constitutions did not reproduce the internal balance of the parent model: 'in brief, that the monarchical and "aristocratical" parts of their constitutions were too weak and the "democratical" part too strong'.[38] Consequently, the Second British Empire became characterized by a new emphasis on the powers of the governor and the nominated council with less emphasis on, and sometimes no provision for, an elected assembly. The government of Hong Kong was to develop from this model.

Under the First British Empire, the elected assembly was much more important than the nominated council. Yet the council rather than the assembly became the forerunner of the future embodiment of colonial legislative rights, the colonial legislative council. By the 1840s, the time of the founding of Hong Kong, this alternative form of colonial government was recognized as 'the Crown Colony system'.[39]

The Second British Empire

The colonies of the Second British Empire possessed a more 'aristocratic' and executive-based government than did those of the first. The Second British Empire distinguished more clearly between settled colonies, which gained dominion status, so possessing responsible government, and those, conquered or ceded, which did not and came to be ruled under the Crown Colony system.[40]

The Anglo-French War (1793–1815) transformed the empire from an Atlantic-based colonization peopled by British subjects, to one that encircled the Indian Ocean and was peopled by individuals from European, African, and Asian nations. The acquisition of land with large foreign populations required that a new type of colonial government be established. The new constitutions of the colonies provided for the abolition of the assembly, with the legislative councils becoming the sole house of the legislature. Four basic principles evolved under this new system:

1. The maintenance of the original laws and institutions of the colony, instead of the grant of English law and the old representative system;
2. The concentration of power in the hands of the governor;
3. The strict control of the governor from a newly established colonial department in London, and government as far as possible under the prerogative without recourse to Parliament;
4. The maintenance by the Crown of the power of legislation by Order in Council.[41]

Henceforth, colonial constitutional progress could be measured not only by the establishment of the organs of government, such as the advisory executive council and the legislative council, but within the legislative council according to the balance between official members (civil servants) and unofficial members (those not civil servants, either appointed or elected). A new classification of colonies could be made according to the following criteria:

1. Those with no legislative or executive councils;
2. Those with no legislative but an executive council;
3. Those having legislative councils with an official majority but an unofficial minority wholly nominated;
4. Those possessing legislative councils with an official majority and unofficial minority partly nominated and partly elected.[42]

Until 1984 Hong Kong was placed in the third category. Chapter 3 will explain why it never progressed beyond this point, and in so doing, provide a context from which to better evaluate its dramatic development in the late-twentieth century.

As Britain expanded and consolidated its empire, colonial constitutional formàts changed significantly. The Crown colonies in general, and their colonial councils in particular, underwent dramatic transformations. Crown Colony government became based on the 'twin pillars of a strong local executive and ultimate imperial control'.[43] At first, local public opinion was purely advisory. Then the governor's advisers divided into legislative and executive councils, establishing the means for a government by consent. Local representatives were admitted to sit with official members. Later, a limited form of election was granted and 'the thin edge of the democratic wedge'[44] was placed into the colonial constitution. A further advance came when the unofficial members of the legislative council became a majority. Differentiation between the colonial legislative councils could now be made according to their function (advisory, legislative, or executive) and their membership (officials, appointed unofficials, or elected unofficials). This classification will be used to delineate the development of Hong Kong's Legislative Council in Chapter 3.

Function

To understand the function of the legislative council in the Crown Colony system, it is beneficial first to examine its relationship with the other colonial organs of government, the governor, and the executive council.

The Governor

The governor is the 'central institution of the Crown Colony system'.[45] He is, first and foremost, the King's representative. The governor is the 'single and supreme authority responsible to, and representative of, His Majesty'.[46] Furthermore, he possesses many of the King's powers. While the president of the United States was seen by Lord Bryce as 'George III shorn of a part of his prerogative,'[47] the governor remained George III, 'with a ministry of obedient officials secured to him by status and functions ... and with a permanent majority of King's friends in the legislature'.[48] The governor's power in the Crown Colony system is so pervasive that it has been noted that 'the Government' shall mean 'the Governor'.[49] His powers and duties are established in the Letters Patent and Royal Instructions for the colony. He is appointed at His Majesty's pleasure, with a tenure of office typically confined to five years.[50]

Besides being the representative and communications conduit for the British sovereign, the governor also serves as the administrative and executive head of government, possessing 'all the authority inherent in the head of the executive government of the territory, whether it rests on prerogative or is inferred from statutes'[51]. In this capacity, he performs many duties, including the granting of lands within the colony, appointing judges, and dismissing or suspending public officials. He is also the commander-in-chief of all military in the colony,[52] and the ceremonial head of the colony. He does have limits to his powers, however, as his acts are subject to the rule of law. Also, unless expressly authorized, the governor cannot declare war or make peace or conclude treaties; he cannot regulate coinage; nor can he confer any honorary distinction or extend the boundaries of the colony by annexing territory.

With respect to the two councils of the colony, his authority is pervasive. He can influence (and in many cases, solely determine) their membership. He appoints not only the nominated official members, but also the nominated unofficials. In this latter capacity, in colonies where there are no elected unofficials, he is given the responsibility for determining, through appointment of unofficials, the local representatives of public opinion. Typically, he is president of the legislative council, exercising both original and casting votes, and therefore predominantly affecting all council activities. This influence is magnified by the fact that by law all money bills, and in practice, all bills, are introduced by his government.[53] In addition, should legislation receive support in council with which he disagrees, he may impede its implementation through the exercise of a veto.[54] Furthermore, he may ignore the legislature by urging the British sovereign to enact ordinances through an Order in Council.[55]

In general, the governor can effectively secure any desired piece of legislation through the influence he possesses in the legislative council. Even when a part of the membership is elected, these members, if they so desire to oppose the administration, find that their power to do so is insufficient. Control over the legislature is exercised 'not by restricting the scope of their authority to legislate but by securing that the powers enjoyed shall be exercised as desired by the executive in any vital manner'.[56]

Executive Council

The executive council consists of the chief executive officers of the colonial government, and in some cases, especially where the legislature contains elected members, representatives of the non-officials from the legislature and the community. All members hold office at the Crown's pleasure, and may be suspended by the governor upon confirmation by the Crown. The council's main function is to aid the governor in carrying out his duties and the governor's responsibility to the council is to consult with it about the performance of all his functions.[57] In addition, the governor in executive council approves all rules promulgated to execute ordinances already passed by the legislative council. Finally, the executive council also determines the outcome of disciplinary questions arising in the colonial service of the colony.

The executive council has often been described as a cabinet, but this is inappropriate because it only advises the governor on the formulation of public policy and has no collective responsibility. The governor may act against the council, but when he does he must report to the British Secretary of State. The governor controls all of the council's proceedings: it cannot meet unless summoned by him, and he determines the agenda. Its proceedings are confidential and the members are bound by oath to secrecy.

The unofficial members of the executive council who are also members of the legislative council serve as a bridge between the executive and legislative organs of government. Members of the legislative council were added to the executive council 'with a view to establishing some harmony between the executive and the legislature, and to facilitate the passing of governmental measures'.[58] The unofficial membership of the executive councils evolved so that the governor might have spokesmen in the assembly explaining and promoting government business.[59] Eventually, however, it was the unofficials rather than the governor who pushed for membership in the executive council, to have some representation in the executive branch. Mixed membership was thought to promote a more stable environment in which to govern:

So long as initiative regarding the formulation of general policy remains vested in bodies from which unofficial representatives are excluded,
it is difficult to see how the tendency can be avoided for the elected
members of the Legislative Council to regard themselves as an opposition,
whose duty it is to criticize measures which emanate from the official
side.[60]

In some self-governing colonies of the nineteenth century,
the executive councils evolved into cabinets responsible to the
legislature. This made the councils ministerial bodies. In other
colonies however, the executive council was overshadowed by
the financial committee of the legislative council when its unofficial members were required to resign their legislative seats
to serve on the council. In those instances where a colony advanced towards self-government and its executive council did not
evolve into a cabinet, it typically ceased to serve any purpose
at all.

So in relation to the other two organs of colonial government,
the governor and the executive council, the legislative council plays
a distinctly subordinate role. Its membership is determined largely
(if not solely) by the governor and its public policy making is
limited to those measures suggested by the governor or his
department heads. Nonetheless, the colonial legislative council
continues to perform critical functions.

The Legislative Council under the Crown
Colony System

Functions

Explaining the functions of the legislative council would be
straightforward if it only had the formal responsibilities described
in the Letters Patent or Royal Instructions. However,

the duties and obligations of the various parts of the legislative council, are
most of them not of a nature to admit of precise definition, and in these, as
in all other mixed political bodies, success in co-operation is to be obtained, not by seeking to define what is in its nature indeterminate, but by
a disposition on all sides not to press opposing powers to what may be
supposed to be their ultimate limits, and to give ample scope and allowance in practice to those elements in the Legislature which have not a legal
predominance.[61]

Lawmaking

The involvement of legislatures in making law has been considered their 'central and most fundamental function',[62] so it is not surprising that the most important legally mandated responsibility of the legislative council is the passage of bills. Through the processes of legislation, debate, questions, and financial appropriations, 'all the affairs of the colony pass across the table of the council, which thus mirrors the life of the colony'.[63] Budgetary measures, relating to both appropriations and revenue, are included in this function. However, this traditional 'power of the purse' is limited, in that unofficials of the legislative council may not increase estimates presented to them.[64] In general, colonial legislatures have the right to make laws for the 'peace, welfare and good government' of the colonies. While this is a broad designation the lawmaking power of the council is in practice limited in significant ways:

- The control of local legislation is exercised through the provision of an official majority in the legislature. Officials exercise a positive form of control in that they typically vote according to the wishes of the governor. Further, only officials can initiate legislation which has a financial effect, with unofficial initiation limited to the presentation of private bills.
- Any bill passed by the legislative council must be presented for assent to the British sovereign or his/her representative. The governor, as the sovereign's representative, is generally given discretion to give or refuse assent to a bill or to reserve it for Her Majesty's pleasure. Assent is rarely withheld because almost all bills have been presented and approved through use of the official majority. Further, should a governor doubt the wisdom of the legislation, he is more likely to reserve it for Her Majesty's pleasure than to formally refuse to assent.[65]
- Similarly, the governor may exercise a reserve power over the legislation, often referred to in terms of a 'certification' of bills. The governor may put a bill into effect any time he thinks fit, even if the bill has not been passed in council; or if passed, he may amend it and then provide his assent.[66] Under such conditions, the governor is required to report to the Secretary of State the rationale underlying his action.
- A law, even if assented to, may be disallowed by the Crown and will cease to have effect. This power depends upon the terms in which it is reserved and on political considerations.[67] It is

doubtful, however, that the Crown would ever disallow legislation not contrary to treaty rights or patently *ultra vires*.[68]

- Legislation cannot be repugnant to any act of Parliament extending to the colony or any other regulation made under the authority of such an act.[69] It is significant, though, that colonial law is not rendered totally invalid because of repugnance; only such provisions as are repugnant are inoperative.[70]
- The bills considered by the legislative council can only apply to the colony itself. The colonial legislature cannot enact any extra-territorial legislation—the power to legislate is local, and the validity of the legislation stops at the territorial waters of the colony.[71]
- Finally, the legislative council cannot 'commit suicide'; it cannot abdicate its functions or extinguish itself, nor can it legislate to become a member of a union or federation. This limitation means 'that nothing save Imperial legislation would avail to dissolve the bond of Empire'.[72]

In summary, a colonial legislature is not a sovereign legislature but it is 'sovereign within its powers'. Its lawmaking powers are limited both in a positive sense (for example, by the control exercised by official majority and the governor's certification powers) and a negative sense (through refusal of assent and disallowance).

Representation

One of the traditional functions of the legislative council has been to provide representation. In most legislatures, this has meant territorial representation, but in the more diverse colonies, where a universal franchise was not immediately attainable, representation was of a communal and/or corporate nature. Communal representation allows different races, ethnic groups, religions, or social orders in the colony to elect members of the legislature. Corporate representation allows sectional interests such shipping, banking, or a chamber of commerce to be represented.

Colonial legislatures are unique in that typically the governor, rather than a publicly based electorate, determines what—or whom—will be represented. In addition, representation in the legislative council serves a dual purpose, as the function of the council is not only to represent the various interests of the community and bring them to bear on subsequent debate about the appropriateness of legislation, but more importantly, to represent to the community the intentions of the administration and the rationale underlying its actions. In this sense, representation also involves the system-maintenance function of legitimizing the government's actions.

System Maintenance

Legitimacy Legislatures can generate support for government programs through their legitimation function. This system-maintenance function may be the 'latent' function of many legislatures, particularly those located in the Third World. As Packenham was to discover about the Brazilian Congress, 'Simply by meeting regularly and uninterruptedly, the legislature produced, among the relevant populace and élites, a wider and deeper sense of the government's moral right to rule than would otherwise have obtained. It also was being exercised when the legislature put its "stamp of approval" on initiatives taken elsewhere.'[73]

The legitimizing function of the legislative council has been seen by some colonial scholars to override—if not make irrelevant—the representative function. During the debate over the future format of the colony of Newfoundland in 1826, it was noted that the old legislative council's 'only function was to shield the governor from full responsibility'.[74] Munslow concluded: 'Legislative councils were not intended to represent the people or make the government responsible to the people. They were expected to act as a mouthpiece for the administration.'[75] Schaeffer, writing about the legislative council in Uganda, similarly suggested that 'the function of the legislative council was not at all to represent the people to the government, still less to make the government responsible to the people, but instead to act as a spokesman for the administration to the people'.[76] And Hopkins, writing about Tanzania, noted that the legislature served as a 'sounding board and forum for extracting approbation and applause for new government policies [rather] than a deliberative body that formulates policies or actually writes legislation'.[77] To ensure that legitimation occurs, however, it is necessary to have the participation of colonial élites in the legislature.

Élite Recruitment 'The legislative councils are often a training ground for the colonial peoples [to learn] the responsibilities of self-government.'[78] One of the 'chief functions of the Empire in the world is to train its subjects in the principles and practices of autonomy'.[79] As Austin opined about the Gold Coast legislative council, 'a colony is led to independence by a gradual process of emancipation through the careful training of the "unofficial" in the techniques of self-government'.[80] As the participation of élites expanded, the unification or integration of the colony was enhanced.

Integration   Integration refers to the 'penetration of the primary, occupational, or geographical groups of a governmental unit by a broader national identification'.[81] Many conquered territories were made up of individuals from diverse ethnic or regional groupings. One way to integrate these individuals into the new colonial structure was to provide their representatives with membership in the legislative council. Another aspect of this function can be labelled mobilization, in which legislators communicate with citizens on behalf of the executive to gain popular support for, as well as compliance with, specific government policies.[82] This type of integration has a symbolic function, as it symbolizes the participation of the relevant ethnic or regional groupings in the rule-making process. Attempting to break down divisive local communal orientations and instilling broad extra-local orientations, the legislative council furthers a sense of political unity and decreases fragmentation and insecurity. However, successful integration is ultimately based on a final system-maintenance function, the resolution of conflict.

Conflict Resolution   Perhaps the primary goal of any government is to ensure that it remains in power. In providing a place to institutionalize colonial élites, potential areas of conflict are managed in a government-sponsored setting, allowing conflict to be adjusted to provide a minimum of disruption and a maximum of public support for the government. According to one British colonial scholar, the early colonial legislatures were little more than 'debating societies', serving as a way in which 'grievances could be ventilated and desires made known'.[83]

In summary, legislative councils have performed many functions; some functions have been legally mandated (such as lawmaking and budgeting), while others have evolved informally (such as representation and the system-maintenance functions of conflict management, integration, legitimacy, and élite recruitment). How these functions have been carried out has depended largely upon the composition of the council.

Membership

The constitutional evolution from colony to dominion status can be measured through membership changes in the legislative council.

Passage from an elementary form of Crown Colony administration
to a complete system of cabinet government was dependent upon
'the changing balance of power between British officials and representatives of the local community' in the legislature.[84] There are
five types of members of the legislative council: the governor,
the ex-officio member, the nominated official, the nominated unofficial, and the elected unofficial.

The Governor

The governor, as noted earlier, possesses substantial legislative
powers. He appoints all members of the council except for elected
members. He exercises, as president of the council, both an original
and casting vote. He acts in a capacity similar to that of the British
prime minister in that he both answers questions and introduces
new proposals.[85] Further, he can, through certification, enact legislation which has not been passed by the legislative council, or he
may amend legislation that has already received a majority vote.
Finally, he can exercise a veto on legislation either indirectly
by recommending that the Crown disallow it, or more directly,
through refusing assent.

Ex-Officio Members

These members hold their seats by virtue of holding certain prescribed offices such as chief secretary, financial secretary, or
attorney general. Their role is to support the colonial government
or the Crown in the legislature.[86]

Officials

Unlike ex-officio members, officials do not hold their legislative
seats by virtue of office, but are appointed by the governor. As
members of the administration they are expected to support the
government's measures, and if need be, to vote against unofficial
opposition.[87] They are responsible for answering questions about
various government policies and for presenting bills for legislative
consideration.

Appointed Unofficials

Unofficials are selected 'in the expectation and in the confidence
that [they] will co-operate with the Crown in its general policy, and
not oppose the Crown on any important question without strong
and substantial reasons'.[88] They typically belong 'to the wealthiest

class in the colony, and for social and other reasons would usually be loyal to the governor and give him their support'.[89] Yet it has been argued that 'in every colony, as it developed politically, the qualification for nominated unofficial shifted from readiness to co-operate with the Crown to representativeness of some aspect of colonial life and opinion'.[90] Nonetheless, should they want to continue as a member of the legislative council, it is expected that they must continue to please the individual who is responsible for their placement, the governor.

Elected Unofficials

Unlike the previous categories, elected unoffical do not owe their seat on the council to gubernatorial appointment or administrative office, but to an electoral franchise. The type of franchise can be either territorial, communal, or functional. It is expected that an elected unoffical will 'vote as he sees fit' and exercise a 'vigilant supervision over the measures introduced by the Government lest in any case local official interests . . . should prevail to the prejudice of public interests'.[91] Nonetheless, the exercise of this legislative role is expected to occur within the context of retaining governmental control of the legislature.[92] To secure this goal, the 'development of committees of the legislative council has provided the great means of canalizing the political activities of unofficials, and of diverting their attention from insoluble general issues by securing their co-operation on limited particular issues'.[93]

Not only can the colony's constitutional progress be measured in the balance between official and unofficial members, but the functional emphasis of a legislative council can only be determined by examining the self-defined roles the members of the legislature play. This will be the focus of examination of Hong Kong's Legislative Council in later chapters.

After the Second World War, most of the colonial territories followed the dominions and became independent sovereign states. The intention of creating an independent ministerial system in the remaining Crown Colonies was first suggested in the *Watson Report* on the Gold Coast in 1948. The report claimed that 'the central purpose of British colonial policy is simple. It is to guide the colonial territories to responsible government within the Commonwealth'.[94] Both in the original West Indian colonies and in the newer African and Asian colonies the progress from Crown Colony to independence was accomplished within a few years.

Typically, this progress commenced when the legislative council, now fully elected, was transformed into a ministerial system. Elected members of the legislature were included in the executive council and made responsible for certain departments of government. Two or three officials served with them as advisers to the governor, who invariably presided over the executive council meetings. The next step towards independence was marked by the removal of official members from the executive council and the appointment of a chief minister to preside over the meetings of a newly constituted cabinet. At a later stage, the chief minister became premier. Upon completion of this stage, responsible government became the basis for independence, which was most often readily granted by the British government upon request from the local legislature.

While one renowned British scholar has argued that 'Parliamentary institutions have, in fact, been incomparably the greatest gift of the English people to the civilization of the world,'[95] others have seen the parliamentary transplant in terms of failure rather than success. This failure has many reasons, not the least of which is the experience of colonial rule itself: 'Colonial rule was not a preparation for operating the Westminster model; it was singularly different from it . . . [based] on undemocratic . . . principles . . . at best paternalist and at worst authoritarian'.[96] Others have gone as far as to argue that colonial history is distinctly anti-legislative: 'The history of colonialism can be retold as the attempt of the colonial powers to prevent the emergence of legislative institutions and the struggle of national groups to create such institutions'.[97] Nonetheless, almost all of the Crown Colonies have progressed during decolonization in the typical constitutional pattern towards independence, even if their post-independence experience has been less than a successful exercise of parliamentary government.

Although it has been concluded that 'history suggests that almost every type of colonial constitution is a stage and not a stopping place',[98] the constitutional progress of one Crown Colony, Hong Kong, had been arrested for almost 150 years. The lack of constitutional advance in the territory has been ironic, as Hong Kong, more than most of the former Crown Colonies that gained independence, has long been ready for the 'burdens and opportunities of independence. . . . It is rich by the standards of colonial territories, it has no problem of inter-racial tension such as exists in the plural societies of Africa, and it has a large cadre of efficient

Chinese administrators'.[99] Yet the lack of local agitation for independence, coupled with Britain's and China's willingness to uphold the status quo, at least until 1982, meant the Colony was to remain a 'living fossil of early colonial government'.[100] The reasons for this arrested development are not only unique, but multiple, and comprise the subject of Chapter 3.

3 Hong Kong's Legislative Council, 1844–1984

Hong Kong became a British Crown Colony in 1841. While the Colony in general can be said to have been ceded, it became a British possession as much by conquest as by cession.[1] Hong Kong was not to be a colony in the usual sense, but a factory similar to the old establishments of the East India Company in India.[2] The island was acquired to further British trade with China. Its purpose was to provide the conditions for healthy trade, namely stability, guarantee of contract, and impartial justice.[3] Hence the Colony was not seen as a territorial gain, but rather as 'the minimum space required for . . . [a] headquarters to British trade, administration, and general influence in the Far East'.[4] It was unique as a commercial rather than a territorial settlement, a place where the British migrated to establish a mercantile way station rather than a home, with the length of their residence, and that of the Chinese, primarily determined by economic considerations. Hong Kong was thus not a community in the traditional sense but a trading post inhabited by a succession of temporary traders. This sense of transience was to have a negative impact on the development of popularly based government institutions.

Throughout much of Hong Kong's history its uniqueness has been emphasized, beginning with Lord Stanley's[5] statement to the new Governor, Sir Henry Pottinger, that there was to be 'no slavish copying of precedents . . . methods of proceeding unknown in British colonies must be followed at Hong Kong'.[6] Nonetheless, how the Colony was constituted was typical of other British Crown Colonies. The basic constitutional documents establishing British sovereignty over the territory are three Orders in Council: The Hong Kong Charter of 9 April 1843, the Order in Council of 24 October 1860, and the Order in Council of 20 October 1898. These Orders in Council do no more than define the territorial boundaries of the Colony and the extent of the Governor's and Legislative Council's jurisdiction. The details of the framework of government were established in the Letters Patent and the Royal Instructions, the former creating the office of Governor as well as the Executive and Legislative Councils, the latter 'filling the gaps left by the Letters Patent' with detailed provisions for the composition, powers, and procedures of the two councils.[7] The Charter of 1843 established Hong Kong as a British Crown Colony with a governor, acting with the advice of a legislative council, making laws for the 'peace, order, and good government' in accordance with instructions and subject to the power of disallowance by the Crown. The Governor was to be 'assisted and advised' by an executive council in keeping the seal of the Colony, making grants of land, and making appointments as well as suspensions of the officers of government. While the first Governor administered the government by proclamation, it was eventually felt that he required formal legislative power to establish law and order in the Colony.[8]

Establishment of Hong Kong's Legislative Council

Legislative power was located in a legislative council consisting of the governor and members appointed by the Crown. The membership of the first Council consisted of three officials, who held office at Her Majesty's pleasure. It was clear from earlier communications that there was to be no popular form of government.[9] The Governor, with the advice of the Legislative Council, was given full authority to make laws for the 'peace, order and good government' of the Colony, subject to three limitations: instructions from London, disallowance by the Queen, and the passage of concurrent legislation by the British Parliament.

Under this framework, the chief executive of the Colony, the Governor, was also the chief legislator, exercising pervasive legislative power. He was made the presiding officer of the legislature and had an original as well as casting vote. He could determine the period of each legislative session with absolute authority, convening and dissolving the Council as he saw fit. The Governor had the power to formulate the Council's standing orders and, significantly, could make and promulgate laws even against the united opposition of the other members of the legislature. The Legislative

Council was effectively subordinated to the will of the Governor by the instruction that 'no law was to be passed or any motion debated unless first proposed by him'.[10] The Executive Council rather than the Legislative Council was to review new legislation. In sum, the Governor was given overriding power to dominate the members of the Legislative Council. He formulated their agenda, chose their meeting times, and ultimately could put into effect legislation contrary to their wishes. Moreover, he selected the members, who were then formally appointed by the Crown. Lessons had been learned from the demise of the First British Empire, namely, that the Governor should not be subordinate to any determinations of the Legislative Council.

While this constitutional configuration mirrored the initial phases of the development of Crown Colony government elsewhere, Hong Kong was never to progress much beyond it.[11] These legislative arrangements were perceived as a prudent response to the take-over of a 'barren island' without a well-established indigenous community demanding political representation. It was a place which was more a military, diplomatic, and trading station than a settlement, and thus strategic considerations for the promotion of British trade in the Far East remained uppermost in the minds of colonial officials. These considerations necessitated that there be a greater degree of imperial control, primarily exercised by the Governor as the Queen's representative, than was normal for most colonies.[12] Yet in practice, this 'administrative absolutism' was much modified, as can be seen in the development of the first Legislative Councils.

The First Legislative Councils

The history of Hong Kong's Legislative Council reflects a constant competition between Great Britain, the colonial government, the British traders, and the Chinese inhabitants for the best compositional membership of the legislature. The composition of the Legislative Council posed a difficult dilemma: if there was to be legitimate representation of the community, the Council needed to include not only the British traders for whom the colony was founded, but the growing number of Chinese inhabitants, who soon became a significant majority of the Colony's population. However, Chinese representation was difficult to achieve, as Council members needed to be conversant in English and possess an understanding and respect for British legal customs. As a consequence, it was assumed from the outset that it would be the government itself who would best represent the Chinese majority. This paternalistic assumption was to remain in force throughout the Legislative Council's history and prevent the development of elected representative government.

Initially, the Council was kept small to allow the Governor to dominate his administration. It was established more as a 'matter of form',[13] that form dictating that it be an advisory tool of the executive rather than a viable legislature exercising the usual legislative functions of policy making, systems maintenance, and representation.

The immediate problem in constituting the Legislative Council was the lack of suitably qualified candidates. Appointees needed to be individuals who held high official positions and were familiar with the day-to-day problems of government. There was an 'acute scarcity of men willing to serve who were reliable and capable of such civic duties as service implied'.[14] The first Council of three officials was actually not constituted until early 1844, whereupon it proceeded to pass an ordinance declaring slavery illegal, which along with a series of loosely phrased ordinances passed that year were disallowed by the Crown.[15] More detrimental was suspicion of the motives of the first Council members, who were known to speculate in land and assumed to be serving their own interests rather than those of the territory. This reinforced the conclusion that only the Governor could be counted on to uphold the public interest,[16] strengthening the belief that representative government was inappropriate for Hong Kong.

The second Legislative Council was instituted under a new governor, Sir John Davis,[17] who tried to increase the size of the Council to five members. Governor Davis criticized the existing arrangement as the Legislative Council and the Executive Council had the same members and they were too few in number. While wanting more legislators, Governor Davis believed that membership should remain restricted to officials, as 'almost every person possessed of capital who is not connected with government is employed in the opium trade'.[18] Lord Stanley, however, refused to allow more members, as he wanted the Council to remain 'deliberately small to strengthen the Governor's position'. It was clear from early communications that the Council was only nominally 'legislative' in that its 'real function was to advise the governor, who was himself the legislative authority, since he had both the first word and the final say'.[19] Yet, it would be erroneous to conclude that the Governor totally dominated the legislature, as a proposed tax on wines and spirits in 1846 had to be withdrawn when it became subject to the unanimous opposition of the Legislative Council members.[20] This established a precedent in which the British Secretary of State would normally not allow ordinances to be passed when there was unanimous opposition in the Legislative Council.

Appointment of Unofficials

The third Governor of Hong Kong, Sir George Bonham,[21] provided the Council with its first unofficial members in 1850. The change was initiated by a report of the 1847 Select Committee of the House of Commons on the China Trade. When the merchants complained about Governor Davis' revenue measures in 1845,[22] they presented a memorial to the Secretary of State demanding a measure of municipal self-government as well as stating their reasons for opposing the taxation plan. The 1847 Select Committee agreed that the Colony's finances should not be based solely on local revenue, as it did not 'think it right that the burden of maintaining that which is rather a post of general trade in the China seas than a colony in the ordinary sense, should be thrown in any great degree on the merchants or other persons who may be resident upon it'.[23] Furthermore, it was sympathetic to the demand for a measure of self-government, concluding that 'a share in the administration of the ordinary and local affairs of the Island should be given, by some system of municipal government, to the British residents'.[24] Two years later, when nothing had been done to implement this suggestion,[25] the merchants petitioned for either elected or nominated representatives on the Legislative Council. The Governor sent the petition to the Secretary of State and noted that he had no objection to the nomination of two inhabitants to the Legislative Council, as they would be a good source of information and, more importantly, could assist the government in explaining public policy to the community. Hence at the outset, the intended function of unofficial appointees was oriented towards systems maintenance. The Secretary of State accepted the principle of nominating two unofficials to the Legislative Council and

Governor Bonham proceeded to make the nominations. He used recommendations from the Justices of the Peace to make the nominations, and in so doing instituted a form of indirect election to the Council.[26] The first unofficials were both merchants, fostering a focus upon merchant concerns within the Legislative Council.

Municipal Self-Government Initiative

The recommendation that there be some form of municipal government came to nothing. The Colonial Office objected for two reasons: first, because the 'English minority can hardly be trusted with powers which it would give them over Chinese and other alien and ignorant ratepayers'; and second, because the existence of a municipal government would be incompatible with the 'decisiveness and energy of proceeding which are almost necessary for the very existence of a European government surrounded by millions of Asiatics'.[27] Yet when the merchants revived the issue of municipal government after 1847, permission was granted by Secretary of State Earl Grey. Governor Bonham then consulted with the Justices of the Peace and offered them control of the police if they would raise additional revenue to make up the deficit in the police rate. The Justices, however, refused because increased taxation was the very condition that had sparked their interest in constitutional reform, hence on the issue of who was to pay the municipal government initiative failed. This led to the conclusion that the motives of the merchants were simply based on considerations of economic advantage rather than political autonomy. Further attempts to initiate a degree of representative government in the late 1860s also appeared be based on popular opposition to a military contribution and attendant taxation rather than on 'abstract principles' of representative government.

Elected Unofficials Initiative

When Sir John Bowring[28] took over as Governor in 1854, he concluded that the Legislative Council was an 'absolute nullity' that had never been consulted on the 'all-important questions of income and disbursement'.[29] Moreover, he argued that the Legislative Council was not acquainted with the concerns of the Colony, did not debate the Blue Book,[30] and could not initiate legislation or review the annual estimates. Bowring thus announced his intention to increase membership in the Council and provide for greater publicity over the disposal of public funds. In advocating legislative reform, Bowring noted that the Colony was now financially self-supporting and so should also be self-governing. He proposed that the Council should consist of eight officials and five elected unofficials, three of the latter being elected by the Justices of the Peace and two by the registered holders of Crown leases.[31] The only qualification for membership was British citizenship, although he did stipulate that unofficials should not be employed by the administration in any official capacity. Bowring argued that there should be a popular element in the Legislative Council so that it could 'represent public opinion with its contribution of local information, its demands for improvement, its interest in social reform'.[32] Governor Bowring was thus proposing a new representative function for the legislature, namely as a conduit of community concerns. Furthermore, he believed that Legislative Council members should be truly responsible to the community, with representation broadened to include the views of Chinese inhabitants.

The new Secretary of State for the Colonies, Labouchere, noted that if the British alone had the power to vote, this would give political authority to a small number of temporary residents over the more permanent Chinese population. However, he also felt that the Chinese population was 'endowed with much intelligence but . . . very deficient in the elements of morality . . . and have not acquired a respect for the main principles on which social order rests'.[33] A further argument against the reform was based on Hong Kong's 'peculiar position', for the 'great commercial interests and future progress of civilization throughout the East are to a great extent involved in the maintenance of British rule and of orderly government in Hong Kong'.[34] Finally, there was the complication of internal insecurity and lawlessness as well as the territory's proximity to China.

Labouchere, therefore, only agreed to a moderate increase in the number of Legislative Council members. He allowed for there to be two more official members and one unofficial, who was nominated by the Governor from a list of names selected by the Justices of the Peace. The proportion of unofficials to officials was thus weakened rather than strengthened, contrary to the Governor's original intention. But the status of the unofficials was enhanced when the Secretary of State declined to increase the number of officials, when he was later requested to do so by the Governor.[35]

The unofficials' power was also better delineated when the financial arrangements for reviewing the annual estimates of income and expenditure were reformed. From 1858, all expenditure had to be placed in the estimates and formally passed by the Legislative Council. The reform meant that the Council exercised a more implicit policy-making function. Yet the initial use of this new power demonstrated its limits. During the first discussion of the estimates, unofficials were critical of the lack of spending on public works, which they wanted extended. The acting Governor though ruled that he could not accept any amendment to the Estimates Ordinance unless it was clearly necessary. Colonel William Caine, who was deputizing for Bowring, pointed out that colonial regulations did not give the Council control over expenditure already fixed and agreed to by the Secretary of State, and asked for a ruling. The subsequent ruling stated that there ought to be a fixed establishment on the Civil List consisting of permanent expenses, with only the remainder placed in the annual estimates for review by the Legislative Council. The ruling substantially diminished the Council's newly acquired 'power of the purse'.

Nonetheless, by the late 1850s 'the Legislative Council had now become an important body which the Governor could no longer override in the way in which had been provided for in the original Instructions of 1843'.[36] Furthermore, the members' freedom of speech in the Council was upheld by the Secretary of State over the Governor's request to make them responsible in the courts for libel. The Secretary of State, when rejecting the Governor's request, added that he was unwilling to sanction an amendment contrary to the Council's wishes.

During the tenure of the next Governor, Sir Hercules Robinson,[37] a second conflict erupted between Great Britain and China. The hostilities arose out of differences in the interpretation of previous treaties between the two countries and was instigated by the boarding of a British ship, the *Arrow*, by Chinese authorities in search of pirates. The Arrow War ended in 1858 with the signing of the Treaties of Tientsin, but renewed hostilities commenced in conjunction with the Chinese refusal to accept a British envoy in Peking. The British troops assigned to fight in the war were temporarily based on a peninsula across from Hong Kong; at the conclusion of hostilities, formally recognized by the Treaty of Peking, this portion of the mainland directly across from the island, named Kowloon, was ceded to ensure a better defence for the Colony in the future.[38]

Early Role of the Officials and Clarification of Legislative Procedures

Distinctions between official and unofficial members were first elaborated upon when Sir Richard MacDonnell[39] became Governor in 1866. Instructions prior to his taking office undermined the Governor's discretionary power of appointment by defining 'officials' as the Chief Justice, Colonial Secretary, Attorney General, Colonial Treasurer, and Auditor General.[40] Additionally, while the number of unofficials was established at four, by *de facto* arrangement, one unofficial was an official by virtue of holding a government office.[41]

Both types of legislators were to hold their seats at Her Majesty's pleasure. Official members were to have precedence over unofficial members, and amongst themselves, according to the office held, as ranked in the instructions to MacDonnell dated 16 October 1865. The Governor or senior official was to preside and was entitled to an original and casting vote. The Governor, with the advice of the Legislative Council, could make, renew, or amend the standing orders of the Council as well as enact ordinances. While the overriding legislative power the Governor had possessed disappeared, he retained the right of initiation, in other words, he alone could propose legislation and determine what subjects would be debated by the Council. Later instructions in 1872, however, provided that members might initiate debate on any subject except finance as long as they were seconded by two members of the Council. In financial matters the role of officials—and hence the Governor—remained predominant. This position was strengthened in 1860 when certain fixed annual charges, such as the salaries of government officers, were placed on the civil list and hence excluded from the legislature's annual vote.

While it was assumed that the official members of the Council would always support the Governor, there was no formal ruling on their voting requirements until 1864. In that year, an official voted against the government's sponsorship of the annual defense payment to Britain. The Secretary of State reprimanded him and subsequently drafted a ruling stating that the opposition of official members to settled policy was 'incompatible with retention of office'. Furthermore, the Secretary noted that they were 'bound . . . to support by their votes and not to oppose by any public act a policy which may originate with the governor'. From that time onwards, the official majority has always supported the measures of the colonial administration, guaranteeing that the opinion of the government would have precedence throughout Hong Kong's history.[42]

The First Chinese Member of the Legislature

Sir John Pope Hennessy, Governor from 1877 until 1882, believed the real interests of the Colony should be equated with those of the permanent Chinese residents rather than the British merchants. He considered that the time was ripe for giving the Chinese greater influence in the Colony's administration. This view was enhanced by the fact that beginning in 1865, Chinese in Hong Kong were no longer subject to Chinese law and the two races were treated equally before the law. The Hong Kong Chinese were providing an increasing contribution to the economic prosperity through their business activities and growing possession of crown leases. By 1877, 130,168 of the 139,144 colonial inhabitants were Chinese. In that year the Chinese were also the largest owners of real property, holding over 90 per cent of the note issues and contributing over 90 per cent of the Colony's revenue. By the time that Hennessy sent to Britain a list of the largest ratepayers in 1881, seventeen were Chinese and only one British.

In 1879 Chinese leaders sent, perhaps at his suggestion,[43] a memorial asking for a share in the management of public affairs through membership on the Legislative Council. Acting upon this, the Governor suggested that a Chinese should fill a temporary unofficial vacancy. The Secretary of State failed to act on the proposal, and the following year, Hennessy again proposed that a Chinese take a temporary appointment to the legislature in the absence of an unofficial. The Governor noted in his proposal that there was a Chinese appointed in the Singapore legislature in 1869 and that he had appointed a Chinese to the Legislative Council of Labuan in 1867 during his tenure there as Governor. This time there was provisional approval. The appointee was a Chinese barrister, Ng Choy, who was a British subject by birth, born in Singapore and educated in Great Britain.

Hennessy then proposed to have the Council permanently re-organized to include Chinese representation. He requested that the size of the Council be increased to eleven members, with the additional unofficial being a Chinese. The Secretary of State rejected the proposal arguing that if the Governor wanted to consult the legislature secretly or if relations with China became strained, the presence of a Chinese member might be 'awkward'.[44] Nonetheless, he left the door open for further attempts at Chinese representation by noting that if a Chinese were appointed in the future, he ought to be a merchant. This was clear official recognition of the mercantile interest, which had initially been enhanced with the appointment of British merchants as the first unofficials.

The 1884 Reorganization of the Legislative Council

It was not until the governorship of Hennessy's successor, Sir George Bowen (1883–5), however, that a Chinese member was permanently appointed. While supportive of Chinese representation on the Council, Bowen noted that selection of the right individual was 'a task of considerable difficulty and delicacy,' because 'I am informed that most of the leading Chinese merchants resident here are not British subjects',[45] and that it 'will not be easy to find among those qualified as British subjects, a native gentleman combining in his own person the proper social position, independent means and education'.[46] The Governor was implying that in addition to being a British citizen there were informal requirements for serving as an unofficial legislator, namely social and economic status. He further complained that most of the Hong Kong Chinese retained their Chinese nationality and therefore allegiance to China, and, unlike Governor Bowring, believed that they were only temporary residents.

However, Bowen did not solely focus on the need for Chinese representation. Rather, he placed this need within the broader context of a comprehensive reform of the Legislative Council. Investigating practices in Ceylon and Mauritius, he concluded that while popular elections were impractical in the Hong Kong community, indirect elections for nomination of two unofficial appointees could occur through the Chamber of Commerce and the Justices of the Peace, as they represented the 'intelligence, education, and property of the Community'. The Governor also suggested the termination of the practice of having a paid government official serve as an unofficial member of the Council.[47] Furthermore, he proposed that the Registrar General and the Surveyor General be added to the official membership and that there be two more unofficials appointed, at least one of whom should be Chinese. Also suggested was a regular annual session for the legislature in November, when a review of the Colony would be provided to the membership along with an outline of the Government's legislative programme. Finally, the Governor highlighted the need for an overlap of membership between the Executive and Legislative Councils, suggesting that all official members of the Legislature serve on the Executive Council 'since they had to support the Executive's policy by their votes'.[48]

The British Secretary of State, the Earl of Derby, accepted most of the broad parameters of the reform, but altered some details.[49] Most importantly, he accepted the need for Chinese representation on the Council, which led to the appointment of Wong Shing, who was exemplary in that he was 'much travelled, speaking good English, and willing to be naturalised', as well as possessing the ability to 'look at Chinese affairs with English and English affairs with Chinese eyes'.[50] However, besides the representation of the Chinese population by an unofficial, it was emphasized that the Chinese would remain best represented by the government itself, particularly by the Registrar General, an official position created in 1858 that included the title of 'Protector of the Chinese'.[51] The indirect election for two unofficial seats took place shortly after the Earl of Derby's communication. With the adoption of Bowen's reforms, the Legislative Council assumed its modern shape and subsequent reforms did not lead to any significant alterations until 1985.

Bowen's reforms recognized the principle of Chinese representation, and thus allowed the government to assume greater control over the majority of citizens by integrating Chinese leaders into the legislature.[52] They also recognized indirect elections as a permanent element in the Colony's constitutional development. They were elections that 'gave great influence to the relatively small groups of important merchants who controlled the Chamber of Commerce and who were also Justices of the Peace'.[53] Hence, representation provided by indirectly elected unofficials remained narrowly defined in terms of mercantile interests.

Governor Bowen enhanced the legitimacy of the Council as a legislative body by printing its minutes together with annual departmental reports and other papers laid before the Council, coming out in an annual series of *Sessional Papers*. Furthermore, the new standing orders drawn up in 1884 provided for the establishment of three standing committees, a Finance Committee[54] consisting of all members of the legislature, except the Governor, with the Colonial Secretary as chairman; a Law Committee, consisting of five members, with the Attorney General serving as chairman; and a Public Works Committee, with five members, and the Surveyor General serving as chairman. The Finance Committee was the most powerful, as all votes on public money were to be considered by it first.

But even with the creation of the Finance Committee, the power of the purse, the ultimate source of all legislative power, remained reactive; it was the power to say no, rather than the power to initiate. Unofficial members remained limited in their financial power, as they could not add to the estimates but simply approve, reject, or reduce financial proposals. This was clearly recognized in the remarks of one appointed unofficial: 'I need not tell you that the unofficial members of the Legislative Council are not representative in any sense. We are nominated by the Government, we have no real power, we cannot exercise any effective control over expenditure and there is left to us only the very modified power of protest'.[55] This limited power was soon to be put into effect.

The 1894 Petition for Representative Government

As in previous initiatives, the demand for a more representative government originated with resistance to increased taxation. In 1894 there were three issues: an increased need for public works, insistence on a greater defence contribution, and a fall in the value of silver, resulting in a devaluation of the currency. The impetus for additional public works came not from within the Colony but from without. Following prison-reform legislation passed in Britain in 1885, the home government pressed for a new prison to relieve the overcrowded conditions in Hong Kong. All unofficials opposed the building of a new prison, with the new Chinese member, Doctor Kai Ho Kai, arguing that the proposed separate cell system was 'unsuited to Chinese temperament'.[56] He chastised his European colleagues in the following manner: 'I say that there is an enormous difference between the European and the Chinese constitution. Of that the Legislature never takes any notice, they simply say that what Europeans require, the Chinese must require and, consequently, they make the mistake of treating the Chinese like Europeans'.[57]

Unofficial annoyance was exacerbated by expenditure proposals to improve sanitation conditions in the colony. In 1890 a plan to reconstruct sewage treatment works was passed over the united opposition of the unofficials. Also, doubling the annual military contribution to Britain and extensive plans to build fortifications and raise a locally recruited force aggravated financial conditions and the relationship between unofficials and the government. The final indignity occurred in 1891 when it was discovered that half the military contribution held over from the previous year had been paid by the Governor on his own authority rather than voted upon in the legislature. The stage was set for a confrontation.

The tensions between the unofficials and the government were aired over the issue of civil servant salaries. Sterling depreciation meant that salaries and pensions were likewise depreciated. In 1890, to meet a demand for increased salaries, a committee consisting solely of unofficial members recommended a salary increase, which was subsequently approved by the Legislative Council and was to take effect the next year. However, in 1891 Thomas Whitehead, an elected unofficial from the Chamber, proposed that the salary increases should be withdrawn because the Colony could no longer afford them. The Governor refused to accept the proposal, noting that the increase had already been approved, and in November 1892 the appropriations containing the increases were carried by the official majority against the unanimous opposition of the unofficials.[58] The unofficials subsequently protested that the vote was unconstitutional and the Appropriations Ordinance for 1893 invalid because the officials had a personal bias in voting for their own salary increases. The Secretary of State did not uphold this protest as 'it would have given the unofficials control of all business by refusing to vote salaries'.[59] The embittered unofficials now felt that the time was ripe for a constitutional initiative.

In June 1894 the indirectly elected unofficials lacking support from all but one of the nominated unofficials organized a petition signed by a majority of Hong Kong ratepayers, asking the Secretary of State to create an unofficial majority in the Legislative Council. Charging that the current Legislative Council was controlled by the official majority, most of whom were residing in the Colony for only a short time, they urged that Hong Kong be placed on a par with the many other colonies that had an unofficial majority in their legislatures. The unofficials argued that it was the 'common right of Englishmen to manage their own local affairs and control the expenditure of the Colony where imperial considerations were not involved'.[60] Specifically, they requested two constitutional innovations: that there be a free election of representatives of British nationality in the Legislative Council and that these representatives constitute the majority of the Council.

The new Governor, Sir William Robinson, noted that the 'real' reason for the attempt to reduce officials' salaries was 'soreness over the increased military contribution' and resentment over the push for a new prison. He believed that the English residents did not necessarily want more elections but hoped to have power through an unofficial majority of nominated members. This would then result in a 'very small alien minority . . . rul[ing] the indigenous majority'.[61]

Secretary of State Ripon's reply noted that 211,000 of the territory's 221,400 inhabitants were now Chinese and that Hong Kong had become a 'Chinese rather than British community' with the Chinese contributing 90 per cent of the colony's revenue. Only 800 male British citizens would be eligible voters[62] and the Secretary of State reasoned that this 'small oligarchy' could not safeguard the well-being of the majority of inhabitants. He believed that the inhabitants could best be protected through the Crown Colony system, which as far as possible made no distinction based on rank or race. He concluded that Hong Kong prospered because it was a British Crown Colony, and unlike other Crown Colonies, such as Cyprus, Malta, or Mauritius, it possessed no traditions, no history, no record of political usage or constitutional rights, and had few lifelong inhabitants.[63]

The unofficials again failed in their attempt at representative government, partly because their main object was prevention of taxation rather than promotion of representation, for they could not abide a truly representative government, which would have given power to the more numerous Chinese. The membership of the Legislative Council was however increased by two, an official (General Officer Commanding) and unofficial (a second Chinese member, Wei Yuk). So, ironically, one outcome of the initiative was an increase in Chinese representation in the legislature, an unintended, and perhaps unwelcome, development for the petitioners. The Council was to consist of the Governor, seven officials, and six unofficial members until 1929.

The most important change as a result of the petition, however, was a concession by the British government to allow some Legislative Council members to sit on the Executive Council. When the Executive Council was established in 1843, it consisted of only senior officials. However, in an attempt to assuage the aspirations of the unofficial Legislative Council members, the British government decided to select two of them to serve on the Executive Council as well. From that time until 1992, there was unofficial Legislative Council representation on the Executive Council, which meant in theory, if not in fact, that Legislative Council unofficials might have some influence in the formative stage of legislation.

To summarize, the attempt to introduce representative government in Hong Kong failed. The British colonial authorities were not willing to accept that constitutional advances in other Crown Colonies should serve as models for Hong Kong. They considered the territory distinct, as its population was overwhelmingly composed of Chinese rather than British inhabitants. Both of the two major British political parties agreed that giving greater political autonomy to the British residents of Hong Kong was 'incompatible' with the moral obligation to protect the interests of the Chinese inhabitants. Furthermore, colonial officials believed that the Chinese were not ready to assume political control, particularly considering the Colony's economic, diplomatic, and strategic importance to Britain. Therefore, the principle of Crown Colony government was even more 'firmly entrenched in Hong Kong as a result of the 1894 Petition'.[64]

The New Territories

This attitude was further strengthened at the end of the century when the New Territories were acquired from China. These territories, which were over twelve times the size of Hong Kong Island, were leased to Britain for ninety-nine years commencing in 1898. The impetus for this acquisition was based on commercial as well as defense imperatives: 'Well-organized opinion at Hong Kong provided the rationale, and imperialist rivalry in China provided the opportunity, for the longed-for extension of Hong Kong boundaries'.[65] This property was seen in terms of 'British counterpoise' for Russian and German acquisitions in Kiaochow (Jiaozhou), Port Arthur (Lüshun), and Talienwan (Dalian). But during negotiations over the territories, it was imperial rather than colonial interests that were given precedence. So, the Chinese were allowed customs privileges, jurisdiction of the Walled City of

Kowloon, and ultimately a lease rather than outright cession, following the form of acquisitions of both Germany and Russia.[66] While initially it was believed that a lease was simply a face-saving disguise for a permanent cession, later events were to prove otherwise.[67]

Unlike the previous acquisitions of Hong Kong Island and the Kowloon Peninsula, the New Territories already had a large indigenous population (approximately 100,000). Therefore, the colonial administration, acting in the British tradition of not interfering with local custom and usage as far as they were compatible with the stability of the colonial government, determined that Chinese rather than colonial law should apply. Although it was found that Chinese law was inadequate to deal with the mass of disputed claims over land ownership, the Governor, Sir Henry Blake, believed that it would be impossible to govern the inhabitants of the New Territories in the same manner as the inhabitants of the older, more urbanized colony.[68] He divided the new land into districts and sub-districts, which were to be administered with village elders. In so doing, he introduced a more geographically based system of representation.

From the legislature's point of view, this was a negative development for two reasons: first, legislative authority in the New Territories was partially given to local inhabitants through a system of committees;[69] second, the fact that no representatives of the new lands were given membership of the Legislative Council undermined its legitimacy as a body truly representative of the whole colony.[70] Furthermore, the new centres of quasi-legislative and quasi-judicial authority were often to be antagonistic towards the legislature.

The nature of the acquisition, as a leased rather than ceded territory, was to have a negative impact on the nature of the legislature's, and eventually the entire Colony's, development, as it was seen in temporary rather than permanent terms. Subsequent governors were to argue unsuccessfully that the British government should make the New Territories a permanent acquisition.[71] By leasing the territories, fears over the intentions of China increased, as it was perceived not only as a potentially hostile neighbour but, possibly, an autocratic landlord. More significantly, the Chinese viewed the treaty which detailed the acquisition to be 'unequal'. By the early 1900s China was demanding the return of the territories, a demand which became unsettling to future colonial development and foreshadowed the eventual takeover of the entire territory in 1997.[72]

Twentieth-century Developments to 1984

The Imperial Conference of 1917, acknowledging the colonies' contribution to the war effort, granted virtual nationhood to the self-governing dominions. In light of these advances, demands for reform of the legislature were once again advocated in Hong Kong. A petition, organized by elected unofficial H. E. Pollock—a member selected by the Justices—was addressed to the Secretary of State asking that the number of unofficials in both the Executive and Legislative Councils be increased, and that the principle of election extend to all unofficials,[73] except the Chinese members ('who stand on a somewhat special footing').[74] Furthermore, the petition requested that the number of unofficials be increased to 10, creating an unofficial majority.[75] The petition protested that unofficials were a 'permanent and hopeless minority ... [as the Legislative Council] simply carries into effect the individual will and judgement of the Governor'.[76] The fact that the appointed unofficial members of the legislature did not sign the petition indicated an early role distinction between appointed and indirectly elected unofficials.

Governor May criticized the petition because he saw no convincing rationale for constitutional change.[77] Furthermore, Pollock's statement that the interests of the Chinese were safeguarded because the unofficial European votes in the Legislative Council would not outnumber the combined votes of the officials and the Chinese members merely 'strengthened the case for continued Crown Colony government which rested on the necessity to protect Chinese interests'.[78] Consequently, the composition of the Legislative Council remained fixed at eight officials (including the Governor), and six unofficials (two elected by the Chamber of Commerce and the Justices of the Peace, and four nominated by the Governor, including two Chinese). While the policy of giving political power to the minority British residents was again decisively rejected, the sentiment for constitutional change remained. This was evident from the launch later that year of the Constitutional Reform Association and the creation in 1921 of the Kowloon Residents Association, both of which advocated greater representation on the Executive and Legislative Councils. The Constitutional Reform

Association sent a petition to the Secretary of State asking for an elected unofficial majority. This request was rejected both in Britain and by local senior civil servants, a rejection which was to be mirrored by concerns in the 1980s: 'What would happen were the government to be defeated by the proposed unofficial majority on some crucial question? The only possible course would be for the government to resign, but that it cannot do, as there are no persons available to take up the offices that would be vacant'.[79]

The Colonial Office was also persuaded by the arguments against the election of unofficials presented by Sir Paul Chater, at that time an unofficial member of the Executive Council who had also served on the Legislative Council (1887–1906). He reasoned that it was already difficult to find Europeans to serve on the Council and that with the possibility of a junior European clerk being elected to the Council over a company head, the difficulty would be exacerbated.

In consulting with the Governor, Sir Reginald E. Stubbs, British authorities were to find further difficulties. Stubbs had two reasons for opposing an unofficial majority: first, an unofficial majority was essentially unnecessary since he, similar to previous governors, 'had invariably given the fullest consideration to the views of the unofficials and refrained from pressing on with proposals to which they were opposed, except when acting upon orders from London'; and second, that an unofficial majority of elected Europeans 'would cause trouble among the Chinese community'.[80] This trouble, he believed, would lead to Chinese agitation for a majority of elected members and ultimately the demise of Hong Kong as a British colony. Stubbs put his comments in the context of political change in China, where 'revolutionary and Bolshevist ideas prevalent in Canton had a very serious influence on the Hong Kong population', and suggested that no constitutional change occur until conditions were more stable. Colonial officials agreed with Stubbs' recommendation and did not reply to the petition. The Constitutional Reform Association finally folded in 1923. Its initiative was the last attempt by the Colony's European minority to grasp power for themselves.[81]

Broader Chinese Representation

When constitutional change finally occurred, it led to greater representation for the Chinese. Following an upsurge in nationalism in China directed mainly against Japan and Britain,[82] Legislative Council Member Sir Shouson Chow was appointed as the first Chinese member of the Executive Council in July 1926, to 'disarm the anti-British sentiment in China and encourage local Chinese loyalty in Hong Kong'.[83] The appointment was made following two general strikes in Hong Kong,[84] which had vividly illustrated the distrust that then existed between the Chinese population and their British rulers.

Two years later, prompted by Pollock's suggestion, two additional unofficials were nominated to the Council, both of whom were from Kowloon, indicating a new basis for representation, namely geography. The increase in the number of unofficials allowed the government to strengthen Chinese representation as well. At the outbreak of the Second World War, the Legislative Council consisted of the Governor, nine officials, and eight unofficials. There were four European unofficials; two were nominated by the Governor, one chosen from the Justices of the Peace, and one chosen by the Hong Kong General Chamber of Commerce. In addition, there were four Chinese representatives, all appointed by the Governor. The growth of Chinese representation was the most significant development in this period. Yet it was accompanied by the view that the government itself must continue to protect the local Chinese community's interests as Chinese legislators were often more active in Mainland China affairs.[85]

The Governor continued to possess not only an original but also a casting vote. He remained not only chief executive but also chief legislator, presiding over the legislature more often as a determined leader than an impartial chairman, making statements on bills and interjecting comments to prompt if not direct the Council's activities.[86] Opposition to the administration's policies occurred infrequently and was 'almost invariably spearheaded by the European members'.[87] The Chinese members often voted with their European colleagues as a 'gesture of solidarity' but did not take the lead in raising controversial matters. They developed a legislative style which emphasized that the 'best way to serve the interests of the Chinese community was . . . quietly and tactfully instead of asking questions and proposing resolutions in the Council'.[88]

The committee structure developed in two ways: the Finance Committee gained power through an unofficial majority, and the Public Works Committee enlarged to include all unofficials. However, the unofficials' committee powers remained circumscribed because their decisions could be overridden in full Council. Hence, it was perceived that a united front against the government would be futile, as the official members on the Council could always vote down the unofficials.

The Legislative Council remained at most an advisory body, comprised of individuals chosen by the Governor more for their ability to provide support and legitimacy for his actions than to prompt him to initiate new policies based on the demands of the populace. The Council's activities were usually characterized as formalistic and routine. Between the wars, it met an average of eighteen times annually, passing approximately thirty pieces of legislation, which were typically incremental changes to existing law. The rapidity with which legislation passed through the Council led to the conclusion that 'the task of protecting civil liberties from the encroachment of the executive was carried out by the Colonial Office instead of by the unofficial members of the legislature'.[89] The next reform of the Legislative Council was not to be made until after the Second World War, and it was to be at the instigation of the government rather than the people.

The Young Plan

Hong Kong fell to the Japanese on 25 December 1941, and for the next three years and seven months the Japanese controlled the Colony, nominally through two councils, the Chinese Representative Council and the Chinese Cooperative Council. These councils were consultative only and were used for system-maintenance activities, mainly as a conduit of Japanese policy to the Chinese population.

With the fall of Japan in 1945, the Colony was surrendered to Rear Admiral Sir Cecil Harcourt, who took it in the name of both the British and Chinese governments. Normal civil administration was restored by May 1946 with the return of Governor Young,[90] whose first formal announcement contained a promise of constitutional reform:

His Majesty's Government has under consideration the means by which in Hong Kong, as elsewhere in the Colonial Empire, the inhabitants of the Territory can be given a fuller and more responsible share in the management of their own affairs ... by handing over certain functions of internal administration ... to a Municipal Council constituted on a fully representative basis.[91]

Impetus for the Young Plan came from many quarters. The victors in the war, led by the Americans, advocated political freedom, which they saw as a primary goal of the war. More specifically, at the Yalta Conference in February 1945, American President Franklin Roosevelt urged in private conversation with the Russian leader Josef Stalin that Hong Kong should be given back to China or internationalized as a free port.[92] Moreover, the United States and Britain had earlier signed an agreement which sought to end the 'unequal treaty' system with China. While at times during the war it appeared that Hong Kong would revert to China, towards the end of the war, with both China and the United States attending to more pressing matters, Britain was able to restore colonial rule.[93] Given the anti-colonial imperatives, it is surprising that the Young Plan ended in failure. To comprehend how this occurred, a brief review of the context of the debate over the plan is beneficial.

The Young Plan provided two major initiatives. First, the Governor proposed the creation of a municipal council to help administer the urban area; two-thirds of its members were to be elected in equal numbers by Chinese and non-Chinese voters, and the remaining one-third, again in equal numbers, by Chinese and non-Chinese representative bodies. The new council was to be financially autonomous, receiving revenue from rates and licenses, which would be used to administer all urban services.

Second, he suggested that the number of unofficials in the Legislative Council be increased by one, with the number of officials decreased by two. The new Council would then consist of seven officials and eight unofficials in addition to the Governor, who as president would retain both his original and casting votes. To broaden the representative basis of the Council, it was proposed that four unofficials should be nominated by community organizations, one each by the Justices of the Peace and Chamber of Commerce, and two by the new municipal council.

Although the plan was initially well received, no concrete steps were taken before Young's retirement in May 1947. Two months later, however, it was announced in the House of Commons that the Secretary of State had given his provisional approval of the plan. For it to be implemented, a series of bills embodying the reform needed to pass the Legislative Council. This format was seen as imperative by British colonial authorities as they wanted to ensure that public opinion, through the unofficial members of the Legislative Council, was properly assessed.[94] The process required much deliberation and took much longer than originally expected. It was not until two years later that the three bills[95] for the creation of the municipal council were given their first reading in the Legislative Council. In the 1949 budget debate, D. F. Landale, the senior unofficial, objected to money being earmarked for the municipal council and urged that reform of the Legislative Council occur first: 'There is I believe a strong body of opinion that does not favour this reform, and would rather see a larger and more representative Legislative Council working in conjunction with a larger and more representative Urban Council than through the cumbersome machinery of the proposed Municipal Council'.[96]

Governor Sir Alexander Grantham replied that he was quite willing to reconsider the proposal and suggested that the unofficials propose their own reform: 'I can assure this Council that it is not the intention to steam-roller through the Legislative Council the existing proposals and any alternative proposals that have the backing of the unofficial members of this Council will be forwarded to the Secretary of State with my recommendations'.[97]

The unofficials then came up with a series of resolutions, abandoning the proposed municipal reform and substituting it with a reform of the Legislative Council. A resolution in June 1949 proposed a seventeen-member Council, with the number of officials reduced to six, part of the remaining unofficials elected and part appointed. In the subsequent debate, one Chinese unofficial, Sir Man Kam Lo, voiced concern over any attempt to make the government more representative. He stated that no electorate devised could do justice to all sections and interests, that the current unofficials represented the interests of the Colony as a whole, and that this remained the justification for the nomination rather than the election of the majority of them. In addition, he argued that an electorate composed of non-British subjects would 'involve long argument and delay'.[98] He proposed that the partly nominated element in the Legislative Council be retained and a new elected element added. The consensus among unofficials during the debate was that it was difficult to ascertain what kind of constitutional reform the community wanted, and many appeared to doubt if any demand for reform existed.[99]

As a consequence of the unofficials' negative reaction to the municipal government initiative and international events, including the Chinese Revolution of 1949, the only reform carried out was an increase in the number of elected representatives on the Urban Council from two to four. There was no change in the Legislative Council, as the time was 'inopportune for other constitutional changes of a major nature'.[100]

The Young Plan has since been characterized as 'still-born'[101] and an 'historical curiosity'.[102] It was unpopular initially with the unofficials, who not unsurprisingly were threatened by the creation of a new municipal body with elected unofficials who might usurp their role as 'representatives of the people' and diminish their political power. The unofficials had similarly attempted to quash the creation of the Sanitation Board and a later proposal to make it into a municipal council. The demise of the Young Plan was hastened by the lack of public support. And ultimately, as had happened so many times since the creation of Hong Kong, events beyond the boundaries of the Colony, particularly in China, required that the status quo be maintained. There was a fear that China would exercise pervasive influence on the Council if elections took place.[103] Colonial authorities feared that the electorate for the legislators would not be British nationals and consequently would have no allegiance to the British Crown. Somewhat paradoxically, authorities also feared that China would be unable to tolerate a more democratic, and hence legitimate, Legislative Council, which could prove much more troublesome than the eager-to-please colonial government,[104] particularly if it was, as anticipated, strongly anti-communist. Furthermore, it was believed that the election of even a portion of the unofficials would inevitably lead the colony on the path to independence taken by other colonies (see Chapter 2).

It has been suggested that the colonial authorities' decision to place the locus of constitutional reform in a new municipal body rather than in the legislature may have been due to an 'attempt by Britain to keep her imperial interests in Hong Kong—the port facilities and the naval dockyard—insulated from the area of activities of any newly emergent Chinese politicians for as long as possible'.[105] This would suggest that systems maintenance was the motivation for the meagre constitutional reforms. The reforms can thus be seen as attempts to ensure the resolution of conflict rather than the promotion of democratic representation.

Furthermore, the Young Plan was instructive as some of its features—for example the proposal to create a body composed of functionally based as well as popularly elected members— were to reappear in reform proposals of the mid-1980s. Also, the reasons for its failure—the jealousy of those already in power, particularly the appointed unofficials, the general apathy of the public, and the external constraints posed by upheavals in China—would be mirrored in future attempts at 'constitutional change.

Over the next few years the Colony was preoccupied with the after-effects of the Chinese revolution. It had to cope with the influx of Chinese refugees[106] and the economic changes necessitated by the loss of entrepôt trade with China.[107] During this time of tremendous upheaval, additional constitutional reform, particularly that aimed at enfranchising the majority of the new Chinese population, was considered unrealistic as well as unwise. It was feared that broader enfranchisement would lead to bitter factional disputes and exacerbate an already unstable climate. Nonetheless, up to 1984 some incremental changes did occur.

When the Legislative Council was reconstituted in 1946, it had nine officials and seven unofficials. Over the next few years, the number of Chinese unofficials began to exceed the number of European unofficials. In 1964 an equal number of official and unofficial members were allowed, although the Governor still retained his casting and original vote so that the unofficials could be voted down. Yet this was to prove to be a symbolic rather than a real majority; the last time the official majority was used to overcome the unanimous opposition of the unofficials was in 1953.

The need for both numerical and substantive broadening of the representativeness of the legislature's unofficials came to light during the 1966–7 riots. The riots, while arising from different issues,[108] revealed a colonial political system that was alienating a sizeable proportion of the population by failing to meet their social aspirations and improve their standard of living.[109] It was clear that the political structure, as exemplified by the Legislative Council, which had first been based on British mercantile interests and then Chinese business interests, failed to take into account the rising working and middle classes.[110]

Following the riots, the government attempted to be more responsive to local needs by broadening the avenues for public opinion to reach the government.[111] They did this primarily through representation on the Legislative Council, a variety of consultative committees and commissions, and the establishment of the City District Offices scheme in 1968. This scheme paralleled in the urban areas the district scheme in the New Territories—both schemes had the goal 'of representing the government at the basic level of society'.[112]

The impetus for a broader representational basis for the Legislative Council was provided by Governor Sir Murray MacLehose. From 1971, and most notably in 1976, the Governor nominated unofficials from a broader range of backgrounds to provide a more accurate assessment of public opinion in the colony. One of the 'class of '76' recently recalled: 'We were chosen to represent a particular body of people, with the Governor trying to balance the groups of the community through his appointments'.[113] The Governor was attempting informally to recognize functional categories of individuals, which were later to be formally instated in reforms during the mid-1980s. Included among these functional representatives were some individuals who were not wealthy, such as a retired health inspector from the Urban Services Department and a former bus driver. This necessitated that unofficials receive some pay, with allowances of $4,800 a month provided to hire clerical assistance.

Conclusion

In Chapter 2, five stages in the colonial preparation process were identified:

1. Division into legislative and executive councils; nomination of unofficial membership to the legislative council;
2. Unofficial members become the majority in the legislature;
3. Majority of the executive council comes from or is related to majority of the legislative council;
4. Nominated officials disappear from the legislative council;
5. Independence with a parliamentary form of government.

Yet by 1984 Hong Kong's legislature had not progressed beyond stage one. As we have seen in this chapter the reasons for this lack of development were many. Originally, Hong Kong was seen as a base for imperial commercial interests mainly in China rather than as a colony. Even as the population grew, the Colony remained defined first and foremost in terms of imperial concerns (later broadened to include defense of British interests in Asia) rather than purely colonial concerns. The population, both British and Chinese, were considered to be temporary rather than permanent residents, so no stable form of representative government was deemed imperative. With the lease of the New Territories the rationale for maintaining the status quo gained new ground, namely, that constitutional development was incompatible with a territory that was predominantly leased rather than ceded. Finally, there was an implicit understanding with China that no fundamental changes would occur in the political system.[114] At all times these various rationales were strengthened by the belief that the population was, for the most part, not only politically unsophisticated but apathetic; it was characterized in terms of its 'utilitarianistic familism, social aloofness and political passivity' which was conducive to a 'minimally-integrated social political system'.[115]

As a body oriented towards the status quo, the Legislative Council would find it most difficult to confront—as well as to shape—a future that was soon to hold dramatic changes: first in the form of the 1984 Sino-British Agreement, which was to re-establish Chinese sovereignty over the territory in 1997; and second, as the political culture changed as more citizens joined the middle class, became more educated, and were therefore more inclined to participate in, if not mould, their political system.[116] Perhaps of all governmental institutions, the legislature was least prepared for these tremendous changes.[117]

Hong Kong was unique among British colonies in that before 1984 there had been little constitutional development. It was also unique among other non-communist industrializing societies in that rapid economic development has not been accompanied by democratic political development. In 1984 the irony of Hong Kong's history was that the legislature was not only the body least prepared and equipped for change—it was also to be the locus of most of the changes that were planned to occur before 1997. It is to these changes that we turn next.

4   The Legislative Council, 1985–1995

This chapter explores political developments from the mid-1980s to two years short of the transfer of sovereignty in 1997. It provides both an historical and political context in which to evaluate the development of the Legislative Council's functions, the subject of Chapter 6, and the development of the political roles of Hong Kong's legislators, considered in Chapter 7.

The major initiatives of the 1985–95 period, including the Sino-British Agreement, the Hong Kong government's series of Green and White Papers, and the Basic Law, are all considered in this chapter. Unlike in other works[1], they are considered in light of the debates on them in the Legislative Council. These debates show the current divisions among conservative and liberal legislators and how the ideological demarcation between them is based on the issue of direct elections. The chapter traces how the consensus nature of Legislative Council proceedings has dramatically, and perhaps irrevocably, changed as the legislature has debated Hong Kong's political future.

Sino-British Negotiations

The period since 1985 has seen the most dramatic changes in the Legislative Council's history. These changes were instigated when China decided that it would regain sovereignty over the colony upon expiry of the New Territories' lease in 1997.[2] The intention of the Chinese government, and the agreement to it on the part of the British government, was announced in the Sino-British Agreement in December 1984. The agreement determined that Hong Kong would not follow the normal path of British colonies to independence, but rather was to become a part of mainland China. While there was some consultation with unofficials during the negotiations over the future of Hong Kong, it was clear from the outset that the future form of government was to be determined by Britain and China rather than by the people of Hong Kong or their representatives in the legislature.[3]

Negotiations commenced after British Prime Minister Margaret Thatcher visited Beijing in September 1982. Her insistence that the treaties founding Hong Kong were legal provoked the Chinese to respond that they were not bound by 'unequal treaties' and would recover Hong Kong when conditions were 'ripe'. Thatcher, unwittingly, had made the fatal error of making Hong Kong the touchstone of Chinese nationalism, resulting in the loss of a rational basis for future discussions.[4] Subsequently, negotiations commenced over the future of Hong Kong, with the British asking for sovereignty or at least a continuation of British administration, and the Chinese insisting that their sovereignty over Hong Kong was not negotiable, and that administration could not be divorced from sovereignty. Initially, Thatcher attempted to insert Hong Kong representatives into the negotiating process on the basis of a 'three-legged stool' concept, but the Chinese were insistent that they alone would represent their Hong Kong 'compatriots'.[5]

During the first year of negotiations Legislative Council members were content to trust British diplomats to negotiate on their behalf and remained passive because of the need for confidentiality. As one commentator noted, 'It made sense then to rally round the colonial Government, to maintain staunchly, in the teeth of accusations of sycophancy and betrayal of the Chinese race, that it was better to be a Colony and free than Chinese and under state dictatorship'.[6] But when it became apparent that China was to regain sovereignty over the territory, members attempted to influence the negotiations through a series of debates.[7] Denied a direct role in the negotiations, they hoped that the concerns voiced in chamber would be heard and acted upon by both negotiating parties. The first such move came on 14 March 1984 when senior unofficial R. H. Lobo offered a motion asking that 'any proposals for the future of Hong Kong . . . be debated in this Council before any final agreement is reached'. Yet this historic attempt to assert deliberative power over Hong Kong's future was criticized by some members of the community as well as the pro-China press, who charged that the unofficials were not truly representative of the community and hence had no role to play in determining Hong Kong's future.[8] Given that all members were appointed by the

Governor, such a charge was difficult to refute. Nonetheless, during the motion debate, Lobo responded:

I make no special claim for the extent to which the Council represents the will of the people of Hong Kong and so far as I am aware, no member of this Council has ever done so. It is not necessary to do so to establish that we have a responsibility to address this issue, and the purpose of this motion is to reaffirm publicly our commitment to that responsibility.[9]

In the subsequent debate, 22 unofficials spoke, most of whom were careful to not offend the Governor or the British government over their handling of the drafting process and simply suggested that Legislative Council be used as a conduit for public opinion. One member went so far as to reassure both negotiating parties that by holding this debate, the Legislative Council was not trying to gain a power of veto or final word over the negotiations but was merely assisting them in achieving the common objective of prosperity and stability in Hong Kong.[10] A few members, however, were more vocal about their exclusion from negotiations:[11] 'We have been silent far too long already. . . . We are a modern people who cannot relish the prospect of an arranged marriage'.[12] Another member argued: 'I feel strongly that if we do not concern ourselves with the future of Hong Kong . . . then we are not worthy of being unofficial members of this Council. [We must] provide some leadership in guiding Hong Kong through this crisis.'[13] Another voiced frustration at their lack of power:

I believe that time has come for China and Britain to lift the veil of confidentiality, and take the people of Hong Kong into their confidence. After all, it is our future. We have the right to know and express what we want. We are only fulfilling our duty and exercising our right as members of one of the highest public bodies as well as asserting the basic right that I believe each and every one of our 5.3 million people has over our future.[14]

The government's response to the motion was calculated to assuage any feelings of mistrust. The Chief Secretary commenced his comments by clarifying the value and function of the Legislative Council: 'This Council's deliberations have provided Hong Kong with a body of laws for the good government of Hong Kong and those deliberations have made a vital contribution, over the years, to the stability and prosperity which those who live there enjoy today'.[15] He then went on to state that all official members of the Council would vote in favour of the motion.

One month after the debate, members were informed that Britain would be relinquishing not only sovereignty but administration over the territory after 1997.[16] Earlier, in anticipation of this decision, one member had called for a fully elected legislature to ensure some local autonomy when the territory was incorporated into China.[17] Now it was apparent that the unofficials must move into the power vacuum left by the British retreat. For the first time they could exercise political power independent of the discredited (by virtue of its failure to prevent the take-over) administration which had appointed them. In quick order, they held a series of additional debates in an attempt to influence the drafting process. One concerned a position paper for issuance to the British government during an upcoming visit by the unofficial members of the Executive and Legislative Council. Another concerned the acceptability of the Sino-British Agreement. Others focused on the future legal, economic, and social systems.

The members' position paper outlined the requirements for a highly autonomous post-1997 Hong Kong and suggested that the essential elements of the future Basic Law be incorporated into the Sino-British Agreement before its passage by the British Parliament.[18] The paper also suggested that Britain should retain some 'residual status' in the colony after 1997 to ensure that the terms of the agreement were fulfilled. A survey taken at the time provided the members with much-needed legitimacy, demonstrating that three-quarters of the Hong Kong people were aware of the position paper and that a majority agreed with it, although one-quarter indicated that it was too cautious and too late.[19] In visits to both London and Beijing during the next two months, unofficials had to defend their views as genuine expressions of Hong Kong opinion, although their unelected status did little to legitimize their claims.[20] At this juncture, China began to realize that it could no longer simply ignore the unofficials, whom they believed to be a small élite close to the British government. Given the public support for their earlier trip to London, China decided that it would mount a twofold campaign: first, accusing the unofficials of 'sabotaging' negotiations by their interference, and second, agreeing to meet with some of them, but belittling their claims to represent the Hong Kong community by only recognizing them in their 'individual', rather than 'Legislative Council', capacity. This was to foreshadow future fights over the power and representativeness of the legislature.

During the August debate, it was revealed that the public's opinion of the agreement would not be sought through the Legislative Council but through an independent assessment office. While the findings were to be forwarded to the British Parliament, their influence was questionable, as the British Foreign Secretary had revealed that no changes to the agreement could be made after it was initialled. Only eight members spoke on the motion, and while they unanimously welcomed an assessment office, they expressed reservations about ruling out a referendum on the agreement. There was an air of futility about the assessment process. Since assessment would not begin until the agreement was initialled, the Legislative Council, and indirectly the Hong Kong people, were informed that their views would make no difference regarding the framework of the future government. As one unofficial stated, 'What choice is really open to us? The plain truth seems to be a choice between an agreement or no agreement at all, leaving China to make its own unilateral declaration, the contents of which would be anybody's guess'.[21]

The Sino-British Agreement

The draft agreement incorporating a joint declaration, initialled on 26 September 1984, provided that Hong Kong would become a special administrative region of the People's Republic of China.[22] The special administrative region was to have its own government and legislature composed of local inhabitants and enjoy a 'high degree of autonomy'.[23] Because members of the judiciary were to be appointed by the Chief Executive, who in turn was to be appointed by the Chinese, it was clear that whatever autonomy the territory was to possess would primarily reside in the elected legislature. Hong Kong's social and economic systems and its life-style were to remain unchanged for fifty years after 1997. The Joint Declaration also specifically stated that China's socialist policies would not be practised in Hong Kong, giving rise to the interpretation that the relationship between Hong Kong and China was to be along the lines of 'one country–two systems'.[24]

Annex I of the Joint Declaration dealt with the future form of the legislature. It stated that

the government and legislature of the Hong Kong Special Administrative Region shall be composed of local inhabitants. . . . The chief executive . . .

shall be selected by election or through consultations held locally and be appointed by the Central People's Government. . . . The legislature . . . shall be constituted by elections. The executive authorities shall abide by the law and shall be accountable to the legislature.

The power of the legislature was defined solely in terms of lawmaking: 'The legislative power of the Hong Kong Special Administrative Region shall be vested in the legislature. . . . The legislature may on its own authority enact laws in accordance with the provisions of the Basic Law and legal procedures'. The explanatory notes accompanying the Joint Declaration noted that laws of the special administrative region, including the common law and laws passed by the legislature, would be valid unless they contravened the Basic Law. All laws, however, would have to be reported to a committee of China's legislature, the Standing Committee of the National People's Congress, 'for the record.'

The immediate reaction within Hong Kong to the Joint Declaration was fairly positive.[25] It was, however, presented as a *fait accompli*, as 'the alternative to acceptance of the present agreement is to have no agreement'.[26] Yet many questions remained unanswered, especially with respect to the legislature. What was meant by 'constituted by elections', and more fundamentally, what was to be the nature of legislative representation? How were the candidates to be selected? Who would participate in elections? Would representation be based on geographic districts, as was common in most Western democracies? Would the electoral districts be single or multi-member constituencies? And would the principle of 'one man–one vote' be instituted?

With respect to legislative powers, what was to be the exact relationship between the legislative and executive branches of government? Would lawmaking now encompass the ability to initiate rather than just approve or reject bills proposed by the executive? Would the legislature be able to override an executive veto of legislation? Would it be allowed to participate in the election of the Chief Executive? Would the chamber be able to elect its own leadership?[27] What would be the nature of executive accountability to the legislature? Would additional powers, such as oversight, including question time, investigation, and even impeachment, be granted to ensure executive accountability? Would the Council's budgetary power be enhanced?[28] And would these powers be exercised within the framework of a new standing committee system which would enhance executive oversight?

Finally, what was to be the relationship between the Hong Kong legislature and China's legislature, the National People's Congress? Would there be a direct link through the election of some local legislators to serve on the National People's Congress? What would be the nature of the 'reporting' function of Hong Kong laws? Would this allow for the National People's Congress to determine the constitutionality or even desirability of local laws, and consequently to exercise a veto over them? Essentially, what comprised a 'high' degree of autonomy?

Many of these questions were asked during the ensuing Legislative Council debate. For on the same day the agreement was initialled, the Governor tabled the document in the Legislative Council, which then held a three-day debate in October. The motion moved this time by senior unofficial Lobo was in the form of an endorsement: 'That this Council endorses the Draft Agreement . . . and commends it to the people of Hong Kong'. The debate came in the form of an endorsement because a majority of the 27 members who spoke believed that the agreement had fulfilled the four requirements specified in the earlier position paper.[29] Yet in endorsing the agreement, members chose to ignore a vital requirement of their own position paper, namely incorporation of key areas of the Basic Law into the agreement. This omission would prove catastrophic for future autonomy, when discrepancies occurred between interpretation of the promises of the agreement and the provisions of the Basic Law.

But at the time most members were happy to endorse the agreement, as they believed that the British government had done its best to secure Hong Kong's future under difficult circumstances. As a normally critical analyst put it:

It is difficult to think of any other nation which could have entered into such long and difficult negotiations over such a sensitive bone of contention as Hong Kong, involving as it did China's acute sensitivity over questions involving its territorial sovereignty, and emerged with such a detailed agreement offering the people of Hong Kong what amounts to a constitution for an almost completely autonomous region of China.[30]

Members were aware that the Chinese government had originally simply wanted a statement of general principles to accompany the announcement of their resumption of sovereignty, but due to British prodding, the final document contained a comprehensive rendering of assurances and freedoms to ensure Hong Kong's 'high degree of autonomy' after 1997.[31] One member, in comparing the agreement with other decisions that had previously determined Hong Kong's future, expressed his pleasure in being able to participate in the endorsement:

I am glad that I live in this era. I do not only have the chance to make an opinion on problems left over from history, but also have the opportunity to take part in the debate . . . on the draft agreement. . . . However, the Chinese in Hong Kong in the 19th century were not so lucky. I believe they had no chance to catch a glimpse of the Treaty of Nanking and the Convention of Peking under which Hong Kong was ceded'.[32]

Yet subsequent debate demonstrated that not all councillors were willing to give blank endorsement to a document that they had not shaped. More critically, even those who were supportive of the broad parameters of the agreement remained fearful that China would ignore it in drafting the new constitution for the territory, the Basic Law, or just disregard what was written in either document and do what it wished in various situations. As one unofficial bluntly stated: 'Given the many discontinuities which have characterized the policies pursued by successive leaderships since the establishment of the People's Republic, what guarantee is there that a future leadership will honour the terms of the agreement?'[33] And one member, noting that this was the 'most important debate in the history of this legislature [as] . . . we are speaking of the lives and destiny of over five million people and of generations to come,' was unwilling to endorse either the motion or the agreement. Stating that Britain did not do all in her power for Hong Kong, he labelled the agreement 'the best of a bad deal'.[34]

At the end of the debate Lobo qualified the statements of his colleagues by noting that 'the Unofficial members . . . have no common position nor platform; we participate in these proceedings as individuals, drawn from a wide spectrum of society, and the views we express are our own in furtherance of how we, individually, perceive the public interest'. Nonetheless, he was able to argue that 'this debate has responsibly reflected the reservations, fears and worries which trouble many people of Hong Kong about the future'. He added that only time and history would tell whether the high hopes for the agreement were justified and whether members had discharged their duties adequately.[35]

The Joint Declaration spawned several initiatives to ease the transition from British colony to a special administrative region of

China. The Joint Liaison Group[36] was established to assist in implementing the Joint Declaration; the Sino-British Land Commission was established to conduct consultations regarding implementing land leases which would be entered into before 1997 but extend beyond that time; and the drafting of the Basic Law commenced. In addition, the Hong Kong government undertook a series of internal reforms, which in an abbreviated and unique form of decolonization, instigated fundamental changes which were to have a significant impact on the form and functioning of the legislature before 1997. Given the widespread doubts which persisted after publication of the agreement, many felt that a better guarantee for Hong Kong's future would be immediate changes to erect a more 'suitable structure of government well before 1997 which will stand the test of time after 1997'.[37] It is to these initiatives that we turn first.[38]

Proposals for the Development of Representative Government

In April 1984, when British Foreign Secretary Sir Geoffrey Howe announced the planned termination of British sovereignty and administration in Hong Kong, he sought to assure the Hong Kong people that China had promised a high degree of local autonomy. Two slogans were commonly used during this time: 'Hong Kong people ruling Hong Kong' and 'one country–two systems'.[39] To ensure this autonomy, Howe promised that in the last years of British rule, the territory's government would 'be developed increasingly [on] representative lines'. The first initiative to realize this promise occurred on 18 July 1984, when the government issued a Green Paper—the document which initiates the consultative process, inviting public comment on several proposals for constitutional reform. The aims of these proposals were: to develop progressively a system of government which is able to represent authoritatively the views of the people and which is more directly accountable; to build this system on existing institutions, preserving the practice of government by consensus; and finally to allow for further development if that should be the wish of the community.[40]

Since there was no precedent for structuring a colony's transfer to another country, the government built on its existing framework to encourage gradual, evolutionary changes which would enhance representativeness and accountability. The reform focused on who was to make the decisions rather than the type of decisions that were to be made. This was because the extent of policy-making power could only be determined by China, which at that time had yet to announce the draft agreement or the Basic Law. Therefore, while the Green Paper proposed no change in legislative powers, it did suggest an increase in the number of unofficials and a change in the way these members were chosen. The proposal noted that the government was one of 'consultation and consensus' based on two separate sources of representation: 'first, those arising from . . . residence; second, those arising from . . . occupations'.[41] These sources were seen as comprising two constituencies, geographical and functional, respectively. To maintain this tradition, it proposed that a substantial number of unofficial members be elected from within these constituencies. Geographical representation would be indirect, with members of the District Boards and two municipal bodies, the Urban and Regional Councils, selecting legislative representatives.[42] Functional representation would be achieved by having members of recognized professions elect one of their number to represent them in the Council. Direct elections based on universal franchise were ruled out as they 'would run the risk of a swift introduction of adversarial politics . . . introduc[ing] an element of instability at a crucial time', but it was indicated that they might be introduced sometime in the near future.[43]

The suggested number of elected versus appointed unofficials varied, with the Green Paper offering proposals (coinciding with the three-year terms of members) for the years 1985, 1988, and two options for 1991 (Table 4.1).

The Green Paper also examined the relationship between the executive and legislative branches, suggesting that four members of the Executive Council in 1988 and then eight members in 1991 (out of a total of fourteen) be elected by unofficial members of the legislature. Additionally, it suggested that future governors be selected by an electoral college composed of the unofficials of the Executive and Legislative Councils, and that a form of ministerial government might be introduced. Finally, the paper proposed that the Governor be replaced as president of the Legislative Council by a presiding officer elected by unofficials from among themselves.

The Legislative Council debated the proposal on 2 August 1984. Nineteen members reacted in a fairly conservative manner to the

Table 4.1 1984 Green Paper Proposals: Composition of the Legislative Council

	1984	1985	1988	1991	
				Option 1	Option 2
Officials	18	13	10	10	10
Appointed members	29	23	16	12	—
Functional constituency members	—	6	12	14	20
Electoral college members	—	6	12	14	20

proposal. One member, for instance, defended the merits of the current appointment system: 'Measured by Western standards, we cannot claim to have a fully representative government, but we do live in a relatively stable and progressive society, enjoying the various essential freedoms we all dearly cherish. The virtue of our existing system of government is the absence of confrontation and adversarial politics'.[44]

Reservations were also expressed about the timing of direct elections to the Legislative Council, the definition of functional constituencies, and the time for consultation on the initiatives. There were repeated calls for gradual change to promote stability. The members' unprogressive attitude was not surprising, given that many of them would have to stand for election or lose their seats after the 1985 election. Furthermore, members supported the concept of indirect rather than direct elections by pointing to the apathy and political immaturity of the people of Hong Kong, reflected in the low turnout in recent District and Urban Council elections.[45] While most acknowledged that a large majority in Hong Kong wanted the status quo to be preserved, there was a growing realization that this would no longer be possible: 'In the past, Hong Kong people were not at all interested in politics. Their attitude was "you'll be the housekeeper, I'll care about earning my own living". Now the times have changed. . . . From now on, everyone should spare some time to help "keep the house".'[46]

A few advocated broader changes than the paper suggested. While no members called for direct elections immediately, several indicated support for their introduction by 1988. In addition, three members spoke in favour of a ministerial system in which the legislature elected members of the Executive Council who would be 'endowed with executive authority' thereby linking the 'people's elected representatives with the administration of this territory'.[47] In general, however, members spoke of the need for gradual change, continuity, and stability, an emphasis mirrored in a subsequent public survey.

Twenty-nine members spoke during the White Paper debate in early January 1985, following a motion by the Chief Secretary that 'this Council welcomes the plans and intentions described in the White Paper'. After public consultation, changes proposed to the initiative were mostly incremental. The number of indirectly elected members was increased from 12 to 24 due to difficulties in determining the allocation of seats. The electoral college was expanded to incorporate ten geographical constituencies, based on one to three districts established in 1977 by the District Board scheme and representing approximately 500,000 people each. Moreover, two special constituencies based on the Urban and Regional Councils were created, resulting in the electoral college returning 12 rather than 6 members as originally proposed. The impetus for this expansion appeared to come directly from the government rather than the public. As one member noted: 'The only conclusion I could draw [regarding the change] is that this is not due to the public pressure in Hong Kong nor the Chinese demand to speed up the process. It could [only] be the product of Her Majesty's Government through the Hong Kong Government to step-up the process of democratization in Hong Kong'.[48]

While the electoral-college scheme appeared to be widely accepted, the functional constituencies proposals caused much controversy, with criticism voiced about the arbitrary choice of interests to be given representation in the legislature. Those selected appeared to ensure that the majority would speak for the upper class rather than the poor,[49] providing an 'over-representation of strategic elites'.[50] The government sought to assure those sectors not included in the new electoral scheme that their interests would be represented through the Governor's appointed members.[51] Ultimately, it was determined that there would be nine functional constituencies returning 12 unofficials in 1985 who would serve for a three-year term. The government noted that these electoral arrangements would be re-evaluated by 1987 to allow for any necessary changes including the direct election of some members.

In sum, the reform attempted to develop a more representative government by instigating a fundamental compositional change in the legislature.[52] While in 1984 all unofficial members were appointed by the Governor, 1985 was to see a fairly large segment elected through the electoral college and functional constituencies. In addition, the ratio of officials to unofficials was to change. In 1984 officials comprised 38 per cent of the membership; after 1985 they were to compose only 18 per cent. Finally, the number of appointed members was to fall from 62 per cent in 1984 to just 39 per cent in 1985. Figure 4.1 depicts the new composition of the Legislative Council for 1985.

Changes in the relationship between the Executive and Legislative Councils, including the election of some Executive Council members by the legislature, were not incorporated into the White Paper. However, it was stated that 'these matters will be considered further at a later stage',[53] and during the White Paper debate the Chief Secretary promised that the 1987 review would consider the introduction of ministerial government and more specifically address the composition of the Executive Council and the position of the Governor.

The Legislative Council held a debate on the White Paper in January 1985. For the most part, the members were fairly supportive of the initiatives.[54] While there was some agitation for direct

Figure 4.1 The 1985 Legislative Council's Fifty-seven Members

President (1)

Officials (10)   Elected members (24)   Appointed members (22)

Electoral College (12)   Functional Constituencies (12)

Urban Council (1)	Commercial (2)
Urban District Boards (7)	Industrial (2)
New Territories District Boards (3)	Financial (1)
Regional Council (1)	Labour (2)
	Social (1)
	Medical (1)
	Legal (1)
	Teaching (1)
	Engineers (1)

elections,[55] most members expressed more concern that the innovations be tailored to Hong Kong rather than transposed from Western settings: 'Should we really transplant…what seems to work well in the West to Hong Kong without due consideration to our own unique circumstances? … What we are most afraid of is the fact that the cry of total democracy will be blindly accepted by the people of Hong Kong … seriously affecting … our own chances of survival and progress'.[56] And even the idea of indirect elections was greeted with reservations, which were to mirror future disputes. Some members voiced concern that electoral politics would elevate legislators who might put sectional interests ahead of the public interest. Warnings were made about ensuring that the 'various functions contribute to the community rather than for the interests of those groups to be protected in the Legislative Council'. A question was raised 'whether elected members would properly look after the interests of the community as a whole … [or] put the long-term interests of their sectors above immediate benefits'; a warning was made that 'elected [Legislative Council] members should speak and act not only in the interest of their respective constituencies but of the people of Hong Kong'.[57] While the Chief Secretary spoke of the need for broader representation, he placed greater emphasis on ensuring that such changes 'minimise any tendency to factional politics and divisiveness'.[58]

The Green and White Papers were not that much different from previous developments in other British colonies (see Chapter 2).[59] However, given the stagnation of Hong Kong's constitutional development, these tentative decolonization steps seemed to many observers like a radical step toward democracy. Local businessmen in particular were fearful that a more representative legislature would result in higher taxation to pay for social benefits.[60] Yet in reality, the proposals backed away from liberal, democratic reforms typical of late twentieth-century development. The elected members would be a minority, as the Council was to be expanded to retain a substantial number of appointed members (22) and officials (10). Furthermore, their mode of selection was archaic. Indirect elections had been a 'common expedient' in a number of underdeveloped colonies, justified when 'illiterate villagers in the bush are capable of choosing one of their number to act as their spokesman at the district level, but are too ignorant of wider public issues to make a sensible choice between candidates competing for seats at the territorial level'.[61] This rationale did not apply to the more sophisticated electorate in Hong Kong.[62] In addition, the fact that one-third of the members of the electoral college were unofficials appointed by the government rather than chosen by the people served to weaken the legitimacy of candidates as 'true representatives' of the people. Not only were appointed members allowed to select a Legislative Council representative, but they were also eligible for election to the Legislative Council themselves, with the result that six of the electoral-college members had an appointed rather than elected mandate. This ensured that a 'substantial majority of the 56-member legislature owed their presence to government largesse'.[63] Moreover, the Governor had retained his casting and original vote and remained president of the Council. Finally, contrary to the movement towards ministerial systems that had taken place in all previous British colonies since the end of the Second World War, the idea of electing some members of the Executive Council was rejected.[64]

Ultimately, the question was why, after 140 years of incremental variations, should the government become an instigator of such dramatic changes? Up until 1984, any attempt to parallel the decolonization moves in other British colonies had been frustrated by fears of offending China and undermining internal stability. Now, however, there was a perception that the executive-led government should have a broader base so that China could not exercise total control after 1997 through her appointed Chief Executive. Colonial status had been acceptable to the Hong Kong people because the local government was accountable to a democratic mother country that treasured freedom and the rule of law. Now Hong Kong was to assume a similar status under a different mother country, one that had no record of promoting the rule of law or protecting liberty. So, it appeared imperative that power be distributed to locally elected leaders who would be better able to guarantee some measure of autonomy, accountability, and civil rights. Furthermore, the colonial government, increasingly a 'lame duck', needed to facilitate participation and power-sharing to maintain its legitimacy. Also, the imperatives to 'exit in glory and to sweeten the Sino-British deal to be "sold" to the British people by a package of liberal political reforms' was also a powerful reform factor.[65] The democratization trend was increased by local pressure as it became evident that Hong Kong had no credible representatives to voice its case during the Sino-British discussions over the territory's future.

The Hong Kong government thus faced an impossible task: 'to devise representative institutions firmly based on popular support . . . strong enough to resist Peking's demands after 1997, while at the same time ensuring that these same institutions [were] not strong enough to prove any danger to the existing social order . . . and also to ensure that these institutions [were] compatible with China's . . . structure of government after 1997'.[66] The government appeared to be working at cross purposes: on the one hand, creating a more broadly based legislature by dividing it by geographic as well as functional interests; on the other hand, hoping that this new development would minimize factional divisiveness and lead to the same consensus as had characterized Legislative Council decisions in the past. These competing demands resulted in reform that was a 'patchwork of short-term improvisations for the simultaneous and partial attainment of a set of contradictory goals'.[67] The government given these reform imperatives reacted schizophrenically: 'conservative and innovative, concessionary and assertive, courageous and timid, far-sighted and short-sighted'.[68] It raised a number of proposals and in the process lifted expectations that would be difficult to meet in future reform efforts.

Far more important than the actual changes that occurred in 1985 was the anticipation of further changes, including the possibility of the direct election of members of the legislature in 1988. These initiatives were the subject of a 1987 political review. During the reform debate, many members of the legislature looked expectantly to the 1987 review to provide answers to questions not yet definitively addressed. These questions included:

1. How can executive authorities be more accountable to the legislature?
2. Should unofficial members of the Executive Council be elected by members of the Legislative Council?
3. Should a ministerial system be institutionalized?
4. Will the number of functional categories be increased to include, for instance, accountants, nurses, and social workers, paramedics and religious groups?
5. Will direct elections be instituted?
6. What should be the Governor's future relationship with the Council?

7. Will the Council have a role in the Governor's selection?
8. Should the total membership of the Council be increased if its functions and powers are to be increased?[69]

However, the 1987 Green Paper review was more notable for its lack of answers than as a definitive guide to the future.

1987–1988 Green and White Papers: Review of Representative Government

On 27 May 1987 the Hong Kong government published *The 1987 Review of Developments in Representative Government*. The Chief Secretary had indicated as early as 1985 that the review would consider whether a portion of the legislators should be directly elected in 1988; what the Executive Council's powers, composition, method of selection, and linkage with the Legislative Council should be; and whether the Governor's relationship with the two councils should be changed.[70] However, these objectives were frustrated by Chinese resistance.

The 1987 initiative sharply contrasted with that of 1984. It did not advocate any specific political or electoral reform but instead invited public comment on a number of rather confusing options dealing with the mode of determining legislative composition, the presidency of the Council, and new electoral requirements and procedures. These options made no reference to reform of the Executive Council. Instead of providing the expected leadership to the community 'who traditionally look to its authority for guidance',[71] the government presented ideas which were 'tedious, confused, and at times illogical'.[72] It was clear that the Hong Kong government had all but jettisoned its aims of developing a more accountable and representative legislature as it did not recommend any particular reforms or reiterate earlier goals.[73] This retreat was due to China's opposition, which it voiced through a series of intermediaries, labelling any modification of the government before 1997 a violation of the Joint Declaration. From China's perspective, any change which would impact on the future special administrative region was to be specified by the Basic Law rather than initiatives in the waning days of colonial government. China wanted no change so as to retain an executive-led government, which would be easier to dominate through its appointed Chief Executive. Furthermore, China was deeply distrustful of democratization, believing it this would be a way in which Britain, and possibly Taiwan, would exert control over the territory in the post-1997 years.[74] 'Convergence' between the Chinese-drafted Basic Law and the form of government up to 1997 became the new priority from China's, and eventually Britain's, perspective.[75] Accordingly, the long-awaited 1987 review on constitutional changes was pre-empted by Chinese authorities, who made it clear that they would accept no further changes in legislative composition unless these changes 'converged' with the upcoming Basic Law. Because the Basic Law was not to be issued until 1991, the need for convergence placed a significant restraint on further reform.

The Legislative Council Green Paper debate, in which 45 members participated, reflected the disappointment of many over the paper's lack of direction and clarity: 'This Green Paper compares very unfavourably with the 1984 Green Paper. . . . [It] lacks direction and purpose. But what it suffers from in substance, it makes up in volume, with the result that it is pretty indigestible'.[76] The lack of government leadership in clearly articulating further democratic reforms was looked upon as a derogation of duty: 'Government has not fulfilled its duties, namely to present clearly ideas on future development in representative government. . . . I do not believe there are too many governments in the world that behave like the Government of Hong Kong, that is when confronted by the issue they look on with folded arms and put the responsibility on its people'.[77] Others looked at the paper as a betrayal in terms of what had been promised not only in the Joint Declaration (that the legislature shall be constituted by elections) but by the British and Hong Kong governments (who promised to develop a more representative government, based on directly elected seats):[78] 'the supporters of direct election for 1988 have sometimes been described as "idealists" and "dreamers". . . . But if we are dreaming, who led us up the garden path and made us dream?'[79] Some members even believed that Britain had 'sold' Hong Kong to China to facilitate smooth trade relations between the two countries: 'Within a short period of three years the Hong Kong Government's attitude towards political development has greatly changed. . . . Where mutual interests are involved enemies can become friends and vice versa. Hong Kong's political developments will inevitably be affected by the Chinese interests and British interests.'[80]

The debate is significant as it is indicative of the changing nature of the Legislative Council, which since 1985 had contained a broader range of views encompassing both ends of the ideological spectrum.[81] The conservatives were against further reform, wanting a retention of the status quo to ensure stability and prosperity: 'The maintenance of this system is far more important to the real interests of the people of Hong Kong than the introduction of a politically oriented system that could divide the community against itself and [lead] . . . into confrontation between differing political groups'.[82] They also argued that more time was needed to evaluate the impact of the 1985 innovations before proceeding in new directions.[83] Some appointed members still appeared to favour the 'old days' rather than those in the new-look Legislative Council: 'In 1985 the system underwent a momentous change . . . but despite longer working hours and greater frequency of meetings, can we honestly say that we have done better than before? Has our productivity increased? Is government more efficient or . . . have we provided better service to the community? In my humble opinion, I honestly doubt we have'.[84]

Conservatives were particularly fearful of the negative consequences of direct elections. One noted that directly elected members would 'create a permanent opposition . . . as frequent objectors of Government policies and actions since they have to prove to the electorate that they, and not the majority, speak for the population'. Dealing with this type of legislator would have negative consequences for governmental accountability:

The need for constant political bargaining with the populist elements to maintain an appearance of effective Government will tend to reduce Government's authority and decision-making flexibility. The tendency will then be to bolster its position again by closing bureaucratic ranks and also by relying more on China to support its dwindling authority in dealing with the opposition. What appears to be a move towards greater democracy could therefore turn out to have the effect of prompting more autocratic rule.[85]

In a similar vein, the advent of direct elections would change the function of the legislature from that of systems maintenance, primarily to secure the legitimacy of government, to a new body which would question that government's authority to act. Arguing that direct elections would lead to adversarial party politics, one member noted that 'the immediate task of those parties not in power is to topple the government. They ridicule the government's policies, harass the government officials' behaviour, discredit the government's decisions, and try to shatter public confidence in the ruling party'.[86] Because members of the legislature would not be serving in the executive branch as in a ministerial system, directly elected members could only be 'representative but not responsible', engaging in behaviour that was 'threatening to Hong Kong's stability and future prosperity'. Allowing elected legislators to engage in such behaviour would result in Hong Kong 'paying the price of confrontational politics without the remotest possibility of reaping the benefits'.[87] Furthermore, from a cultural point of view, this type of defiance is 'at variance with the Chinese tradition and mentality'.[88] A final warning was that direct elections could 'lend themselves quite easily to "Patriotic Front" movements of the type we have seen coming to power in Eastern Europe'.[89] Ultimately, most conservatives believed that Hong Kong's future could only be ensured by keeping China happy by converging with the Basic Law. This belief, along with their natural inclination for durability, led the conservatives to advocate either no change or a very incremental change in the number of seats indirectly elected.

The liberals believed that the freedom to choose one's government is a 'basic human right'.[90] Direct elections were the 'litmus test' to determine if the British and Chinese governments were genuine in their intention of assuring the territory's future 'high degree of autonomy'.[91] For them, the issue of direct elections was symbolic, taking on magnified importance: 'Without direct elections we would not have a democratic political system. Without a democratic political system', one said,

the policy of 'Hong Kong people administering Hong Kong' cannot be genuinely practised. Without 'Hong Kong people administering Hong Kong' there will not be high autonomy. Without high autonomy we cannot realise the 'one country, two systems' policy. Without the realization of the 'one country, two systems' policy, it would only be one country, one system and then there would not be any stability and prosperity.[92]

Yet some liberals were careful to point out that direct elections only helped realize a larger goal: 'direct election is not an end in itself, but only a means to an end . . . [which] is to implement successfully the policy of one country, two systems [with] a high degree of autonomy. As a positive measure, we should introduce direct elections in 1988 to ensure that our Government, both before and after 1997, will be more responsive to the people it governs, and will therefore have their support and will be able to defend their rights and freedoms'.[93] Another echoed that direct election would help 'consolidate the "one country–two systems" concept which has been promised to us'.[94] In sum, those who supported direct elections believed that legislators so elected would provide a bulwark against future Chinese interference, ensuring that Hong Kong would indeed enjoy a high degree of autonomy as promised in the Joint Declaration.[95]

Hence, the issue of direct elections to the legislature in 1988 proved to be the ideological demarcation line between liberals and conservatives, providing concrete evidence that the Legislative Council was no longer a consensus-oriented body. Of the 46 unofficials, 18 were opposed, 18 supportive, and the remainder noncommittal on this issue.[96] Many arguments offered by both sides were both repetitious as well as contentious: 'Indeed, it seems to me that never before in Hong Kong have so many said so much to express so little to so few'.[97] The Legislative Council itself had earlier demonstrated its division and gave up any pretence of leadership when it issued a report on constitutional development, which merely established the parameters of debate rather than providing firm recommendations: 'They set out the rules of the game but they refused to get in involved with the game itself'.[98] So rather than rely on the legislature, the government decided another form of assessment would be needed to ascertain the range and depth of feeling about the issue within the community. Consequently, a survey office was established to receive and record all views about the Green Paper so that refinements could be made to the White Paper before its publication.

In November 1987, the report of the Survey Office was introduced to the Legislative Council. Over 130,000 direct submissions were received (compared with 364 received in response to the 1984 Green Paper); as well as material from 170 public opinion surveys and 20 signature campaigns. Ninety-six per cent of all submissions commented on the issue of direct elections.[99] Given the turgid style of the office's subsequent report, it would have been expected that the direct election controversy would have been dealt with definitively. But the report only obfuscated the issue, heightening controversy. The office itself commissioned two public opinion surveys which rigidly followed the myriad of options set out in the Green Paper, listing as a first option for all innovations 'no change'. In the end, this methodological confusion resulted in almost half the respondents being unable to understand the complex questions and giving no reply. Where other surveys had found between

41 and 62 per cent in favour of direct elections, the office's surveys showed that between 12 and 15 per cent were in favour.[100]
Additionally, while the quantity of submissions might lead to the
assumption that the findings were thorough and legitimate, the
subsequent Legislative Council debate revealed a controversy over
their format and analysis.

The main source of contention was the handling of submissions
on direct elections. The Survey Office decided that 230,000 petition signatures for direct elections would be excluded but 70,000
mimeographed letters against them would be allowed. Based on
the survey findings and the other submissions, the office reported
that 94,270 individuals were opposed and 39,345 in favour of direct
elections in 1988. Both the deletion of petition signatures and the
methodology employed in framing the surveys angered the liberals.
One liberal concluded that 'these two surveys had been conducted
for and on behalf of the Government of Hong Kong with the sole
object of ensuring that the results would not justify the introduction
of direct elections in 1988'.[101] Another charged that the report 'was
not worth the paper it is written on, as the public would consider
their opinion raped'.[102]

In February 1988, the government issued the White Paper, calling it *The Development of Representative Government: The Way
Forward*. It was most noteworthy for what it did not say rather than
what it did. Noting that change must be both 'prudent and gradual',
the paper found that while there appeared to be a strong public
desire for further representative developments, there was no clear-
cut consensus, particularly on the timing and extent of direct elections to the legislature. It promised that by 1991 (the year that the
Basic Law was to be published) 10 (of 60) members of the legislature would be directly elected from geographical constituencies.
But these new members were to replace rather than join the members selected by the electoral college. In the short term, the only
change advocated in the White Paper was an increase in the
number of members elected from functional constituencies from 12
to 14, with an equal reduction in the number of appointed seats.[103]
The issue of removing the Governor as president of the Council
was not directly examined, but it was suggested that he be allowed
to appoint a senior official member to preside in his absence. While
the government had acted positively in establishing some seats for
direct election, its decision to wait until 1991 indicated to most
observers that it would no longer pursue its original goal of representative government unless China approved.[104]

The debate over the White Paper was one of the most acrimonious in the Council's history. Significantly, the Chief Secretary, rather than an unofficial, moved that 'this Council takes note of the plans . . . in the White Paper', which allowed members to neither endorse nor reject the paper. Forty-three members then spoke during the two-day debate, which saw two amendments offered but the motion in its original form carrying by voice vote.[105] The main source of controversy during the debate was the government's decision to postpone the introduction of a segment of directly elected members until 1991. It was charged 'that the Government lacked the courage of its convictions [behaving] . . . as a lame duck';[106] that the paper was a 'stop sign' to the development of representative government;[107] and that it was a 'betrayal and misrepresentation' of what the majority in Hong Kong wanted.[108] The government was excoriated for being more eager to please China than the people of Hong Kong and allowing diplomatic deference to become political subservience. It was said to be raising a 'white flag' to make it easier to merge with the 'red flag' of socialism. The critics, however, were in the minority, and in turn drew fire from their colleagues, some of whom accused them of degrading Hong Kong's international image and consequently undermining its prosperity and stability by the use of such confrontational tactics.[109] Dismayed by the uproar, the senior unofficial warned the members that 'unless we get our own act together, there is little chance of a successful transition and a secure future for Hong Kong'.[110] Another member put it more colourfully: 'Aggressive or not, satisfied or not, we are in the same boat. This boat has a full load and the water is not particularly tame. Our primary duty at this time is to keep the boat steady with as many rowers as possible so that it can glide smoothly towards 1997. . . . Let us keep the sailing smooth by not rocking the boat'.[111] Yet the waters were to be even more turbulent as the Legislative Council debated the Basic Law, the first draft of which was issued just two months later.

The Basic Law

The drafting of the Basic Law[112] was the responsibility of the National People's Congress, which in 1985 established the Basic Law Drafting Committee composed of 23 members from Hong

Kong and 35 from China.[113] While the constitutional drafting was specified as 'purely an internal affair of China', several Legislative Council members sat on the committee, and assurances were given that the constitution would be primarily based on opinions gathered from the people of Hong Kong.[114] The collection of these opinions was helped by the locally based, 176-member Basic Law Consultative Committee.[115] Composition of both the committees was skewed: in favour of the mainland drafters on the Basic Law Drafting Committee and business and professional groups on the Basic Law Consultative Committee. The appointed liberals were overwhelmingly outnumbered by mainland drafters and their conservative Hong Kong supporters.[116]

Unlike most constitutional drafting exercises in other localities, the first draft of the Basic Law presented options, rather than a framework, for several critical areas of the new constitution. Annex II to the draft listed four alternatives for legislative composition; all of these had legislators selected for a four-year term from multiple sources including districts, a grand electoral college, functional bodies, and direct elections.[117] By providing a broad definition of 'elections' it was clear that China wanted a weak legislature with a membership that was more indirectly than directly elected, allowing for better control over the institution. This mixed electoral basis reduced the effectiveness of the legislature, as it insured that it would be much more difficult to forge a consensus. In addition, it undermined the accountability and ultimately the legitimacy of the legislature.

The proposed legislature was also weak in terms of its powers. The draft retained many of the Legislative Council's colonial features, with its main function to endorse executive initiatives rather than exercise wider policy-making powers, especially those of initiation and oversight. While members, either individually or jointly, could introduce legislation, they would first need the approval of the Chief Executive.[118] Legislation passed by the Council would only become law after it was signed and promulgated by the Chief Executive; moreover, any law could be revoked by the Standing Committee of the National People's Congress.

The scope of legislative powers was quite normal and clarified by concrete specifications: to enact, amend, or repeal laws according to the Basic Law; to examine and approve budgets submitted by the government; to approve taxation and public expenditure; to hear and debate the policy addresses of the Chief Executive; to raise questions on the work of the government; to summon persons to testify or give evidence; to hold debates on any issues concerning public interest; to endorse the appointment and removal of judges; to receive and process complaints from Hong Kong residents; and, with a two-thirds majority, to pass a motion of impeachment. However, these powers were limited by the extensive powers given to the chief executive.

The Chief Executive was given Draconian powers: if he considers that a bill passed by the legislature is 'incompatible with the interests of the special administrative region', he may return it to the Legislative Council to be reconsidered. If the legislature passes the original bill again by a two-thirds vote, the Chief Executive must either sign and promulgate it or dissolve the legislature. With respect to the 'power of the purse', the Legislative Council was saddled with its current colonial constraints. The legislature could only accept or reject the budget as a whole. Refusal to pass the budget would lead to the legislature's dissolution; in this case the Chief Executive could secure temporary appropriations. In sum, the Legislative Council was not to be a legislature in the usual sense, but merely 'a deliberative assembly with no authority "on its own" to make laws' concerning public policy or the budget'.[119]

Executive accountability to the legislature simply meant making regular reports and answering questions posed by the members. The Chief Executive was given the power to determine whether government officials should testify or give evidence before the Legislative Council, circumscribing legislative oversight and the power of investigation. He was also was given total discretion in choosing members of the Executive Council, making it clear that no ministerial form of government was envisioned.[120]

Finally, impeachment powers were applicable only to the Chief Executive, not inferior officers. Impeachable offenses were limited to a serious breach of law or dereliction of duty. While legislators were given the right to participate in the removal of the Chief Executive through the initiation of impeachment proceedings, an independent investigating committee, chaired by the Chief Justice, would determine if impeachable offenses had occurred, and only the Central People's Government was empowered to remove the Chief Executive from office. In sum, instead of the executive being accountable to the legislature, as specified in the Joint Declaration, the Basic Law made him accountable to China and ensured that he could control the legislature through use of his extensive powers, including the threat of dissolution.[121]

A final limitation on legislative powers was the provision that the State Council may apply laws enacted by the National People's Congress relating to defence, foreign affairs, and 'national unity and territorial integrity'. The very vagueness of the last two areas raised concern over the scope of the special administrative region's future legislative autonomy. In sum, the draft appeared to emphasize Chinese sovereignty, as embodied by the Chief Executive, rather than Hong Kong's autonomy, as realized through the legislature. The draft made it apparent that Hong Kong's promised 'high degree of autonomy' would be superseded by claims of Chinese sovereignty entitling the central government to intervene in any matter which might affect China's interests.[122]

The Legislative Council's July 1988 debate on the first draft was in the form of a noncommittal motion that simply stated that the Council 'takes note' of the draft and urged the public to express their views on it. Surprisingly, given the draft's shortcomings and inconclusiveness, the mood of the members was tentative but hopeful. The senior unofficial member opened the debate by remarking: 'Who could have conceived 50, 20, or even five years ago that a Government of China would one day publish the draft of such a law, widely promulgate its text, and formally invite public comment on it?'[123] Members had delegated more detailed scrutiny of the draft to a constitutional development panel. As the panel had not yet made its report, most comments offered in the debate were tentative suggestions so as not to impede the consensus that was being worked out in the panel discussions. According to the convenor of the panel, members had three general concerns: that the Basic Law be consistent with the Joint Declaration, not only in letter but in spirit to promote 'one country–two systems' and 'a high degree of autonomy'; that the Basic Law provisions be both justiciable and enforceable; and that during the next nine years, the political system be allowed to evolve.[124]

Most of the debate, however, was again dominated by statements concerning legislative composition. Members spoke both for and against functional constituencies;[125] for and against universal suffrage and direct elections;[126] and for and against[127] a new grand electoral college,[128] which would choose part of the legislature as well as the chief executive. For the first time in chamber, the hope was expressed that the members of the pre-1997 legislature remain in place after 1997 to minimize uncertainty and disruption; this arrangement was labelled the 'through train'.[129]

Members also addressed specific questions concerning legislative powers and executive accountability to the legislature. For instance, some were concerned with the adequacy of their oversight powers, advocating the extension of impeachment powers over executive officers;[130] others wanted the Basic Law to specify standing panels to ease executive oversight,[131] and in general provide better powers of investigation.[132] Enhanced executive accountability was suggested by having three-quarters of the Executive Council members come from the legislature[133] and having the Chief Executive elected from among members of the legislature and then formally appointed by China.[134] While several members voiced disquiet about the draft being more concerned with promoting China's sovereignty than Hong Kong's autonomy[135] and attempting to retain a colonial framework that was no longer appropriate for Hong Kong,[136] most exhibited a cautious optimism that the final draft would better reflect their concerns.[137]

The five-month-long consultation period (April–September 1988) did not yield any consensus on the form or function of the legislature. A series of composition models were presented for public discussion, but the one ultimately adopted by the Basic Law Drafting Committee did not appear in the Basic Law Consultative Committee's five-volume consultation report. This model, adopted in January 1989, postponed the introduction of a fully directly elected legislature for at least 15 years after 1997. It suggested that only 27 per cent of the members of the 1997 legislature be directly elected, with the remainder elected by functional constituencies. By the year 2007, directly elected and functional constituencies were each to form 50 per cent of the legislature. A referendum held in the year 2011 would determine if a one man–one vote direct election for all seats in the legislature and the position of Chief Executive should occur.

Disillusionment with this model was expressed by many, most prominently by the liberals, who now believed that China had destroyed any pretense of a fair and open drafting process in the push to destroy democratic initiatives. The adoption of this new model was seen as 'high-handed, procedurally improper and politically unjustified'.[138] The liberals attempted to shift the referendum forward to a date before 1997 but this suggestion was rejected by China as an infringement upon its sovereignty. It was clear that the Chinese, like the British during deliberation over the Joint Declaration, had no intention of commissioning a public-opinion survey or a referendum to allow an assessment of local views. The high-handed tactics adopted by the Basic Law Drafting Committee and the perceived inflexibility of the Chinese towards any democratic initiatives hastened a legitimacy crisis not only for the Hong Kong government, still smarting from criticism of its 1988 White Paper, but for the Chinese government as well. The extent of this crisis was evident from the increase in Hong Kong people emigrating, up from 18,300 in 1981 to 45,800 in 1988; people who were not given the opportunity to shape their present and future governments by a vote with their hands were 'voting with their feet'.[139]

The new compositional model for the legislature was one of the main changes incorporated in the second draft of the Basic Law released in February 1989. The draft also stipulated that the president of the legislature be elected from among the members of the Council. Limitations on legislative power remained extensive. The draft stated that members could not propose bills relating to public expenditure or the structure and operation of government and further, that the written consent of the Chief Executive would be required before bills relating to policy could be introduced. In addition, the draft limited legislative power by specifying that all laws enacted by the legislature be presented to the Standing Committee of the National People's Congress 'for the record'. If the Standing Committee were to consider that any law does not conform with the Basic Law, it would return that law, at which time it ceases to have force.

Another significant provision in the new draft was for the selection of the Chief Executive, who was to be chosen by an election committee of 800 members composed of individuals from various industrial, social, and professional sectors, as well as public officials, including members of the Legislative Council. The Chief Executive would then be formally appointed by the Central People's Government. In sum, the draft favoured a strong Chief Executive who would dominate the other branches of government and be accountable to, and possibly controlled by, Beijing. Generally, the new provisions in the second draft heightened local distrust and led to widespread scepticism about life in the special administrative region.[140] The drafting process and the provisions of the Basic Law clearly showed that Beijing's rulers have no intention of creating a truly autonomous special administrative region.[141] It was in a climate of distrust, dismay, and skepticism that public consultation over the draft re-commenced. This final consultation period was to have lasted five months, although circumstances were soon to require an extension.

Public consultation began with a Legislative Council debate on 31 May. Before the debate, the Council members unanimously put forward their own framework for the composition of the Council calling for one half of the Council to be directly elected by 1997 and 100% by 2003 (Table 4.2).

In addition, unofficials, now referred to as OMELCO members after the Office of the (non-governmental) Members of the Executive and Legislative Councils which assists them in their work, urged that the Chief Executive be popularly and directly elected no later than the year 2003. They further stipulated that 'if he needs to be elected by elections committees before 2003, these committees should be democratically elected and the election procedures used by the committees should be democratic'.[142]

This was a significant attempt by the legislature to mould its future and that of the Chief Executive's office. Clearly, lessons had been learned about the meaning of Chinese 'elections', which could denote forms of participation not found in the West. The members also acknowledged for the first time the superiority of a directly elected legislature *vis-à-vis* a functionally based legislature—a

Table 4.2 OMELCO Consensus on the Pace of Democratic Reform (Number of Members and Percentage of Total Membership)

	1989	1991	1995–1997	1999	2003
Directly elected members	—	20 (33%)	no fewer than 30 (50%)	60 (67%)	90 (100%)
Functional constituency members	14 (25%)	20 (33%)	no more than 30 (50%)	30 (33%)	—
Electoral college members	12 (21%)	—	—	—	—
Appointed members/ Officials	30 (54%)	20 (33%)	—	—	—
Total	56	60	60	90	90

Source: OMELCO Annual Report, 1989, Appendix 2.

conclusion at odds with the draft's proposal. The consensus model also reflected a widely held perception that the Basic Law was contrary to the spirit if not the letter of the Joint Declaration, with its promise of autonomy and its stipulation that all members of the legislature be elected. This concern was coupled with fears of Chinese autocracy, which strongly intensified when, in early June, tanks of the People's Liberation Army killed pro-democracy demonstrators in Tiananmen Square.

The push for democracy on the mainland in the previous two months had been strongly supported in Hong Kong, where the people were beginning to realize that their own fate was intrinsically linked to political developments in mainland China: 'To many of them, the plight of the Beijing masses in pursuit of democratic reform *vis-à-vis* the CCP/PRC party-state was too close a real-life parallel to their own uphill battles in the still ongoing Basic Law drafting process and the abortive attempts for constitutional reforms in 1987–88'.[143] Ironically, it was the events in Beijing that finally galvanized the Hong Kong public into a political collectiveness, with one in five (1.5 million) Hong Kong people protesting the events in China in various marches. One march was led by two elected legislative councillors, Szeto Wah and Martin Lee. The impact of the protest, so unprecedented in size and intensity, brought Hong Kong squarely onto the world stage, as leaders in democracies throughout the world voiced outrage over China's repression and concern for Hong Kong's future. The effect of the bloodshed at Tiananmen Square on the Hong Kong people, already jittery over the years of Sino-British machinations on their political future, was overwhelming. As one local newspaper editorial said of China, 'ten years of winning confidence through its "open door" policies and economic reform have been wasted in one night of slaughter'.[144]

Chinese leaders were quick to react to the public outpourings in Hong Kong. In his report on the student protest to the National People's Congress, the mayor of Beijing charged that the students were working 'in collusion with foreign forces' to force China to 'give up its socialist road'. The notion that Hong Kong was 'polluting' China with its free market and more pluralistic political ways became a frequent theme over the next few months.[145] Warnings were repeatedly given to Hong Kong 'compatriots' to stop subversive activities if they wanted the pledge of autonomy granted in the Joint Declaration to be honoured.

The aftermath in Hong Kong was a heightened political consciousness and an attempt by Legislative Council members and the public alike to exert more control over their future. Local liberals formed a massive umbrella coalition, the Alliance in Support of the Patriotic Democratic Movement in China, linking many pro-democratic organizations and civic groups into a co-ordinated network. Not only did several members of the Basic Law Drafting Committee and Basic Law Consultative Committee take part in subsequent protests, but two Hong Kong members resigned from the Basic Law Drafting Committee and two liberal members of the Legislative Council boycotted its proceedings. So the period after the second draft changed from one of consultation to one of confrontation.[146]

British authorities moved quickly to shore up confidence in the local government, which was harshly criticized for 'kowtowing' to the Chinese too much in the past. They planned to speed up the pace of democratization before 1997, enact a Hong Kong bill of rights, and offer British citizenship to a number of local British Dependent Territories passport holders. While the British government did enact a British passport scheme[147] and subsequently the local government did pass a bill of rights, it was less successful in realizing its plan for a more democratically based legislature. By early July, the House of Commons Foreign Affairs Committee released a report on Hong Kong calling for one-half of the Legislative Council to be directly elected by 1991; and for all of it to be directly elected by 1997. The Legislative Council held a motion debate on the report in early July, but most of the debate examined the committees' proposals to provide British citizenship to a limited number of British subjects in Hong Kong and to enact a bill of rights, rather than its proposal for a more democratic legislature. Most members spoke out in support of a quicker pace for democratic reform, but the familiar cautions of not moving too hastily were also voiced. Since the motion was in the form of 'taking note' of the committees' report, no specific action was urged.

In late 1989 the Chinese authorities strongly criticized local democrats, insisting, for instance, that Basic Law Drafting Committee members Szeto Wah and Martin Lee 'explain, repent and account for their past activities which are subversive' if they wanted to resume their work on the committee. It was ironic that the Chinese were attempting to use membership of a committee intended to promote confidence in the future as a means of forcing conformity.

In this confrontational climate, Legislative Council members pushed the British to include their consensus package in diplomatic discussions of the Basic Law. The model, issued in October under the title 'Comments on the Basic Law', had to be sent via British diplomats to Chinese authorities, as China continued to refuse to recognize the Legislative Council as a legitimate source of local opinion. Members met British diplomats and members of Parliament to gain backing for their electoral framework.[148]

Despite these efforts, the future political structure of Hong Kong adopted in the Basic Law failed to match the OMELCO consensus model. The final draft, issued on 16 February 1990, provided that only 20 seats in the 1997 Legislative Council be filled by directly elected members.[149] Of the remainder, 30 seats were to be allocated to functional constituencies and 10 seats to be chosen by an electoral college. The number of directly elected seats was to be increased to 30 by 2003. Although the Basic Law stated that the 'ultimate aim' is election by universal suffrage, the only provision for further change was through an amendment process requiring a two-thirds majority of the Council and approval of the Chief Executive. The compositional changes of the 60-member legislature from 1991 to 2003 are seen in Table 1.1.

The Legislative Council debate over the final version came in the form of two separate motions. The first motion, offered by senior unofficial (appointed) Mr Allen Lee, stated 'that this Council expresses disappointment that the OMELCO consensus has not been adopted in the formulation of the future political model and urges the community, in the interest of Hong Kong, to be united in its efforts to achieve a successful democratic system'. In addition, Mr Jimmy McGregor, a functional constituency member, moved 'that this Council deplores the extremely undemocratic political model proposed for the Basic Law . . . [and urges] accept[ance] of a more democratic political model . . . based upon the OMELCO consensus'. These two motions were debated together on 28 February and 1 March. Most of the 32 members who spoke expressed their strong disappointment that the OMELCO consensus model had not been adopted. Although they recognized that the parameters of the Basic Law had been determined, nonetheless, the members urged greater democratization for the future political system. Yet the majority was unwilling to risk the ire of China by supporting McGregor's motion. He was later to remark with bitterness: 'China disapproved of the OMELCO model and, when the chips were down, so did OMELCO. What leadership, what dedication, what an example to our confused and anxious people, what encouragement to China's leaders . . . what vindication of the value of bullying and intimidation, what a blow to democracy and democratic values and, ultimately, what lack of courage'.[150] Upon the rejection of McGregor's motion Lee's was passed. A more comprehensive debate on the Basic Law was held one month later.

On 4 April Mr Martin Lee, a functional constituency member, moved that 'in light of the promulgation of the HKSAR [Hong Kong special administrative region] Basic Law . . . this Council urges the Chinese and British Governments to . . . amend the relevant clauses of the Basic Law according to the recommendations of [the] OMELCO "Comments on the Basic Law (Draft)".' Lee argued that even though the Basic Law had just been promulgated, it was nonetheless timely and appropriate to urge amendments to it. He castigated the Basic Law Drafting Committee for ignoring the strong local opposition to several divisive issues and neglecting the widely heralded OMELCO model.[151] Lee was especially critical of a new provision in the Basic Law which imposed a 20 per cent ceiling on the number of legislative councillors who could be non-Chinese or with a right of abode in foreign countries. But he was most censorious of how the Basic Law deviated from the Joint Declaration: 'I wonder how many people in Hong Kong, when they read the promises in the Joint Declaration that the HKSAR shall have an elected legislature to which the executive is accountable, would have envisioned the present scheme . . . providing for a legislature which is only one-third democratically elected, whose members cannot introduce any bill without the chief executive's written consent, and which can be unilaterally dissolved by the chief executive for failure to pass any "important bill".'[152]

Another member expressed outrage at the Basic Law's final contours, charging that it 'strait-jacketed future political developments' by turning the legislature into a 'mere consultative body', confining its powers to the extent that it was 'impossible to check and balance the executive authorities or hold them accountable'.[153] Other members expressed dismay not only at the contents of the Basic Law but the fact that all three governments ignored the Legislative Council's legitimate demand to help shape the future Hong Kong government.[154]

Both the British and Hong Kong governments were denounced

for being as guilty as the Chinese in ignoring the Legislative Council: 'On the one hand, China refused to accept the views of OMELCO which it regarded as part of the British political structure. On the other hand . . . we realized that the British Government had not taken the views of OMELCO seriously. Nor did the Hong Kong Government attach much importance to the views of the OMELCO Constitutional Development Panel in formulating details of the 1991 election'. This member went on to warn that continuing to ignore the Legislative Council would provoke difficulty for the government's future efficiency, effectiveness, and legitimacy: 'It is . . . imperative that the Hong Kong Government . . . improve [our] relationship . . . otherwise, the acceptability of the Administration's policies and the degree of support they will get from the public will surely be adversely affected'.[155]

Despite the air of futility, a 20-member majority supported the motion, with 6 against and 16 abstaining.[156] While unable to sway the Chinese government to provide for more directly elected legislators in the Basic Law, the British and Hong Kong governments were able to make some amends. Shortly after the motion was passed, the Hong Kong government announced that the number of directly elected seats for 1991 would be increased from 10 to 18. This increase was made only after Britain had secured China's agreement in an exchange of letters between the British and Chinese foreign secretaries.[157]

The Basic Law had left unspecified two critical areas which had to be clarified before the 1995 election: first, the composition of the new Electoral Committee which would elect 10 members; and second, the form of the nine new functional seats. When the Basic Law was adopted, the British government promised that if the elections in 1991 were successful, they would push for more directly elected members in the Legislative Council in 1995. This issue resurfaced after the British general election in April 1992, when the British government reaffirmed its support for a faster pace of democratization in 1995.[158] The Chinese government reacted in typical fashion, emphasizing that they would not allow any amendment of the Basic Law before 1997 and accusing Britain of imperiling the Sino-British relationship and undermining Hong Kong's stability and prosperity. Yet it was not until Governor Chris Patten took office in July 1992 that the issue came to a head.

Patten's Proposals

China expected that Patten would discuss these matters when he visited China in mid-October 1992.[159] Yet the Governor took the initiative and suggested an ambitious electoral reform in his inaugural address to the legislature on 7 October. While noting that he did not have a free hand to create local democracy due to 'the ink of international agreements and the implacable realities of history, geography, and economics',[160] he promised to broaden participation of the community as well as ensuring that a 'vigorous and effective' executive branch was better accountable to the legislature. His initiatives covered two areas: changes in the executive–legislative relationship and electoral changes for the 1995 Legislative Council elections.[161]

Executive–Legislative Relationship

The Governor proposed a separation of the Executive Council from the Legislative Council, which necessitated that all six of the Legislative Council unofficials currently serving in the Executive Council resign. The Governor stated that no legislative member, appointed or elected, would serve on the Executive Council, and in so doing avoided any possible Chinese criticism should he appoint a member of the territory's winning party in the last election.[162] To make the Legislative Council more autonomous, he proposed that the legislature have its own secretariat and elect its own president. He also proposed the creation of a government–Legislative Council committee, composed of the policy secretaries and Legislative Council members, which would discuss the handling of the government's legislative and financial programmes. To ensure better accountability to the legislature, the Governor also promised to attend the Legislative Council at least once a month to answer questions from members on the government's policies.

1995 Electoral Arrangements

The Governor's plans for the 1995 Legislative Council elections were even more innovative. While promising that 'the British Government will continue to press with vigour the case for more directly elected Legislative Council seats', he suggested several creative innovations to facilitate democratic participation. He proposed lowering the voting age from 21 to 18 and adopting a single-seat and single-vote electoral system. Moreover, Patten suggested a radical alteration to the narrowly based functional system by expanding the franchise of existing constituencies, and replacing all forms of corporate voting with individual voting, which would result in a fivefold increase in eligible voters. In addition, he proposed the creation of nine new functional constituencies to include all working people, which would enfranchise 2.7 million workers. The Governor's final democratic initiative was the creation of an Election Committee (should the push for more directly elected members in 1995 fail) that would be comprised of directly elected District Board members.

China's Response

After the Governor's 7 October speech to the Legislative Council the Chinese mounted an unprecedented campaign to ridicule both the speaker and the speech, setting China and Britain on course for the worst political crisis since Hong Kong's future was determined in 1984. After having spent the two previous weeks trying to stop the address, China responded vehemently.[163] They argued not only against the specific proposals, but belittled the Governor himself, chastising Patten for being 'irresponsible and impudent'[164], a plotter of the 'evil roots' of disorder,[165] a 'petty thief',[166] a 'prostitute',[167] and a masquerading 'saviour'.[168] The Chinese were particularly upset with Patten's 'unilateral decision-making style' as he broke precedent by going public with suggestions without prior approval from China.[169]

The Chinese stated that the proposals were in total contradiction to the Basic Law. They believed that giving the District Board members electoral responsibility violated article 97 of the Basic Law, which stated they were not to be 'organs of political power'.[170] They labelled the government–Legislative Council committee a '*de facto* Executive Council' in violation of articles 55, 62, and 74 of the Basic Law.[171] The proposal to have direct election through nine new functional constituency seats was portrayed as a violation of the functional concept and a blatant attempt to 'bring democracy through the back door'.[172] Yet they were careful not to let their rhetoric be seen as undemocratic: Zhou Nan, Hong Kong director of the New China News Agency, prefaced his criticism of the reform by stating 'as is well known, during the last 150 years of British rule, Hongkong was under the dictatorship of a Governor. We, on the other hand, are greatly in favour of introducing democracy to Hongkong'.[173] He argued that the essence of the political changes was 'not whether to hasten the pace of democracy,' but rather 'the essence of whether there will be co-operation or confrontation'[174] governing the relationship of Hong Kong and China. The dispute was characterized as entailing whether both sides should abide by understandings reached in the past, not whether Hong Kong needed more democracy.[175] Lu Ping, Director of China's Hongkong and Macau Affairs Office, accused Patten of instituting a 'diplomatic fraud', charging that it had been previously agreed upon through diplomatic channels that the Election Committee would incorporate what was specified in Annex II of the Basic Law.[176]

After returning from a trip to China, Patten addressed the Legislative Council and admitted that 'major differences remain'. He was philosophical over what had become a diplomatic disaster: 'It's hardly a state secret that we did not see eye to eye on everything, but I rather doubt that anyone thought that we would'.[177] Patten was not allowed to visit Chinese Premier Li Peng, who normally met visiting Hong Kong governors, unless he compromised on his reform proposals, something he was unwilling to do. His trip to Beijing was rife with additional public insults. His counterpart, Lu Ping, failed to meet him at the airport; his meeting with Qian Qichen, China's Foreign Minister and State Councillor, was framed by Qian's accusation that Patten was jeopardizing co-operation between China and Britain, injuring the prosperity and stability of Hong Kong, and placing obstacles before the smooth transition of Hong Kong in 1997.

Patten countered that he believed his proposals would command support in Hong Kong and China and, further, that they promoted rather than undermined political stability. In the face of adamant Chinese opposition to more directly elected Legislative Council members, Patten neatly side-stepped the issue and came up with democratic initiatives that he believed were not precluded by the Basic Law: 'I say, to my great shame as a Christian, that I have read the Basic Law and Joint Declaration more than I have read the New Testament . . . [and] I am confident that my reforms do not breach either of them'.[178]

He also stated that if the Chinese did not like his proposals, it was incumbent upon them to forward alternatives. The Chinese response to this suggestion was blunt: all 'concrete proposals concerning constitutional arrangements were included in the Basic Law. We do not have to put forward our own proposal'.[179] Patten then noted that 'the Chinese interpret co-operation as meaning that one side—theirs—has the right of veto'.[180]

After Patten's return from Beijing, the Chinese changed their tactics. They announced that they would delay approval of financial arrangements to build a new Hong Kong airport at Chek Lap Kok[181] and also hinted that they might deny airspace rights to planes using it before 1997.[182] They attempted to manipulate the business community by stridently criticizing anyone who publicly sided with Patten[183] and implied that future contracts and franchises extending beyond 1997 might not be honoured, in direct violation of article 160 of the Basic Law.[184] Moves such as these led to the inevitable conclusion that China would pick and choose what sections of the Basic Law it would honour.[185] Ultimately, China threatened to derail the 'through train' in 1997 by dissolving the 1995 legislature and thus preventing legislators elected in 1995 from serving terms due to expire in 1999. Lu Ping went so far as to warn that lack of convergence in the 1995 election would mean no 'through train', not only for the Legislative Council but for the judiciary and possibly the civil service: 'If Mr Patten does not take our views into account then, when the time comes, we will form the first legislative council, the first government and the first judicial organizations of the special administrative region'.[186] China even hinted that such unilateral decisions could occur before 1997, with the establishment of a 'second kitchen' for Hong Kong.[187]

The controversy highlighted the concept of the 'through train' and its future implications. The 1987–8 push for convergence was based on the premise that Hong Kong should not do anything about legislative composition that would diverge from what was to be mandated in the Basic Law. The importance of this concept was established by the fact that the term for the first legislature would begin in 1995 and extend to 1999. Yet it remained unclear what this concept actually entailed. Was it simply a symbolic stop on the track in 1997 to acknowledge the change in sovereignty, allowing existing legislators to take a new oath of allegiance to the Basic Law and China rather than the British Queen? Or did it imply that an inspector could board and throw off those people who were not looked upon favourably by China, particularly those who had participated in the pro-democracy rallies in 1989? Or did it imply that one carriage would be exchanged for another—that the legislature elected in 1995 would be replaced by a new one in 1997? Patten argued that his proposals helped secure a through train: 'What these arrangements should give us, therefore, is a 'through train' of democracy running on the tracks laid down by the Basic Law'.[188] When the Chinese implied that pursuit of his proposals would lead to derailment, Patten argued that his proposals were necessary even if convergence was dismantled: 'I don't think anyone should want a through train to run carrying discredited goods'.[189] Later he was to add more strongly, 'I was not prepared to do what China wanted and demanded that I should do—which was to rig the 1995 elections. It is imperative to have clean election arrangements in 1995. I don't want to see a rubber stamp legislature'.[190]

Critics of the Governor's proposals were not limited to China. Some local commentators expressed dismay over his proposals, although their concern was more about the lateness of the push for more democracy than about its substance.[191] Even in Britain, the Governor did not remain unscathed. Britain's 'old China hands', particularly those who were intimately involved in the Sino-British negotiations ten years earlier, charged that the proposals were harming Sino-British, as well as Sino-Hong Kong, relations. In the House of Lords, criticism of Patten came from Lord MacLehose, a former governor of Hong Kong, and Baroness Lydia Dunn, the senior non-government member of the Executive Council.[192] However, public opinion surveys showed that these critics remained in the minority. Patten also garnered substantial international publicity and support in Japan and the West.

The dispute over Patten's proposals also highlighted a larger issue: the extent of future autonomy for Hong Kong. What appeared to matter most was not whether Patten's specific proposals converged with current Chinese thinking or even whether they were totally accepted; but that the government to 1997 and beyond was more accountable through a more democratically based legislature. The struggle, therefore, was over more than just reform for one election; it was over the meaning of a 'high degree of autonomy' and the actual 'extent to which one country, two systems can and will be allowed to actually operate'.[193]

The Legislative Council's New Role

Patten's approach was different from that of his predecessors. Instead of presenting the Legislative Council with the usual pre-ordained mandate for electoral reform, he decided that the Legislative Council, rather than the British or the Chinese governments, should be the final decision maker.

The Governor pointed out that it was a matter of both 'fact and principle'[194] that the Legislative Council would ultimately determine the outcome of his proposals: fact because legislation had to be enacted by the Legislative Council as stated by law; principle because the British government believed that the Legislative Council had the duty to decide whether the Governor's proposals correctly reflected the aspirations of the community.[195] Patten was also careful to emphasize that these were proposals, not decisions, and that the administration would abide by the legislature's judgement, and warned China that they must also be prepared to accept it.[196] The new proposals represented a major test for the legislators: 'They are going to have to stand up and be counted, rather than relying on British paternalism'.[197] The proposals left the Legislative Council with a unique and distinctly uncomfortable choice: whether or not to back Patten even if the plans were strongly opposed by China. 'They will find themselves sandwiched between a blueprint popular with the people and backed by a Governor high in opinion polls, and the future sovereign of Hongkong'.[198]

Patten charged that Legislative Council members would have to answer to the people of Hong Kong if they voted down his plans for political developments. The Governor gave a warning: 'If the legislature representing the people of Hongkong gives those proposals the thumbs down, then they will have to explain that to the people of Hongkong and live with that, not just in 1993, but . . . afterwards'.[199] Legislative Council responses were along the usual liberal and conservative divisions.[200] According to conservatives, 'a good Sino-Hongkong relationship is . . . even more important than . . . political reforms'.[201] In contrast, the liberals believed that legislators should ignore the pressure from China and decide their own internal affairs as had been specified in the Joint Declaration: 'How we want to frame our own election laws is for us to decide. We feel it is important for Mr Patten to follow Hongkong opinion'.[202] Liberals argued that the reforms should be supported even if they were inconsistent with the Basic Law, as that document itself was inconsistent with the Joint Declaration's promise of an elected legislature with a chief executive accountable to it.

The legislature moved quickly to act on parts of the reform. Before Patten had even left for Beijing, members agreed via a voice vote to a motion pledging support for his concept of the Election Commission. The mover stated that it was his intention to demonstrate to China the widespread support enjoyed by Patten's proposals 'when taking on such difficult discussions in Beijing, how much better it would be if the Governor should know he has our support'.[203] Early the next month, the government indicated that it was dropping its planned government–Legislative Council committee. The committee was scrapped mainly because members were having difficulty in deciding who should sit on it. The divisions and lack of cohesion in the Legislative Council were such that there was no agreement on how the committee should be formed or operate.

A more wide-ranging motion was offered in late November calling on the Hong Kong and British governments to adopt fair, open, and acceptable principles when discussing political development with the Chinese government. The mover, a Patten appointee, Christine Loh, noted that 'democracy in Hong Kong has been regarded, by London and Beijing alike, not as a value but as a commodity—something to be bartered, bargained over, managed and exploited'.[204] Implicit in the wording of the motion was the desire for the two governments to abstain from the secret negotiations of the past and engage in an open dialogue so that the Hong Kong people could influence deliberations through their opinions. Four amendments were offered to the motion: one calling for pre-1997 political development to converge with the post-1997 model; another pledging support for Patten's reforms; a third urging the British and Chinese governments to engage in constructive discussion; and a fourth asking the government to consult with the public before negotiating with the Chinese. A total of 45 councillors spoke during the debate, with the motion finally passing by a 32 to 21 vote as amended to include a pledge of support for the Patten proposals. Analysis of the debate indicates that the directly elected members were firmly behind the move, although some argued that the Governor's reforms did not go far enough. They were joined by about half the functional constituency members. By contrast, most appointed members and those from business constituencies were either critical or non-committal.

The more routine parts of the reform were easier to pass. In July 1992, before the reform proposals, the members had already endorsed a one-vote, one-seat district for selection of directly elected members. In doing so, they cast aside recommendations from their Select Committee on Legislative Council Elections which had advocated a multi-seat constituency system. The majority agreed that multi-seats were 'unfair and undemocratic' and favoured making the constituencies single-seat, single-vote mirroring Patten's suggestion.[205] By the end of the year legislators had moved to establish the Boundary and Election Commission[206] to set up electoral boundaries and handle the administrative work of organizing and supervising elections.[207]

Yet at the beginning of the new year controversy resurfaced over a third motion urging Patten to withdraw his political proposals and resume talks with China to seek a more acceptable alternative.[208] The intention of this motion was not to question the merits of Patten's proposals but their timing, or to 'question the wisdom of reforms that have no chance of surviving beyond June 30, 1997'. Its author stated that it was the 'last chance for responsible legislators to save us from disaster'.[209] Most members were unswayed, believing it unnecessary to engage in further debates on the constitutional reform package before the bills were tabled. During the debate, an independent member urged: 'We must not enter into discussions with a view to placating China but with a view of what's best for Hong Kong. Patten's proposals . . . will be fully decided in open in this council. I hope China will understand this democratic process . . . and accept [it]'.[210] Another member put the reform in a broader context by noting that it was not merely a question of electoral arrangements but of whether 'Hongkong people administering Hongkong' would really occur.[211] The final vote had 15 abstentions, including 12 conservative members; only 2 votes were in support and 35 were against. Although the Governor gazetted the electoral bills in March 1993, he had not yet formally introduced them when negotiations recommenced between the British and Chinese.

Sino-British Negotiations

On 13 April 1993 it was announced that there would be a resumption of Sino-British talks on the 1995 electoral plan. The diplomatic breakthrough was due to compromise on both sides: Beijing dropped its precondition that Patten retract his proposals and Britain backed down on having Hong Kong participate as a 'full partner' at the negotiating table.[212] It appeared that China had retreated the farthest, possibly due to their desire to forestall what they considered a greater evil (and what Patten considered a main aim of the exercise): the elevation of the Legislative Council into a decision-making body.[213] The role of the Legislative Council itself had become the main impediment to commencing the talks.

China had initially stated that it would not talk unless the reforms were withdrawn. When it became apparent that Patten would not withdraw his proposal, the Chinese countered that the new impediment was the role of the Legislative Council, which they saw as an attempt to resurrect the 'three-legged stool' concept. The Chinese disparaged the Legislative Council as a British-invented institution whose majority was controlled by the government. Beijing maintained that only China and Britain should decide the 1995 electoral package. But the British were adamant that any attempt to cut off the legislature would be unpalatable. Eventually, both sides ignored the question of the Legislative Council's status and Patten's proposals by simply 'agreeing to disagree'. Yet this forebode trouble, as these seemingly intractable issues would have to be dealt with if there was to be any hope for future convergence.

So while there was elation in Hong Kong that the Chinese had agreed to talk, no one was underestimating the difficulties involved. The 'make or break' part of the negotiations remained centred on whether China would allow the 'through train'. For the British, the only reason to hold the talks was to implement the through train— allowing those elected in 1995 to serve through a four-year term until 1999. For the Chinese, it appeared unthinkable to accept automatically anyone elected in 1995 under British colonial rule as a member of the first special administrative region's legislature. Therefore, as of this writing, the outcome of the talks remains unpredictable.

Conclusion

The 1985–95 period has witnessed tremendous changes that have shaped the future of Hong Kong, and in turn, the structure and composition of its legislature. Legislative composition itself has proven to be the key political issue in the years leading to the 1997 change in sovereignty. Review of the Joint Declaration, the White Papers of 1985 and 1988, and the Basic Law demonstrates that the Legislative Council had been effectively excluded from the process of deciding its own future. The 1992 Patten proposals not only intensified the debate over what is a legitimate legislative composition but highlighted the need for the legislature itself to participate in decisions that will determine its own future. Whether the legislature will participate in these decisions will depend not only on the outcome of the British and Chinese negotiations, but the courage and discipline of the Legislative Council's members.

To summarize, this chapter has provided a contemporary context with which to evaluate the legislature's evolution. An actual look at how the Legislative Council operates within this highly politicized context will be the subject of the next three chapters, commencing with investigation of the legislative staff in Chapter 5.

THE COUNCIL TODAY: STAFF,
MEMBERS, ROLES, AND FUNCTIONS

5 The Staff of the Legislative Council

With the transformation of the Legislative Council in 1985, changes were made to the size, type, and function of the Legislative Council's staff. The most important of the staff bodies is the Office of the (non-governmental) Members of the Executive and Legislative Councils, or OMELCO. Its function is to enable the non-governmental members of the Executive and Legislative Councils to meet among themselves to discuss matters of policy and important issues and to receive complaints and representations from members of the public. The significance of OMELCO has heightened with the compositional changes in the legislature. In 1984 OMELCO had 76 staff members; by 1985 the number had increased to 137.[1] While previous research[2] has focused on the complaints function of OMELCO, this chapter places emphasis upon the servicing function it provides for legislators. It also examines two other staff groups, the Clerk of Council's Office and the members' personal staff. To evaluate the effectiveness of these three entities in providing support for the Legislative Council, the chapter will begin with a brief comparative look at the nature of legislative staff and their functions.

The scope, magnitude, and complexity of modern government activities have dictated increased specialization and division of labour in legislative systems.[3] The most obvious by-product of legislative specialization has been the development of legislative staff. Beginning in the nineteenth century, and increasing at a dramatic rate in the two decades since 1970, the numbers and functions of legislative staff have multiplied in Western and non-Western legislative settings alike. The legislative staff structure, its nature, and the extent to which it has become bureaucratized differs somewhat with each polity and its legislature.[4] The amount, type, and function of staff indicate the degree of institutionalization of the legislature. Institutionalization implies organizational autonomy, internal specialization (which takes shape in greater complexity), and the evolution of standardized procedures and universal criteria for ordering the legislature's affairs.[5] A well-institutionalized legislature is stable and promotes an effective counterbalance to executive expertise. With the development of legislative staff bodies, political scientists have become increasingly interested in describing and analysing their activities, role, and impact on the legislative institution.

Functions of Legislative Staff

Research has emphasized that the most important function of legislative staff is providing information.[6] The impact of this function pervades the entire legislative institution. For instance, in terms of the legislative process, a well-developed system for providing information can save time, improve accuracy, promote cost savings, and enable easier absorption of increased legislative workloads. With the traditional legislative function of representation, staff can improve the ability of legislators to service requests from constituents, performing an ombudsman's role,[7] and serve as a conduit for constituent views about various political issues. Wolman and Wolman identified four models of staff influence on the functions of representation and policy. They saw staff as

1. an intervening variable between constituency attitudes and a legislator's perspective of constituency attitude;
2. an independent variable with impact on the roll-call behaviour of legislators;
3. an independent variable with a direct impact on public policy;
4. a conduit for constituency demands.[8]

More exclusively, in terms of the function of legislative policy making and oversight, the information provided by the legislative staff facilitates better policy analysis and provides a good basis for legislative deliberations of the policies promoted by the executive branch. Indeed, such information increases the capacity of the legislature to be independent of the executive. Staff may also be a source of innovation to form the basis of legislative-led initiatives in crucial areas of public policy. The degree of innovation that staff can provide for the legislature depends on the issues under consideration, legislative leadership, and staff style.[9]

Besides providing information and innovation, staff can also serve as a source of systematic integration, and as such, assist the legislature in performing systems-maintenance activities. For instance, the development of an efficient and expert staff improves cooperation between governmental institutions, particularly the bureaucracy and the chief executive. In addition, staff can promote intra-committee, inter-chamber, and inter-institution (executive–legislative) integration.[10] Lastly, legislative staff have been found to be a crucial component of the 'iron triangle',[11] linking legislative committees with executive agencies and interest groups.[12]

Factors that generally promote staff capability include good pay, high morale, professional status, expertise, and specialization. Furthermore, as the staff develops it assumes unique norms of behaviour, resulting in greater institutionalization. These norms include limited advocacy, loyalty to committee chairmen, deference to members of the legislature, anonymity, specialization, and limited partisanship.[13]

Three sub-fields of research on legislative staff have been identified: comparative studies, studies of American state politics, and studies of the United States Congress, reflecting the American-dominated bias of legislative staff research.[14] However, much more emphasis of late has been placed on the development of comparative legislative staff research.

Comparative Legislative Staff Research

Since the early 1970s, comparative research has been undertaken in a variety of settings. Most of the comparative literature has provided an institutional-level focus. For instance, central staff agencies of non-partisan professionals serving the entire legislature were the focus of studies in Brazil, Lebanon, and Costa Rica.[15] One of the most important findings of the studies was that 'neutral' staff may not be adequately responsive to legislators' needs nor sufficiently sensitive politically. Staff in these settings were civil servants insulated from partisanship, working on 'generally legislative' matters such as assembling information and providing background for legislative proposals. Because of their civil service background, the staff did not work on private bills, constituency service, or the re-election of legislators.

The informational needs of legislatures and the effect of different staffing patterns have also been investigated. The findings highlighted that legislative information requirements may vary according to the country's stage of development; important variables are the 'legislature's prominence *vis-à-vis* other institutions of government', the opposition parties, and the society's 'affluence'.[16]

Legislative institutionalization has been the focus of studies that investigated the autonomy and independence of legislatures in developing countries. In a study of Pacific Basin legislatures, it was concluded that 'legislative staff can significantly enhance progress toward institutionalization; staff help maintain procedures and give the institution more visibility and autonomy'. Furthermore, staff were found to be especially important in pre-modern legislatures, as 'members have few other sources of aid (such as interest groups or political parties) and legislatures are generally undifferentiated from other political subsystems'.[17]

All of the comparative studies have borne out conclusions reached in American-based studies, namely, that legislative staff agencies increase the efficiency and effectiveness of the legislature as a whole and individual legislators in particular. The independence of the legislature is enhanced by staff and reflected in the tradition of an autonomous legislative staff bureaucracy responsible to the legislature. Central staff, committee and party staff, and members' aides provide various research and system-linkage services. This is especially true in Asian legislatures where there are 'poorly developed interest group structures, almost no professional lobbyists, and political parties without organizational apparatus, [hence] the legislator must perforce look to legislative staff for assistance'. For these reasons, even beginning legislative bodies today 'need staffs far larger and more diverse than ever served the early sessions of currently functioning, fully institutionalized legislatures'.[18]

The data and conclusions from studies by Ryle, Campbell and La Porte, and Blischke[19] suggest questions for further research. How do the political system and local traditions affect legislative staffing? As a counterpoint, how does legislative staffing affect the political system and the place of the legislature in that system? Are there patterns of evolution for legislative staffing? What is the role and effect of legislative staff composed of civil servants in contrast to independently hired personal assistants?[20] All these provide a good context within which to investigate the legislative staff of Hong Kong's Legislative Council.

Office of Members of the Legislative and Executive Councils

The Hong Kong legislature's staff agency was established in 1963 and known as UMELCO (Unofficial Members of the Executive and Legislative Councils). In 1986 the office's name was changed to OMELCO to reflect the Governor's desire to change the terminology of non-government councillors from 'unofficials' to the symbolically more significant 'members'. In 1992 the Governor separated the non-government members of the Legislative and the Executive Councils, so that currently the staff agency only serves legislators, although the name has remained the same pending future restructuring.

OMELCO is served by a secretariat that is independent of the government, although it is funded from public money. While the agency is composed of some independently recruited staff, mostly clerical, the majority is seconded from the government, typically for a three-year assignment. The OMELCO secretariat is headed by a secretary general, and is divided into a Committees Division, Complaints Division, Administration Division, and a Legal Unit, comprising 167 individuals. The structure of OMELCO is portrayed in Figure 5.1.

The agency basically has two functions: to conduct research and provide staff assistance to the members; and to assist the public in their grievances and difficulties with government departments. Priority has traditionally been given to the second function.

Complaints Division

Unlike the statutory grievance systems provided in some countries, the OMELCO redress system is neither confined to, nor defined by, law. It handles all public complaints, appeals, and representations made to members alleging maladministration by government departments and complaints objecting to government policies and decisions. From the outset, there was recognition that, due to a weak political culture,[21] the population would be extremely reluctant to use the services of the office: 'There is some reluctance among the people of Hong Kong to come forward with complaints.

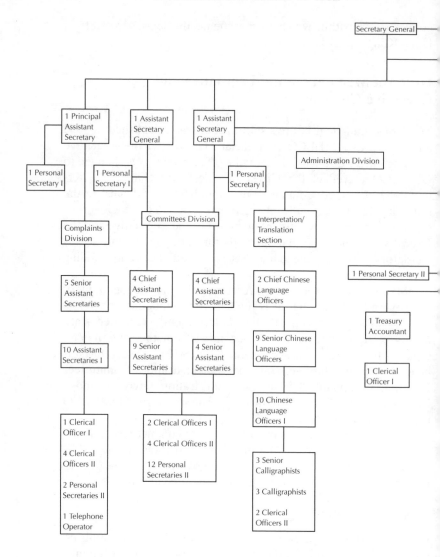

Figure 5.1 The Structure of OMELCO, 1993

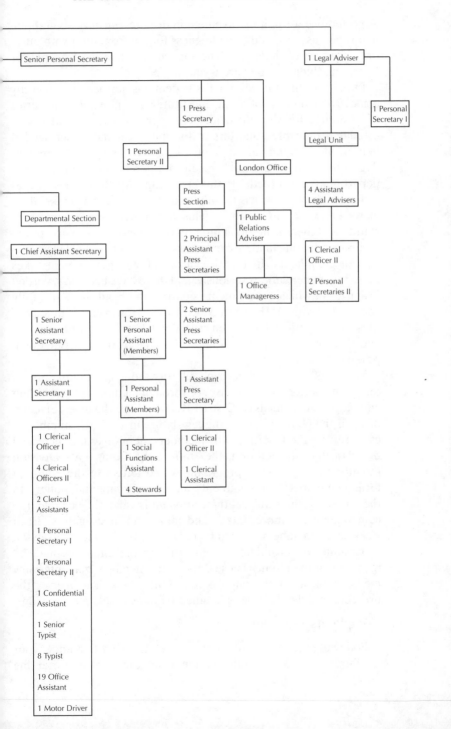

A preference for non-involvement in disputes, anxiety about poss-ible repercussions, and unwillingness for confrontation with auth-ority are part of the cause. The capacity of most local people for tolerating things as they are is another'.[22]

In light of this, the complaints system has not been confined by a narrow definition of what constitutes a complaint. The terms of reference for the office include 'representations', and it was estimated that three-quarters of the initial callers in fact needed help in overcoming various types of difficulties with government departments that were not a result of a dereliction of duty by the departments concerned.[23] In this broad capacity, the office serves as a 'forum through which members of the public can make their views known to members'.[24] This function is not governed by statute and there is no obligation on the government to accept the recommendations made by members as a result of their examina-tion of complaints. In practice, however, the government takes these recommendations seriously, and there have been no recorded instances in which government departmental heads have not fully cooperated with OMELCO investigations. However, the quality of these investigations have been crucially determined by the amount and type of OMELCO staff and the range of their jurisdictional powers.

Members of the public can put forward their complaints by telephone, letter, personal visit, or through members of the Urban and Regional Councils or District Boards. Since the direct election of 18 of the 60 members of the legislature in 1991, the number of cases referred to OMELCO by members themselves has increased dramatically.[25] In addition, the staff of the Complaints Division monitor radio phone-in programmes and letters to the editor in local newspapers for comments about governmental policy. In these cases, if the staff feel the complaint is valid, they contact the complainant for more details and mount an investigation. Each week seven members, chosen by roster, are on duty to oversee the complaints system and take in any further representations made by members of the public. These duty-roster members may interview members of the public who ask to see them as well as oversee the progress of individual cases handled by the Complaints Division.

Complaints Procedure

Following the receipt of a case, OMELCO staff first endeavour to obtain all relevant information from the person presenting the case and from the government departments concerned. When necessary, members will meet with government officials to clarify or seek additional information on the handling of a particular matter. At times, members or OMELCO staff will make site visits to be able to judge the merits of the complaint better. The case is then examined in light of the information obtained from both the complainant and government. This information is used to measure the appropriateness of given government policies and procedures.

In some cases, members may conclude that they are unable to help a complainant because they consider the complaint unjustified. In such cases, the reasons for the decision are explained fully, often in person or by correspondence, to the individual or group who initiated the complaint. Although the definition of what constitutes a complaint is broad, there are, nonetheless, several matters that OMELCO does not cover: disputes between employees and employers, disputes between individuals, matters which are the subject of litigation or involve possible criminal charges, or matters over which a statutory appeal has already been initiated or on which the Governor or the governor-in-council has made a decision. Since 1989 complaints alleging maladministration by government departments have been referred to the Commissioner for Administrative Complaints for investigation.

The steps taken by the Complaints Division of OMELCO in handling the casework are displayed in Figure 5.2.

It is estimated that the Complaints Division staff spend one-third of their time on intake (initial interviewing), one-third on investigation, and one-third presenting the case to OMELCO members.[26] In determining the outcome of cases that appear before them, the OMELCO staff and members may exercise three important rights.

Right to Information   This right allows the secretary general to call for files and copies of correspondence, procedures, and instructions, and policy papers related to the case in question. The normal procedure is that each time a case arises, the background procedure and policy papers that pertain to it are examined. If necessary, the actual departmental file relating to that case can be perused.

Right of Access to Government Files   This right can be exercised by the members themselves or by the secretary general. Frequently the head of department or assistant head of department is involved. Hence, the request for departmental files leads to the

Figure 5.2 Steps in the OMELCO Complaints Procedure

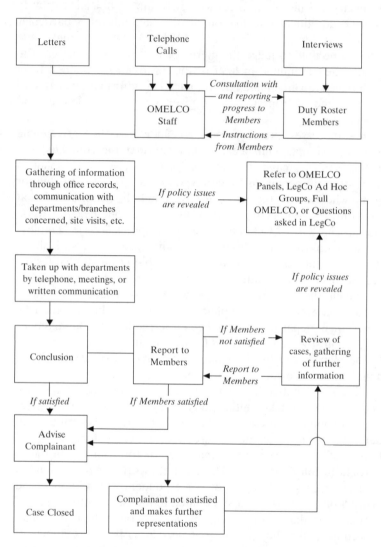

Source: 1987 OMELCO Annual Report

highest level of departmental review, and at times can result in a reversal of a case decision.

When all of the relevant information is assembled, the secretary general makes a report to the members. With routine affairs, the members simply ratify the decision. However, all matters of current public concern, petitions, cases involving points of principle or policy, and cases involving particular hardship or having special features are discussed by members before a decision is reached on the action to be taken. At times, a case may indicate the need for a review of a policy or decision. In this instance, members may exercise a third right, the right of challenge.

Right of Challenge   Members can raise the matter with the head of department, branch secretary, or the Chief Secretary. Questions may be asked in Executive Council[27] or notice given of a question or of an adjournment debate to bring the matter before the Legislative Council. Cases raising matters of policy and cases that are 'particularly difficult or complex'[28] are assigned to an appropriate OMELCO panel for consideration. If members consider a case to be justified, they may ask a government department to reconsider the initial decision or the procedures which instigated the complaint. On other occasions, they may decide that a policy change is in order, and ask the appropriate policy branch to initiate changes, which may require drafting legislation to be considered in the Legislative Council.

Following the appointment of an administrative secretary and the restructuring of the office, the number of cases increased from an average of 52 per month from June to December 1970 to 80 per month from January to June 1971. Since that time, the number of cases dealt with by OMELCO has risen substantially.[29] During the year beginning on 1 October 1991 and ending on 30 September 1992, 2,546 case files were completed. Figure 5.3 illustrates the nature and outcome of cases completed during this period.

'Cases resolved' refers to those cases which were wholly or substantially resolved or settled to the satisfaction of the complainants; 'cases where other assistance was given' describes cases in which the request was not resolved or acceded to but in which other suitable forms of assistance were given. 'Cases in which explanation was given for not pursuing cases further' were those which were first taken up but were not pursued, or cases which were considered unreasonable and groundless at the outset. Of these cases, 69 were the subject of discussion in the Legislative Council panels during the 1992–3 session.[30]

Figure 5.3 OMELCO Redress System: Nature and Outcome of Completed Case, 1991–1992

Nature of Completed Cases

Complaints	708	27.8%
Appeals	60	2.4%
Requests for assistance	1,082	42.4%
Proposals/views	486	19.1%
Enquiries	130	5.1%
Matters which are not related to the work of the Administration or which are subjudice	60	2.4%
Civil service matters	20	0.8%
Total	2,546	100%

► Nature of Completed Cases

Resolved	357	50.4%
Other assistance given	78	11.0%
Explanation given for not pursuing cases further	273	38.6%

► Outcome of Appeals Cases

Resolved	17	28.3%
Other assistance given	2	3.3%
Explanation given for not pursuing cases further	41	68.4%

Overall Outcome of Completed Cases

Resolved	933	36.6%
Other assistance given	180	7.1%
Information given/ referrals made	724	28.4%
Explanation given for not pursuing cases further	709	27.9%
Total	2,546	100%

► Outcome of Requests for Assistance Cases

Resolved	499	46.1%
Other assistance given	90	8.3%
Information given/ referrals made	221	20.4%
Explanation given for not pursuing cases further	272	25.2%

Note: Cases from 1 October 1991 to 30 September 1992.

While most staff attention has traditionally been given to complaints, much more attention of late has been centred on servicing the members themselves.[31]

Committees Division

Unlike the Complaints Division, whose work primarily involves dealing with the public, the Committees Division performs functions typically associated with a legislative staff agency, namely, looking after the members individually. This division assists members in their duties and activities arising from the work of the Legislative Council. Its staff arrange meetings of members, undertake research, prepare information and discussion papers, keep minutes, and take actions arising from meetings. They also assist members in handling public representations on draft legislation or policy matters and organize visits to pertinent areas in the territory.

The growth of the division can be traced to the change in the Legislative Council's composition in 1985. In 1984 the division, known as the Members Division, consisted of one chief assistant secretary and four administrative officers. By 1993 it had expanded to include two assistant secretaries general, eight chief assistant secretaries general, thirteen senior assistant secretaries general, twelve personal secretaries, and six clerks as depicted in Figure 5.4.

As seen in Figure 5.4, the division is divided into eight teams with each team assigned to approximately seven legislative councillors. The assignment of staff to Council members is based on the staff's subject experience—the experience they gained from their previous assignments in government[32] as well as their compatibility with the temperament and style of individual members.[33] This latter factor is taken into account to enhance rapport between staff and members. All assignments are made by the Secretary General after informal consultation with the relevant staff. At the end of each Legislative Council session the staff assignments are re-evaluated. Often, however, changes are made in the interim due to staff turnover. There is no stable staff–member relationship due to the normal turnover of staff and the limited tenure of most members.

While the staff members perform such personal services as writing speeches, providing information, drafting letters, and giving advice on various policy matters, priority is given to servicing the more formal legislative institutions, the standing committees, the

Figure 5.4 Organizational Chart of the Committees Division, 1993

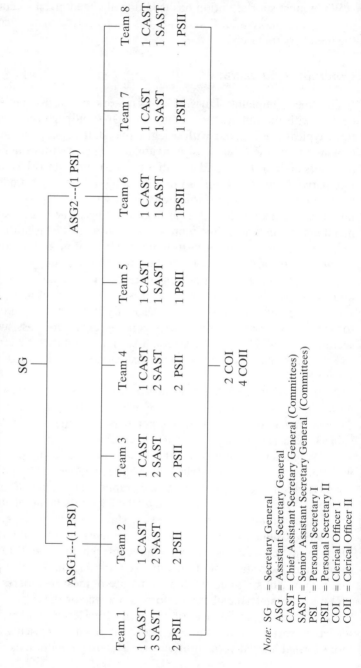

	Team 1	Team 2	Team 3	Team 4	Team 5	Team 6	Team 7	Team 8
	1 CAST	1 CAST	1 CAST	1 CAST	1 CAST	1 CAST	1 CAST	1 CAST
	3 SAST	2 SAST	2 SAST	2 SAST	1 SAST	1 SAST	1 SAST	1 SAST
	2 PSII	2 PSII	2 PSII	2 PSII	1 PSII	1PSII	1 PSII	1 PSII

SG

ASG1--(1 PSI)   ASG2--(1 PSI)

2 COI
4 COII

Note: SG   = Secretary General
ASG = Assistant Secretary General
CAST = Chief Assistant Secretary General (Committees)
SAST = Senior Assistant Secretary General (Committees)
PSI   = Personal Secretary I
PSII   = Personal Secretary II
COI   = Clerical Officer I
COII = Clerical Officer II

Bills Committees, and the select committees and policy panels, all of which will be investigated in Chapter 6.[34] In addition to taking minutes and performing correspondence chores for the panels and committees, the division staff are responsible for overviewing specific policy areas corresponding with their assignments. Their policy responsibility entails corresponding with the secretariat[35] whenever an issue comes up, taking minutes in the panel that investigates the policy, helping to draft questions to be put forward by the members to the administration, keeping records on the policy's development, and preparing status reports to those members who are concerned with its resolution. However, due to the rapid institutionalization of the Legislative Council, with two standing committees created since 1991[36] and the Bills Committees beginning work in 1993, the staff's time is increasingly being devoted to servicing these new entities rather than performing any policy research or providing services for individual members. For instance, in 1988 over 50 per cent of staff time was devoted to providing personal services for members,[37] but by 1993 servicing the committees and panels was taking up 70 per cent of their time.[38] It is envisioned that personal services for members will diminish further, if not disappear altogether, as the division concentrates solely on servicing the committees.[39]

Even with fairly rapid turnover of personnel, the development of staff norms suggests that the Committees Division staff is becoming more highly institutionalized. The staff see themselves as a bridge between the administration and the members. They are deferential to members, desire that their contribution, be it writing of questions or speeches, remains anonymous, and work at all times to promote consensus among the members themselves. Furthermore, they believe that it is essential to treat the members equally and when asked to oppose an idea broached by another member, to listen but not respond.[40] According to a senior member of the division, 'The Golden Principle is that we maintain strict neutrality and impartiality.'[41] While staff loyalty is developing, it is a loyalty to the integrity of the Legislative Council as an institution, rather than a personal loyalty to individual members.

Enhancing the stature of the Legislative Council members as a whole is also an important function carried out by the press section, and more particularly, the public relations advisor, all of whom are part of the third division of OMELCO, the Administration Division.

Administration Division

The Administration Division consists of a number of units. Unlike the staffs of the Complaints and Committees divisions, most of the staff in the Administration Division, with the exception of personnel in the press section, are recruited directly rather than seconded by government. Two of the units, the interpretation and translation unit and the departmental section, perform routine jobs. The interpretation and translation unit translates all the Legislative Council questions and speeches, all papers which originate from OMELCO, and any other documents which may be required. All these documents appear first in English, which is the official language of the government. In addition, the section provides simultaneous interpretation for the Legislative Council meetings. The departmental section provides general office services and looks after housekeeping functions. Less routine are the functions performed by the press section and, more particularly, the public relations adviser.

Press Section

Essentially, the press section performs a two-way communications function: providing information to members about what the media is saying, and disseminating information to the media about the Legislative Council activities.[42]

Providing media feedback to members This daily function has assumed the highest importance in terms of OMELCO time and effort, involving not only personnel from the press section, but the upper echelon of OMELCO, including the secretary general.

Each morning from 7:30 to 9:00, press section staff read all major newspapers and decide what reports will interest members. They compile a daily headlines summary, giving a short review of pertinent articles. These summaries are then sent to the members by special dispatch, arriving in their personal offices sometime before lunch. In addition, the section also provides special reports on current issues. These reports are updated daily for the period that the issue is topical.

Disseminating information to the media Upon compilation, the daily reports are reviewed by the Secretary General and members of the secretariat in his office for one hour commencing at 9:00 a.m. This meeting is seen as one of the highest priorities of the day by the Secretary General. The purpose of the meeting is to assess what the media and public are saying about certain issues or actions taken by the Legislative Council; to ascertain the public-relations impact of a particular course of action for the members to take in response; to take forward a decision, usually in the form of a press release, should action be required; and finally, to monitor the public reaction to this response.[43]

Public Relations Adviser

Concern about the public image of the Legislative Council led to the creation of a public relations adviser post in April 1987. The rationale for this post was to have an individual independent of the press section and independent from government, who could spend more time exclusively promoting the image of the Legislative Council.[44] There are two major functions provided by the adviser: image building of the Legislative Council and educating members about the importance of public relations. With image building, the adviser attempts to make the members 'look good' and counsels them on how to present themselves to the media. The second function—to 'make members aware of outside perceptions in terms of their own credibility'—is seen as the most important.[45] It focuses not just on the members' public speeches, but their activities in the committees and panels.

Most of the advice is provided on a one-to-one basis, although the adviser attends committee and panel meetings when asked. However, it is not totally informal. The adviser meets daily with the Secretary General in what is termed a 'public relations caucus'.[46] The meeting, the same one in which the daily headlines are reviewed, involves developing public-relations strategies to protect as well as promote the proper image of the Legislative Council. In addition, the public relations adviser operates according to a specific strategy paper, prepared by him and formally approved by the public relations panel and ultimately at an in-house meeting of members.[47] This paper establishes points of strategy, emphasizing the importance of the public-relations function, its various components, and the methods by which good public relations can be achieved. The strategy paper is reviewed on an annual basis. According to the adviser, facilitating public relations at this point in Hong Kong's political development is seen as crucial because when the 'legitimacy of government is being questioned the public relations aspect is more important than ever'.[48]

Legal Unit

The function of the Legal Unit is to provide legal advice to members on all aspects of their job as legislators. Specific duties include:

1. scrutinizing all bills and subsidiary legislation coming before the Legislative Council, with particular reference to technical and drafting aspects of the legislation;
2. providing legal advice to members on all bills and subsidiary legislation;
3. providing any additional legal support or advice needed by the Legislative Council committees and panels;
4. assisting members with the preparation of amendments and additions to legislation with the law draftsman of the Attorney General's chambers;
5. translating all new bills into Chinese;
6. providing any additional legal advice needed on Legislative Council matters.[49]

Essentially, the legal staff vets bills (with most attention given to subsidiary legislation) and assists members with any legal matter connected to their public duties. However, in performing these duties, the staff is careful to only look at the technical, legal aspects of the legislation rather than the substantive merits: 'Our duty is to look at legislation and spot legal defects ... We don't look at the actual policy but rather, like an ends-means distinction, we just focus on the means'.[50] But ignoring policy implications proves exceedingly difficult: 'The problem is that I cannot divorce policy from law, but on the other hand, I must try not to influence members about policy. My main function is to advise members on whether the bill itself as a legal vehicle accurately reflects stated policy intentions'.[51]

In carrying out these duties, the staff of the Legal Unit attend committee meetings and panels when requested. Before these meetings, the legal adviser makes a full report on bills to be considered, which is circulated to all the members. If, after reading the report, members believe that an amendment is needed, the legal adviser then helps them to frame an amendment. His work is aided by three assistant legal advisers. Much of the unit's work must be accomplished in coordination with the Clerk of Council's Office.

Clerk of Council's Office

The Clerk of Council's Office currently employs 70 individuals, approximately one-half of whom are assigned to the production of *The Hansard*, the official record of all the Legislative Council meetings.[52] *The Hansard*, published since 1890, provides a comprehensive report of all business conducted during the Legislative Council's weekly sitting, including speeches, questions, debates, and votes.[53]

Twelve of the staff of the clerk's office provide security for the Legislative Council building. These uniformed individuals ensure that all visitors have a pass to attend the Legislative Council sittings, panels, or committees. They also provide crowd control when a petition or protest is held outside the Legislative Council building.

The rest of the staff are assigned to look after the business of the main sitting of the Legislative Council. This entails issuing notice of the Council sitting; processing questions and motions that will be asked; arranging the Council's order papers, and in general, ensuring that all wording in questions, bills, and motions remains relevant. In addition, the clerk is responsible for keeping the minutes of the committee, as well as the Council, proceedings. The minutes record the members attending, decisions taken, and details of any division or vote held. On a daily basis, the clerk is also responsible for keeping an order book that shows all future business of the Legislative Council of which notice has been given.

In sum, the work of the Clerk of Council's Office is mainly to ensure that the legislative process, including bills, motions, and adjournment debates, occurs according to the stipulations of the standing orders. While OMELCO staff, primarily the Committees Division, is involved in servicing individual staff and their panels and committees, the Clerk of Council's Office provides procedural support for the Council sittings. Personal staff provide more individual support for members.

Personal Staff

As of 1993, members were allotted a salary of HK$39,400 per month and an allowance of HK$32,700.[54] This latter amount is to cover staff salaries and the cost of maintaining an office. Recent interviews with members indicate that the overwhelming majority employed their own staff.[55] This was true regardless of their method of selection (Table 5.1).

A typical staff office is made up of one or two professional administrators or research assistants and one clerk. Of those members who have staff, most (41 per cent) have two staff; over one-third have one staff member; and one-fourth have more than three staff members. Those who employ more than one staff member typically fund them through outside sources, often using staff from the member's principal occupation or sharing them with other Legislative Council colleagues. With the recent development of political parties, additional staff is being made available to members, although the staff organization remains rudimentary.

Most members indicated that researching legislative issues was the most important staff function, followed by clerical duties. A third function was meeting with constituents to assist in taking representations about government policies or procedures (Table 5.2).

While 'legislative research' might indicate that staff assisted in the formulation of policy by investigating issues and drafting legislation, in reality, the function is more clerical in nature. According to subsequent interviews with a small sample of the personal staff and comments from the members themselves, this function primarily involves keeping up-to-date files, comprised mainly of newspaper clippings pertinent to legislation being reviewed by the legislature. As one staff member put it, 'research for us is really passive and routine. We don't have time to dig into the issues so we just spend most of our time simply keeping up with the Legislative Council agenda'.[56] Other paperwork that would be grouped under this function includes over 1,000 papers issued each session by

Table 5.1 Members' Employment of Personal Staff (Percentage by Type of Member

	Appointed Members	Directly Elected Members	Functional Constituency Members	All Members
Yes	73	100	93	88
No	27	0	7	12

Source: Author's tabulations from interviews conducted in 1992 and 1993.

Table 5.2 Functions of Personal Staff (Percentage of Time Spent)

Function	Percentage of Time Spent
Legislative research	30
Correspondence	28
Meet constituents	17
Casework (complaints)	13
Speech writing	9
Visiting constituency	3

Source: Author's own tabulations from interviews.

OMELCO as background information for legislation. These papers consist of minutes from panels and committees and a multitude of background information provided by the Finance Committee. And further, while the papers are kept and filed for future use, they are seldom referred to again, as 'it is easier to contact OMELCO staff directly with a particular inquiry'.[57]

This last comment would imply a steady relationship between personal staff and OMELCO staff, but according to interviews with both types of staff, rarely do exchanges occur between them. What contact the staff have has more to do with locating the member than exchanging information. As one staff member noted, 'We have an OMELCO "nanny" who assists us just in terms of scheduling'.[58]

The key difference between the functions of personal staff of different types of members is that geographically elected members employ at least one staff member to deal directly with constituents. Constituency relations include taking complaints and representations, organizing events in the constituency, and providing information to the member about what constituents are saying as well as to the constituents about the activities of their member. Almost without exception, directly elected members indicated in interviews that they wanted to employ more staff to cover constituency relations in their district, but were limited in doing so by insufficient financial resources.[59]

For members from functional constituencies, while some staff support was devoted to constituency relations, the focus was much more on communicating what the member was doing, typically in the form of a newsletter. It may be that, due to the smaller size of the constituencies, the functionally based members are better able to know the views of their constituents directly rather than through their staff. In addition, many functional members remarked that they often solicited the views of their constituents on controversial matters either informally, through weekly luncheons or banquets, or more formally, through polling.

Only appointed members did not volunteer any complaints concerning the current staffing allowance. Many of these individuals do not employ legislative staff directly but rather rely on staff support from their outside employment to assist in legislative duties. What staff they do employ are usually part-time or 'shared' with other members. Without a constituency, appointed members have less need for staff to provide the services typically provided to their elected colleagues.[60]

One of the key difficulties both members and personal staff highlight in interviews is staff retention. From the members' perspective, their staff perform much needed clerical functions that make their legislative jobs much easier. Rarely, however, do members have their staff assist them in substantive terms by, for example, drafting legislation and writing speeches. From the staff perspective, the job is an interim one with no long-term career possibilities. The pay is low and requires little training. Unlike most OMELCO staff, who see their job as a temporary assignment in their civil service career, personal staff see their job solely as a 'stepping-stone', often to maximize their own political aspirations on the way to becoming members of other political bodies, such as the District Boards or even the legislature itself. Since 1991 a 'new breed' of personal staff—albeit a minority—has evolved. These individuals are motivated to become staff members because of the current political situation in Hong Kong. They have specific goals, typically revolving around the promotion of greater democracy. They have joined members' offices to promote this goal through a member with a similar ideological commitment. Yet they also see the job as short-term and their issue-orientation highlights a new factor in the retention problem.

The problem of turnover was emphasized by the staff members themselves. One noted that the job was frustrating as it lacked rules, procedures, and professionalization. This individual was the longest-serving member of the staff of a combined office of three legislative councillors, and he had only been there for 15 months.[61] What staff loyalty does exist is to the individual member rather than to the legislative institution, as contrasted with OMELCO staff. This loyalty is at the expense of having one's own work recognized, as personal staff can only vicariously enjoy the success of a proposal or speech written by them. The average working day of a personal staff member is detailed in Figure 5.5.

In conclusion, personal staff primarily perform routine clerical functions. Staff whose members are elected geographically spend a considerable amount of their time facilitating casework, which entails assisting constituents with their problems with the government. Those staff that are active in 'research' approach their job in a clerical fashion as well, with their primary activity being filing the data provided by OMELCO, or through OMELCO, by the government. Generally morale is low and this results in frequent turnover, impeding the development of expertise.

Weaknesses in the Legislative Staff System

Since the signing of the Joint Declaration, many have looked to the future legislature to ensure local autonomy. Consequently, developments that strengthen the legislature during the transitional period have been of particular interest. Key to realizing

Figure 5.5 Average Working Day of Personal Staff

Activity	Percentage of Time Spent	Description
Reading newspapers	10%	Looks for territory-wide as well as constituency-peculiar news; looks at press coverage given to the member
Communication	50%	Performed primarily by phone: with constituents for complaints and representations; organizing community events; scheduling of the member's activities
Research and compilation	40%	Compiling of information from Council meetings in-house, panels, *ad hoc* groups, standing committees, etc.; drafting of questions for the member; finding information for speeches, etc.

the goal of a strong legislature is adequate provision of legislative staff. In investigating attempts at legislative reform in other
settings, it is frequently found that greater provision of staff
is the major component of reform, as it increases legislative
information and strengthens the legislature's autonomy and
independence.[62]

While there has been a substantial increase in the number of staff
serving Hong Kong's Legislative Council, the potential for using
staff significantly to strengthen the legislature's autonomy and independence has remained unfulfilled. Weaknesses in the current
legislative staff system are revealed by investigating the issues of
independence and functionality.

Independence

Until recently, OMELCO has been a temporary assignment
for most staff members, even for those who are given the most
significant 'legislative' jobs in the Committees Division.[63] Because
most of these individuals are seconded from government, they
are subject to several constraints that inhibit the development of
loyalty to either the members or the institution. 'While our loyalties are supposed to be to OMELCO members, this is problematic,
as we know we will soon go back to government, and want to retain
our primary loyalty to [that] body'.[64]

Many administrative officers assigned to OMELCO view the
posting as a bad one that may hurt their career. This is because they
are working for an institution whose watchdog role requires it to be
critical of government. But being critical of future employers can
be short-sighted, if not risky: 'In our minds there is the possibility
that we will be posted to a branch in the future and that they won't
like us, especially if the Legislative Council has recently been critical of the workings of that branch'.[65] Another staff member cited a
more specific case, in which a colleague previously assigned to
OMELCO was having difficulty adjusting to her new government departmental assignment: 'Her boss was constantly telling
her that OMELCO was nothing but a bunch of yes-men and shoe-
shiners, who were no good at normal government work. He kept
telling her to 'get over her OMELCO mind set' and get on with her
job'.[66]

At the very least, those assigned to OMELCO will soon have to
return to work with government officials who are suspicious of, if

not hostile to, their previous work. Staff perceive that government officials view their OMELCO activities as provoking members to be critical of government so that the member can gain personal publicity. On the other hand, the staff realize that they are often viewed by the members themselves with suspicion. They are seen as having divided loyalties, if not outright allegiance to their primary employer, the government: 'Some members think that we are posted here [at OMELCO] as plants; that we will tell the respective government department of their intentions, even before they are able to ask a question or make a speech'.[67]

An appointed member echoed this perception: 'The staff is typically not acting on my behalf. In one instance, I was planning to ask some questions about a department and had asked a particular OMELCO staff member to provide me with information for the question. I found out later that the department had the benefit of knowing in advance that my question would be asked, and hence the government spokesman in the Legislative Council meeting made me look foolish. Not unsurprisingly, I suppose, two years later this OMELCO staff member has been promoted to that very department that I had been critical of'.[68]

Independence of staff, therefore, appears crucial, for as previous research has shown, 'neutral' civil servant staff may not be adequately responsive to the legislators' needs nor sufficiently sensitive politically.[69] What these studies highlight is the contradiction between 'political legislative values and bureaucratic administrative values', leading to the conclusion that staffing government bureaucrats in central staff agencies 'may end up weakening the institution they were supposed to strengthen'.[70]

There have been recent moves to make OMELCO more independent. In 1991 the members decided that the OMELCO secretariat should be financially autonomous and administratively separate from the executive branch. To achieve this, OMELCO was incorporated into a non-profit company on 2 August 1991. By 1993 further movement was made in the direction of independence, with an increasing amount of the staff independently recruited rather than seconded by the government (Table 5.3).

Accompanying this independence initiative has been employment of more executive officers rather than administrative officers, perhaps to counteract some of the difficulties just highlighted. For instance, in 1985 there were 13 administrative officers in OMELCO; by 1993 only one remained, the secretary general.

Table 5.3 Origins of OMELCO Secretariat: Government-seconded Versus OMELCO Staff, 1993

Rank	OMELCO	Government-seconded
Secretary general	—	1
Assistant secretary general	1	1
Legal adviser	1	—
Principal assistant secretary	—	1
Senior assistant legal adviser	1	—
Assistant legal adviser	2	1
Public relations adviser	1	—
Chief assistant secretary	1	8
Senior assistant secretary	—	18
Accountant	1	—
Assistant secretary I	2	8
Assistant secretary II	—	1
Office manager	1	—
Assistant secretary (social functions)	1	—
Senior social functions assistant	1	—
Press secretary	—	1
Principal assistant press secretary	—	2
Senior assistant press secretary	—	3
Assistant press secretary	—	1
Chief Chinese language officer	—	2
Senior Chinese language officer	—	8
Chinese personal secretary	—	1
Personal secretary I	—	5
Personal secretary II	9	9
Senior calligraphist	—	3
Calligraphist	—	3
Senior typist	—	1
Typist	6	2
Clerical officer I	3	1
Clerical officer II	13	2
Clerical assistant	3	—
Accounting clerk	1	—
Office assistant	17	—
Social functions assistant	1	—
Steward	5	—
Telephone operator	1	—
Motor driver	—	1

Source: OMELCO Statement of Establishment and Strength, 1 February 1993.

From 1 April 1994, all staff members will be independently recruited, reporting to an independent Legislative Council Secretariat, headed by the president of the Legislative Council, an individual elected from among the members.

For many staff, this move towards independence is a welcome one, giving them more 'legitimacy' and allowing them to develop more trust with the members.[71] As one staff member noted, the move 'makes us more responsive and a lot more divorced from the administration. In the past we have been looked upon as "government spies". Now we are beginning to be accepted as loyal employees'.[72]

Yet independence also means that staff must attempt to deal impartially with the disparate and often hostile groupings within the legislature itself. As one high-ranking staff member laments: 'My job is to find a common ground for distinct groups in the legislature. No other parliamentary staff in the world must serve both the government party and the opposition! In addition, we have China to worry about. But while the politicking goes on, I have to keep the machinery ticking'.[73] Another noted that the job was one of being a 'facilitator or mediator, not an innovator'. The main responsibility is to 'steer the members back from the rails'.[74]

The disparate groupings within the legislature have also aggravated the need for independence and neutrality in OMELCO's dealings with members' staff. As one OMELCO staff member noted, 'we now must deal with over 100 staff aides—both from personal offices as well as parties. We are in a "whole new ball game" in which we have to assist both teams on the field!'[75] An additional issue regarding independence and neutrality of staff is the 'China factor'—China's hostility towards the legislature. Working in a body which is responsible for overseeing the work of a Chinese-appointed Chief Executive—who may become a focus of legislative criticism about China's interference into Hong Kong affairs—has concerned several staff members. These people have indicated that they and others will opt to serve in a government department with a 'lower profile' and therefore less likely to provoke Chinese anger and possible retaliation.

In addition to the problem of maintaining neutrality when dealing with the legislature's members, the separation of OMELCO staff from the government has provoked supplementary problems. First, the independence initiative occurred without the support of

Table 5.4 Unofficials' Views on OMELCO Independence, 1987–1988

Should OMELCO be independent from government, hiring independently recruited staff?

Yes	42%
No	47%
Undecided	11%

Source: Interviews with 42 of 46 non-government members of the Legislative Council, 1987–8.

all legislature members. When asked in interviews before the initiative if OMELCO staff should be composed solely of non-civil servants, the members appeared to be unsure, and less than three years before the decision, the majority were not in favour of a separation (Table 5.4).

While those who were in favour of a staff independent from the executive branch cited increased oversight and investigation, the majority of members believed that the existing arrangement produced staff who, through their contacts in government, were able to provide the best service to members and the public. And even after the independence decision had been made, members remained ambivalent, with one-fifth responding 'no' or 'don't know' when asked if OMELCO should be staffed by non-civil servants.[76] Some members expressed concern that information from the executive branch would no longer be as easy to secure, as their staff would not have sufficient contacts with civil servant colleagues. Furthermore, because OMELCO staff will no longer be part of the civil service, members fear they will not have the sophistication to determine where the information is located or the ability to analyse it once it is provided. These fears highlight a second, more critical concern, namely the calibre of staff. Since OMELCO staff will no longer have the career prospects offered by the civil service, members fear that the job will be perceived to be a 'dead end' resulting in frequent turnover, low morale, and little professionalism.

It is estimated that by the end of the decade Legislative Council staff will number no more than 250. The number of senior staff positions and therefore promotion opportunities will be limited, possibly deterring high calibre professionals. The calibre of staff, as well as their recruitment, remains a critical problem for members. In recent interviews, many members indicated that the current staff allowance, particularly for those members who are directly elected, is insufficient. With the need for at least one and, depending on the geographical size of the district, up to three district offices, some members are using their salary as well as outside funding sources to supplement their staff allowance. The personal staff who are employed remain crippled by low pay, overwork, and often, low morale. According to one staff member, 'I am frustrated with the amount of issues we have to cover—we are spread too thin and we can't specialize in anything!'[77] As seen earlier, all these factors impinge on the capability of legislative staff, stifling expertise and professionalism. What is really crucial though is not the number of staff or their independence but their function.

Function

Most members primarily use OMELCO staff to coordinate the timing and turnout of panel and committee meetings. A second major use is as a 'reference' service; further probing in interviews indicated that this involved providing routine information, such as copies of minutes for the panels and committees (Table 5.5).

Table 5.5 Use of OMELCO Staff

Function	Percentage of members responding
Coordination of committees	38
Technical and legal activities	29
Reference	17
Secretarial	5
Complaints	5
Other	6

Source: Author's own tabulations from interviews.

What is revealing in these responses is a lack of any appreciation of what are normally the legislative staff's major functions. Previous research has revealed that legislative staff fill multiple functions that are crucial for increasing the effectiveness and autonomy of the legislature: providing information for effective oversight of the executive branch, promoting integration within the legislature, and providing innovation to assist the legislature in evaluating policy options. Yet members use OMELCO staff as they use their personal staff, primarily to do clerical work, and this suggests that neither staff is being used to fulfil informational, integrational, or innovative functions. In addition to being unacquainted with the potential of their legislative staff, members tended to under-use those services that are available (Table 5.7).

With little comprehension of the functions that can be performed by a legislative staff, coupled with under-utilization of what services are provided, it is perhaps not surprising that members were divided as to the merits of its independence. For, ultimately, the issue of the utility and independence of the staff is based on the role of the legislature in the political system. The quality of the legislative staff depends upon the expectations members and the greater community have of the legislature. If it is true, as one staff member suggests, that the OMELCO staff were originally established solely 'to control the members' rather than to assist in the performance of their legislative duties, then fundamental changes must occur in the aspirations and expectations of both the staff and the members. Perhaps the current staff norm of 'neutrality' in all matters among members and between members and the govern-

Table 5.6 How Often Members Use OMELCO Services

Description	Percentage of members responding
Often	40
Occasionally	22
Rarely	35
Never	3

Source: Tabulation from responses of 39 members, 1992–3

ment will become one of 'advocacy' of oversight rituals or policy initiatives as the staff becomes independently recruited. Further-more, the more traditional complaints function provided by OMELCO may take on less significance as more members be-come directly elected from geographical constituencies and open more ward offices to handle casework to secure their 'electoral connection'.[78]

In summary, as long as the Legislative Council was simply an executive advisory body whose members were appointed by the chief executive, it seemed logical that the staff provided for this body would emanate from the executive branch. The Council was perceived primarily to fulfil a systems-maintenance function, so most of the staff assisted in the processing of public complaints about the government. The small amount of staff provided to assist the members in their legislative duties were also civil servants, who were rotated out of OMELCO after a three-year posting. This rotation impeded the development of strong member–staff relations and frustrated the development of expertise and specialization.

With the signing of the Joint Declaration came the realization that the legislature, as the only basis for future autonomy in Hong Kong, must become more than simply a part of the executive branch. While the future political system enshrined in the Basic Law concentrates most powers in the executive branch, it is increasingly apparent that an autonomous legislative branch is needed to make that executive accountable. Hence, parallel to the move to make the Legislative Council's membership more representative and so more legitimate was a move to make its staff independent of the government. At this juncture, the staff is only beginning the process of becoming an independent entity. Yet it is crucial that even these initial moves take place with full awareness of the legislature's changed functions. As the legislature broadens the basis of its members and more actively pursues its legislative responsibilities, other functions are becoming apparent, including representation and to a degree, policy making, particularly over-sight, all of which will be explored in Chapter 6. It will be necessary for the staff not only to be aware of these new functions but actively to participate in their fulfilment if they are to play an effective role in the Legislative Council's evolution. But it will only be when the members themselves arrive at a consensus about their own role and realize how crucial a professional staff is to achieving their goals that the potential of OMELCO and personal staff alike will be realized. To understand better the need for more effective use of staff services, we next turn to an examination of the functions the Legislative Council currently fulfils.

6 Legislative Functions

The function most typically associated with legislatures is their ability to make law. But as we saw in Chapter 1, just focusing on the enactment of legislation within the chamber fails to illuminate the true extent of legislative powers. Consequently, we will broaden our focus to encompass all aspects of the Legislative Council's policy-making powers, assessing their exercise according to the context and stage of policy development. Furthermore, the chapter will assess the development the Legislative Council in terms of how it has performed the other traditional legislative functions of representation and systems maintenance.

Policy Making

The invention and enactment of public policy has traditionally been thought to be the essential legislative function. However, as surveys have uncovered, most legislatures are not active in policy initiation, although they may play a role in shaping the law. The extent of their policy-making powers depends on their ability to constrain the unilateral policy making of others, typically the executive.[1] The form of this constraint can be strong (legislative rather than executive initiation of policy; negation of executive policy), modest (modification and/or delay of executive policies), or weak (no ability to initiate, negate, or modify, but some ability to establish the parameters of the policy).

Legislatures can be classified by measuring their policy-making power and the degree of support they receive. The degree of support depends upon the extent to which the legislature is looked upon as a valued and popular institution. While in the absence of specifically tailored public opinion polls it is extremely difficult to measure, events and the public statements of political actors indicate the presence or absence of support. But the basic measurement of support is the institution's continuity. The presence of *coups* or other extra-constitutional attacks on the integrity of the legislature obviously indicate the legislature's instability, and, if the public allows these steps to be taken, its lack of support. By measuring the policy-making strength of the legislature and the degree of support the legislature receives from the public as well as from political élites, legislatures can be classified into one of five categories: active, vulnerable, reactive, marginal, and minimal (Figure 6.1).

Figure 6.1 A Typology of Legislatures

Policy-Making Power	Less Supported Legislatures	More Supported Legislatures
Strong	*Vulnerable Legislatures*	*Active Legislatures*
	Philippines, Uruguay, Chile, Italy, France, Weimar Germany	U.S. Congress and American state legislatures, Costa Rican Congress
Modest	*Marginal Legislatures*	*Reactive Legislatures*
	Thailand, Pakistan, S. Vietnam (pre-1975), S. Korea, Kenya, Uganda, Malaysia, Colombia, Peru, Brazil, Afghanistan, Iran, Ethiopia, Syria, Jordan, Zambia, Nigeria, Argentina, Bangladesh, Guatemala, Lebanon	United Kingdom, Canada, Australia, New Zealand, India, Israel, Mexico, Norway, Sweden, Denmark, Finland, W. Germany, Belgium, Netherlands, Switzerland, France (Fifth Republic) Austria, Ireland, Japan, Turkey
Little or None		*Minimal Legislatures*
		Former Soviet Union, Poland, Tanzania, Singapore, Tunisia, Taiwan, Ivory Coast, Ghana

Source: Comparative Legislatures (1979) by Michael L. Mezey, p. 36. Copyright 1979 by Duke University Press. Reprinted by permission.

Additionally, policy making can be classified in terms of arenas, which is to say the physical setting within which policy makers interact. The arenas outside the legislature (such as executive departments and the cabinet) are extra-parliamentary, and arenas within the legislature, parliamentary. Parliamentary policy-making arenas can be further distinguished depending upon whether it is by plenary session, during which all legislators participate, or by committees, which involves a subset of legislators.

Finally, policy making consists of three stages: formulation, deliberation, and oversight. Formulation involves the identification of demands for government action, the framing of preliminary responses in the form of policy proposals, fact-finding procedures to generate relevant information, and consultation among affected members of the public as well as political élites. It culminates with the formal introduction of a proposal to the decision-making body able to make final determination of the policy's parameters. The second phase, deliberation, involves discussion of the merits of alternative proposals. Amendments may be considered, compromises sought, and ultimately a majority coalition formed either to approve or reject the policy proposal. Oversight, the final stage of policy making, involves determining how well the policies are working, involving measurement of their impact and effectiveness.

Policy Making in the Legislative Council

As seen earlier, the power of the Legislative Council to formulate legislation has been effectively circumscribed by the requirement that all legislation that imposes a charge on revenue must receive the Governor's approval before introduction.[2] But even lacking initiation, does the Legislative Council have a role in amending or even rejecting government-ordained legislation? In terms of formal naysaying powers, for most of its history the Council could offer little or no constraint over executive policies, as government members (officials) dominated.[3] The numerical breakdown between officials and unofficials (non-government members) is seen in Table 6.1. The table reflects the legal number of positions, with the actual number appointed given in parentheses.

Table 6.2 shows that until 1964 there were more officials than unofficials. Between 1964 and 1976, the numbers were equal, but the Governor, possessing two votes (original and casting) could

Table 6.1 The Composition of the Legislative Council: Officials and Unofficials, 1843–1991

Year	Officials[a]	Unofficials	Total
1843	4	—	4
1844	6	—	6
1845	4	—	4
1850	4	2	6
1857	6	3	9
1858	6	3	9
1865	6	4[b]	10
1884	7	5	12
1896	8	6	14
1929	10	8	18
1946	10	7	17
1947	9	7	16
1951	10	8	18
1964	13	13	26
1973	15	15	30
1976	23 (20)	23 (22)	46 (42)
1977	25 (21)	25 (24)	50 (45)
1980	27 (23)	27 (26)	54 (49)
1983	29 (19)	29 (29)	58 (48)
1984	29 (17)	32 (30)	61 (47)
1985	11	46	57
1991	4	56[b]	60

Note: [a] Includes all *ex-officios* as well as the Governor, who as president possesses both original and casting votes, enabling the government to retain numerical control until 1976. [b] Excludes deputy president who was appointed by the Governor to officiate. His appointment was reaffirmed when he was formally elected president by members of the legislature in February, 1993.

Sources: Author's tabulations, from tables compiled by G. B. Endacott, *The Government and People in Hong Kong*, Appendix B, and Norman Miners, *The Government and Politics of Hong Kong* (4th edn.), p. 124.

always ensure that the government's views would prevail because the officials were required to support the government. Therefore until 1976, the executive branch was able to retain control of the Council and ensure that any policy promoted by the Governor would be enacted by the official majority. Even after 1976, although the full complement of officials was not appointed, the Governor could easily appoint additional officials if he felt that he needed their votes. It was not until 1984 that the unofficials were able to dominate, possessing both *de facto* and *de jure* superiority. However, governmental policies were not constrained by the united opposition of the unofficials. From 1985, as the numerical superiority of unofficials increased, their ability to act as a unified opposition to or constraint on government policy making was hindered by the diverse sources of their selection.

Up until 1991, the officials allied with appointed members and conservative functional constituency members and almost always ensured that what the Governor wanted prevailed.[4] This was demonstrated in debates about Hong Kong's political future and even when controversial and unpopular measures, such as the Public Order Ordinance[5] and the Daya Bay agreement,[6] were considered. It was only with a majority of elected members in 1991 that open opposition to government initiatives became more frequent. Yet only rarely has the government had to back down.[7]

There has been little formal constraint of the executive, but the question remains: Has legislative constraint been imposed informally? This question can best be answered by examining the role of the legislature in each policy-making stage, beginning with formulation.

Formulation

Activities in the formulation stage have always taken place outside the legislature, in extra-parliamentary arenas, most prominently in the bureaucracy. Bill proposals originate in the departments, due to the prohibition on unofficial initiation noted earlier.[8] After the department formulates some tentative legislative suggestions, the bills are formally drafted by the Government Secretariat, composed of the Chief Secretary and various secretaries of the policy and research branches of government. While most bills are routine matters of administrative detail, more substantive measures are subjected to extensive consultation. Consultation typically takes place with advisory bodies before the introduction of the legislation.[9] Should the consultations reveal support for the bill, it is then submitted to the Executive Council.[10]

The Executive Council is similar to the cabinet in parliamentary systems in that both are the final decision makers on government policy.[11] Distinct from the cabinet, however, its members are not selected by the legislature but are chosen by the Governor, promoting if not ensuring their compliance with most government measures. Upon submission of the draft bill, the Executive Council may approve, reject, or amend it. Up to 1992, this was the first time that legislative involvement would occur, albeit informally outside the legislature, with the few unofficials in the legislature who sat on the Executive Council providing comments about the legislation.

In sum, policy formulation is an almost exclusively executive prerogative, and encompasses deliberation as well, for it is during this time that most changes are made to the legislation according to views offered by various interests. It is difficult to judge the weight given to unofficial legislators' views, as the meetings of the Executive Council are not open to the public. Yet given the part-time nature of their job, and the resulting lack of time and expertise, it can be surmised that the legislators also serving on the Executive Council have functioned primarily as forecasters of the success of the measure in the legislature rather than as drafters of any substantive details.

Deliberation

Deliberation proceedings are initiated when the bill is published in the *Government Gazette*, along with explanatory memoranda detailing the general aims and financial implications of the legislation. Formal legislative deliberation commences with the introduction of the measure by an official member, typically one from the department or policy branch where the bill originated.[12] The first reading is short, with the Clerk of Council simply reading aloud the short title of the bill. A motion is then offered by the official member in charge of the bill that it be read a second time. The official follows the second reading with an introductory statement on the general merits and purpose of the bill. Then the debate is adjourned and the bill is sent to the House Committee. The House Committee, consisting of all non-government members except the president, determines how to study the legislation and can exercise one of two options: to refer the legislation to a Bills Committee for further study; or if noncontroversial, to refer it to the Legal Unit, which examines the bill to determine the policy implications of the proposal and considers whether what the government intended is really accomplished by the legislation.[13]

The Bills Committee considers the general principles as well as the detailed provisions of the bill, and may also consider any relevant amendments.[14] Once the Bills Committee has finished its considerations, it notifies the House Committee, providing a written summary of its deliberations.[15] The House Committee in turn reviews the actions and suggestions taken by the Bills Committee, but this review is for informational purposes only and no amendments may be offered.[16] The chair of the House Committee then informs the official in charge of the bill that the Council is now ready to resume the second reading of the bill. The official, after a review of the amendments, gives notice to the Clerk of Council, who puts the legislation on the agenda for the next meeting of the Legislative Council. Upon resumption of the second reading, the Council goes into a committee stage at which time the bill is read clause by clause, with each clause and any amendments offered voted upon separately.[17] After this stage, the full Council resumes deliberation, at which time the Attorney General reports that the bill has gone through committee with or without amendments. The president proposes a third reading, which typically involves a reading of the short title of the bill with no subsequent debate, after which the bill is considered approved by the legislature.[18] It is then referred to the Governor for his assent. The legislative process is depicted in Figure 6.2.

While legislative deliberation appears fairly elaborate, it is important to note that detailed scrutiny of legislation by the Bills Committees only began in 1992. For approximately 20 years before this innovation, *ad hoc* groups were formed to study legislation affecting a new policy or making important amendments to existing legislation.[19] And before that, for the overwhelming majority of the Legislative Council's history, Council deliberation was typically informal and cursory. Furthermore, those bills subject to the more detailed scrutiny of either the *ad hoc* groups or the Bills Committees remain a small minority of the total legislation passed by the chamber. Until quite recently, then, most actual deliberation on legislation occurred outside the chamber during discussions between bureaucrats and advisory groups.

Oversight

Legislative oversight of the administration occurs through several devices: parliamentary panels and committees, annual debates over the Governor's policy speech and the budget; and the use of questions, motions, and adjournment debates.

Figure 6.2 The Legislative Process

1. Gazetting
2. First reading and moving of second reading
   a. House Committee
   b. Bills Committee
3. Debate on resumption of second readings[a]
4. Second reading
5. Committee stage[b]
6. Third reading
7. Governor's assent

Notes:

[a] Normally held two weeks after first reading. The gap may be longer if the bill requires careful scrutiny or public representations have been received; if this is the case, it is referred to the House Committee which in turn assigns the legislation to a Bills Committee for detailed scrutiny.

[b] Normally held the same date as the second reading but may be held at a later sitting if required.

Panels

Panels are non-statutory bodies that oversee government policy. While they possess no formal powers, having no status under the standing orders, informally they monitor the work of the branches. The subjects discussed by panels may be initiated through complaints from the public, proposals presented by the administration, or through the members themselves. All non-government members are free to join panels and may enroll in as many as they desire at the start of each session. In the 1991–5 session, 16 panels were created to deal with different aspects of government business and public administration. These panels and their correspondence to government policy branches are depicted in Figure 6.3.

Panels were created in the early 1970s to enhance the legislature's ability to oversee the administration of government policy. By 1984 there were 16 panels with the average number of meetings held at 2.5 per panel. But by 1991, while the number of panels remained the same, the number of meetings per panel now averaged 10, with a total of 160 meetings that year.[20] Even considering the increased membership, it is clear that members were spending much more time performing oversight activities on panels.[21]

In addition to the more discrete policy activities of the Legislative Council panels, there are also two occasions annually in which the whole range of government activities are open for scrutiny: the debate over the Governor's annual policy speech at the outset of each new legislative session in October; and the debate on the territory's budget, which occurs in March.

Policy and Budget Debates

The first debate is technically framed to be a motion of thanks to the Governor for his address, but often members use the occasion to comment on a whole range of government activities. They divide the policy areas to avoid duplication in their responses. Almost all members take this opportunity to speak on the floor about a particular policy concern, but their speeches have historically been

Figure 6.3 Legislative Council Panels

Panel Name	Policy Branch/Department
Community and New Territories Affairs	City and New Territories Administration
Constitutional Development	Constitutional Affairs Branch
Culture, Recreation, and Sports	Recreation and Culture Branch
Economic Services, and Public Utilities	Economic Services Branch
Education	Education and Manpower Branch
Environmental Affairs	Planning, Environment, and Lands Branch
Finance, Taxation, and Monetary Affairs	Finance/Monetary Affairs
Health Services	Health and Welfare Branch
Housing	Housing Department
Lands and Works	Planning, Environment, and Lands Branch
Manpower	Education and Manpower Branch
Public Service	Civil Service Branch
Security	Security Branch
Trade and Industry	Trade and Industry Branch
Transport	Transport Branch
Welfare Services	Health and Welfare Branch

Source: Report by Working Group Arising from Winding Up of OMELCO, February 1993.

couched in polite language with infrequent, tentative suggestions. To those speeches requiring a response, the official members typically reply by the next meeting, which ends with a ceremonial 'vote of thanks' to the Governor for his address. However, 1991 witnessed a dramatic change to these formal, polite renderings. Instead of delivering polite recaps of given policy initiatives, many members used the occasion to attack the government's record.[22] A directly elected member, expressing dismay over the contents of the Governor's policy speech and the rather sparse, often uninformative replies of the officials to members' queries, even called for a division, and was joined by 12 other members who also failed to endorse the routine vote of thanks.[23]

The budget debate is similarly structured. It commences in March when the Financial Secretary presents the Appropriations Bill and the Draft Estimates of Expenditures for the following financial year. Before the debate, members form internal working groups to study the detailed proposals of the draft estimates and then determine who will speak on which subject in reply. Often the basis of the members' speeches comes from the knowledge gained through participation in two standing committees: the Finance Committee and the Public Accounts Committee.

The Finance and Public Accounts Committees

All non-government members sit on the Finance Committee, whose power rests in its ability to veto any items of government expenditure.[24] The committee is chaired by the Chief Secretary, who is joined by the Financial Secretary. Since 1984 the committee has met in public.[25] To assist in its work, two subcommittees have been instituted: the Establishment Subcommittee, which reviews the staffing needs of the civil service; and the Public Works Subcommittee, which monitors the government's building programme.[26] The Finance Committee's main responsibility is to scrutinize all proposals for public expenditure. While it meets throughout the year,[27] the committee is most active during consideration of the Appropriations Bill and the Draft Estimates of Expenditures in the spring.

Yet, as seen earlier, the financial power of the unofficials remains limited: according to paragraph 24 of the Royal Instructions, unofficials are forbidden to move any motion or amendment which would have a financial obligation except when approved by the Governor. In practice, such permission is never asked nor granted. Up until 1991, an additional limitation was that the members' financial oversight was confined to more technical details; their powers were limited to either accepting or reducing the amount of funds allocated in discussion on the budget through internal working parties. But commencing in 1991, the policy secretaries and department heads had to explain policy decisions directly to full meetings of the Finance Committee; further, members could submit questions that required written answers to be given two weeks before the budget debate in chamber.

The financial powers of the members are more informal than formal. Even in those days when officials were the majority in Council, they would not override a negative decision taken by the committee in the full chamber. Members now scrutinize fund allocations before the submission of the budget, with the Finance Branch supplying written answers to members' questions two weeks before the budget debate. Despite the greater scrutiny, however, the ultimate decision to increase the level of expenditure still remains with the government.

Directly linked to the work of the Finance Committee is the Public Accounts Committee,[28] which determines how effectively public monies have been spent in the past. This seven-member committee is responsible for reviewing the report of the Director of Audit.[29] The goal of the committee is to insure that public monies have been spent efficiently for authorized purposes and that the administration has not been faulty or negligent in its conduct of financial affairs. In pursuing these tasks, the committee has the right to call heads of departments and other pertinent officials to testify before it.

The committee is reactive in that it must await the report of the Director of Audit before undertaking any oversight. Furthermore, its recommendations are not binding on the administration, for the Finance Branch rather than the legislature has been given the responsibility of taking remedial action when problems are uncovered in the report.[30] Even with these restraints, the committee has recently proved to be an effective watchdog rather than the 'lapdog' of earlier proceedings. In 1992 the committee persisted in a comprehensive investigation into cost overruns in the establishment of a new tertiary educational institution in the territory,

not only embarrassing the government but signalling more stringent exercise of financial oversight in the future.[31]

Motions

Before 1980, motions were rarely offered by non-government
members; in recent years, however, they have been more frequently used by both officials and members, becoming 'the instrument by which most of the business of the Council is transacted'.[32]
Motions are used to advance a bill through the legislative process;
they are also used to amend certain ordinances, and recently have
been used by members to express their views on subjects or
expressly to call upon the government to take a certain action.
While in the 1984 session there were 3 motions offered by non-
government members, by 1985 the number of motions had risen to
7, to 11 by 1988, and 43 by 1991. Motions are now used as an
extensive oversight vehicle to inform the government about the
members' views on a variety of policies. The government is required, in turn, to give a verbal reply to the motion; this exchange
enhances the legislature's ability to influence and oversee the administration. Because motions always end with a vote, the government becomes acquainted with the degree to which the motion
carries the support of the Council.

Adjournment Debates

Debates on adjournment are also used by the legislature to oversee
administrative actions. First introduced in 1966, these debates occur at the end of a chamber meeting and involve members giving
their views on and asking questions about governmental policy.
Official members then reply to the views expressed on behalf of the
government.[33] This procedure allows areas of public interest to
receive legislative attention without being subject to a specific action (as mandated in motion) or limited by wording restrictions (as
mandated in the use of questions). The use of this tool has varied
greatly through the years. Throughout the 1970s there were approximately four debates annually. In 1984 three debates were
held, increasing to six in 1985, with only one in 1988, but 17 by
1991.

Questions

Perhaps the most extensively used tool of oversight is asking questions. The steady growth in the number of questions is shown in

Table 6.2 The Number of Questions Asked in the Legislative Council, 1960–1992

Year	Questions	Supplementaries	Number of Unofficials at Session
1960–1	11	1	8
1961–2	25	0	13
1962–3	2	0	13
1963–4	35	7	13
1964–5	17	12	13
1965–6	28	19	13
1966–7	6	2	13
1967–8	45	9	13
1968–9	102	66	13
1969–70	85	89	13
1970–1	135	96	13
1971–2	166	155	13
1972–3	171	96	14
1973–4	176	120	15
1974–5	118	104	15
1975–6	181	157	15
1976–7	284	318	22
1977–8	290	578	24
1978–9	163	306	24
1979–80	137	214	24
1980–1	131	231	26
1981–2	157	271	27
1982–3	194	348	27
1983–4	180	286	29[a]
1984–5	179	350	29
1985–6	296	797	46
1986–7	206	505	46
1987–8	245	729	46
1988–9	272	830	46
1989–90	269	990	46
1990–1	226	755	46
1991–2	479	798	56[b]

Notes: [a] Actual number of unofficials; some discrepancy with other tables due to when in the year recorded. [b] Does not include deputy president, who was appointed by the Governor to officiate at Council proceedings.

Sources: UMELCO Annual Report 1984, Appendix 11; OMELCO Annual Report 1992, Appendix 7.

Table 6.2. Questions are offered by members to seek information from the Government about particular problems, policies or actions. Questions may require the government officials to respond either orally or in a written reply. Members may follow up their initial question by supplementary questions to elicit specific responses to their concerns. The immediate post-war years saw little use of this procedure, averaging only two questions annually during the 1950s, increasing to thirty-five annually in the 1960s. Since then, the use of questions has proved an increasingly attractive tool, going up from an average of 1.3 per member in 1960 to 6.2 per member in 1984 and 8.5 per member by 1991.

Yet the use of questions is fairly well restricted.[34] While it would be expected that the number of questions will grow even more in the future, the restrictions will probably keep them at their present level; the number of supplementaries, which are less restricted, may steadily increase. None of these restrictions, however, relate to a new innovation to establish better accountability of the executive branch, namely, the Governor's question time.

Question Time

In 1992 Governor Patten initiated a monthly question time. During question time, the Governor addresses the Council on matters of public concern[35] and then allows members to ask him questions on his discourse or other subjects.[36] The intent behind this innovation was better to fulfil the Joint Declaration by making the executive more accountable to the legislature. There were practical reasons as well for its creation: since the Governor was no longer president of the Legislative Council and legislators no longer served on the Executive Council, there was a need to maintain a link between the two branches to ensure accountability and to assist in the passage of government measures.[37]

Staff Agency

The legislative staff agency, OMELCO (reviewed in Chapter 5), functions as another legislative oversight mechanism. Oversight activities are enhanced by the Complaints Division, which takes complaints from the public and mandates governmental responses, and the Committees Division, which assists the legislators in performing their policy-making functions more effectively.

In conclusion, compared to the previous two stages of policy making, oversight of the administration appears to occur in a fairly institutionalized way. While legislative oversight has substantially improved since the 1970s, several weaknesses remain, at least up until 1984.

Policy Making in the Legislative Council until 1984

Most of the legislature's policy-making activities up until 1984 were pre-ordained, formalistic, and routine. There were structural, cultural, and substantive reasons for this.

The structural make-up of the Council enabled the Governor to dominate its proceedings. The Governor determined when the Council would meet and when its session would end. The Governor not only presided but also possessed his dual vote, a power he did not need to exercise during most of the Colony's history, as he was already supported by the official majority. Even in more recent times when the number of votes possessed by officials and unofficials has been equal, however, formal divisions were seen as a past exception rather than a present rule. Since the Second World War the official majority has been used only twice to overcome the unanimous opposition of unofficials.[38] This lack of division was intentional, as the government took 'great pains to avoid having any contested votes as all'.[39] Finally, the Governor's pervasive powers over the legislature were also manifested in the structural requirement that all bills must have his assent before introduction and further, that no bill can become law without his assent. Oversight was also constrained by structural limits. Given the dominant influence of the officials on the Finance and Public Accounts committees, both in terms of number (an earlier phenomenon) and informational sources (a continual phenomenon), it would appear that the committees were only advisory, with the inevitable result that they would 'strengthen rather than weaken the hands of the government officials . . . becoming a kind of private appendage of the department[s], bound to secrecy, giving advice but unable to say in public what that advice was or to carry criticism of the department into public'.[40] Furthermore, the panels and committees were weak in that both were infrequently used and their work remained limited to giving advice, as they lacked the ability to formulate any remedies or initiate any new policies.

Plenary debate within the legislature remained highly structured and controlled by the executive. The debates were rarely spontaneous, with the administration given sufficient notice to be aware of the nature, if not the exact wording, of the questions that were to be asked. In preparing its response, the government was able to set the context of the debates, controlling the extent of the debate not only by the amount of information that it was willing to provide but restricting debate by limiting the number of questions the individual member could ask as well as the total number of questions allowable per sitting. More fundamentally, the questions asked typically focused on incremental non-substantive changes in policy. The basic premises of the policies and practices of the government were never questioned.

The nature of the questions asked can be attributed to the orientation of the unofficials, characterized as conservative individuals who aimed to maintain the status quo: 'past Governors used their power of nomination to appoint to the Council only those . . . who were prepared to support the fundamental assumptions of the administration about the proper limits of official activity, the desirable level of public spending, the incidence of the burden of taxation, and the present distribution of privilege and power between employers and employees'.[41] In sum, executive domination in all aspects of policy making occurred to the extent that it was concluded that the 'Governor is both legislature and chief executive in Hong Kong'.[42]

From a cultural perspective, the unofficials by 1984 were overwhelmingly Chinese (27 of the 29 unofficials), which resulted in a chamber characterized by a Confucian restraint from any form of adversarial politics. This is typical of many Asian cultures where

people tend to see power as status...when power implies the security of status, there can be no political process. Contention and strife cease. All are expected to devote themselves to displaying the proper respect and honor for others, according to their station. Any criticism of leaders becomes an attack upon the social system. Hence to criticize is to display bad taste, to be less than worthy.[43]

As one Chinese unofficial put it, 'Hong Kong is the lifeboat; China is the sea. Those who have climbed into the lifeboat naturally don't want to rock it'.[44] There has been a clear preference given to harmony rather than adversity in dealing with government. Typical of this belief was the statement of another Chinese unofficial who remarked, 'In Hong Kong we do not want politics of any kind'.[45]

Consequently, 'vigorous articulation of interests on behalf of the common people and against the interests of the government is relatively rare, and an atmosphere of harmony between the government and the Chinese élite prevails most of the time'.[46]

There has not always been a passive atmosphere in the Chamber; the reform initiatives in 1845, 1894, and 1916 were exceptions, but they were all at the instigation of European unofficials. Before 1984 no Chinese unofficial, even when they commanded a majority among unofficials, had openly pressed for a more representative and responsible form of government.[47] Nor had Chinese unofficials used their votes in Council to embarrass or rebuff the government's unilateral policy making.[48] In sum, until 1984 the passivity of unofficials could be attributed to cultural norms as well as structural factors. These norms resulted in formalistic if not ritualistic meetings with their outcomes a foregone conclusion.

The lack of adversarial politics was also linked to the fact that members owed their office to gubernatorial selection. Legislative oversight is vigorously pursued only if the legislators have compelling reasons to do so, with comparative studies revealing that the most important reason is the member's re-election.[49] In many countries, the oversight of executive agencies is infrequent and ineffectual unless the constituency interests of the legislator are directly involved.[50] Until 1985 Hong Kong's legislators were unelected which enabled them to remain free to promote interests that they often saw as coinciding with the individual who selected them, the Governor. To retain their office, they had to support rather than be critical of their benefactor:

Inasmuch as the Chinese élite members are co-opted into the bureaucratic polity individually by the government, they are dependent on it for official recognition. To an individual élite member, official recognition of élite status is of enormous symbolic importance in enhancing his overall social status and prestige in the Chinese society. And, if he is an industrialist or merchant, official recognition is also a very important asset in establishing business connections.[51]

Unofficials have seen their tenure on the legislature not as a means to realize a particular policy goal but rather as an end in itself: 'for most members membership is [merely] a decoration and an honour'.[52] Therefore, they lacked the motivation to engage in any comprehensive and critical oversight. So, for structural, cultural, and motivational reasons, policy making, particularly oversight, remained sporadic and rarely effectual.

Finally, from a substantive viewpoint, the overwhelming majority of measures were matters of minor administrative detail, requiring little legislative participation. With those measures which were more substantive, it was exceedingly difficult for the unofficials to offer comprehensive improvements or even marginal refinements to the legislation. This was due to time constraints as well as the nature of the legislation itself, which had become more legalistically complex, placing the part-time unofficials on an unequal footing to compete with the superior information and expertise of bureaucratic officials.[53]

Accordingly, before 1985 the executive branch (the Governor and executive departments), operating in extra-parliamentary settings (the departments, the Government Secretariat and the Executive Council), clearly dominated. The pre-legislative stage remained the most important for the success of legislation. In terms of deliberation, the executive was again dominant, with most deliberation occurring in the Government Secretariat, which approved all policy proposals, and the Executive Council, which approved all draft bills before their submission to the Legislative Council. The weakness of the deliberative function of the legislature can also be seen in terms of statistics. While the legislature had become much more active since the Second World War, this trend could not overcome the essential weakness of their deliberative format. By 1984 the legislature met only twice monthly, except in August and September when there was a recess, and had just 27 public meetings, averaging only two hours in duration. It typically took only four weeks for the bills to pass through all three readings and adoption. Of the 89 bills passed that year, only 24 were subject to amendments which were mostly incremental in nature. What policy making took place in the legislature, in the form of questions, motions, and debates, was by definition both general and public, characteristics that are disadvantageous to effective policy participation.

A minimal prerequisite for effective policy participation is that legislative arenas become a source of expertise comparable to that which is present in the bureaucracy. This level of expertise can only be maintained through the division of the legislature into substantive committees, which are then able to ensure legislative participation during all three policy-making phases. Yet the committee system in Hong Kong remained inadequate, consisting of just two committees possessing the limited power of advice rather than enactment. Therefore, up until 1984, the Legislative Council did not make public policies or laws, it merely endorsed and ratified decisions that have already been taken elsewhere.[54] Unofficials lacked not only the ability but the inclination fundamentally to change the unilateral policy making of the executive branch. But this orientation was to undergo a dramatic transformation with the introduction of new types of legislators in 1985.

Policy Making in the Legislative Council: 1985 to the Present

Since 1985 the legislature has become much more active in the making of public policy. This can be seen in the change of policy-making activities from the dominance of extra-parliamentary settings before 1984 to the assertion of parliamentary settings since 1985.

While structurally the Governor continues to exercise pervasive power, these powers have diminished. As noted earlier, the Governor can no longer assume that his proposals will command majority support, as most of the membership is now elected. Furthermore, as of 1991, the appointed members of the legislature are no longer beholden to the Governor as he cannot reappoint them for the next term.[55] Finally, the Governor has relinquished the presidency of the Council, and in the process has given up both a casting and original vote as well as other prerogatives that have camouflaged dissent in the past.[56]

Perhaps the most remarkable transformation has been the institutionalization of the Legislative Council's meetings and the proliferation of committees[57]. The chamber has moved to exert better control over its proceedings[58] and, in establishing an independent Legislative Council secretariat, ensured that it has an identity distinct from the executive. It has also developed new structures to assist in its policy work. These have included the addition of a House Committee to assist in the administration of its work and the creation of a Bills Committee system to formalize and regularize deliberation over legislation. In addition, old structures, most notably the Finance and Public Accounts committees, have refined their practices and now exercise more extensive oversight.

In 1991 there was an attempt to exert a stronger policy-making power with the creation of new standing committees to assist in deliberations.[59] This attempt to revamp the committee system revealed the ideological divisions among legislators paralleling their mode of selection. The liberals (primarily directly elected) desired the creation of permanent standing committees to vet both legislation and policy over time, while the conservatives (primarily appointed and from functional constituencies) preferred incremental changes to the *ad hoc* structures that simply vet legislation so as not to denigrate 'executive-led' government.[60] China also voiced misgivings about a standing committee system. They feared it would lead to a 'legislature-led' political system, which they would have to dismantle after 1997.[61] The conservatives won the initial round of this engagement, with the decision to set up Bills Committees simply to vet bills. These committees are temporary and go out of existence once legislation has passed. Yet further refinement came in February 1993, with the publication of a report suggesting that there be a membership overlap between panels (which are ongoing bodies that monitor policy) and the Bills Committees, to maximize expertise.[62]

A second structure to expedite and refine the deliberative function, the House Committee, was instituted in 1992. This committee oversees the allotment of bills to committees and serves as a forum in which the members can discuss the position and progress of the panels and Bills Committees. Hence the new members, in pushing for the creation of these structures, which now possess the power to summon witnesses and call for testimony,[63] enlarged the grounds upon which to engage in deliberation.

While the lack of formal standing committees, with a permanent membership, possessing expertise that would be gained from weekly committee meetings, remains a critical deficiency, these refinements have resulted in much more effective legislative oversight. Furthermore, motion and adjournment debates have more closely defined the parameters of executive policy making. But perhaps more than any other tool, it has been the use of questions, vigorously articulated and ruthlessly pursued, that has made the government more accountable.

For functional transformation has come not just from the changes in structures and tools of policy making but the orientations of the legislators themselves. Culturally, while the membership is now almost totally Chinese, the norms of deference to authority have given way to a new-found identity in a fuller legislative role. Since 1985, and particularly since 1991, members have been more active during all three stages of policy making.

While initiation remains an executive prerogative,[64] members now attempt to assert themselves in the formulation stage by holding adjournment debates on areas requiring revised or new policies. They have increased their control over deliberation by using their powers to negate or veto those policies with which they disagree. They have also increased their use of private member bills. In November 1993 a bill was introduced and passed, over the opposition of officials, to stop the government from employing expatriate civil servants on local terms. Further private bills are expected to be tabled during 1994 concerning sexual harassment and access to information.

The legislators have become much more active in scrutinizing legislation, as witnessed by debates over the Complex Commercial Trials Bill,[65] the Daya Bay discussions,[66] and the Film Classification Bill.[67] Finally, they are increasingly exercising more stringent oversight, as was seen in April 1993 when members threatened to invoke the Powers and Privileges Bill to break government silence on the causes and costs to taxpayers of the resignation of the Provisional Airport Authority's chief executive. Their zeal has been enhanced in some instances by the controversial nature of the measures, particularly those dealing with the future of the political system (see Chapter 4).

But even with less controversial issues, it is clear that the most dramatic change in legislative policy making came with the change in membership, particularly with the introduction of directly elected members in 1991. Voters demand accountability from their elected legislators; in turn the legislators demand more accountability from the government. As one policy secretary recently observed, 'In the dim and distant past the dealings of the Finance Committee were behind closed doors. Now the doors are always open and we are trying to convince legislators who are accountable to the public'.[68] This process has resulted in not only a more responsive legislature but a more responsive government, as new legislators have been the main catalyst for reform within the civil service. This new orientation clearly occurred when the legislature ceased to be a totally appointed body. To put it simply: changes in the way members were selected in 1985, and particularly 1991, have resulted in a corresponding change in the policy-making role of the legislature, which has enhanced the accountability of the government.

One of the most dramatic examples of this new orientation is how the members exercise their power of the purse. In 1991, for instance, one elected member moved to amend clause 3 of the Inland Revenue (Amendment) (No. 3) Bill 1991 to raise the personal tax allowance. On the same day, another moved to amend to reduce a proposed vehicle tax.[69] While both amendments were defeated, they demonstrated the growing clout of members in the exercise of financial powers.

The potential exercise of these powers was again demonstrated in the 1992 'battle of the budget'. Within 36 hours of the introduction of the budget, the liberals (primarily directly elected) declared that the budget needed to be amended to assist 'the sandwich [middle] class'; without government concessions, they threatened to vote against the Appropriations Bill. A record 935 questions were asked about the 1992 budget during these hearings.[70] As the Financial Secretary was to remark at the close of debate, the budget had been 'the subject of unusually intense scrutiny and debate', and he argued that 'we cannot become embroiled in a protracted series of negotiations after the Budget Speech'.[71] Due to pressure from the members, however, the Financial Secretary promised that the following year's budget would substantially increase salaries-tax allowances and review tax bands. Yet even with this pledge, which represented a substantial concession by government, the Appropriations Bill was subject to a division, rather than the usual unanimous voice vote, and only carried by a vote of 36 to 18, with elected members comprising the overwhelming majority of those who voted against it. Financial oversight has also increased. For the first time, legislators are beginning publicly to reject finance papers, as seen in December 1991; over the next three months, several papers were withdrawn in anticipation of possible legislative rejection.[72] In related financial matters, in November 1992 the legislature voted to cancel an increase in fees payable to the Labour Tribunal, and in February 1993 legislators reduced the charges for vehicles using government tunnels.

A second more dramatic instance of the Legislative Council exercising its deliberative powers came with the debate over the Court of Final Appeal. For the first time in history, the Legislative Council rejected an agreement reached by the British and Chinese governments. This agreement, a product of the Joint Liaison Group, provided for only one overseas judge on the new Court of Final Appeal. The legislators voted 34 to 11 in support of a motion that demanded the make-up of the court be more 'flexible,' with provision for more overseas judges.[73] The mover, a member from the legal functional constituency, noted that the Joint Liaison Group cannot make unilateral decisions and 'then expect us to endorse them automatically' as the Legislative Council was no longer a 'rubber stamp' assembly.[74] A directly elected member, speaking in support of the motion, observed that the partnership the Governor called for between the government and the legislature appeared to be a mockery: 'May I ask the administration whose partner? Or does it say that it is partner to both—Beijing being the predominant partner, the administration being the subservient partner, and this council being only a partner in name only? I say, "Shame on you, partner" '.[75] Ultimately, the legislature rejected the government's bid for the future court's funds until it better reflected the chamber's views. This was the first time in the 150-year history of the legislature that the government had been defeated in a vote in Council. 'The Court of Final Appeal was something of a watershed,' according to a recent statement by a British Foreign Office official. 'We found that we had a Legislative Council that was not grateful for all our efforts—but on the contrary, thought that the agreement we struck with Beijing was poor, and asked why they had not been consulted.'[76]

In sum, elections held since 1985 have turned out a new breed of dynamic legislator who refuses to take public policies and fund allocations for granted. While there has been some disquiet regarding the loss of efficiency of the Council, its effectiveness appears assured.[77] The chamber has become more assertive and aggressive than at any other time in Hong Kong history. Yet it is important to point out that the new-style legislature does not have any more policy-making power than before, but rather has matured in the ability to exercise those powers. The more active posture towards policy making can be seen in some gross indicators of legislative activity.

Table 6.3 indicates that while the number of sittings has not dramatically increased, their duration has, particularly since 1991.[78] This can be seen in the increase in the number of pages in the *Hansard*: from 1456 in 1984–5, to 1769 in 1985–6, 2347 in 1988–9, and 4519 in 1991–2. Even taking into account the increased number of members, the statistics clearly demonstrate a much more active legislature, at least in terms of its work in chamber.[79] Less clear an indication of the changing policy-making function of the Legislative Council is seen in a review of their handling of bills, particularly the number of bills amended at the committee stage.

Table 6.3 Number and Duration of Legislative Sittings, 1984–1991

	1984	1985	1988	1991
Sittings	28	32	31	32
Hours	56[a]	86	111	220

Note: [a] Approximate average for this year was two hours per meeting. The other hourly statistics were compiled by OMELCO staff.

Source: OMELCO annual reports, OMELCO staff statistics.

Table 6.4 Number of Bills and Amendments, 1984–1991

	1984	1985	1988	1991
Bills	83	68	66	80
Amendments	25	20	27	30

Source: OMELCO reports.

Table 6.4 shows that the number of bills has slightly reduced but the number of amendments offered has grown. Comparing 1984 with 1991, the number of amendments has increased 20 per cent. But these statistics camouflage a substantive difference: namely, the types of amendments offered to the types of bills considered. Since 1985, the Legislative Council has been much more willing to involve itself in highly controversial, substantive matters, from bills dealing with political rights to the budget. Furthermore, the types of amendments have changed from incremental stylistic alterations more characteristic of pre-1984 deliberations to the more substantive amendments highlighted above. In addition, the fact that the number of bills has slightly declined could be interpreted as further evidence that the members are exercising more deliberation in the passage of legislation.[80] While much more legislative attention has been devoted to deliberation, even more has been given to legislative oversight. This can be seen by comparing the post-1984 membership in a variety of legislative policy-making dimensions. First, in terms of questions, Table 6.5 clearly demonstrates that elected members are most active in posing them.

Table 6.5 also demonstrates that elected members are more active in asking questions than are appointed members;[81] this is particularly true of those members who are directly elected from geographical constituencies. Directly elected members are almost twice as likely to pose questions than members from functional

Table 6.5 Average Number of Questions Asked by Each Member of the Legislative Council, by Type of Member, 1984–1992

	1984	**1985–6**[a]	**1988–9**	**1991–2**
Appointed members	6.17	4.2	6.0	5.6[b]
Functional constituency members	—	6.2	5.1	7.0
Electoral college members	—	10.6	6.3	—
Directly elected members	—	—	—	13.1
Number of questions asked	179	296	272	480

Notes: [a] To simplify, from 1985 the first session of each term is used only. [b] Excludes deputy president, who is barred from asking questions.
Source: Author's tabulations from Hong Kong *Hansard*, 1984–5; 1985–6; 1988–9; 1991–2.

Table 6.6 Average Participation in Adjournment Debates: Number of Speeches per Debate by Type of Member, 1984–1992

Year (Number of Adjournment Debates Occurring)

	1984 **(3)**	**1985–6** **(6)**	**1988–9** **(1)**	**1991–2** **(17)**
Appointed members	6.3	7.6	4.0	2.4
Functional constituency members	—	5.3	5.0	2.9
Electoral college members	—	6.8	2.0	—
Directly elected members	—	—	—	4.4

Source: Author's tabulations of speeches offered in each adjournment debate. Compiled from information in Hong Kong *Hansard*, 1984–5; 1985–6; 1988–9; 1991–2.

constituencies, and almost three times more likely than appointed members. The fact that newer members are more active is also seen in their use of adjournment debates (Table 6.6). While the average participation per member does not show a critical difference between them, nonetheless the rise in the total number of debates can be attributed to the advent of elected members. Furthermore, a series of informal rules mandate that the participation in debates be distributed according to previous participation: members who have not participated in the past are given precedence. Time-limits also restrict the number of members who may participate. Finally, the number of motions offered by various types of members also demonstrates role variations (Table 6.7).

Table 6.7 Legislative Council Motions by Type of Member, 1984–1992

	1984	**1985–6**	**1988–9**	**1991–2**
Appointed members	2[a]	7	6	10
Functional constituency members	—	—	5	13
Electoral college members	—	—	—	—
Directly elected members	—	—	—	19
Officials	n.a.	28	34	28
Total	n.a.	35	45	70

Notes: [a] Until 1991 it was customary for the senior unofficial, always an appointed member, to move motions on behalf of the non-government members.

The motions show that the government was clearly in charge of determining the Council's agenda until recently. While the number of official motions, the vehicle for introduction and movement of bills through the legislature, remains sizeable, the number of unofficial motions is increasing over time as legislators use this device to assist in their policy-making activities.

The Legislative Council has seen a tremendous growth of policy-making activities, particularly oversight, led by the directly elected members. Their endeavours to restructure the legislature—from the direct election of the president to the refinement of the committee system—and the way in which they have become involved in all three stages of policy making reflect their desire for an independent legislature that will guarantee better government accountability, both now and after 1997. In the pursuit of these activities, however, many members argue that they are using a means (policy making) to an end, that end being the function of representation.

Representation

As noted in Chapter 1, the philosophical history of the legislature is rooted in popular choice—not government by the people, but of and for the people. A descriptive basis of representation was provided by John Adams, who argued during the American Revolution that a representative legislature 'should be an exact portrait, in miniature, of the people at large, as it should think, feel, reason, and act like them'.[82] From this perspective, the Legislative Council has been vastly unrepresentative. Perhaps the biggest criticism voiced throughout the history of the Legislative Council has not been so much its lack of policy-making powers or its disinclination to use those powers as its unrepresentative nature. From the outset, the Council was perceived to be composed of individuals quite different from the common Hong Kong inhabitant. It was initially perceived as an executive creature, and so it remained, with official domination, at least formally, until 1984 (see Table 6.1). Additionally, Chapter 3 highlighted that the racial representation on the Legislative Council was predominantly European for much of its history. This can be attributed to the fact that until quite recently almost all civil servants who comprised the official membership were British expatriates. Yet even looking at the racial composition of the non-government appointees, it is clear that while Chinese representation eventually occurred, it was never in proportion to the Chinese population until recently (Table 6.8).

Moreover, even with the growth of Chinese representation, these members, similar to their European colleagues, were unrepresentative of the population in terms of occupation and social class. Both Chinese and European unofficials were wealthy merchants and barristers rather than representatives of the more numerous working class.[83] A study of the Chinese unofficials before 1964 noted that they were from 'established rich families and are among the small circle of élite in the Chinese community'. After the mid-1960s, the study found that the Chinese unofficials were from a new category, namely the 'new rich representing the ever-increasing industrial force'.[84] The appointed members represented only a narrow segment of society, predominantly voicing the interests of big businessmen, industrialists, and in general, the wealthy. While attempts were made to address this bias, particularly in the mid-1970s, until 1984 the legislature remained unrepresentative in terms of social and economic class. This bias was reinforced by the informal requirements of the job:

The Governor's choice of unofficial members is limited by the members' status. They must also be British subjects, otherwise they cannot take the oath of allegiance. They must be men of some substance, otherwise they cannot afford the time to attend meetings. Furthermore, the unofficials are subject to the test of competence, social prestige and interest in public affairs. Thus it is very doubtful whether the appointed unofficial members . . . are representative of the man in the street.[85]

Table 6.8 Racial Background of Members, 1850–1991[a]

Year	Chinese	Indian	Portuguese	Other European
1850	—	—	—	2
1857	—	—	—	3
1865	—	—	—	4[b]
1880	1	—	—	3
1884	1	1	—	3
1896	2	—	1	3
1906	2	—	—	4
1929	3	—	1	3
1952	4	—	1	3
1954	4	1	1	2
1959	4	—	1	3
1960	4	1	—	3
1966	9	1	—	3
1969	10	—	—	3
1971	11	—	—	2
1973	11	—	1	3
1976	17	—	1	4
1977	19	—	1	4
1980	19	—	1	6
1984	25	—	1	3[c]
1985	43	—	—	3[c]
1988	43	—	1	2
1991	53	—	1	3[c]

Notes: [a] Members refers to non-government members, previously referred to as unofficials. [b] Includes a member of the government (official) who sat as an unofficial. [c] Includes an individual who is Eurasian.

Sources: Author's tabulations from Endacott, *Government and People of Hong Kong*, Appendix D; and Miners, *Government and Politics of Hong Kong* (3rd edn.), p. 127.

In spite of attempts to broaden the basis of representation by including more Chinese members, the composition of the legislature remained quite distinct from the general public.

It is ironic that as the legislature gained in terms of racial representation, these gains were more symbolic than real, and should be seen in terms of appeasement if not co-optation rather than constitutional advance. The integration of Chinese community leaders into the system of governance allowed the maintenance of executive-led government. The closed decision-making system that emerged meant that 'the Legislative Council failed to develop into a representative assembly because those who might have promoted such a development were themselves part of the power structure . . . [hence] they had nothing to gain by seeking a more powerful and expanded structure'.[86] This was clearly seen in debates over political reforms surveyed in Chapters 3 and 4 that revealed that the majority in the Council itself were often against further democratization and broader representation.[87] Yet since then, the business-oriented, conservative bias of the legislature has been transformed through the creation of multiple bases with which to choose members of the legislature. The first change occurred in 1985.

Elected members

Clearly a broader basis of representation was established with the election of 24 of the 57 members of the legislature in 1985. Of those 57 members, 12 were elected by functional constituencies representing key economic and professional sectors[88] and 12 were elected through geographical districts from an electoral college composed of members of the District Boards, Urban and Regional councils.[89] Just 24,803 people voted in the functional constituencies and 403 in the electoral college; less than 1 per cent of the total population. Nonetheless, this electorate, while small, was to set in motion a new representational trend that fully blossomed in the 1991 elections.[90]

For the first time, the 1991 legislature had a majority of elected members. The abolition of the electoral college and its replacement by direct elections resulted in 750,467 individuals voting in the nine, double-member geographical constituencies,[91] yet this comprised only 39.1 per cent of registered voters, who in turn comprised only 50 per cent of the eligible voters. Participation in the functional elections was not much better: only 47 per cent of the 48,756 registered voters in the functional constituencies bothered to vote, and some constituencies recorded a voting turnout as low as 16 or 17 per cent.[92] While some commentators argued that participation was sufficiently low to warrant the election being labelled 'unrepresentative', others reached different conclusions.[93] Analysts were quick to point out that the statistics were misleading, suggesting that the real turnout in the direct elections was as high as 55 per cent[94] and that the low figures could be attributed to an out-of-date electoral register and insufficient incentives to vote.[95] Low turnout for the functional seats may have been because the majority (12 of 21) of elections were uncontested.

Regardless of the rate of participation, what was significant about this election is that it was the largest election in Hong Kong's history and provided a valid indication of the public's political preferences. It resulted in a liberal landslide, with approximately 67.5 per cent of those who voted casting their votes for liberals.[96] One party, the United Democrats, won 12 of the 18 directly elected seats; all but one of the remaining directly elected seats were filled by liberals, either from among the independents or from other political parties. Liberal ideology in this election was equated with fighting for more autonomy and standing up to China.[97] The strong anti-communist vote reflected mounting apprehension over events since the signing of the Joint Declaration, from allowing 'convergence' to stifle democracy to the means and ends obtained in provisions of the Basic Law. The elections, therefore, can be seen as partial realization of the demand for a referendum on events which have shaped Hong Kong's future, and they sent a clear message: 'The election results were a vote against the Chinese government and against communism but also . . . a negative judgment on the facile role the British and Hong Kong governments played in failing to introduce representative government [and] insist on autonomy'.[98]

Yet Governor Wilson's response to this mandate was quickly to appoint conservative individuals to 'better balance' the legislature, in the process denying that body a truly representative nature. Coupled with the overwhelming conservative bias of the functional constituencies, this maintained a fundamentally conservative body, now shown to be out of touch with the majority of the public's views.[99] In so constructing the legislature, the Governor insured that disharmony rather than consensus would characterize the Council's proceedings.

While the debate continues over the most suitable basis for choosing Hong Kong's legislators, what is apparent is that since 1985 a new electoral format for part of the members has enhanced the representativeness of the legislature along a wide variety of descriptive dimensions. As previously noted, the body had become much more racially representative; by the early 1990s Europeans became a minority, not only due to the reduction of official members, but because those appointed and elected were almost all Chinese. Additionally, one of the most obvious changes has come in terms of occupation. A unique feature of Hong Kong's legislature is that some of its members (50 per cent after 1997) are chosen by occupational functions, ensuring that certain sectors and professions are explicitly represented.[100] But enhancing the breadth of representation has been the myriad of other occupations as is depicted in Table 6.9, represented from members chosen by the electoral college as well as those who are directly elected.

The electoral changes also resulted in a younger legislative body. While the average age of members was 50.3 in 1984, it decreased in 1985 to 49.8, dropped further in 1988 to 49.3, and fell most dramatically in 1991 to 46.3. The lowering of the average age can be attributed to several factors. Members no longer have to be at the top of their profession to obtain gubernatorial recognition and appointment to the Council. While in the old days service on the Legislative Council was seen as an 'honour'—a tribute to one's success, typically at the end of one's career—today's member is often at the beginning or just approaching the mid-level of career status. Being younger, the individual has more time and energy to participate in campaigning; being less committed to a career allows more time to devote to the legislative responsibilities, resulting in the increased policy-making activities seen earlier. This increased devotion to the requirements of the job is most graphically depicted by the seven members of the 1991 session who declared that serving as a legislator was their principal occupation. Their average age was 36.

From a variety of perspectives the legislature has become dramatically more representative of the Hong Kong public.[101] In looking at the pre-1985 legislature, we can easily see that it was a business-dominated conservative group. But ultimately, a discussion as to the representativeness of Hong Kong's Legislative Council up to 1984 must be put in a broader context. Throughout Hong Kong's history, the Legislative Council has been only one body representing the Hong Kong people, and perhaps not the most significant one at that. More direct representation came from groups such as the District Watch Committee,[102] the Tung Wah Group,[103] the District Boards, the Heung Yee Kuk, and the Urban Council. Yet these institutions, like the legislature, were oriented more towards maintaining the power and legitimacy of the government than representation; they were a principal means by which

Table 6.9 Representation in the Legislative Council by Occupation, 1984–1991 (Number of Members and Percentage of Non-Civil Servant Members)

Occupation	1984	1985[a]	1988	1991
Business	15 (53)	16 (35)	15 (33)	12 (18)
Banking	—	2 (4)	1 (2)	3 (5)
Law	3 (10)	6 (13)	7 (15)	8 (14)
Engineering	—	1 (2)	1 (2)	1 (2)
Healthcare	—	—	1 (2)	1 (2)
Social welfare	—	2 (4)	2 (4)	1 (2)
Education	4 (13)	9 (20)	9 (20)	10 (18)
Public relations	2 (6)	1 (2)	2 (4)	2 (4)
Medical doctors	2 (6)	3 (7)	2 (4)	4 (8)
Accountancy	3 (10)	2 (4)	2 (4)	2 (4)
Religion	1 (2)	—	—	1 (2)
Architecture	—	—	1 (2)	1 (2)
Surveying	—	—	1 (2)	1 (2)
Transport	—	1 (2)	—	—
Trade unions	—	2 (4)	2 (4)	2 (4)
Legislators	—	—	—	7 (13)

Notes: Total percentages may not add up to 100 due to rounding. [a] One non-civil servant seat was vacant at the time report was filed.

Source: Author's compilation from OMELCO annual reports and membership directories.

the government could 'exercise its control and influence over the Chinese population by co-opting its natural leaders'.[104] Thus co-optation rather than representation appeared to be the *raison d'être* for the unofficials, revealing that the real function of the Legislative Council up to 1984 was systems maintenance.

Since 1985 the legislature has become much more representative, yet it has remained unrepresentative ideologically. The conservative functional constituency members coupled with Governor Wilson's conservative appointees formed a dominant bias against the liberals chosen by the electorate in the first direct elections. Members themselves saw this division in terms not so much of ideology as of what should be the appropriate response in dealing with China. When they were asked to define what the divisions were in the Legislative Council, over 67 per cent said the main division was not ideology but 'how to deal with China'. Conservatives think that it is imperative that nothing be done to antagonize the future sovereign power, even at the expense of further democratization. Liberals believe that now is the time to push for more democracy so as to have a more effective 'legislative bulwark' to protect and promote the public interest after 1997. These divisions were clearly apparent during the debates over the constitutional reform outlined in Chapter 4 and have become even more striking as the legislature debates the Patten proposals. It appears that the conservative majority, like the members of the old Legislative Council, is attempting to maintain stability at all costs—a key ingredient systems maintenance.

Systems Maintenance

The term *systems-maintenance activities* relates to the ability of the legislature to promote integration of the political system, mobilize support for its policies, and legitimize those who are in power. These activities rely less on specific legislative action and more on the legislature just 'being there'.[105] The performance of this function by the Legislative Council is not entirely surprising, for as seen in Chapter 2, in other colonial legislatures systems maintenance— at least for as long as the unofficials were in the minority—was the predominant function. For instance, Sir Hugh Clifford, remarking upon the Nigerian Legislative Council observed: 'It was clear that the function of the legislative council was not at all to represent the people to the government, still less to make the government responsible to the people, but instead to act as a spokesman for the administration to the people'.[106]

Integration involves 'penetrating the primary, occupational or geographical groups by a broader national identification'.[107] The Legislative Council can be seen as just one of the organizations which used the Chinese élite to link the people to the government. It was a mechanism 'whereby the decision and wishes of the government are unilaterally transmitted to the Chinese society'.[108] Yet integration by the legislature was not totally successful, as Hong Kong society, at least to the early 1980s, remained 'minimally integrated'.[109] Furthermore, most Hong Kong citizens showed little support and even less knowledge of the legislature's activities. In a survey of Chinese residents in the late 1960s, respondents were asked if they were satisfied with the present form of government or if they would prefer Hong Kong to be governed by an assembly elected by the people. The findings showed that 21 per cent of the respondents wanted the status quo, 22 per cent wanted an elected assembly, while the majority, 51 per cent, replied that they just 'didn't know'. When asked if the Legislative Council paid attention to the opinions of the majority of people in Hong Kong, only 20 per cent replied affirmatively, with 24 per cent stating no, and 56 per cent replying that they did not know.[110] As the 1960s riots demonstrated, one of the clear deficiencies of the colonial system was the lack of integration of mass groupings, particularly the Chinese working class, into the legislature and other governmental structures. Consequently, reforms undertaken in the 1970s attempted to promote better integration with the colonial regime and hence led to a growth both in the number and background diversity of legislators.

Integration, however, was most easily achieved with élite groupings of the wealthy Chinese and Europeans. This level of integration was acceptable because up until 1984 the majority of Hong Kong citizens were apolitical, had a low sense of political efficacy, and could be characterized as possessing 'utilitarianistic familism with an orientation towards the realization of short-term economic rather than political goals.'[111] Most knew very little about the Council. They did not know its function or composition. Furthermore, most thought the Council had insufficient representation, with 25 per cent stating that Legislative Council members did not represent their opinions, 22 per cent saying they did, and the rest undecided.[112] Hence in terms of integration, although the Legislative Council in the past did not provide for integration of the mass public, it did integrate the élite well which was what the government desired, in the process providing a legitimizing function.

Legitimation refers to increasing the level of diffuse support for those in power.[113] Legitimation is particularly important in Hong Kong where it is crucially needed to provide stability for an alien, colonial government. Unofficial co-optation into the bureaucratic polity by the government meant that the non-government members legitimized the political system to the extent that an 'administrative absorption of politics' occurred in which the government 'co-opt[ed] the political forces...into an administrative decision-making body, thus achieving some level of elite integration; as a consequence, the governing authority is made legitimate'.[114] In characterizing the pre-1985 Legislative Council, one observer noted: 'The old Legco [Legislative Council] Chamber was something of a cosy club. Its debates were conducted in an atmosphere of genteel subservience. Together, the councillors constituted a defensive team without any star players'.[115] So up until 1985, the legislature's main function was systems maintenance, in which it generated support for government-sponsored proposals, and in the process of granting legislative approval provided for the government's legitimation. But this function, like the functions of policy making and representation, also changed with the new membership from 1985.

Since 1985, the Legislative Council has ceased to be the consensus body it was in the past. Now there is more open opposition both within the legislature and between the legislature and the government in debates. Resolution of disputes is often arrived at through a public vote in chamber rather than behind-the-scenes compromises. The newly elected members quickly became a 'de facto opposition' with members arguing [about] rather than condoning policies'.[116] Rather than a government based on 'consultation and consensus' it is beginning to look like a government based on 'assault and dissensus'. All of this has had a destabilizing effect. Lacking consensus, the legislature is unable to promote stability and continuity; lacking unity, it is increasingly factionalized if not fractionalized.

Ironically, the government mandates that delineated the Legislative Council's structure in 1985 and 1988 ensured at the same time that the government itself could no longer rely upon the Council to secure its legitimacy. This is because the government created disintegrative forces when it opted to provide multiple bases for the legislators' selection. By recognizing specific occupational sectors (and by ignoring others) the government created members who would find it difficult to promote the public interest over their explicitly defined private interest. By mixing these with members selected by the Governor and members who have wide-ranging geographical districts with multiple and often conflicting demands, the government ensured that integration would be difficult. Furthermore, by not providing sufficient enfranchisement for the growing middle class through direct elections, the government promoted wide-scale dismay and distrust. These disintegrative factors resulted in weakening the legitimacy of its rule.

When Governor Wilson tried to mould a pro-government majority of conservative appointees and functional constituency members to overcome a possible 'opposition' party of twenty-one liberal members in 1991, his efforts were not totally successful. This was evident in the conservative defections in the earlier Court of Final Appeal dispute and at the outset of the 1992 budget debate. More paradoxically, it has been the arrival of a new, more liberal Governor in 1992 that has led the conservatives (primarily appointed and functional constituency members) to become the 'opposition party' with the liberals (primarily directly elected members) appearing more 'pro-government'. In the process, the function of systems maintenance, performed by conservative members in the past for the colonial regime, is now being performed by them for the future sovereign, China, even as this sovereign is engaged in disputes with the Hong Kong government.[117] The Chinese have effectively courted the conservatives by raising the spectre of Chinese nationalism and economic profit. China, in a era that has seen the globalization of political values, has found itself increasingly isolated and has eagerly looked to others, in this instance, the conservative Legislative Council members, to help justify its legitimacy.

Moreover, under the current structure of the Council, the government is operating without a majority party. For although the legislature has become more representative, it has not become more responsible, as policy portfolios are not open to legislators. The government is uncomfortably aware of this anomaly, as the Chief Secretary has remarked:

We all recognize that it may not always be easy to gain support of a majority of the members of the Council because . . . this Government . . . has no political party, annual conference, nor a manifesto, from which to develop and propagate policy. . . . In this Chamber we have no party machine or whip system to give us the guaranteed majorities that support governments in more developed democracies. Nor do we have elected ministers to provide a popular public face.[118]

In this perilous climate the Chief Secretary pledged that the government would try to be more responsive to the legislators and allow the Legislative Council to be more active in formulation rather than just deliberation of policy. Nonetheless, he asserted that 'an appointed Executive, working through an apolitical Civil Service, balanced by an elected legislature is a fair and workable system, provided everyone is committed to making it work in the interests of the Hong Kong people'.[119]

But the pursuit of the 'public interest' appears to differ according to one's definition, with legislators differing among themselves and with the administration over its proper definition. Furthermore, these disintegrative forces have occurred in a climate of rapid political development and controversy, conditions that would prove perilous even to the most secure government structure. It would indeed be an anomaly if the Legislative Council should vigorously pursue 'maintenance' during a context of rapid and fundamental changes.

The legislature's new combative role has generally been praised by the public. In a large number of polls that measure popularity among members, the directly elected members, who have been the most combative, have overwhelmingly been the public's favourites.[120] Other polls indicate that the public backs the Legislative Council's hard-line stance towards the government, particularly during the 1991–2 budget battles.[121] And more than half of those surveyed in a recent poll believed the Legislative Council was 'right to take on China'—from disputes over the Court of Final Appeal, and the setting up of the committee system, to support for the Patten proposals.[122] The Legislative Council's popularity has increased to the extent that when the public was recently asked which they would prefer, a vote for the 1995 legislature or HK$100,000, more opted for the vote than the money.[123]

Therefore, while the legislature itself has gained in legitimacy, it appears that this gain has been at the expense of both the present and future sovereign. This could be indicative of difficult legislative–executive relations in the future.[124] Furthermore, recent activity in the Council clearly shows the increasing functional importance of policy making and representation over that of systems maintenance.

Comparative Classification of the Legislative Council

The preceding assessment of the legislative functions of policy making, representation, and systems maintenance in the Legislative Council demonstrates that up until 1984 the Legislative Council would, from a comparative perspective, be classified as minimal. The Council had low support from the masses, high support from the government élite, and little policy-making power. Minimal legislatures are dominated by executive-centred élites whose influence permeates the entire policy-making process. The most important limitation on the effectiveness of the legislature's policy making, particularly oversight, goes to the basic defining characteristic of the institution: 'The minimal legislature exists by the grace of the executive . . . and only exercises the authority that [the executive] cares to allow it'.[125] The control of the executive, in this case the Governor, is reinforced by his dominance in legislative recruitment as well as his overwhelming legislative power. In terms of function, the behaviour of members of minimal legislatures best conforms to the requirements of the system-maintenance functions, as 'legislators and executives agree that the major activities that legislators are expected to undertake are those that are designed to increase support for regime policies and legitimize the regime in the eyes of its citizens'.[126]

Yet ironically, as a body oriented to the status quo, the Legislative Council found it most difficult to confront—as well as shape—a future which held such dramatic change. But as elected members joined the legislature, they provoked a dramatic evolution in the way in which the Council performed all of its major functions. The Legislative Council participated more in the shaping of public policy; it broadened its representation, not only on a descriptive basis but more importantly in terms of legislative activities; and it became less bound by traditional systems-maintenance mandates. Public support for the legislature grew but was not overwhelming. One year after the 1991 election, only 47 per cent of the public felt the Legislative Council was 'effective' and 50 per cent felt that the Legislative Council had 'done a good job monitoring the government'.[127] Since then the Legislative Council's approval rating has ranged from 46 per cent to 51 per cent.[128] Yet approval appears tentative, with the public equally divided as to whether the Legislative Council should cooperate with the government in promoting the public's interest or if it should put the public's interest first even if it means confronting the government.[129]

Public opinion is also divided over what the Legislative Council's role should be towards China, at least with respect to the Patten proposals. While initially supportive, as China's attitude became more combative, the Hong Kong public was quite willing to let the future be determined by China and Britain rather than by their representatives in the legislature.[130]

In turn, the government is exhibiting less support for the Legislative Council than previously—it has become increasingly frustrated with a body it no longer can control. According to one senior official, the new legislature has become 'problematic' for the government: 'Sometimes the more we give, the more they use this to attack us. Then we tend to close up when the information is used in this way. This is ultimately self-defeating for the legislature in terms of accountability; leading to a government which is less open, more cautious, and therefore less accountable'.[131]

In terms of measuring legislative support, the views of the future sovereign are even more pertinent. China has not only undercut the Legislative Council's future effectiveness through restrictions over its powers in the Basic Law but has also attempted to restrict its membership to those who are 'loyal compatriots' or at least amenable to manipulation. Ultimately, China's refusal to recognize the Legislative Council as a legitimate representative body portends serious conflicts in the future.

So while the policy-making power of the Legislative Council—or rather the use of that power—has resulted in the legislature being given a 'modest' rating, public opinion remains fairly divided as to the Council's future format and effectiveness. More importantly, élite support in Hong Kong for the Legislative Council appears to be waning, and China remains hostile if not threatening. So, the Legislative Council today must be classified as a marginal legislature.

In marginal legislatures, policy formulation is dominated by the executive, although there is some form of consultation with a selective subset of legislators before formal introduction in the chamber. While marginal legislatures are more capable of deliberating than formulating, they often perform these activities in a climate of wide-scale giving of favours by the executive and under the omnipresent threat of extra-constitutional sanctions. The giving of favours here means providing support in elections or jobs, funds, political influence, and prestige to elicit responsible behaviour from appreciative members. Committees in marginal legislatures are more effective at deliberation than any attempt at formulation but are hindered by the lack of legislative expertise, the fluidity of committee membership, and the absence of competent professional staff. Members are assigned to committees almost at random and frequently change their assignments, as seen in the Bills Committees. Even those committees that exercise some degree of influence on the shape of legislation are not really autonomous. The Public Accounts Committee and the Finance Committee, for example, are both reliant on the government for all of their information. In sum, the deliberative activities that take place in the committee arenas of marginal legislatures can be characterized as 'generalized rather than specialized, occasionally rather than regularly significant and usually subordinate rather than autonomous'.[132]

Plenary sessions of these legislatures are generally free to criticize and amend government proposals as long as they remain within the parameters established by the executive-centred élites who run the political system: 'The most important of these parameters is that the government not be defeated on legislation that is important to it; however, there is reason to believe that the government in certain instances may well back off even from important proposals if confronted by strong opposition from the legislature'.[133] One way these governments protect themselves from legislative opposition is through constitutional and political provisions that restrict the scope of legislative activity, as is clearly seen in restrictions in the Royal Instructions and the Basic Law.[134]

Question time or the use of questions is the customary vehicle for oversight in plenary arenas of marginal legislatures. The heavy volume of questions is attributable to three factors: 'the ineffectiveness of committees' oversight activities, a parliamentary form of government which requires the presence of government in Parliament, and the formal designation of a particular period as question time'.[135] Yet oversight is often limited due to the lack of adequate support staff and the fact that ministers are responsible to the executive rather than the legislature. Finally, if political parties are present in marginal systems, they are multiple and weak, in that they cannot take over executive positions.

To conclude, marginal legislatures can impose certain constraints on executive-centred élites although they are generally dominated by these élites. Yet exercising constraint over executive activities is accompanied by some risk, for the marginal chamber constantly faces the prospect of closure or other extraconstitutional reactions from the executive. In Hong Kong this threat is more appropriate to a post-1997 scenario, particularly should the Legislative Council refuse to pass the budget or 'an important bill'.[136]

For several reasons, this classification may change in the future. First, the classification is functionally based on the legislature's policy-making ability, which has been—and barring constitutional amendments will continue to be—constrained by the inability of legislators to initiate policies. Yet the legislature may become more active in policy making through its naysaying and oversight powers, as depicted in recent trends, and these may provide significant limits to executive policy making in the future. Moreover, the Legislative Council is moving to strengthen both its policy deliberation and policy oversight through the development of a variety of structures leading to a more highly institutionalized body.

Second, the classification is based on measurement of public support, which in Hong Kong remains incomplete if not inadequate. While there have been fairly extensive appraisals which measure respondents' attitudes towards government,[137] few surveys have directly attempted to measure the level of specific support for the legislature[138] and, more significantly, none to date have measured diffuse support.[139] Thirdly, while most indicators suggest that the Legislative Council best fits the marginal classification, the fit is imperfect.[140] And fourth, this classification may be inadequate, as it has been concluded that for most legislatures, the function of representation rather than policy making is the more meaningful,[141] and hence a more useful classification might be based on legislatures' representative features.

Conclusion

This chapter has traced the development of the Legislative Council as it has performed the functions of policy making, representation, and systems maintenance. Until 1985 the Council was a minimal legislature, receiving little support from the public but enjoying support from the governmental élite who perceived its function as being to legitimize their rule.

While the Legislative Council has witnessed a rapid evolution in its representative and policy-making functions, it remains limited by its present and future constitutional context. Recent modest increases in the exercise of its policy-making power allow the Council to be reclassified as a marginal legislature. Although the classification allowed for only 'less' or 'more' determination of support, the Legislative Council's support has progressed in two opposite directions: support of government élites has waned, but the public appears to be not only more aware of but more supportive of its activities.

Yet for the Legislative Council to be more than a marginal legislature it must pursue both internal and external reforms. Internally, it must institutionalize a stronger and more competent staff with research capabilities to provide a counterbalance to the informational expertise of the executive (a subject explored in Chapter 5). In addition, the Legislative Council must develop a stronger committee system that allows legislative independence to occur through standing committees with powers over both policy and bills, possessing a stable membership and benefitting from frequent meetings to allow for development of expertise. This reform also implies that the legislators must make a full-time rather than part-time commitment to the job.

But it is the external reforms that will be much more difficult to accomplish. The Legislative Council must push to have some of its members provided with policy portfolios so that they may exercise better formulative as well as oversight power over the governmental branches. In addition, the Legislative Council must try to promote amendments to the Basic Law to eliminate the restrictions over its membership composition and exercise of policy making. But developments such as these will depend not only on what the current and future sovereign powers want but, perhaps more critically, the aspirations of the legislators in the pursuit of their legislative roles. It is to these aspirations that we turn in Chapter 7.

7 Legislative Roles

The most significant assurance of a degree of local autonomy after 1997 was the Joint Declaration's promise that the executive would be accountable to a legislature composed of elected members. This assurance led to two common assumptions: that the most effective check to Chinese influence and possible domination of Hong Kong affairs would be the locally based legislature, and that the legislature, as the most representative branch of government, would be the most responsive to the wishes of the people.

Yet as was evident in Chapter 3, up until 1984 there was no strong legislative tradition in Hong Kong. The Governor appointed all members of the Legislative Council and chose them more for their conservatism and willingness to support his initiatives than their representativeness. The main function of the legislature up to 1984, as described in Chapter 6, was to secure the legitimacy of the colonial government. Since the signing of the Joint Declaration, however, aspirations for local autonomy centred on transforming the legislature into a body which would not only be more representative of the people but would in turn possess the power and inclination to make the post-1997 government more accountable. Consequently, determining the format with which to choose future legislators became the key political issue of the next decade and aroused the most extensive political debate in Hong Kong's history.

Legislative composition was the subject of two White Papers and the key issue during the drafting of the Basic Law (see Chapter 4). Since Governor Patten suggested reforms in 1992, it has been the subject of an acrimonious dispute between Britain and China. The argument is centred on the best compositional format for the future legislature.[1] Implicit in this argument is the assumption that how the legislator is chosen determines the type of legislator he will become—what will be his conception of his legislative responsibilities, his view of the function of the legislature—in essence, his role concepts. The aim of this chapter is to build upon this assumption by investigating the current membership of the legislature and examine what, if any, difference it makes in terms of role conceptions. Ultimately, it is assumed that these beliefs will guide subsequent legislative behaviour. Hence examining role concepts will help us determine whether the legislature will continue primarily to perform the systems-maintenance traditions of the past or if it will endeavour to be more active in policy making and representation as recent trends suggest. If the latter, legislators will help to ensure better responsiveness and accountability in the post-1997 government.

Acting upon these assumptions, 52 members of the Legislative Council were interviewed between May 1987 and June 1988, and another 52 members between May 1992 and February 1993. This chapter analyses the variations in purposive, representational, and interest group roles uncovered by the interviews. The results are summarized in Figure 7.1.[2]

To discover which of these orientations was adopted, the following question was asked: *How would you describe the job of being a legislator—what are the most important things you should do here?* Table 7.1 shows the gross breakdown of responses.

The responses make clear that most Legislative Council members primarily define their roles in terms of two functions, lawmaking and representation. Yet already, at this simple functional level, differences in orientation appear depending on how the member was selected. For the appointed members 'lawmaking' is perceived as their principal function, yet fewer than half of the elected members in 1988 and significantly fewer in 1993 share this perception. This indicates that the change in membership has transformed the perception of what is significant legislative activity. While only a few of the appointed members perceive representation as their primary function, this is the most popular function for elected members.[3] A significant portion of directly elected members and an even larger group of functional constituency members believe they serve in the legislature to represent others. Moreover, some appointed members revealed their orientation towards two functions that none of their elected colleagues mentioned: supporting the administration in the passage of its legislation and mediating between conflicting interests. Directly elected members also expressed a unique priority: promotion of democracy. In addition,

Figure 7.1 Role Conceptions of Hong Kong Legislators

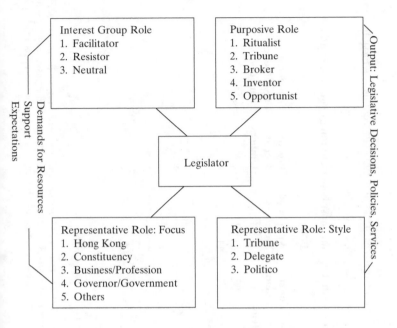

Feedback

a new category of activity has developed in the latest survey, reflecting a major development in Hong Kong's political development, namely, the promotion of specific political parties.

These functional distinctions are also seen in the members' descriptions of their activities, although they are less strong. In response to the question, *What problems occupy most of your time?* 46 per cent of appointed, 47 per cent of functional constituency, and only 25 per cent of electoral college members noted in 1988 that they debate and amend bills; this increased to 64 per cent for appointed, 50 per cent for functional constituency, but only 38 per cent for directly elected members in 1993. No appointed, but 6 per cent of electoral college and 12 per cent of functional constituency members, indicated in 1988 that they 'express people's views' compared with 7 per cent of the appointed members, 14 per cent of the functional constituency members, and 31 per cent of the directly elected members who noted they do so in 1993. Further, 4

Table 7.1 Legislative Councillors' Descriptions of Their Purposive Roles, 1988 and 1993 (Percentage of First Responses Received)

Q: How would you describe the job of being a legislator—what are the most important things you should do here?

	1988			1993			Average
	Appointed Members	Electoral College Members	Functional Constituency Members	Appointed Members	Directly Elected Members	Functional Constituency Members	
Lawmaking	60	50	43	61	15	28	43
Representation	5	10	50	11	33	54	26
Affecting public opinion[a]	5	—	7	—	—	—	2
Supporting the executive[b]	15	—	—	7	—	—	4
Checking the executive	—	10	—	—	15	—	5
Broadening oneself	10	10	—	—	—	—	4
Serving the public	—	20	—	—	15	6	7
Mediating[c]	5	—	—	7	—	—	2
Promoting democracy	—	—	—	—	15	—	2
Protecting the economy	—	—	—	7	—	6	2
Promoting a political party	—	—	—	7	7	—	2
Educating members[d]	—	—	—	—	—	6	1

Notes: Percentages are rounded to nearest whole number. Average combines responses from both surveys. [a]Affecting public opinion denotes trying to lead or mould the views of the people. [b]Supporting the executive involves assisting the administration in the passage of legislation. [c]Mediating involves the balancing of various interests, promoting compromise and consensus. [d]Educating members is viewed as assisting new members to learn how to become good legislators.

per cent of appointed members, 6 per cent of electoral college members, and 12 per cent of functional constituency members in 1988 noted that they 'intercede with the government on behalf of members of the public,' but by 1993, none of the appointed and functional constituency members, and 15 per cent of the directly elected members volunteered they were busy with this activity.

Further variations are also apparent in how the legislators perceive their interactions with the public in comparison with those of members of the administration and members of other consultative bodies. 'Representing the citizens' is seen as a clear distinction from civil servants by half of the elected members but by only 27 per cent of the appointed members.[4] Furthermore, a surprising 9 per cent of the appointed members see no difference between their job and that of civil servants. These distinctions are also apparent when legislators consider the difference between the ways in which they and the Governor deal with the public, with 17 per cent of the appointed but none of the elected members seeing any difference. What appears to be emerging at this initial stage of the data analysis is that appointed members have a less clear definition of their legislative role, and furthermore, that they distinguish their role primarily in terms of its lawmaking function, whereas a significant proportion of elected members see their role primarily in terms of representational activities. These distinctions become more apparent when analysing their verbatim responses which provide the basis for classifying the members' purposive roles.

Purposive Roles

Since lawmaking has traditionally been perceived as the central function of legislatures, the investigation of legislators' roles initially focused on their participation in this activity. Priority was given to determining the basic premises of decision making by uncovering the purpose of legislators' behaviour. This investigation revealed five orientations toward the legislator's job.

The institution of the legislature is a product of a long and slow growth over centuries, which has give rise to a maze of rules, procedures, privileges, duties, etiquettes, rituals, informal understandings, and arrangements. Every phase of the lawmaking process has gradually become circumscribed by appropriate strategies and tactics. The legislator may orient himself to the job of law-making by becoming knowledgeable about parliamentary rules and routines rather than other legislative functions. Moreover, the legislator may focus on knowing the particulars of the bill's content rather than assessing the merits of its intent. If he does so his orientation to his legislative role is that of a *Ritualist*. This role may be especially appropriate for those members who are new, and was particularly prevalent in 1991, when 33 of the members were first-termers:

As a new member, I try my best to know more about what I am supposed to do in the Legislative Council—how to run with it, how to get things accomplished. I feel that I have had an apprenticeship period of two years in which we need to spend our time learning the practices of the body, the standing orders, and the strategies and rules we need to know.

Yet this orientation is not confined to new members, indeed it was held by some of the longest serving appointed members. As one senior member notes, 'Our job, quite simply, is to make laws. It is really amazing how many laws we pass, though the media never focuses on lawmaking, or what we are actually doing. So much of what we do is just routine legislative work that it doesn't interest the media.' Another appointed member carefully explained all the stages of lawmaking and noted what work occurred at each stage. Through this simple recitation the member believed that he was making it clear that his function was to 'assist in all stages with the legislation that the administration wants enacted'. Another was content to note that 'we do what are our prescribed duties . . . we enact law and approve of public finances'. Finally, one notes that his main job 'is to help with the legislative process, to involve myself with the committees as they look at the bills and to act as a sounding board as the bills work their way through committee and chamber action'. A shared feature of these comments is the members' need to fulfill the constitutional responsibilities of the legislature by immersing themselves in the process or mechanics of legislation.

A second orientation was initially perceived to be rooted in the conflict that many colonies had with the imperial powers. In the course of the dispute the colonial legislature came to be viewed as the instrument through which local interests could be defended against royal or executive encroachments. This orientation was revealed in Chapter 2 when investigating the activities of the lower houses of the American colonial legislatures in their fight for independence from the British. In this context the members of the legislature were expected to be advocates or defenders of popular demands. This role orientation is that of *Tribune*—the individual who 'fights the people's fight' against a chief executive or outside, but controlling, imperial power. One functional constituency member clearly delineated this role, and in the process contrasted it with that of the ritualist:

Officially we do what is written in the constitution—primarily the legislature decides an amendment or establishes new ordinances and laws. Unofficially, and more importantly, we are the representatives of the people, we make sure they have a voice, that they are heard and that their needs are being expressed. We monitor the government for the people.

An electoral college member also clearly reflected this orientation when he noted 'the most important thing [we do] is to try to reflect—and protect—the people from the government. We have to scrutinize the bills the executive hands down to us and to speak out strongly against a bill—to challenge it effectively—if we believe it is not in the public interest'. The number of members holding such beliefs substantially increased after 1991 with the direct election of 18 members. Some of the directly elected members were former social activists and still maintained their adversarial attitudes towards governmental policy: 'I am a point man of public pressure to demand changes from government'. One directly elected legislator notes that his constituents are a 'microcosm of Hong Kong' and his role is to 'represent and protect their interests'. Another directly elected member noted: 'I represent the people and I bring their problems to key decisionmakers for resolution. I also oversee government policy and make it more reasonable, responsive, and responsible'.

The popularity of this role has been enhanced with the territory's political transformation: 'I see myself as a participant—and protector—at this critical period of development in Hong Kong. As a legislator, I have a responsibility to make sure of a smooth transition for Hong Kong's future after 1997'. Another legislator noted that his role was to 'make sure the Joint Declaration is fully implemented so that in 1997 we will have "Hong Kong people ruling Hong Kong" with a high degree of autonomy'. This orientation led one legislator to be critical of the legislative body itself:

I believe that legislative councillors should look at the interests of the Hong Kong people. The trouble is that to get what I think is right, I have to fight the majority in the legislature because essentially I am fighting a system based on conservative appointees and narrowly elected business members. Britain now runs Hong Kong and soon China would like to, but neither of them have Hong Kong's interests first. My job is to protect those interests.

A third role orientation, that of *Broker*, developed in response to the rise of interest groups and the attendant increase in conflicting demands for legislative action. As legislatures become a major integrating force in pluralistic societies, a mediator is needed to balance these interests and make the best possible decision in light of competing demands. It appears that appointed members can most easily adopt this orientation towards their legislative job. Indeed they consider that it has become imperative with the increase in numbers of their more highly politicized, constituency-based colleagues: 'With no constituency, I can take a broader view of things. The legislature is becoming too parochial, therefore I am needed to balance these interests with a broader perspective'. Another appointed member was particularly critical of the elected members in that they are 'too parochial, too inward-looking regarding Hong Kong, and they fail to see the international context. At the end of the day, we must do what is best for all of the territory, not just for some specific interests'. This concern for keeping in mind the public interest rather than particular interests was reflected by another who noted: 'What we do in the Legislative Council is just a game of compromise. At the end of the day, nobody really wins, we just all win a little'. This view was mirrored by another, who said: 'Politics is the art of compromise, the art of the possible. Our job is to bridge and facilitate a two-way communication between the people and their government'.

While one might expect this orientation to be strongest in electoral college and particularly directly elected members, who have broader interests in their districts than functional constituency members, nonetheless a surprising number of functional constituency members also adhered to this orientation. As one functional member noted: 'In my constituency, there are bound to be differences of opinion and conflicts of interest. My constituents are a mixed bag of people—highly intelligent, vocal, international, and self-interested. It is difficult to represent them all fairly as there are many conflicts of interest. My job is to provide compromises'.

The present stage of constitutional development in Hong Kong has added a new dimension to the Broker role: 'In politics the important thing is to reach an agreement so as not to wreck the integrity of government. In this time of political challenge, it is important that we [in the legislature] "live and let live"—compromise continually—in order to protect the system of government'. Furthermore, given the political context, the interests being brokered may not only be internal—those interests within the body politic of Hong Kong—but also external, between Hong Kong and other countries, as seen in this functional constituency member's comment: 'I serve as a bridge between Hong Kong and China. This bridge has two-way traffic; China needs to know and understand our interests and we need to know more about hers'.

A fourth major orientation has originated in most legislatures at a later stage of development when the legislature has asserted itself as an institution capable of performing independent policy-making functions. When the legislature is looked upon as an instrument of governance rather than an instrument of obstruction, some of the legislators have assumed the role of *Inventor*, a policy maker sensitive to public issues, discovering potential solutions and exploring alternatives both with respect to means and ends. Given the Legislative Council's limited policy-making role, one would expect few Inventors, yet a surprising number of members adopt this orientation. One typifying this view was a functional constituency member:

The job of the the Legislative Council member is to probe the intentions and likely effects of any piece of legislation proposed by the administration onto Hong Kong as a whole. We need to look at the objectives of a piece of legislation and determine whether that objective is the right objective. Having examined and decided that it is the right objective, we need to look at its effect upon the community. If the impact is negative—or if it doesn't do what it is supposed to do—then we have to pose some alternatives to the administration.

An appointed member proposed a more specific Inventor role: 'I believe that I was appointed so that I could formulate ideas that would improve on present policies; to help formulate remedies which are not currently available to meet special problems'.

Another member, acknowledging that he could not play an inventive role given the current legal parameters of the Legislative Council, nonetheless expressed the desire to assume this orientation should the parameters change:

I believe that we should take a role in making policy. Now if I think of something, I have to give it to a secretary. If he does not take it up, then I have to ask questions in the Legislative Council or even take up the matter in an adjournment debate. This is the extent of our current policy making role. In the future, though, I would like to see us obtain the ability to initiate our own policies.

While this last comment came from an interview in 1988, prior to the passage of the Basic Law, since that time, even with the new restrictions on legislative policy making after 1997, the aspiration to become an Inventor remains strong, particularly among those who are directly elected. As one notes: 'Even with no political power, nonetheless, I continually try to influence policy. As I have the mandate of the people, I must help formulate policy'. Another promises: 'I am someone who is active in participating in politics but right now I can't come into power, I can never become a minister or government policymaker. I understand this context, but I aim to change it'.

A final role is that of the *Opportunist*. It is adopted by the legislator who holds the office without really 'taking' the associated role, who accepts the bare minimum of expectations, such as voting and attending committee meetings, but always as a passive participant, who uses his position on the legislature to achieve other, essentially non-legislative goals. For instance, one member voiced concern with restraining the legislature rather than enhancing its ability to act, in the process revealing this orientation: 'As a businessman, I realized that it was time to get organized, to protect our economic development by making sure that the legislature doesn't just increase taxes for more social services. I am here to make sure that economic growth occurs first and foremost'. Another member noted that serving in the legislature helped him in publicizing his ultimate goal: 'My aim is not to be a legislator but to use the Legislative Council to publicize and push for my goals; a means by which I can make government aware of my beliefs'.

To summarize, five major purposive roles were identified in interviewing Hong Kong's Legislative Councillors, as depicted in Table 7.2. The data clearly supports the contention that the mode of selection influences the role orientation of the member. While the Broker was held by a subset of all types of legislators in 1988, by 1993 the newer, directly elected legislators gave this role no priority. Further, a major component of those who adhere to this role are the appointed members, who will no longer be serving in

Table 7.2 Legislative Councillors' Purposive Roles, 1988 and 1993 (Percentage)

	1988			1993			Average
	Appointed Members	Electoral College Members	Functional Constituency Members	Appointed Members	Directly Elected Members	Functional Constituency Members	
Ritualist	45	10	17	38	—	13	23
Tribune	15	60	58	—	69	27	34
Broker	20	30	17	30	—	27	21
Inventor	20	—	8	13	31	33	19
Opportunist	—	—	—	19	—	—	3

Notes: Percentages are rounded off to nearest whole number. Average combines evaluations from both surveys.

the legislature after 1995. Also apparent is the distinction between the number of appointed members who are Ritualists in both 1988 and 1993 (45 per cent and 38 per cent respectively) versus the smaller percentage amongst the other types of legislators, particularly the directly elected members. It would appear that most legislators are engaging in other types of activity, some of which are extra-parliamentary in nature, primarily in their districts. This activity, particularly for the directly elected members, is that of a Tribune who must be aware of and then articulate the needs of the people to the government. Finally, the popularity of the orientation of Inventor by both the directly elected and functional constituency members suggests that this role will become more prevalent over time when these legislators each comprise 50 per cent of the post-1997 legislature.

It would appear that in terms of their major legislative role orientations, variations among legislators are clearly based on their mode of selection. This also was true with a second major role orientation, the representational role.

Representational Roles

As we have seen, the philosophical history of the legislature is essentially rooted in popular choice—not government by the people but of and for the people. Legislatures connect the people to their government in special ways. Every member of the legislature claims to stand for some of his fellow citizens and all members together presume that they are acting for their fellow citizens collectively. To quote Loewenberg and Patterson: 'Citizens expect from legislatures a special responsiveness to their demands; legislatures expect from the public a special respect for their words and deeds. These claims, presumptions, and expectations signify that special relationship which can exist between legislature and citizens. The word representation describes that relationship.'[5]

The problem of representation is central to all discussions of the functions of legislatures and the behaviour of legislators. For it is through the process of representation that legislatures are empowered to act for the whole body politic. Of the three branches of government, the legislative branch is supposed to be the most responsive and representative of the views of the public. While this is a traditional function, the ways of assessing it have undergone a dramatic transformation. Sometimes the adjective 'representative' denotes nothing more than the publicly approved process by which representatives are chosen—with the typical distinction made between a 'representative body' as a group of individuals elected by specific modes of popular election and a 'non-representative body' denoting a group of individuals selected by royal or executive appointment, entailed inheritance, or some other non-electoral process. Chapter 6 established that Hong Kong's Legislative Council was 'non-representative' at least until 1985; even since then a sizeable portion of its members remain 'non-representative' as they are appointed. Moreover, the majority of those 'elected' are chosen from bodies which are not based upon universal suffrage. Nonetheless, interviews reveal that all Hong Kong legislators see themselves as 'representatives'. Therefore a key question to be addressed is 'who' they represent (focus), and 'how' that representation is carried out (style).

Focus concentrates on who is represented. There are many 'publics' that constitute foci for the representative, so his focus may be something other than an electoral unit or district. Rather, in an increasingly plural political and social order, focus may incorporate the whole body politic, a political party, pressure group, or administrative agency, to give but a few examples. Indeed, given the peculiar context of Hong Kong's political identity, the focus may also include political powers outside of the territory, namely Britain and China. Of course different foci of representation need not be mutually exclusive. They may occur simultaneously. Furthermore, the distinction between focus and style of representation denotes a concern not with what decisions are made but how they are made. The representative here can act either on the basis of his own judgement or he may rely upon the 'mandate' or instructions of his constituency.

Representation of electoral units, which in most countries means geographical areas, introduces a certain amount of ambiguity into the relationship between representative and represented. Part of this ambiguity involves the widely held expectation, contested by Edmund Burke but shared by many citizens and politicians alike, that the legislator is a spokesman of the presumed 'interests' of his district.[6] Implicit in this expectation is the assumption that the constituency has interests that are distinct and different from those of other units. This assumption has been challenged on a variety of grounds: that the geographical boundries of an electoral unit are artificial; that it cannot and does not generate shared interests by its residents; that it has no unique interests, and so on. It may be assumed that electoral schemes based on more 'natural' interest groups, such as minority, skill, or economic groups, would provide better representation of diverse interests. This leads to the hypothesis that the focus of functional constituency members will be stronger than that of appointed, electoral college, or directly elected members. The responses to the question *How would you define your constituency?* validated this hypothesis (Table 7.3).

Over one-quarter of all appointed and electoral college representatives cited 'Hong Kong people' as the individuals they believe they represent, with only 17 per cent of the functional constituency members noting this in 1988. These views had changed dramatically by 1993, with most of the appointed members now citing the public as their focus of representation. This change may have occurred as the appointed members themselves became more politicized. This focus may also reflect an attempt to rationalize why they were serving in the legislature, particularly because they had to defend their representative legitimacy to the directly elected members who claimed that only they had the mandate of the people. As one appointed member complained: 'I am tired of having to constantly defend my legitimacy to a bunch of directly elected members who were only chosen by a minority of the voters. They are no more representative of the public than I am!' Moreover, it was the appointed members who had the most variegated representational focus. Many believed they were appointed to represent a particular business or professional sector; some believed they represented China, while others more simply delineated their focus as the Governor or themselves. Perhaps the most unusual representational focus came from the appointed member who believed he represented not any one aspect of Hong Kong but rather 'a world view to Hong Kong,' in stating that 'I reflect how the world at large reacts to us'.

Elected members, not unsurprisingly, had a much narrower focus, namely their electoral constituency. While some also designated 'the Hong Kong people', it is clear that the electoral process concentrated their representational focus on their constituencies. Furthermore, the directly elected members have a much stronger sense of their constituency than did their predecessors, the electoral college members, one-third of whom cited Hong Kong people rather than their constituents as their focus. Perhaps

Table 7.3 Legislative Councillors' Focus of Representation: Views of Their Constituency, 1988 and 1993 (Percentage of First Responses Received)

Q: How would you define your constituency?

	1988			1993			Average
	Appointed Members	Electoral College Members	Functional Constituency Members	Appointed Members	Directly Elected Members	Functional Constituency Members	
Hong Kong people	26	30	17	63	15	19	29
Constituency	n.a.	60	75	n.a.	70	81	43
China	10	—	8	6	—	—	4
Oneself	32	—	—	—	—	—	8
Business or profession	16	10	—	19	—	—	8
Geographical area	5	—	—	—	—	—	1
Governor	5	—	—	12	—	—	4
Grass roots	—	—	—	—	15	—	2
Other	6	—	—	—	—	—	1

Notes: Percentages vary as different amounts of each subset did not answer all questions. Percentages are rounded off to nearest whole number. Average combines responses from both surveys. n.a. = Not applicable.

most surprising were the directly elected members who differentiated their focus in terms of the working class or 'grass roots'. But of
all members, it was the functional constituency members who had
the most unidimensional focus of representation, namely, their
functional constituency.

A second way in which to distinguish the focus of representation
is to contrast one focus of representation with another. This was
accomplished by asking, *If you had to make a choice between the
views of the Hong Kong people and your constituents, which one
would you choose?* The answers to this question are detailed in
Table 7.4.

Table 7.4 is most useful for comparing the responses of the
directly elected with the functional constituency members. Many
appointed members, with a broader and often less defined characterization of their constituency, had trouble in distinguishing between the two foci, and indeed, often see 'their constituency' as
that of the 'Hong Kong people'. However, with the elected members, their constituency, at least from an electoral point of view, is
well defined, and can be easily distinguished from that of the 'Hong
Kong people'. One-third of the directly elected members and almost 40 per cent of the functional constituency members represent
the interests of their constituency even in opposition to the views or
interests of the Hong Kong people. Many of the electoral college
and directly elected members perceive their constituency as a
reflection of the general public, and so they had difficulty in recognizing that a difference between the two would ever exist. Nonetheless, when pushed into a hypothetical situation in which such a
difference was measurable, a sizeable proportion were willing to
promote that constituency's interests over those of the Hong Kong
public. The actual strength of commitment to constituency views
relates to the member's representative *style*, which was measured
by the following questions:

1. *If you had to make a choice between the views of your constituents and your personal convictions, which would you choose?*
2. *Do you think a legislative councillor should do what the people of
   his constituency want no matter what his own opinion is?*
3. *Do you think a legislative councillor should follow his own
   judgement because he knows more about what is best for the
   constituency?*

Responses to these questions can be seen in Table 7.5.

Table 7.4 Legislative Councillors' Focus of Representation: Forced Choice, 1988 and 1993 (Percentage of First Responses Received)

Q: If you had to make a choice between the views of the Hong Kong people and your constituents, which one would you choose?

	1988			1993				Average
	Appointed Members	Electoral College Members	Functional Constituency Members	Appointed Members	Directly Elected Members	Functional Constituency Members		
Hong Kong people	68	73	58	75	63	54		65
Constituents	—	9	17	—	32	38		15
Depends on circumstances	32	18	25	25	8	6		20

Note: Average combines responses from both surveys.

Table 7.5 Legislative Councillors' Style of Representation, 1988 and 1993

Q: If you had to make a choice between the views of your constituents and your personal convictions, which would you choose?

	1988			1993			Average
	Appointed Members	Electoral College Members	Functional Constituency Members	Appointed Members	Directly Elected Members	Functional Constituency Members	
Constituents	5	36	27	6	31	26	19
Personal conviction	80	64	55	81	62	56	69
Depends on circumstances	15	—	18	6	7	6	9
They are the same	—	—	—	6	—	12	3

Q: Do you think a legislative councillor should do what the people of his constituency want no matter what his own opinion is?

	1988			1993			Average
	Appointed Members	Electoral College Members	Functional Constituency Members	Appointed Members	Directly Elected Members	Functional Constituency Members	
Yes	—	18	—	12	46	7	14
No	90	82	73	88	54	93	81
Don't know/It depends	—	—	27	—	—	—	3
Not applicable	10	—	—	6	—	—	2

Q: Do you think a legislative councillor should follow his own judgement because he knows more about what is best for the constituency?

| | 1988 | | | 1993 | | | Average |
	Appointed Members	Electoral College Members	Functional Constituency Members	Appointed Members	Directly Elected Members	Functional Constituency Members	
Yes	80	91	100	95	46	82	85
No	—	9	—	5	46	9	10
Don't know/It depends	5	—	—	—	8	9	2
Not applicable	15	—	—	—	—	—	3

Note: For each question, average combines responses from both surveys.

Table 7.5 demonstrates that most of the members are certain of their ability to make the right decision for their constituency. The appointed members manifest the most confidence in the merits of their own judgement, probably because the size of their perceived constituencies is much larger than those of other members, making it more difficult to determine any monolithic constituency views. For several appointed members these questions pose no problem, as they define their constituency as themselves.

The functional constituency members are also assured that they 'represent' perhaps not the views, but certainly, the best interests of their constituencies, as seen in their responses to Question 3. This may be attributed to the fact that most functional constituency members have a homogeneous constituency and that, as members of their functional profession, it is easy for them to have the same views and desires as their electors. Yet these members are determined to pursue their own judgement even when this judgement collides with the known judgement of their constituents. Many of the functional constituency members indicated that this would never be a problem, confident that they could educate their constituents and transform their opposition into support for their point of view.

Electoral college and directly elected members appeared less assured of knowing and reflecting the views of their constituents. Moreover, if put into a situation in which the views of their constituents were known, many felt obliged to act upon those views, even if they were against their own convictions. This role attribute may be due to the fact that, unlike the functional constituency members, their constituency is much more diverse and harder to represent. This explanation is supported by responses to the statement *I seldom have to sound out my constituents because I think so much like them that I know how to react to almost any proposal.* While 67 per cent of the functional constituency members agreed with this statement,[7] less than 25 per cent of the electoral college and directly elected members did so. If it is harder to discover the views of their constituents, the electoral college and directly elected members may rationalize that once these views are known they must follow them. And finally, these members exist in a more competitive electoral environment than their functional constituency counterparts[8] and hence may be much more willing to sacrifice their own convictions in the interest of remaining popular and so re-electable. In sum, of all the members of the

Legislative Council, a greater proportion of the members elected from geographical districts are more willing to follow the dictates of their constituencies, even if they have to go against their own judgement.

Yet the findings from Table 7.5 also reveal some inconsistencies. For instance, one would have expected that a legislator who chose 'Personal Convictions' as the response to Question 1 would have responded 'disagree' to Question 2 and 'agree' to Question 3. While a trend is evident, there is less than a 100 per cent correlation in the responses. There are several reasons for this. First and most importantly, the majority of respondents are new to the legislature and are just beginning to define their role. So, there might be some inconsistencies as they attempt to adopt appropriate role behaviour in a new environment. Secondly, many of the legislators noted that they had never been placed in a situation as described by Questions 1 and 2 (where their constituents' views are different from their views) and consequently had not given it much thought. Finally, some distortion is expected in an interview process that measures attitudes of the moment rather than actual behaviour. Regardless of the cause, in order to construct the representational role classification for the members, emphasis was placed on a qualitative rather than quantitative analysis of their comments. By using open-ended questions, the interviewer was able to probe more accurately the representational orientation of each member. Consequently, the verbatim responses to the same question used in constructing the purposive role, namely *How would you describe the job of being a legislator—what are the most important things you do here?* and follow-up questions to the more direct representational questions previously cited were used to determine three major representational-role orientations of the Legislative Council members: Trustee, Delegate, and Politico.

Trustee

The *Trustee* orientation finds expression in two major conceptions of how decisions ought to be made. These conceptions may occur separately or jointly. First, from a moral point of view, the Trustee sees himself as a free agent in that he claims to follow what he considers right or just: his convictions and principles, the dictates of his conscience. Reasons for this may include the Trustee's ideas, attitudes, or legislative objectives, which he sees as the same or in harmony with those he represents. According to one appointed member:

While I really just represent myself, in the end I am also voting for the public interest. I vote for things as I see best. I generally know what the public wants—I hear all of the public's opinions and then I select what is the best. I analyse things as they are presented to me, and I believe that I have the public at heart as the basis of my vote.

This role is obviously more natural for appointed members who have no constituency to be accountable to: 'I don't represent anybody and yet I think I represent everybody. Because I am not elected, I don't have to do things that are popular'. Yet this was an orientation held by a subset of elected members as well, as exemplified by one functional constituency member who simply remarked: 'There is never any conflict between what I like and what my constituency wants'.

Second, if the representative as a man of principle finds himself in conflict with the constituency he represents, he believes he should try to persuade them to adhere to his convictions rather than submit to their judgement. The Trustee in this context sees himself as 'mentor'. As one electoral college member noted: 'I would consult, discuss, listen, and inform—and then make my own judgement'. Another put it more simply: 'Since the voters elected me, they have given me their mandate, which is to vote in the way I think best. If possible, before I vote, I try to educate them as to my point of view'. And a directly elected member noted: 'As elected members we have the responsibility to consult with our constituencies, express their views, but then to reach our own judgement about the matter, explain to them why we have reached this decision, and then to vote according to our own personal views'.

Third, the Trustee may follow his own judgement because he cannot afford to allow himself to be influenced by persons who are either uninformed or ill-informed. According to one appointed member:

For most of the bills we vote on, the Hong Kong public is ignorant. Or worse, ill-informed. Therefore I can vote against public opinion and for my own convictions because the public is not always right. If a legislator feels that he has to vote for the opinion of the people of his constituency no matter what his personal conviction is, he might just as well be a computer—or a post box!

Another appointed colleague agreed:

As a member of the Legislative Council the most important thing to bear in mind is that you are serving the public but also you should be aware that the public is ignorant of most issues and policies. The questions you must ask yourself before each bill or issue is decided is if it is good for Hong Kong as a whole. As a Legislative Council member, you must have integrity and not do things simply because the public wants it.

Finally, an important aspect of the Trustee's role orientation is that he should be willing to accept the political consequences of his refusal to be swayed by public opinion. As one elected member said: 'In general I know what is best and I act upon it. Should my constituency disagree with me, then they have the option of kicking me out'.

In sum, a great variety of representational conceptions are involved in the role orientation of the Trustee. The supposition that the represented do not have the information necessary to give intelligent instructions, that the representative is unable to discover what his constituents may want, that preferences remain unexpressed, that there is no need for instructions because of an alleged harmony of interests between representative and represented—all of these circumstances may be acknowledged as sources of the role orientation of Trustee, at times even forced on the representative against his own predilection for a mandate.[9]

Delegate

In contrast, *Delegates* feel that the job of being a legislator requires them to follow the dictates of their constituents. They believe that they should not use their independent judgement or principles and convictions when making decisions. Some observe that they try to consult with their constituents and others before making a decision; in so doing, they imply that such consultation has an inevitable effect on their behaviour. As one functional constituency member notes: 'On most things my constituency does not seem to have an opinion. But when they do, I will of course follow their wishes as their duly elected representative'. Others frankly acknowledge that instructions are necessary or even desirable to make a decision. As one functional constituency member said: 'My constituency is narrowly defined in interest and small in number. This makes my role easier. I can easily find out their views, and represent them in the Legislative Council, through speeches in the council and voting'. Finally, there is the delegate who not only feels he should follow instructions, but also believes that he should do so even if these instructions are against his own judgement. Another functional constituency member observed: 'I cannot freely express my own views; normally I must express the views of my constituents. I have a sophisticated constituency; I don't need to explain things to them; they just tell me what they think. Therefore in voting, I always put the views of my constituents first'.

In contrast to the functional constituency Delegates just cited, it is the very diversity of the district, and in this instance the competitiveness for the seat, that makes some directly elected and electoral college members Delegates.

My biggest concern as a Legislative Council member is in trying to keep in touch with my constituents. I spend a lot more of my time than appointed or functional constituency members attending various functions in the district. I see myself as being very close to the views of the people and I take it as my duty to represent those views—even above those of my own.

Perhaps one unique context that promotes some Delegates in the Legislative Council is that until recently, legislators serving on the Executive Council felt bound to abide by the rule of collective responsibility, which meant that once the Executive Council had taken a view on a policy they felt bound to vote to support it no matter what their personal opinion. Consequently, for some, the Executive Council rather than their constituency posed the most severe constraint on their ability to reach independent judgements on the issues of the day. As one member of both councils put it: 'As an [Executive Council] member, I am part of the government. I am a junior partner without portfolio. I must support any government policy which has gained Executive Council support, even if this is against my personal judgement'.

Politico

Depending on the circumstances, a representative may hold the role orientation of Trustee at one time, and the role orientation of Delegate at another. Or they may be taken simultaneously producing role conflict. Legislators who express both orientations, either simultaneously or serially, are labelled *Politicos*. In contrast to Trustees or Delegates—relatively 'pure' types—Politicos exhibit a certain amount of flexibility in their representational relationships.

This orientation may be pertinent if the legislative issue being determined affects all of Hong Kong or only the member's constituents. As one functional constituency member notes: 'If there is a conflict between my views and those of my constituents, I generally would go with my own views unless the measure actually affected my constituency—such as licensing—and then I would go with the majority of my constituents'. An electoral college member put it similarly: 'It depends on the topic. If it affects my constituency, then I would go with my constituents' views'. Another member said: 'If the majority of my constituents actually had a view on the matter—such as direct elections to the legislature—then I would follow their dictates'. More recently, a large number of directly elected members exhibit this orientation, noting that their decision 'depends' on the importance of the issue for their constituents.

According to this analysis, therefore, the representational roles of Hong Kong's legislators can be put into three categories (Table 7.6). Again, the distinctions between the types of members are significant. While the Trustee orientation is held by all three types of members, it might be expected that it would be a particularly appropriate role for appointed members. In fact, the overwhelming majority of appointed members appear not to feel 'bound' to follow the mandate as expressed by their constituency, however defined, but rather believe that they should use their own best judgement in the performance of their legislative duties. Indeed, in response to the question, *Almost no one in my constituency cares about the big policy issues unless a bill happens to touch his personal or business interests*, over 65 per cent of the appointed members agreed versus only 14 per cent of the elected members. Furthermore, in response to the question, *Most of my constituents have either no knowledge of nor opinion about the issues we discuss in the Legislative Council*, over 50 per cent of all appointed members agreed, versus less than 25 per cent of all elected members. It is apparent that appointed members have a less clearly defined view of what their constituents want, as over one-third agreed with the statement, *My constituency includes so many different kinds of people that I often just don't know what the people there want me to do.* Yet none of the elected members agreed with this statement. For these members the views of their constituents are fairly well-known and these views, for some, can restrict their legislative behaviour—in 1993, 28 per cent of the functional constituency and

Table 7.6 Representational Role Classification of Legislative Councillors, 1988 and 1993 (Percentage)

	1988			1993			Average
	Appointed Members	Electoral College Members	Functional Constituency Members	Appointed Members	Directly Elected Members	Functional Constituency Members	
Trustee	85	40	50	88	19	50	56
Delegate	—	30	17	—	37	28	19
Politico	15	30	33	12	44	22	25

Note: Average combines evaluations from both surveys.

37 per cent of the directly elected members could be classified as Delegates. Additionally, elected members show more flexibility in their representational approach with 30 per cent of the electoral college, over one-quarter of the functional constituency, and 44 per cent of the directly elected members adopting the representational role of Politico.

In analysing the differences between elected members, it would appear that the electoral college, and particularly the directly elected members, may feel more constrained by the views of their constituents than their functional constituency counterparts. If the views of their constituents are known, they appear to be more likely than their functional constituency counterparts to follow these views, even if they conflict with their personal convictions. Ironically, however, the views of their constituents are less well known to them than the views of the functional constituents. In general, the functional constituency member exhibits much more confidence than his elected counterpart—confidence in his ability to understand his constituents; certainty in his ability to vote for their best interests; and faith in his ability to persuade them to adopt his point of view.

Finally, as has been found in previous studies, the focus and style of representation are likely to be influenced by the character of politics at a given time and the demands of contemporary political circumstances. The current political context of Hong Kong may dictate the type of role taken, at least for some members of the legislature. Under the conditions of heightened political tension in the territory many constituents' views on major political issues are expressed and known to Hong Kong's legislators. This in turn obligates some of those legislators to be 'more representative' of those views, and take a more restricted role as a result. However, this would only significantly affect legislative behaviour if the members of the legislature were actually taking a role in determining Hong Kong's future. But as was seen in Chapter 4, the legislators have played no significant role in shaping that future—a source of frustration to many interviewed.[10] When the Patten proposals are put before them, legislators will be in the new position of determining, at least in the short-term, the compositional make-up of the Council. Being aware of and possibly acting upon the views of their constituents will delineate the parameters of their representational style.

Interest Group Roles

Until recently, Hong Kong had not had political parties and consequently, any group of citizens who wanted to influence public policy could only do so by forming pressure groups. The parameters of the political system and the political apathy of the population have dictated that few associations have played the role of 'interest articulator' and 'interest aggregator'.[11] But with the rise of a better educated, more demanding middle class, coupled with the expansion of the service-delivery role of government, there has been a substantial growth in the number of pressure groups.[12] While originally there was a predominance of groups concerned about business, professions, and unions, more recently, given the political transformation since 1984, there have been an increasing number of 'grass roots' groups striving for the advancement of local democracy and improvements in different aspects of people's livelihood.

In most countries, the once-prevalent view that 'special interest groups' are a threat to the general 'public interest' has generally given way to a belief that interest groups now constitute a legitimate source of information and demands in the legislative process.[13] In the last twenty years, a substantial body of literature has been devoted to analysing the effects of pressure-group activity on the legislative process, particularly in the committee arena.[14] For the legislator, a key difficulty is how to balance these interests and subordinate them to the unarticulated public interest. To do his job a legislator must answer such questions as: How much, and in what way, should one consider the activities, demands, and attitudes of all these groups and their agents? What behaviour is appropriate for the legislator in encounters with lobbyists? How can one evaluate the comparative merits of diverse and competing demands coming from different groups?[15] To inquire into these questions and thereby to explore analytical issues about the function and process of representation, an additional role orientation must be examined, namely that relating to pressure groups. The Legislative Council members' orientations to pressure groups were identified by posing two forced choice questions: *On the whole, the Legislative Council would work better if there were no interest groups and lobbies trying to influence legislation*; and, *Under our form of government, every individual should take an interest in government directly, not through an interest group.* The pressure-group orientation was constructed by re-sponses to these questions, which revealed members' friendliness or hostility toward pressure-group activity. From this, a classi-fication of Facilitator, Resistor, and Neutral emerged as seen in Table 7.7.

The most dramatic change over time is the views of the appointed members. While in 1988 almost three-quarters were Facilitators, in 1993 the majority of appointed members held either neutral or negative attitudes towards group activity. The reason for this may be that the number of interest groups, and the extent of their activity, has steadily increased over the past five years. It would appear that this phenomenon has been greeted with mixed emotions by the appointed members. While in inter-views many acknowledged the need for the information the groups provided, most also expressed dismay over their growing clout.

Another change revealed in the analysis was the slightly more favourable attitude given to interest-group activity by the func-tional constituency members. Yet functional constituency mem-bers remain almost equally divided about the merits of interest-group activity with over half holding either negative or ambivalent views about their influence. Given that the functional constituency members themselves represent a specific interest group, it may initially seem startling that these members would not be more tolerant of such activity. This may reflect the fact that the func-tional constituencies are mostly monolithic, essentially represent-ing 'interests' which are deemed by the government as meriting some form of representation in the legislature. The hostility of these well-defined interest groups may arise because they see other interest groups as competing with them.

The strongest supporters of interest-group activity are the directly elected members. Given the broad range of interests repre-sented in their districts, these members appear to be most familiar and comfortable with the pressure-group activity. Furthermore, they may forecast their future electoral success in terms of being responsive to the needs of organized interests with clear, articulated goals.

Despite the growing significance of these relationships, relatively little research has been devoted to the degree to which legislators actually represent interests in the legislature. The question asked of legislators in this research concerned if they had to choose between

Table 7.7 Forced Choice: Attitudes of Legislative Councillors Toward Pressure Groups, 1988 and 1993 (Percentage)

Statement 1: On the whole, the Legislative Council would work better if there were no interest groups and lobbies trying to influence legislation.

Statement 2: Under our form of government, every individual should take an interest in government directly, not through an interest group.

	1988			1993			Average
	Appointed Members	**Electoral College Members**	**Functional Constituency Members**	**Appointed Members**	**Directly Elected Members**	**Functional Constituency Members**	
Facilitator	71	70	40	20	71	47	53
Resister	23	30	50	13	14	27	22
Neutral	6	—	10	67	14	27	25

Notes: Evaluations based on responses to the two statements. Average combines evaluations from both surveys.

the views of an interest group and their constituents, or an interest group and their personal convictions, which would they choose? Responses revealed that, for 85 per cent of all elected legislators, personal convictions or constituents' views would command their loyalty over the views of an interest group. These responses clearly indicate the nascent stage of interest-group activity in Hong Kong.[16] The weakness of interest groups as a representational focus was also evident from the fact that no legislator specified an interest group as his focus of representation.

Summary: The Different Roles of Members

This research has confirmed the original hypothesis, namely, that the way in which legislators are selected does indeed affect their orientation towards their legislative work. Clearly, in examining the key roles of the members, glaring distinctions become apparent, particularly between those members who are appointed and those who are elected. These distinctions can best be summarized by providing abstracts[17] of each type of legislator.[18]

Appointed Members

Appointed Legislative Council members appear to be primarily oriented towards the mechanics of legislation and the rituals or routines of the legislative process. The Ritualist orientation, held by the plurality of these members, is that of an insider—'the legislative specialist and substantive expert'—and is typically held by the most senior members of the legislature.[19] In terms of representation, appointed members express diverse views about whom they represent, and even once defined, their 'constituency' appears to remain fairly amorphous and does not exercise a constraining influence on their legislative activity. If anything, their broad representational focus enables a sizeable number of them to perform brokerage functions, allowing for the balancing of interests to occur in the process of legislating. Yet, somewhat paradoxically, they remain a conservative group, with ambivalent or negative feelings about the merits of interest-group participation in the legislative process.[20] While appointed members exhibit a degree of confidence in their legislative work, it is a confidence often operating in a vacuum, with no clear conception of whom they represent or of what their legislative goals are.

Functional Constituency Members

The functional members expressed a variety of views about their purpose as legislators, with an almost equal division between Broker, Tribune, and Inventor roles. This variation is not apparent, however, with regard to their representational activities, with half of them adopting the Trustee role, and an overwhelming majority possessing a unidimensional focus toward their constituency. While the fact that 27 per cent are Brokers would appear to conflict somewhat with the neutral to negative views which 54 per cent exhibited towards interest groups, interviews clarified this orientation was one that involved balancing interests within their constituency rather than between their constituents and other organized interests.[21] Functional constituency members, therefore, exhibit a high degree of certainty about whom they represent and do so through a variety of purposive orientations. Nonetheless, their focus remains conservative, with most of their legislative work protecting their functional interests rather than promoting specific legislative goals.

Directly Elected Members

The majority of the directly elected members, like their electoral college predecessors, possess Tribune orientations. The Tribune exemplifies the legislator-as-representative: 'the reflector, articulator, and champion of the needs or wishes of [the] public'.[22] The directly elected members were similar to the electoral college members in their favourable attitude towards interest groups. However, there the similarity ends, for while a sizeable number of electoral college members were Brokers, this orientation did not find favour with the directly elected members; additionally, almost one-third of all directly elected members but none of the electoral college's members saw themselves as Inventors. The directly elected members, like the functional constituency members, have a strong orientation towards representing their district, yet in the process of representation they tend to be either Politicos or Delegates rather than Trustees. Compared to their functional constituency colleagues, they are less certain of the views of their more disparate constituency, as seen in the response to the statement, *I seldom have to sound out my constituents because I think so much like them that I know how to react to almost any proposal.* While 67 per cent of the functional constituency members agreed, only 25 per cent of the directly elected members did so. As a consequence, their more diverse and highly competitive constituency environment appears to exercise a significant restraining influence on their legislative activity.

Official Members

Role classifications are less informative about those members of the legislature who are also part of the executive branch. Officials tend to be a monolithic group who conceive of their role in terms of the ritualistic procedures of policy making, but this activity occurs within the context of mediation of a variety of interests. In terms of representation, stylistically they are Trustees, and focally they see themselves as primarily representing the government, although some argue that in this capacity they are really representing the interests of the Hong Kong public. Most perceive no role conflict in being a member of both the executive and legislative branches since 'we dominate the legislature'. Further, it is seen as a 'normal part of my job, a way in which I can get my policies implemented'. Their views toward interest groups range from Facilitators to neutral.[23]

President of the Legislative Council

The role analysis of members detailed above is not applicable to one special member of the legislature, the president of the Council. This position, created in 1993, was instituted to enable someone other than the Governor to preside over the chamber sessions.[24] The president's role is similar to that of a speaker under the Westminster system. He has a casting vote in Council but does not take part in deliberations in the House Committee meetings, *ad hoc* groups, or the Bills Committees.[25] The most essential requirement for his job is to maintain impartiality since this enables him to retain authority and legitimacy.[26] He has to appreciate the need for keeping debate on an impersonal and rational level, as 'the enemy of debate is passion'.[27]

While at present the president is an appointed member, in the future he will be a member of the legislature and therefore by definition either directly elected or chosen by the Election Commission or a functional constituency. Yet the constraints of his job—to maintain impartiality at all times, to be above politics, and not to participate in committee deliberations—would seem to place him in an untenable position, given his electoral imperatives to represent his constituents' views in the course of his legislative responsibilities.

Roles in a Comparative Context

How do Hong Kong legislators' role priorities compare with those of legislators in other countries?[28] One of the best ways of understanding how the functions of legislatures differ is to study the priorities their members give to various aspects of their job.[29]

Purposive Roles

Role studies of United States legislatures[30] reveal that lawmaking is the most popular function mentioned by United States congressmen and state legislators;[31] it remains the most popular function even with legislators from emergent legislatures in developing countries, such as Kenya, Korea, and Turkey.[32] What makes the Legislative Council members different from legislators in these other countries is that they increasingly appear to believe lawmaking is less important, with only 43 per cent citing this as a primary function, compared with 58 to 72 per cent of American state legislators, 42 per cent of Korean legislators, 48 per cent of Kenyan legislators, and 49 per cent of those in Turkey. This view is particularly evident with the elected members, with only 15 per cent of the directly elected and 28 per cent of the functional constituency members citing lawmaking as the primary function they perform.

This finding suggests several interpretations. It could be that the Legislative Council members' lawmaking activities remain so tightly constrained and dominated by the executive branch that they believe it is more important to be active in other functions. Furthermore, the newer members are clearly unhappy about the Legislative Council's inability to initiate policy, with 36 per cent of the functional constituency members and an overwhelming 87 per cent of the directly elected members agreeing that the Legislative Council should be an 'equal partner' in the making of Hong Kong law. Another interpretation is that the elected members believe that they were chosen to represent their constituents through a variety of functions, not just pass laws.

This interpretation is given credence by the responses of legislators who were asked what they spend most of their time doing. Recording just their first responses, while 64 per cent of the appointed members noted that they spend most of their time passing laws, only 50 per cent of the functional constituency members and 38 per cent of the directly elected members noted this as their most demanding activity. Rather, over 20 per cent of the functional constituency members noted that they were explaining policies to constituents and expressing their views to government. Directly elected members did not mention explaining policies so much as expressing constituents' views (31 per cent), interceding with the government on their behalf (15 per cent), and resolving conflicts within the constituency (15 per cent). An additional interpretation could be that the elected members, as the newest members of the legislature, are still undergoing an apprenticeship, so do not engage in lawmaking activities as much as they will in the future when they gain more expertise. In general, therefore, it would appear that legislators in Hong Kong are spending more of their time in representational activities than legislators in other countries.[33] But are their focus and style of representation also unique?

Representative Roles

Most research on legislative role orientations has been devoted to representational roles. In terms of representational focus, it appears that Legislative Council members have a much more simplified focus than legislators in other countries. Members either perform their legislative activities according to the perceived or known views of their districts or in terms of how they define the public interest. Yet in other countries, an important component of representational focus is a political party[34] or an interest group,[35] religion, or the monarchy. The Legislative Council members' narrower focus can be attributed to two factors: first, that members are new to the job of legislator, and so focus simply on representing those who elected them; and second, the relative youth of most political parties and interest groups. The Hong Kong polity is at a nascent stage of development, after years of a moribund colonial status. With the upcoming change in sovereignty coupled with the growth of the middle class, it can be expected that more citizens will be active in parties and interest groups, and that legislators will soon reflect these developments in terms of a more diversified representational focus.

Much more emphasis has been placed on uncovering representational style than focus. Wahlke *et al.* found that the Trustee orientation was the most common one in all four state legislatures; with the Delegate orientation adopted by less than 20 per cent of all legislators. Later studies in several other state legislatures have found a greater diversification of role orientation, with a rise in the number of Politicos and, in some states, an almost even division between the three orientations.[36] From a comparative Asian viewpoint, the Trustee classification was found to be the most common orientation in the Philippines,[37] India,[38] Japan,[39] and Korea.[40] This is also the most popular orientation for Hong Kong legislators; however, two contradictory factors may affect its popularity over time. First, it could be expected that the number of Trustees might decrease over time as the number of directly elected legislators increases. This assumption is based on the fact that less than one-fifth of these members adhere to this orientation. Yet another assumption may indicate that this role will retain if not increase its popularity. Some tentative findings from previous research indicate that legislators are more likely to be Trustees if they are well educated, come from less competitive districts, are elected from at-large rather than single-member districts, have had previous political experience at a lower level of government, and have more legislative experience.[41] Considering these findings, it can be surmised that as members serve for greater lengths of time in the Legislative Council and become more confident in their abilities, they will adopt a Trustee orientation. This trend is likely to be strengthened by the fact that government policies are becoming more technical and complex and hence the average citizen's input into the policy process is decreasing.

To summarize, comparing the Legislative Council members' roles with those of legislators in a variety of other settings yields some crude but useful distinctions. More Legislative Council members place importance on functions other than lawmaking, which has been the traditional emphasis of most legislators. Additionally, more Legislative Council members, particularly the directly elected members, are inclined towards a Delegate rather than a Trustee orientation, which is more common in other settings. Finally, the focus of representation remains narrowly defined, due in part to the number of new legislators, the recent introduction of political parties, and the development of interest groups. Yet it must be emphasized that any conclusions about these distinctions and future role trends are highly speculative. Both the purposive and representational roles are, as Wahlke *et al.* noted, greatly influenced by 'the character of politics at a given time and by the

demands of contemporary political circumstances on the representative as decisionmaker'.[42] Given Hong Kong's current political
environment, forecasting trends is difficult. Yet it is with this endeavour that we will conclude this discussion.

Conclusion

Ultimately, the question must be asked: What does this data foretell for the future of Hong Kong's legislature?[43] This question is
addressed from three perspectives: the relationship between the
executive and legislative branches; the relationship between the
members; and the future functioning of the legislature.

Relationship between Executive and Legislative Branches

The interaction between the executive and the legislature has
recently been confrontational rather than cooperative. The reasons
for this changed context are both attitudinal and structural. As seen
in Chapter 6, Legislative Council members are engaging in a wider
variety of functions since the compositional changes began in 1985.
The members' willingness to engage in policy making, particularly
during the deliberative and oversight stages, has been substantially
increased. But this development has been imbued with discord and
dissension, with newly elected members taking on the role of the
opposition. Not unsurprisingly, interviews with officials revealed a
heightened sense of criticism and distrust. While on a theoretical
level officials are supportive of the more representative legislature,
on a practical level they lament the passing of the old days when
their policy-making was rarely constrained. As more members
take on the role of Tribune, and indeed Inventor, the policy-
making environment becomes more turbulent, leading to a loss of
efficiency and an undermining of the legitimacy of government.
The result of this more contentious atmosphere is a 'yo-yo' response: 'Sometimes when we give information to members,
they use this to attack us. As a result, we tend to close up, and
ultimately this is self-defeating for the legislature in terms of insur-
ing accountability'.

The more highly politicized legislative environment has meant
that the official must become a politician in order assure the
passage of his policies through the legislature: 'We are in a curious

system. I am a civil servant yet I have to do things that should be done by a politician'. However, their bureaucratic backgrounds have left them ill-prepared for their new political role: 'I am an official, but in the end, I am a civil servant. Because I have had no briefing about how to behave in the Legislative Council, my behaviour there is an extension of my behaviour as a civil servant. I am polite, unevasive and self-effacing—qualities which may not make for a good legislator'. The new-look legislature has put officials in an untenable position; they are subject to increasingly critical scrutiny yet they lack a ministerial system with which to defend themselves: 'We are a strange animal. We have power but no ministerial responsibility. With no party to back us, we have to stand alone'. The result of this change is that civil servants are behaving more like politicians who attempt 'to insure that the public relations side of an issue is covered as much as the substance,' and who no longer appeal to a closed group of sympathetic legislators but more often go 'over the heads of the Legislative Council to the Hong Kong people to pressure the members to do what we want'.

Besides being critical of the attitude of some newer members, officials also expressed concern over their qualifications: 'the new members are unable to understand the breadth and complexity of government policy'. When asked directly if the qualifications of the members were better, worse, or the same since 1985, 40 per cent of the officials responded 'worse'. While the majority conceded that since 1985 the government was more open with information (80 per cent), more willing to grant amendments (70 per cent), and that the Legislative Council was providing better service to the public (67 per cent), only 30 per cent said the Legislative Council was better at handling policy, with 30 per cent replying it was the same and a plurality of 40 per cent replying it was worse.

The crux of the current discordant relationship between the two branches lies in differing conceptions about the appropriate function of the Legislative Council. While 30 per cent of the officials believe that the Legislative Council should 'legitimize' government decision making and a further 10 per cent believe that it should 'represent the government's view to the people,' only 16 per cent of the 1993 legislators agreed with the legitimizing function and 4 per cent with the idea of representing government's views. More importantly, the overwhelming majority of those responding in this fashion (85 per cent) were appointed members who would be absent in the future.

The policy-making role of the members was also the subject of varied views, with no official acknowledging that the Legislative Council had a role in the invention or formulation of public policy, but nearly one-third of elected members aspiring to be Inventors.[44] Furthermore, while the majority of the Legislative Council members agreed that the Legislative Council and the executive branch should be equal partners in the making of public policy, the majority of officials disagreed.[45]

Hence the perceptions and roles taken by both officials and members of the legislature foretell the continuation of a turbulent future relationship. These problems have been exacerbated by the 1992 split of Executive Council from the Legislative Council. With no overlap in membership between the two bodies, a vital link is lacking to help integrate these disparate points of view. The government no longer has legislators to assist in the passage of its policies within the chamber[46] and the legislature no longer has a voice on the Executive Council so that the government might be informed on the parameters of its policy-making powers.

The only remedy to this situation is to reintegrate the membership. But further, considering the aspirations of many of the Legislative Council members to be more active at the formative stage of policy making, those legislators who sit on Executive Council should be given ministerial portfolios, responsibility over a defined area of public policy. This move would not only strengthen the relationship between the branches but fulfill the aspirations of some of the Legislative Council members to be more intimately involved in the formulation of government policy. This initiative would not only be popular with the newer members of the legislature but would also be applauded by 82 per cent of the official respondents. This reform in turn could enhance accountability and ensure that the Legislative Council not only behaves responsively but responsibly.

Relationships between the Members

Interactions among the members are now characterized more by dissension than consensus. As seen earlier, members expressed fundamental disagreements over what their appropriate roles should be, and these disagreements are fairly well determined by the type of member. The most fundamental differences are between the elected and appointed members, particularly in terms of representational activities and the appropriate relationship with the executive branch. However, there are also differences between directly elected and functional constituency members and these are more significant for the future when these members comprise the entire legislature. As seen in Table 7.1, from a general descriptive view, the directly elected members differ from their functional constituency counterparts in terms of their linkage with political parties and their desire to promote democracy. Table 7.2 revealed that in terms of purposive roles the appointed members were more likely to be Ritualists and Brokers, whereas their elected counterparts were more oriented towards representation. But by comparing the directly elected members with the functional constituency members it is clear that the latter exhibit a fairly even distribution between four role orientations while the former are overwhelmingly Tribunes (69 per cent). Moreover, Council members not only disagree about their roles, they disagree about the fundamental role of the legislature as well (Table 7.8).

Perhaps the most glaring distinction is found in the 1993 sample, where the overwhelming majority of appointed members believed the Legislative Council should promote systems-maintenance activities but most elected members thought that the Council should concentrate on policy making.[47] Within the elected component the distinctions are not as great, with most members generally supporting increased policy-making and representational functions. However, the directly elected members differ from their functional constituency colleagues in their emphasis on policy formulation.[48] This was most clearly depicted in responses to a forced choice statement: *Legislative Council and the executive branch should be equal partners in the making of public policy.* Only 36 per cent of the functional constituency members but an overwhelming 87 per cent of the directly elected members consented to this statement. Moreover, the functional constituency members are much more likely to advocate systems-maintenance activities, particularly championing the executive branch and promoting stability in Hong Kong.

These role distinctions have led to a breakdown in the norms, or rules, under which the legislature operates.[49] Those members who served before 1985 were able to list several norms which governed the Legislative Council proceedings in the past, such as deference to authority, serving an apprenticeship before actively participating in proceedings, keeping arguments private rather than airing disputes in public, never personalizing disputes, operat-

Table 7.8 Members' Perceptions of the Roles of the Legislative Council, 1988 and 1993 (Percentage)

	1988			1993			Average
	Appointed Members	Electoral College Members	Functional Constituency Members	Appointed Members	Directly Elected Members	Functional Constituency Members	
Policy making: Oversight	16	25	36	6	27	22	18
Policy making: Formulation	5	13	18	6	40	28	24
Representation	37	68	50	6	27	22	18
Systems Maintenance: Stability	5	—	—	25	—	11	14
Systems Maintenance: Integration	16	—	—	25	7	6	10
Systems Maintenance: Support	—	5	—	32	—	11	16

Notes: Evaluations derived from responses to a number of questions. Average combines responses from both surveys.

ing by consensus, never disputing a decision once the majority has taken it, showing respect for each other, and promotion of seniority by only electing senior members to leadership positions. By 1993, however, when members were asked if there were any informal 'rules of the game' in operation, they were not able to cite one norm, making the Legislative Council a unique legislative body operating under no apparent normative system.[50] This is a critical flaw in the operation of the legislature, for rules of the game have been found to perform significant functions. For instance, they compensate for the absence of common experience or 'uniform anticipatory socialisation'.[51] Norms have also been found to perform six peculiar functions: they promote group cohesion and solidarity, promote predictability of legislative behaviour, channel and restrain conflict, expedite legislative business, give special advantages to individual members, and promote desirable personal qualities to facilitate interaction.[52] While the Legislative Council has been successful in developing new structures and formal rules to guide its proceedings,[53] lack of the informal codes of conduct will continue to inhibit effective interaction between members and ultimately the effectiveness of the Legislative Council as an institution.

Future Functioning of the Legislature

While the external or systemic functioning of the Legislative Council has been reviewed in Chapter 6, the role analysis of this chapter now allows us to assess its internal functioning. First, the significance of the appointed members should be acknowledged. While it is easy to decry their lack of representativeness, it is also too easy to overlook their past contributions. Although much of their work has been done in private behind closed doors, it is nonetheless clear that the appointed members have performed significant legislative functions. Their roles have included promoting the general public interest and, since 1985, advocating compromise among the diverse interests of their elected colleagues. It would appear that their place would best be taken by members who are elected at-large rather than strictly according to a geographical or functional demarcation. With the loss of appointed members in 1995, the legislature will lose those individuals who perform the most integrative function, that of Broker, with respect to both external and internal interests in the legislature.

Table 7.9 Members' Perceptions of the Most Difficult Job of the Legislative Council, 1988 and 1993 (Percentage)

| | Q: What is the hardest job for the legislature? | | | | | | | |
| | 1988 | | | | 1993 | | | |
	Appointed Members	Electoral College Members	Functional Constituency Members	Average	Appointed Members	Directly Elected Members	Functional Constituency Members	Average
Getting members to agree on sound policy	11	20	9	13	50	50	38	45
Preventing adoption of government policies that might hurt people	26	40	27	30	—	17	6	7
Preventing selfish interests from blocking policies	21	10	9	15	31	25	38	32
Getting constituents to accept policies essential for economic development	5	20	27	13	13	—	12	9
Unable or unwilling to rank	37	20	27	29	6	8	6	7

Note: Percentages are rounded off to nearest whole number.

A number of questions were asked that provide a basis from which to investigate the internal dynamics of the Legislative Council. As seen in Table 7.8, there is a wide variation of functional priorities according to the different types of members. Another forced choice question asked members to evaluate which of four jobs was the hardest for the Legislative Council to accomplish. Table 7.9 provides their responses.

What is most remarkable about Table 7.9 is the variation in responses from 1988 to 1993, which dramatically demonstrate the growing lack of cohesion in the legislature. While *Preventing adoption of government policies which might hurt people* was the most popular response in 1988, almost half of the 1993 respondents indicated that *Getting members to agree on sound policies* was the major problem for the legislature. Moreover, one-third of these respondents noted that *Preventing selfish interests from blocking policies* was a key difficulty. For a change, these perceptions received popular backing, even across membership types. What they indicate is an increasingly fractious, divisive body, lacking in shared values over their method of operation, their priorities, their roles, and their function. Until some consensus can be reached over these vital components, the legislature will continue to operate as a marginal institution in Hong Kong's political system.

8   Conclusion

A brief summation of this research provides some premises from which to evaluate the Legislative Council's development as well as make suggestions for its future. In addition, this review provides the basis with which to place Hong Kong's evolution in the context of the globalization of political values.

Research Findings

The Legislative Council's development has been framed by the exigencies of geography and history, as was shown in Chapters 2 and 3. Its stagnation at the first stage of colonial council development was due more to fears of offending China than British reluctance to grant it power and independence. Lessons from past colonial history may prove instructive at this juncture of the Legislative Council's evolution. First, grave difficulties occur when a legislative body is imbued with representativeness but denied responsibility in the operation of government. The fight for autonomy by the lower houses of American colonial legislatures led to increased instability and eventually to a war for independence. While such a scenario is unlikely, if not impossible, given the parameters of Hong Kong's 'David and Goliath' relationship with China, nonetheless, it is important to be aware of past problems governing similar executive–legislative relationships.

Past colonial history also reveals the problems that arise when a bridge is lacking between the executive and the legislature. In 1839, while investigating the tensions between the governor and the colonial legislatures in Upper and Lower Canada, the Earl of Durham noted the inevitability of the 'collision between the executive and the representative body' when 'an immovable executive confronted a potentially irresistible legislature'.[1] Durham concluded that the governor should only select individuals who have the support of the legislature to sit on the executive council, a recommendation that began the evolution to dominion status for many colonies. This suggestion may prove an appropriate compromise should the development of ministerial government, as recommended in Chapter 7, not occur.

Chapter 3 revealed that Hong Kong's development has occurred within the confines of an autocratic colonial system. However, colonial rule has been tempered by the infusion of democratic values and benevolent practices that have allowed for 'consultation and consensus' to occur before any governmental action. The initiatives that led to Hong Kong's vitality were formulated and executed in extra-parliamentary arenas, primarily the government departments.[2] One of the key ironies of Hong Kong history is that it developed a highly sophisticated and mature economy yet politically remained a neophyte. On the eve of the Joint Declaration, the legislature was a conservative, passive body totally appointed by the Governor and oriented towards the maintenance of the status quo.

From the Legislative Council's perspective, the signing of the Joint Declaration signalled not only the transfer of sovereignty between Britain and China but the beginning of a revolutionary transformation. While the Joint Declaration provided that Hong Kong would be vested with executive, legislative, and independent judicial power, it made it clear that China would exercise pervasive power in determining who would occupy the executive and judicial branches. The Chief Executive appointed by China was, however, to be accountable to the legislature whose membership would be based on 'elections'. So, it was apparent that the extent of Hong Kong's future autonomy would be dependent on the power and representativeness of the legislature. Yet as Chapter 4 demonstrated, the way in which electoral decisions about legislative composition were made undermined the legitimacy of the legislature. For the reforms enacted to make the Legislative Council more representative—from the Joint Declaration and the Basic Law to the internal White Papers—were all formulated in extra-parliamentary settings and presented as *faits accomplis* for pre-ordained legislative approval.[3] Chapter 5 revealed that while the Legislative Council is becoming more highly institutionalized, with the creation of structures within the legislature and the development of an independent staff agency to assist in its work, the

potential use of these resources remains undeveloped, due perhaps
to lack of clarity over the role of the legislature.

As Chapter 6 depicts, post-1984 changes in the Legislative Council's membership led to a diversification in members' expectations
and behaviour. The Council was transformed from a passive body,
noted for its solidarity, into a vocal—if not vehement—body, often
divided rather than unified in its activities, which now encompassed
policy making and representation as well as systems maintenance.

The discovery of members' roles charted in Chapter 7 proved
most helpful in analysing the current and likely future functioning
of the Legislative Council.[4] Several findings are suggestive. First,
the wide variety of orientations towards legislative roles broadly
matches the members' method of selection. Because there will
be no appointed members after 1995, the dramatic differences in
orientation that exist between appointed and elected members will
disappear. However, the unidimensional focus most functional
constituency members demonstrate towards their constituents,
coupled with the broader-based Tribune orientation of a majority
of the directly elected members, foreshadows difficulties in achieving future consensus.[5] Moreover, new party groupings appear to
strengthen these divisions, which are also reinforced ideologically:
the liberals, primarily directly elected members, belong to one
political party, and the conservatives, primarily functional constituency members, belong to another.[6] The fact that so few elected
members appear to be Brokers raises concern over the chamber's
ability to integrate interests, thus impeding the effectiveness of the
Legislative Council. However, this may change. Unlike many other
countries, Hong Kong is not beset by the intractable divisions of
race, religion, or culture. Additionally, its small size makes the
geographical constituency divisions largely artificial. Therefore,
while diversity will continue, political maturation may allow for
compromise between these interests and their subversion to the
public interest.

Members were found to differ not only in their personal
orientations but also in their beliefs about the role of the
legislature. The appointed members favour systems-maintenance
activities whereas their elected colleagues show a greater predilection towards policy making and representation. Additionally,
elected members exhibit important disparities. The directly elected
members differ from their functional constituency colleagues in
their policy-formulation aspirations.[7] Yet under current and future

constitutional constraints these aspirations appear misguided. Members with policy-making aspirations will do better to concentrate their attention on checking executive influence through more elaborate deliberative and oversight activities.[8]

Distinct expectations about the Legislative Council's role were also apparent in contrasting the views of officials with those of the legislators, as officials believed the Legislative Council should have a more restrictive policy-making role, and further, that its main function should be systems maintenance. These disparate orientations foreshadow the continuation of a divisive relationship within the legislature as well as between it and the executive.[9]

When members were asked to explain what they thought were the sources of controversy or division within the legislature, 67 per cent asserted that the most fundamental division occurs over the issue of how Hong Kong should interact with China.[10] Follow-up analysis revealed that this division was reinforced by ideology: self-designated liberals tended to believe that China would only respect them if they continued to fight for the protection of civil liberties and the promotion of Hong Kong's autonomy; conservatives tended to believe that China should be placated as much as possible, and that this approach would lead over time to greater local autonomy. The issue, according to members of both factions, was one of confrontation versus cooperation.[11] Obviously, a key determinant of the future functioning of the Legislative Council will be its relationship with China.

China's Relationship with Hong Kong

The twenty-first century has already been dubbed 'the Chinese Century'. The Chinese economy is expected by many to be at the forefront of a shift of economic activity from West to East.[12] Economic growth has come from a liberalization and decentralization of economic policy making from Beijing to the coastal regions, particularly to the special economic zones.[13] Hong Kong has had a key role in this transformation becoming 'the doormat of China's open door'.[14] The ultimate paradox of Hong Kong's reintegration into mainland China is that the two provide such clear contrasts both in economic and political values and yet are each other's largest trading partners and sources of external investment.[15]

While China's economic relationship with Hong Kong has

strengthened considerably,[16] the fundamental approach guiding the relationship remains political.[17] The recovery of Hong Kong has now taken on added nationalistic significance. The current Chinese regime is one that is 'struggling to justify its legitimacy and one moreover which has shed much of its ideological *raison d'être* in the pursuit of staying in power, appealing to Chinese nationalism [in pursuit of the recovery of Hong Kong] has become a refuge in an otherwise lonely world.'[18] The fundamental problem for Hong Kong is that China does not want decolonization; it simply wants a transfer of sovereignty.[19]

China is keenly aware of Hong Kong's social, cultural, and lately, political, influence on the mainland. The events at Tiananmen Square in June 1989 turned world opinion sharply against China but also produced a vast change in China's perception of Hong Kong. Up until that time China had perceived the population to be apolitical and passive about their future. The widespread protests in Hong Kong after the crackdown coupled with support given to the dissidents by Hong Kong people alarmed the Chinese leadership. Since then, the reactions of China's leaders to various developments in Hong Kong indicate that they place a higher premium on political control than they do on either economic prosperity or their own credibility.[20] Chinese leaders will not allow political changes in Hong Kong to go beyond those that they are eventually prepared to accept for the rest of China. In the words of a former American ambassador to China, 'Beijing wants to preserve Hong Kong's prosperity, but it will not sacrifice its own political survival to do so.'[21]

China maintains that the push for local democracy is a 'Western conspiracy', part of a planned strategy by the United States and Britain to exert pressure on an increasingly powerful China.[22] In this context, Hong Kong is seen as a bridgehead for an international conspiracy of the Western nations against China. The rationale behind such a move, China believes, is to break, or at least weaken, the Chinese government's power by introducing the highly contagious and destabilizing forces of democracy and human rights. To some, the quarrel between Britain and China over Hong Kong's future is not over more democracy for Hong Kong but the linkage of human rights and democracy to China's economic prosperity. According to this view, 'the West would like to try to get China to be more like South Korea or Taiwan: open, multi-party, with a distribution of power within the country that makes it less totalitarian and less of a threat to the world.'[23] In this context, Hong Kong is 'a crucial pawn in this Machiavellian game.'[24] This conspiracy theory was given new impetus with the introduction of the Patten proposals.

The Significance of the Patten Proposals

The Patten proposals have been interpreted by some to be less a struggle over Hong Kong than a struggle over the development of China.[25] Calls from some opinion leaders for Patten to 'internationalize the issue' did much to reinforce the conspiracy fears of the Chinese.[26] The Governor's highly publicized trips to Japan, Canada, and later the United States were seen by Chinese leaders as a blatant attempt further to isolate China and force her into concessions.[27]

Yet looked at closely, Patten's proposals are nothing more than an attempt to provide a modest measure of democracy through provision of a broader-based legislature that would make the future government more accountable.[28] But the Governor's efforts illuminated that for Hong Kong the real issue was not so much more or less democracy but rather how much autonomy will be allowed in the future. In many respects, the Patten proposals accomplished a temporal impossibility—1997 came in 1993, forcing Hong Kong to confront its first great test of political autonomy.[29] The 1997 deadline has lost meaning in terms of economics: the southern Chinese and Hong Kong economies have become so interwoven that local and foreign investors alike think of Hong Kong and Guangdong as a single unit.[30] Similarly, the Patten proposals forced the issue of political autonomy: as the Governor was to remark: 'The argument is whether what Hong Kong has been promised—a substantial degree of autonomy—actually means that. If we don't stand up for Hong Kong before 1997, why should we expect anybody else to stand up for Hong Kong? Secondly, what chance is there of Hong Kong standing up for itself after 1997?'[31] Another analyst remarked, 'Mr. Patten has simply brought out into the open and brought forward a bit, what was bound to come anyway: the polarization and politicization of Hong Kong, and its absorption—in fact, if not yet law—into China.'[32]

The Legislative Council is faced with the most important decision in its history. Its handling of Patten's proposals affects not only its future format but to an extent determines its future role. For the first time the Legislative Council is in a position to demonstrate leadership in shaping Hong Kong's future: 'If the territory is to stand any chance of having a civil society strong enough to support a major role in the international market economy after 1997, then it must be seen to win a battle with Beijing before 1997.'[33] Are the legislators equipped to meet this new challenge? Some are doubtful: 'This will require more leadership and courage than some legislators have shown themselves to possess'.[34] The debate over Patten's initiatives is thus a crucial test of the legislature's maturity.

The reactions from China and the West to the Patten proposals highlight the radically different views each have concerning the function of the legislature. For Britain and the West, legislative approval is a key requirement to legitimize representative government. For China, the legislature should not have a final say in any determination; rather its purpose is purely to legitimize decisions taken elsewhere, to act as a rubber stamp.[35] According to a Chinese government spokesman, 'The Hong Kong Legislative Council, in its capacity as a consultative body to the governor, has no right to approve any resolution to overthrow the agreements and understandings reached by the Chinese and British governments'.[36] This view highlights another reason why the proposals have been so distasteful to China: they democratize a body which China wants to control and then give this body the final say over its own composition. Hence, one of China's strategies in the talks over the Patten proposals has been to downgrade the role of the Legislative Council; one of the Governor's aims has been to build it up.[37] These different conceptions of the legislature demonstrate a fundamental difference in political values.

Patten's Proposals and the Globalization of Political Values

Patten's proposals have brought Hong Kong to the forefront of the world-wide democratic revolution. They deal most fundamentally with the electoral process of the legislature and represent 'just the sort of Western liberal democratic philosophy which has been making great strides in East Asian countries.'[38] The Governor's initiatives brought into high relief the late-twentieth century debate over the globalization of political values.[39] The struggle over Hong Kong goes deeper than an ideological clash between Western democracy and a communist state. It is an irreconcilable clash of values—absolute rule through a monolithic state government based on the personality of those in power versus a belief that for a government to be legitimate, it must be based 'of, by, and for the people' with elected leaders exercising authority according to the rule of the law. The contrast is between a government by men versus a government by law. It is a conflict between the 'descendants of Hobbes and Locke, with their emphasis on human rights, democracy, and rule of law,'[40] and a Beijing regime that 'not only rejects but is threatened by these values.'[41] These disparate values lie at the heart of the issues involved in considering the democratization of Asia.

Asian Democracy

Democratization[42] came to Asia after the Second World War primarily through the process of decolonization.[43] More recently there has been a consistent pattern of economic and political development in East Asia. Export-led economic growth has produced a large urban middle class which, in turn, has demanded political liberalization and democracy. Since the mid-1980s this has been evident in the Philippines, South Korea, Taiwan and Thailand. Yet this process has not been smooth and has often involved reversals as transplanted institutions without sufficient roots in local cultures attempted to cope with the problems stemming from economic development and nation building.[44] The more recent rise of democracies in the region demonstrates that future democracy in Asia will be more closely shaped by the interactions of economics and cultural values.[45] Yet many prevailing Asian values not only differ fundamentally from those of the West but by Western standards are not conducive to democratic development: 'Confucian culture and its variants emphasize the supremacy of the group over the individual, authority over liberty, and responsibilities over rights.'[46] Many Asians have come to reject the Western democratic concept that 'the clash of ideas and ideals [will result in] good government.'[47] Nonetheless, from this distinctly Asian context a democratic variant is emerging, as Huntington notes:

The East Asian dominant-party systems that may be emerging seem to involve competition for power but not alternation in power, and participation in elections for all, but participation in office only for those in the 'mainstream' party. This type of political system represents an adaptation of Western democratic practices to serve Asian or Confucian political values. In this context democratic institutions work not to promote Western values of competition and change but Confucian values of consensus and stability.[48]

Such institutions are distinct from their Western counterparts. They exhibit a communitarian sense that teaches that the individual is important as part of a group rather than heralding the individual as the centerpiece of democracy. Together with this is an emphasis on consensus as the central feature of decision making and a greater acceptance of and respect for authority and hierarchy coincident with a dominant political party and a strong centralized bureaucracy.[49] These differences appear to delineate a unique 'Asian democracy' but one which nonetheless retains the key defining characteristic of democracies in the West: free and fair elections to select political leaders.

Where, in the midst of all this, does the future of China lie? China has proved the exception from the usual mechanistic connection between economic freedom and political freedom.[50] Some authorities argue that an open economic system cannot flourish with political repression. It may be possible for a while, they suggest, but eventually a more pluralistic political system will evolve to go with the more decentralized decision making in the economic system. 'China's chaos-fearing leaders will...eventually fail in their bid to achieve order without opposition, affluence without openness, modernity without pluralism.'[51] Others counter that China's century-long obsession with political order and national strength make support for pluralist democracy even weaker today than when the democracy movement began.[52] Hence, China's push for a decentralized Western-style market economy has occurred simultaneously with the exercise of centralized controls to preserve its political culture. As China evolves economically, it will also evolve politically, but this evolution will not necessarily be a Western-style democracy.[53] At present China remains a hybrid along the lines of capitalist totalitarianism or free-market authoritarianism. Consequently, Hong Kong and China remain the ultimate paradoxes: they have begun to complement each other economically, but politically, culturally, and ideologically, they remain a threat to each other's vital interests.[54]

Finding Hong Kong's Voice: The Role of the Representative

The documents that have shaped Hong Kong's history—from its founding treaties to the scripts of the 1984 Sino-British negotiations to the Basic Law—have all been written without the direct participation of the Hong Kong people. The people have never been allowed to play a meaningful role as masters of their own destiny.[55] It is this fact more than any other which defines Hong Kong's unique past and present.

However, the 1991 elections demonstrated that Hong Kong is now 'part of a world trend towards democracy'.[56] The development of Hong Kong's democracy will ultimately depend on the aspirations of the people and the political will of their legislators. The legislators will need the 'courage of their convictions' to insist on the rights promised in the Joint Declaration and Basic Law.[57] Only by acting in this manner will the legislators be able to safeguard Hong Kong's freedom, way of life, and livelihood.[58] What China fails to realize is that for Hong Kong to be stable and prosperous as well as be a helpful partner in China's future, the people need a sense that they can determine their own destiny.

Will there be a Hong Kong 'democracy' in the future? Much will depend on how Hong Kong legislators relate to China. For both liberal and conservative members, the fundamental challenge will be to think only of Hong Kong's interests: 'For the liberals that means abjuring involvement with mainland politics . . . ; for the business-linked groups, that means showing less short-term greed and more political nous.'[59] Both groups also need to learn compromise, so that the ideological extremes of each will give way to the more moderate political beliefs of the public. In sum, the Legislative Council needs to be more representative of the people. In clarifying its focus it will be able to exert more power as it speaks in a more unified manner. If Hong Kong is to preserve its status in the fifty years after 1997, it needs a 'legislature that is so clearly representative of its people . . . that Beijing will adopt the "hands off" approach it promised.'[60]

In the end the truism is that Hong Kong is neither Western nor Asian,[61] neither British nor Chinese; it is simply Hong Kong. The current battle between the once and future sovereigns is ossified by their own long-cherished traditions, with Hong Kong the 'quirk' the two cultures produced: 'It thrives on all possibilities that are pre-judged to be impossible in the parent cultures.'[62] Hong Kong democracy is not the same as a demand for sovereignty, though this may come in time. For the moment, it relates to ensuring that a legislature elected by universal suffrage occurs sooner rather than later.[63] A legislature so constituted will be more representative, more responsive, and consequently more unified and powerful. This development remains the best way to achieve success in one of the world's most unique political experiments: a relationship of 'one country–two systems'. The principle of 'Hong Kong people ruling Hong Kong' is not so much idealism as realism: 'It is, of course, we the people of Hong Kong who know best how to run our own city. We understand what the problems are and how to solve those problems far better than any outsiders do.'[64] The long-term stability and prosperity of Hong Kong will lie in asserting and defending the unique cultural, political, and economic identity of Hong Kong that so clearly sets it apart from the mainland.[65] Legislators need to be aware of the features of both Western and Asian democracies but then develop their own unique variant. Giving voice to the people's democratic aspirations within the unique context of Hong Kong will be the most important function of the future legislature.

Epilogue

In the time that has elapsed since this book was written, events have continued to transform the discussion of many of the issues previously illuminated. This epilogue will briefly highlight the intensified controversy surrounding the concept of Asian democracy, and then narrow the focus to the democratic aspirations evident in the working of Hong Kong's Legislative Council.

Democratic Values in the Asian Context

Over the past two years, the discussion of the relative merits of Western versus Asian values has achieved greater prominence in academic and journalistic arenas. After the collapse of communism, 'anticlimax has succeeded initial euphoria', particularly in light of the continuing struggles for stability in Russia and the former Yugoslavia.[1] The increasingly vivid illustrations of Western decadence—particularly the attention given to violent crime and the deterioration of the family structure—have been heralded as indicators that the application of Western democracy is fraught with danger.[2] Debate has encompassed the broader characterization that all future world-wide disputes will be based on a 'clash of civilizations', in which, as Samuel Huntington has written, 'the efforts of the West to promote its values of democracy and liberalism as universal values ... engender countering responses from other civilizations'.[3] But others have responded that democracy is not alien to Asian cultures, for, as Kim Dae Jung maintains, 'there are no ideas more fundamental to democracy than the teachings of Confucianism, Buddhism, and Tonghak'.[4] Political analysts have pointed to the durability of the belief that 'democracy works best'.[5]

Although democracy appears to be 'on a winning streak in Asia'[6] there remains much dispute over its merits, and some Asian leaders have begun to proclaim that their economic success is due to the superiority of 'Asian values' over those of the decadent West.[7] These Asian leaders see Western-style democracy as a threat to national and regional stability, and as unsuited to Asia's political culture and traditions. They recommend a 'discipline-for-development' alternative which would replace democracy as an aspiration for Asian nations—a form of 'Confucian capitalism'.[8] This view has gained credence, for it is practised by leaders of some of the region's most rapidly expanding economies—those of Singapore, Malaysia, and, notably, China. The architects of the world's fastest-growing economy remain distinctly anti-democratic, rigidly maintaining an autocratic form of government presided over by an aged patriarch. Yet the danger of basing a government on a 'rule of man' versus a 'rule of law' is apparent in the continual discussions over Deng's succession.[9] His death is likely to bring power struggles, possibly widespread social conflict, and inevitably instability. This event, as well as the larger philosophical issues it raises, has a direct relationship to the future development of Hong Kong's legislature.[10]

A Legislature Comes of Age: The 1993–1994 Session

From the moment the Governor opened the legislature with his policy address, it was clear that this session would be the most assertive in Hong Kong's history. Almost immediately after the address, the Governor was criticised by conservative legislators: he announced revisions to his electoral package to make it more palatable to China, and was accused of 'giving in to Beijing at the expense of Hong Kong'.[11] This was to be just the first of many criticisms of his administration during that session. The next week witnessed a motion urging the scrapping of the law which prevented New Territory women from inheriting land. This motion led to the passage of a bill, in June, which secured women's inheritance rights in the New Territories. Later that autumn, legislators demanded an explanation after the deputy director of the Independent Commission Against Corruption (ICAC) was sacked. They conducted an enquiry into the matter using their previously dormant authority under the Powers and Privileges Ordinance.

Early in the new year legislators wielded their financial power too. They refused to approve the government's call for a 60 per cent increase for vehicle and driving licenses, which they scaled back to 35 per cent. Although the Financial Secretary presented a rosy forecast for revenues and reserves in his March budget address, officials were still bombarded by more than 1,570 written and 233 supplementary questions concerning the government's spending estimates for the next financial year.[12]

The growing authority of the council's policy-making powers became even more evident through the use of two legislative devices. First, members used private members' bills to amend or alter—in some cases fundamentally—government policy. As related in Chapter 6, Martin Lee became the first non-official legislator to introduce public legislation when he proposed an amendment to the Electoral Provisions Ordinance aimed at ensuring that each geographical constituency contained an equal number of people. This past year, functionally elected member Michael Ho introduced a private member's bill which amended the Immigration Ordinance to ensure that foreign workers would be permitted to enter Hong Kong for employment only—in accordance with rules approved by the Legislative Council. Tam Yiu-chung, as convenor of the Council's public service panel, offered a private member's bill entitled Public Officers (Variation of condition of Service) (Temporary Provisions). This bill was used to block a government proposal to allow expatriate civil servants to change their overseas conditions of service to local terms. And Lau Chin-shek offered an amendment seeking to lift the $180,000 ceiling on employees' severance pay.[13]

But the most significant legislative initiative came with the introduction of an Equal Opportunities Bill, which became the first private member's bill covering an entire area of law. It banned discrimination based on sex, sexuality, age, and race. A similar breakthrough was made with an Access to Information Bill.[14] Both these initiatives represented a tremendous amount of research, and draftsmanship[15] of legislation which contained hundreds of provisions.[16] Furthermore, they demonstrated that legislators can be active rather than merely reactive. They can wield policy-making power by forcing the administration to face issues head-on—even those they were not inclined to address. As member Anna Wu noted, introducing legislation was a way of 'breaking the gridlock of the executive branch of government'.[17] In all, the legislature asked 595 questions (excluding supplementary questions; 146 were oral and 449 were written), and passed 104 bills during the session—the most important of which related to the Governor's electoral reforms.

Sino-British Negotiations on the 1995 Legislature

After seventeen rounds and 160 hours of discussion over an eight-month period, the Chinese and British negotiators reached an impasse. The strength of the divisions between the two sides proved too difficult to reconcile. The only area in which a consensus emerged was the lowering of the colony's voting age from 21 to 18. Other areas of dispute, however, remained intractable.[18] The Chinese rejected the principle of 'single-seat, single-vote' in elections for the legislature.[19] They believed that the 1995 functional constituencies should incorporate 130,000 voters rather than 2.7 million (the entire working population of Hong Kong);[20] that the Election Committee for ten seats in 1995 should follow the four-sector model set out in the Basic Law (paragraph 2 of Annex 1);[21] and they mandated that the 'through-train' would entail requirements such as a ban on 'subversives', and the ability to judge behaviour retroactive to the 1997 transition.[22] Beijing's insistence on determining which of the legislators elected in 1995 would be allowed to serve beyond the handover was the crucial issue which doomed the talks.[23]

The British subsequently published a 36-page White Paper, and the Chinese a 17,000-character account, detailing the contents of the talks and their breakdown. The White Paper, presented to the British Parliament, was issued in order to justify the Hong Kong government's decision to push ahead with the Patten proposals. Upon publication, China's Foreign Ministry countered with its version of the events. Both sides appeared to engage in 'double vision'.[24] China charged that Britain 'lacked sincerity and deliberately complicated the issue' during the talks, and had no right to transplant its parliamentary structure into what would be sovereign Chinese territory in three and a half years.[25] Britain portrayed China as 'rigid and uncooperative', making only 'minor adjustments' accompanied by 'significant gaps and ambiguities'.

Consequently, by the end of 1993, the British determined to proceed unilaterally with electoral legislation governing the 1994 District Board and the 1995 Legislative Council elections. The first package of legislation—lowering the voting age from 21 to 18, abolishing appointed seats on local government bodies, and establishing single-seat constituencies for the legislature—was gazetted on December 10.[26]

On 24 February 1994, the Legislative Council overwhelmingly approved these proposals by voice vote, changing only the title of the bill. The final vote on the measure was taken at 1.20 a.m., at the end of more than nine hours of a debate later labelled 'the most significant in the history of Hong Kong's legislative council'.[27] In the interim, five motions were offered to amend or delay parts of the bill. The first motion was offered by functional member Elsie Tu in order to adjourn the debate. Arguing that 'I do not believe in a power struggle that leads the community into a state of fear and anxiety about the future', Mrs Tu urged her colleagues to delay action claiming that China was willing to resume talks.[28] Liberal members quickly countered that a delay at this point would be futile and 'naïve', and would turn the legislature into 'a laughing stock'.[29] Mrs Tu's characterization of Hong Kong as the 'children' of divorcing parents whose dispute 'makes the children feel unhappy and insecure' proved an ineffective hyperbole to use with an increasingly assertive legislature.[30] In voting against the delay, legislators were attempting to obliterate this paternalistic relationship prevalent in past debates over Hong Kong's future. One member, Dr Leong Che-Hung, retorted that if China was the 'parent' and Hong Kong the 'child' who should obey his elders, then 'I fail to see the function and the use of this Council.'[31] Member Jimmy McGregor noted that, if the Council failed to act that day, it would in effect 'give way to the worst kind of bullying' and would seem to 'concede that this Council accepts that instruction replaces debate'.[32] After a three-hour debate, Mrs Tu's motion was defeated by 36 to 23.[33] Following this defeat, four additional motions were offered to amend parts of the bill; all but one concerning technical details were defeated.[34]

Later that same week, Governor Patten proceeded to offer the second—more controversial—part of his electoral reform. This new legislation broadened the base for functional constituencies to include all 2.7 million Hong Kong workers in thirty functional constituencies. Furthermore, the Election Commission to select an additional ten legislators, would be composed of all elected members of the district and municipal bodies. In a marathon twenty-hour session on 30 June 1994, the Legislative Council approved the final portion of the Patten electoral reforms by a margin of 32 to 24 votes.[35] The crucial vote came earlier in the debate, when conservatives, backed by pro-China legislators, proposed an amendment to slash the number of functional constituency voters to 220,000.[36] In that vote, the Governor prevailed by the small margin of 29 to 28, saved by two abstentions and reliance upon the votes of the three official members. An additional issue in the debate was the introduction of a private member's bill by independent member Emily Lau, which called for all legislators to be directly elected in 1995.[37] This bill was also defeated by just one vote—many felt support for it would be futile since it violated the Basic Law, and the Governor had said he would not assign assent, even if it were passed.

In shaping the parameters of electoral reform the legislature have played a decisive role in determining their future, even if it is just for the short-term. As one commentator Margaret Ng noted, 'Fate, for once, if only for a moment, was put into our own hands.'[38] Legislators proved they had the will and discipline to speak for themselves, even under adverse pressure from their future sovereign: 'China has drawn a line and Hong Kong's local politicians collectively crossed it.'[39] The reform proposals provided a platform which allowed the Legislative Council at last to become a 'self-assertive parliament'.[40] As noted by the Governor in his October address, the march of democracy would only go as far as the legislators themselves were willing to take it.[41] After the vote, he noted that 'the process of Hong Kong making that decision does have its considerable consequence for Hong Kong's future, and it is another reason for us to be more hopeful than less hopeful'.[42]

As for the time remaining before the transfer of sovereignty, Patten has said that his main role is one of 'working himself out of a job': 'The future lies with the legislative leaders emerging in the Legislative Council, and the executive leaders emerging in the civil service. It is important that in the next three years I delegate as much as possible.'[43] Yet even though his electoral reform package was approved, the Governor's popularity with the legislature remains tentative. During the same time period in which the legislature discussed and approved his initiative, the Governor, as well as the governments of China and Britain, was subjected to legislative censure.

China, Britain, and the Governor Rebuked by the Legislature

The extent of the legislators' new boldness became apparent in May with passage of a motion voicing the 'grave concerns of the

Hong Kong people' over both Britain and China's handling of Hong Kong's transfer of sovereignty.[44] In a display of growing independence, the Legislative Council voted 23 to 0 (with four abstentions and thirty-three absences) in support of the motion. The resolution reflected mounting anxiety that Anglo–Chinese quarrelling was destroying the smooth transition towards Chinese rule. Additionally, some legislators voiced the suspicion that behind the highly publicized antipathy, Britain and China were quietly colluding in order to dilute the freedoms they had promised in the Joint Declaration.[45] According to the motion's sponsor, Szeto Wah, 'We have reason to believe that the British and Chinese sides have ganged up to destroy the spirit of the Joint Declaration. We are being betrayed.'[46]

In an even more daring departure the following month, the legislature moved to censure the Governor for refusing to back its demand to freeze a proposed tax-rate increase. Since it involved the use of government money, the Governor had used his discretion, under the Royal Instructions, to block an amendment against the government's proposal to increase property rates.[47] The governor was in this instance ignoring the lessons of the past (as uncovered in Chapter 2) namely, that there should be 'no taxation without representation'.[48] In a motion offered in early June the Council 'reproved' the Governor for 'acting against the will of the public'.[49] This event reinforces the prognosis for the future noted in Chapter 7, that due to the lack of a linkage between the legislative and executive, and in light of the policy-making aspirations of the elected members, conflict between the legislative and executive branch will over time become exacerbated.[50]

Representation and rights without responsibility will continue to aggravate relations between the branches of government, and thus the legitimacy and stability of the government, into the future.

OMELCO Update

The increasingly independent stance taken by the legislature was boosted from 1 April 1994 by the independent recruitment of staff. These staff members report to a new Legislative Council Secretariat, headed by the President of the Legislative Council, an individual elected from among the members. The Secretariat was formed from the merger of OMELCO and Clerk of Council offices, and is directed by an independent Legislative Council Commission, created by statute on 30 March 1994. While some legislators noted that the separation of the Secretariat from the executive branch was a 'milestone in the history of Hong Kong's constitutional development',[51] others cautioned that it would only be successful if sufficient additional resources were provided.[52] Since the executive retains the ability to determine finances for all publicly funded entities, there remains concern, previously noted in Chapter 5, over how to ensure that staff are funded at the level the legislature desires—particularly after 1997. Given the oversight activities the legislature may conduct over the executive in the future, there is recognition that its staff may not be popular and that guarantees must be made for their financial autonomy from the executive.

The Legislative Vortex

The future sovereign's response to the dramatic transformation of the Legislative Council—particularly after its passage of the electoral reforms—was in the form of a strong rebuke. Shortly after the passage of the first package of electoral reforms, China stated that all local councils and the legislature would 'definitely be terminated' after 1 July 1997.[53] This pledge was strengthened in late August when the National People's Congress passed a regulation to abolish Hong Kong's political structure when it takes sovereignty.[54] The legislative 'through train' was derailed. In conjunction with the demise of the 1995 legislature, Beijing announced that it would appoint its own 'Civil Legislative Committee' *before* 30 June 1997.[55] In December it was announced that a 'provisional legislature' may be established for one year or more after the transfer. Its membership would be 'elected' by an appointed 'recommendation committee'.[56]

There are many questions still to be answered about the future legislative format. What kind of law-making authority will replace the Legislative Council? What electoral rules will govern the selection of its membership? And how soon will elections be held?[57] The job of drafting a new electoral law will be left to the Preparatory Committee, a Beijing-appointed structure which will not be instituted until 1996. There is some speculation that the committee itself may serve as an interim legislature.[58] A precursor of this committee is the Preliminary Working Committee[59] which, if it proves to be a model, portends a radically different legislature than that elected in 1995. Delegates on the committee currently favour proportional representation and keeping the size of the functional constituencies small.[60]

Rather than dissolve the entire legislature in 1997, China may take the more rational course of abolishing only those legislative seats it considers invalid—namely the nineteen seats elected either through the Election Committee or the wider-based functional constituencies. If China holds new elections for these seats but retains the other forty-one members of the legislature—elected for a four-year term in 1995 by a previously sanctioned method—it would do much to promote stability, and guarantee legitimacy of the post-1997 body.

Summary: The Voice of Hong Kong

If any conclusion can be reached in assessing the dramatic evolution of Hong Kong's legislature—particularly as it has developed through this past legislative session—it is that Hong Kong legislators have at last found their voice. While the voice of the legislature is hardly united—fractures remain along conservative and liberal lines—their views are still discernible. What remains unclear, however, is whether or not they will have the chance to be heard in the future.

In the ten years since the Sino-British Declaration, the people of Hong Kong remain apprehensive about their future.[61] Promises of autonomy are still as elusive as ever. Fears continue unabated that the 'rule of men' rather than the 'rule of law' will prevail in post-1997 Hong Kong.[62] These fears are not without justification. By its recent actions, China demonstrated a disregard for the letter and spirit of the Joint Declaration as well as of the Basic Law. Yet China needs to be aware that silencing the voices of Hong Kong's legitimate representatives can only be self-defeating—in terms of the stability of the territory, and, consequently, its utility to China. To paraphrase the late U.S. Supreme Court Justice, Hugo Black: the freedom to speak about public questions is as important to the life of government as is the heart to the human body. If that heart is weakened, the result is debilitation; if it is stilled, the result is death. The future of Hong Kong, under its own unique brand of democracy, holds much promise. But this promise will only be fulfilled with a Chinese guarantee of autonomy and respect for the rule of law, as realized by a truly representative legislature.

Kathleen Cheek-Milby
December 1994
Tokyo, Japan

APPENDIX

Appendix: Research Design

Methodology

Roles are the basic analytical units of all political, including legislative, systems.[1] Political roles consist of a pattern of expected behaviour for individuals holding particular positions in a system. *Role*, for any individual legislator, refers to a coherent set of 'norms' of behaviour which apply to all persons who occupy the position of legislator.[2] The concept postulates that individual legislators are aware of the norms constituting the role and consciously adapt their behaviour to them in some fashion. Assumptions of this research, taken from general role theory, are that the office of legislator is a clearly recognizable position, that legislators associate certain norms of behaviour with that position, and that a significant portion of the behaviour of legislators is role behaviour consistent with legislators' role concepts.

The role concept links personality to social structure, and role expectations form the normative structure for system behaviour. In a legislative system, role expectations contain the rules that regulate members' political behaviour, which involve policy making, representation, and system maintenance. A system's *institutionalization* can be assessed by the degree of acceptance and commitment the members have toward a set of norms guiding their behaviour. Institutionalization connotes the gaining of organizational autonomy, internal specialization which takes shape in greater complexity, and the evolution of standardized procedures and universalistic criteria for ordering affairs. Consensus of role expectations among members of a system determines the level of institutionalization; the greater the conformity of norms, the greater the institutionalization, and hence stability, of the system.[3]

Since the 1962 publication of *The Legislative System*, a study of four US state legislatures, much of the research on legislatures has employed roles and role orientations as the principal method of investigation.[4] The 1962 study defined a number of role sectors (purposive, representational, areal, and partisan) and specific role orientations (ritualist, tribune, broker, inventor, and opportunist with respect to purposive roles; trustee, politico, and delegate with respect to representational roles). By using role as the organizing concept, the study integrated behavioural and institutional findings and defined the boundaries of the legislative system. In the years since its publication, studies of legislative roles have proliferated in the US and internationally. Role analysis has been found to be a useful concept not only to differentiate members of a legislature, but also for comparing legislatures cross-nationally. Two foci of this research have evolved: the delineation of role orientations and role patterns in different legislative systems, and the development and maintenance of role orientations of legislators. One of the best ways of understanding how the functions of legislatures differ is to study the priorities that their members give to various aspects of their job. Moreover, one way to forecast the current effectiveness, as well as future stability, of a legislature is to measure the degree of role consensus held by its members.

Research Design

The fundamental working hypothesis of this study is that a significant proportion of legislators' behaviour is role behaviour, that this behaviour is substantially congruent with their role concepts, and consequently that insight into the working of the Legislative Council can be gained by studying the role concepts of its members. The decision to approach the problem of legislators' role concepts by using data obtained from interviews is justified by the theoretical assumptions underlying role theory. It will be the task of Hong Kong's legislators to create and institutionalize a set of roles containing the rules of politics which will accommodate the demands and pressures on the system as the polity evolves. The enormous difficulties of observing overt behaviour in real life, as well as collecting behavioural data in a legislative context where voting on legislation, the prime mode of behaviour in other settings, was, until recently, frequently unanimous, and where access to other forms of behaviour within a committee setting was unobtainable due to 'closed door' committee work and restricted access to records of that work—all of these limitations pointed to the utility of the interview method in Hong Kong. Consequently, the primary purpose of this research was not to secure data about overt behaviour, but rather to secure data about legislators' perceptions so that we could inferentially construct portions of their cognitive and evaluative map.

A basic premise underlying most of the political debate since the signing of the Joint Declaration on the Future of Hong Kong has been the assumption that how the individual members of Council are selected will affect the type of legislator they are, essentially how they will behave as legislators. Legislative composition was the subject of two White Papers as well as the key issue during the drafting of the Basic Law. More recently, it has been the focus of the most severe dispute between Britain and China since the Joint Declaration, with divisive views as to what is the best compositional format for the future legislature. Implicit in this debate has been the assumption that how the individual is chosen for the legislature determines the type of legislator he will become: his conception of his legislative responsibilities, his view of the function of the legislature—in essence, his role concepts. The aim of this research, therefore, was to build upon this assumption by investigating the current membership of the legislature to examine what, if any, difference it makes in terms of role conceptions. Ultimately, it is assumed that these beliefs will guide subsequent legislative behaviour. These orientations are determined by personal interviews with members of the legislature. To clarify distinctions between as well as among the various types of legislators (appointed, electoral college, functional constituency, and official and directly elected), role analysis has been employed.

The Interview Schedule

Acting upon these assumptions, interviews took place with members of the Legislative Council from May 1987 through June 1988, and from May 1992 through February 1993. The two time periods allow analysis of trends within as well as between different types of members. Of the 57 Council members in 1988, 9 of the 10 official members, 20 of the 22 appointed members, 10 of the 12 electoral college members, and all 12 of the functional constituency members were questioned. In total, 52 of the 57 members were interviewed. During the 1992–3 interviews, 52 members were again consulted, including 17 of the 18 appointed members, 16 of the 18 directly elected members, 18 of 21 functional constituency members, and 1 of the 4 officials. The schedule of questions was a formidable one, requiring an average of one hour to complete, though the interview times actually ranged from 35 minutes to $4\frac{1}{2}$ hours. A total of 89 questions were asked, which encompassed 167 variables. However, since not all members answered each question, there will be variations in totals and percentages provided by the tables in the chapters of this book. More than 50 per cent of the questions were replicated from a comparative survey of legislators in Kenya, Korea, and Turkey.[5]

The interview opened with a series of questions that explored the perceptions of the member in terms of his legislative behaviour and role, the distinctions of his work from that of the Governor, members of the civil service, and District Board members. The respondent was asked what he devoted most of his time to as a legislator, and then was queried if he thought he should spend more or less time on several activities. Representational focus was then probed by asking about the types of individuals the respondent believes he represents, hears from, and meets with. In a series of forced choice questions, the legislator was asked if he had to make a choice between the views of the multiple groups (including his own personal convictions) which he would choose. After several questions dealing with past issues faced by the Legislative Council and the individual's role in resolving them, the focus of the interview switched from personal perceptions to general perceptions about the role of the legislature. In particular, 12 questions were devoted to measuring the individual's perception of the effectiveness of the Legislative Council since 1985. Finally, the respondents were asked to answer 24 agree/disagree questions designed for the construction of various measures and scales.

Notes

Notes to the Preface

1 A slightly different perspective on this phenomenon has been suggested by Evan Luard who argues that the globalization of politics means that the welfare of individuals no longer depends on their own governments but on international bodies taking action collectively. See Evan Luard, *The Globalization of Politics: The Changed Focus of Political Action in the Modern World* (New York: New York University Press, 1990).

2 See Joseph S. Nye Jr., 'What New World Order?' *Foreign Affairs*, Vol. 71, No. 2 (Spring 1992), pp. 83–96.

3 In a recent report Freedom House notes that 61 countries can now be called democratic, including 39 per cent of the world's people, a higher percentage than ever before. Moreover the proportion living in free countries has crept upwards in recent years, and the share of the world's population living in advanced Western countries has declined, denoting that democracy is spreading in non-Western nations. See Joshua Muravchik, *Exporting Democracy* (Washington, DC: The AEI Press, 1992), p. 68.

4 For an analysis of the basis of democratization, see Dankward A. Rustow, 'Democracy: A Global Revolution?' *Foreign Affairs*, Vol. 69, No. 4 (Fall 1990), pp. 75-91. See also John Lewis Gaddis, 'Toward the Post-Cold War World,' *Foreign Affairs*, Vol. 70, No. 2 (Spring 1991), pp. 102–22. Gaddis argues that the rivalry between democracy and totalitarianism has been replaced by a contest between the forces of integration and fragmentation, with the end of the Cold War bringing not an end to threats but rather a diffusion of them.

5 For more causes of the democratic revolution, see Larry Diamond, ed., *The Democratic Revolution* (New York: Freedom House, 1992), pp. 22–4.

6 See Rustow, "Democracy: A Global Revolution?", p. 90.

7 See Muravchik, *Exporting Democracy*, p. 78.

8 This was postulated by Francis Fukuyama, in 'The End of History', *The National Interest*, Summer 1989, pp. 3-18. The author argued that the death of communism meant the definitive triumph of Western liberalism, the end of ideology, and the coming of a rather boring era of material concerns and unheroic squabbles.

9 There are other exceptions, for instance North Korea, Burma, and, more significantly, parts of the Arab world where Islam rather than democracy has gained adherents. China and Hong Kong, however, are the most significant because they exhibit unique patterns of development and present such contrasts, particularly with respect to political values. Hence their integration presents one of the most unique political experiments at the end of the twentieth century.

Notes to Chapter 1

1 Known formally as the Joint Declaration of the British and Chinese Governments on the Future of Hong Kong.

2 Article 31 of the Chinese Constitution of 1982 provides for the establishment of special administrative regions, stipulating that 'the state may establish special administrative regions when necessary. The systems to be instituted in special administrative regions shall be prescribed by laws enacted by the National People's Congress in the light of specific conditions'.

3 Jean Bodin analysed the idea of sovereignty, which he determined related to a person or group which possessed supreme legislative power, someone who can change existing law. See Carl J. Friedrich, *Constitutional Government and Democracy* (Boston: Ginn and Company, 1950).

4 These two phrases were frequently used during the drafting of the 1984 agreement. The first relates to having a locally based government. The latter implies that Hong Kong could have a Western-style democracy within a socialist superstructure.

5 The Chief Executive is first to be selected by 'election or through consultations held locally' and then appointed by the Central People's Government of the People's Republic of China. The appointment or removal of 'principal judges' will be made by the Chief Executive with the endorsement of the Hong Kong special administrative region legislature and reported to the Standing Committee of the National People's Congress for the record.

6 By 1984 all other Crown Colonies had a fully elected legislative council except Hong Kong. Most had moved from partially to wholly elected legislatures in the period between 1945 and 1960.

7 Until 1964, official members were greater in number than unofficials. From 1964 to 1976, they were of equal number, yet the Governor had both an original and casting vote in case of a tie. While from 1976 to 1984 the Royal Instructions allowed the number of officials and unofficials to be equal, the Governor allowed for some official seats to be vacant giving the unofficials a *de facto* majority.

8 The government established a myriad of advisory bodies including not only the Executive and Legislative Councils, partially comprised of community leaders, but also the Urban and Regional councils, District Boards, and a series of advisory committees attached to governmental departments and quasi-governmental bodies. In 1992 for instance, over 5,500 citizens were appointed to serve on a total of 351 boards and committees.

9 Harvey Stockwin, 'Two years on at the Sovereignty Arms', *The South China Morning Post*, 26 September 1986.

10 *1984 White Paper on Representative Government, 1988 White Paper on Further Representative Government* (Hong Kong: Government Printer, 1984, 1988).

11 The Basic Law Drafting Committee was officially established on 18 June 1985 in Beijing. It was composed of 58 members, all selected by the People's Republic of China, with 23 members from Hong Kong and the remainder from China. The final version of the Basic Law was promulgated in April 1990.

12 The 1988 reform provided for the creation of 10 directly elected seats. This was changed to 18 seats in 1990 after the promulgation of the Basic Law.

13 The election committee was to be one of the main issues of the dispute between Hong Kong's Governor Chris Patten and China during 1993. While the Basic Law did not specify the how this committee was to be constituted, the Chinese government assumed that it would parallel the election committee for the Chief Executive, which consists of 800 people from various sectors as well as past and present political leaders. Patten suggested that the election committee for the 10 seats of the legislature consist of all elected members of the district boards, a suggestion that China vehemently resisted, labelling such a move as a violation of

the Basic Law. For further review of this dispute, see Chapter 4.

14 Article 68 of the Basic Law notes that 'the ultimate aim is the election of all members of the Legislative Council by universal suffrage'.

15 Those members of the Legislative Council serving terms from 1985–8 and 1991–5 have been examined.

16 J. Blondel, *Comparative Legislatures* (Englewood Cliffs, NJ: Prentice-Hall, Inc., 1973), p. 2.

17 At the outset, Parliament was regarded as a high court finding and applying traditional law on a case-by-case basis. The first commoner members of Parliament came to bring up local cases of legal dispute, and eventually carried back the King's proclamations to their community, as well as ratifying the imposition of taxes by the King. This function, however, was seen as a matter of political and administrative convenience, rather than a legislative right. See for instance Hanna Fenichel Pitkin, ed., *Representation* (Berkeley: The University of California Press, 1969), p. 3. One of the best treatments of the history of Parliament is by A. F. Pollard, *The Evolution of Parliament* (London: Longmans, Green, 1926).

18 Gerhard Loewenberg, 'The Role of Parliaments in Modern Political Systems', in Gerhard Loewenberg (ed.), *Modern Parliaments: Change or Decline?* (New York: Aldine and Atherly, Inc., 1971), p. 5.

19 For a fuller explanation, see Pollard, *The Evolution of Parliament*, chap. 9.

20 John Locke, *Second Treatise on Civil Government*, C.B. Macpherson, ed. (Indianapolis, IN: Hackett Publishing Co., 1980), chap. 13, para. 149.

21 Locke, *Second Treatise*, para. 150.

22 Baron Montesquieu, *Spirit of Laws*, Thomas Nugent, L.L.D., translator, London: George Bell and Sons, 1878, Book XI, Chap. 6.

23 James Bryce, *The American Commonwealth* (London: MacMillan & Co., Ltd., 1888), p. 193.

24 A. B. Lowell, *Government and Parties in Continental Europe* (Cambridge, MA: Harvard University Press, 1986).

25 Blondel, *Comparative Legislatures*, p. 6.

26 A good analysis of communist legislatures can be found in *Legislative Studies Quarterly*, 5, 2 (May 1980). The entire volume is devoted to communist legislatures and communist politics.

27 *Comparative Legislatures,* p. 6.

28 C. Hollis, *Can Parliament Survive?* (London: Hollis and Carter, 1949); Gerhard Loewenberg (ed.), *Modern Parliaments, Change or Decline* (Chicago: Aldine-Atherton, 1971).

29 See, for instance Abdo I. Baaklini, *Legislative and Political Development: Lebanon 1842–1972* (Durham, NC: Duke University Press, 1976), p. 11.

30 *Comparative Legislatures,* p. 126.

31 G. R. Boynton and Chong Lim Kim, eds., *Legislative Systems in Developing Countries* (Durham, NC: Duke University Press, 1975), p. 17.

32 Michael Mezey, *Comparative Legislatures* (Durham, NC: Duke University Press, 1979), p. 25.

33 Mezey, *Comparative Legislatures*, p. 8.

34 Legislatures have delegated their authority to the bureaucracy as the issues have become more numerous, pressing, and technically complex. This thesis is best expounded by Theodore J. Lowi, *The End of Liberalism* (New York: Norton, 1979).

35 Although Walter Bagehot enumerated the expressive, teaching, and informing function of parliament much earlier. See Walter Bagehot, *The English Constitution* (Ithaca, NY: Cornell University Press, 1966), chap. 4.

36 Robert B. Stauffer, 'Philippine Legislators and Their Changing Universe', *Journal of Politics*, 28 (1966): 556–91; Ann T. Schulz, 'A Cross-National Examination of Legislators', *The Journal of Developing Areas,* 7 (1973): 571–90; and Donald

R. Matthews, 'Legislative Recruitment and Legislative Careers', in Gerhard Loewenberg, Samuel C. Patterson, and Malcolm E. Jewell (eds.), *Handbook of Legislative Research* (Cambridge, MA: Harvard University Press, 1985), pp. 17–55.

37 Stauffer, 'Philippine Legislatures'; Abdo I. Baakalini, *Legislative and Political Development: Lebanon 1842–1972* (Durham, NC: Duke University Press, 1976); Richard Sisson and Lawrence L. Shrader, 'Social Representation and Political Integration in an Indian State: The Legislative Dimension,' in Albert Eldridge (ed.), *Legislatures in Plural Societies* (Durham, NC: Duke University Press, 1977).

38 J. Grossholtz, 'Integrative Factors in the Malaysian and Philippines Legislatures', paper prepared for delivery at the 65th Annual Meeting of the American Political Science Association, New York, Sept. 1969; Abdo I. Baakalini, *Legislative and Political Development*, 294, 296; Richard Sisson,'Comparative Legislative Institutionalization: A Theoretical Exploration', in Allan Kornberg (ed.), *Legislatures in Comparative Perspective* (New York: David McKay, 1973).

39 Joel D. Barkan, 'Legislators, Elections and Political Linkage', in Joel D. Barkan and John J. Okumu (eds.), *Politics and Public Policy in Kenya and Tanzania* (New York: Praeger, 1979); Raymond Hopkins, 'The Influence of the Legislature on Development Strategy: The Case of Kenya and Tanzania', in Lloyd Musolf and Joel Smith (eds.), *Legislatures in Development* (Durham, NC: Duke University Press, 1979).

40 Robert A. Packenham, 'Legislatures and Political Development', in Allan Kornberg and Lloyd D. Musolf (eds.), *Legislatures in Developmental Perspective* (Durham, NC: Duke University Press, 1970); Jay E. Hakes, *Weak Parliaments and Military Coups in Africa: A Study in Regime Instability* (Beverly Hills, CA: Sage Publications, 1973).

41 For fuller discussion, see Mezey, *Comparative Legislatures*, pp. 9–11.

42 R.B. Stauffer, 'Congress in the Philippine Political System', in Kornberg and Musolf (eds.), *Legislatures in Developmental Perspective,* p. 355.

43 Discussed in Mezey, *Comparative Legislatures,* p. 10; quote from Jean Grossholtz, 'Integrative Factors', p. 94.

44 Thomas Hobbes, *English Works*, ed. Sir William Molesworth (London: Longmans, Brown, Green and Longmans, 1839–45), Vol. III, p. 148.

45 Pitkin, *Representation,* p. 5.

46 As quoted in Carl J. Freidrich, *Constitutional Government and Democracy* (Boston, MA: Ginn and Company, 1950), p. 325.

47 A.B. Lowell, 'The Influence of Party Upon Legislation in England and America', *American Historical Society Annual Report*, 1901; Stuart Rice, *Quantitative Methods in Politics* (New York: Alfred A. Knopf, 1928); Julius Turner, *Party and Constituency* (Baltimore, MD: Johns Hopkins University Press, 1951); David B. Truman, *The Congressional Party: A Case Study* (New York: John Wiley and Sons, Inc., 1959); Lewis A. Forman, Jr., *Congressmen and their Constituencies* (Chicago: Rand McNally & Co., 1963).

48 These assumptions were employed in the seminal work regarding legislative roles: John C. Wahlke, Heinz Eulau, William Buchanan, and LeRoy C. Ferguson, *The Legislative System: Explorations in Legislative Behavior* (New York: John Wiley and Sons, Inc., 1962), p. 29ff.

49 Malcolm E. Jewell, 'Representative Process', in Gerhard Loewenberg, Samuel C. Patterson, and Malcolm E. Jewell (eds.), *Handbook of Legislative Research* (Cambridge, MA: Harvard University Press, 1985), p. 110.

50 Institutionalization connotes the gaining of organizational autonomy, internal specialization which takes shape in greater complexity, and the evolution of standardized procedures and universalistic criteria for ordering affairs. For further discussion of institutionalization and stability, see Samuel P. Huntington, *Political Order in Changing Societies* (New Haven: Yale University Press, 1968).

Notes to Chapter 2

1 Martin Wight, *The Development of the Legislative Council* (London: Faber and Faber, Ltd., 1946), p. 7.

2 See Lionel H. Laing, 'The Transplantation of the British Parliament', *Parliamentary Affairs*, 11 (1957–8): 405.

3 T. O. Elias, *British Colonial Law* (London: Stevens and Sons, Ltd., 1962), p. 49.

4 The colonies examined include the transatlantic colonies which were settled from the seventeenth century.

5 F. J. C. Hearnshaw, *Democracy and the British Empire* (London: Constable and Company Ltd., 1920), chap. 2.

6 A. Berriedale Keith, *The Constitution, Administration and Laws of the Empire* (London: W. Collins & Sons Co., Ltd., 1924), p. 267.

7 Charter of Virginia, 10 April 1606, cap. xv.

8 For an excellent background of these early colonial distinctions, see Sir David Lindsay Keir, *The Constitutional History of Modern Britain since 1485*, 9th edn. (London: Adam & Charles Black, 1969).

9 Instructions of 20 November 1606, Charter of Virginia of 1606, cap. vii, as quoted in Wight, *The Development of the Legislative Council*, p. 26.

10 Keir, The *Constitutional History*, p. 347.

11 During this period the Privy Council acted as an advisory council for the King. It served multiple functions, administratively connecting the government departments and directing their work, and as an instrument of legislation and taxation. It was the 'regular engine for the conduct of normal business'. See Sir David Lindsay Keir, *The Constitutional History of Modern Britain since 1485* (London: Adam and Black, 1969), p. 113.

12 Wight, *The Development of the Legislative Council*, p. 24.

13 Wight, *The Development of the Legislative Council*, p. 30.

14 *The Cambridge History of the British Empire* (Cambridge: Cambridge University Press, 1940), Vol. II, p. 146.

15 Wight, *The Development of the Legislative Council*, p. 26.

16 A. F. Madden, ' "Not for Export": The Westminster Model of Government and British Colonial Practice', *The Journal of Imperial and Commonwealth History*, 8, 1 (October 1979): 13.

17 This theme is skillfully developed by Jack P. Greene, *The Quest for Power* (New York: W. W. Norton and Company, 1963).

18 Included in this classification was Jamaica, captured from Spain in 1655, New York, captured from Holland in 1664, Gibraltar, taken from Spain in 1704, Minorca, also taken from Spain in 1708, and Nova Scotia, taken from France in 1710.

19 For additional background information on the rights of inhabitants of settled colonies, see D. L. Keir and F. H. Lawson, *Cases in Constitutional Law*, 4th edn. (Oxford: Clarendon Press, 1954), pp. 469ff.

20 Typically, existing laws and institutions were maintained until the Crown provided a change. These newly annexed territories were subjected to royal control yet 'extreme diversity marked their constitutional character'. See Keir, *The Constitutional History*, p. 351. In Canada, with its large French population, the Quebec Act of 1774 established a governor and nominated council with power to legislate but no power to tax. The constitutional difference between these two varieties of colonies was emphasized in the decision of *Campbell v. Hall*, which held that where the Crown had established a representative legislature it could not fall back on its prerogative power to tax.

21 Keir, *The Constitutional History*, p. 322.

22 Wight, *The Development of the Legislative Council*, p. 353.

23 Wight, *The Development of the Legislative Council*, p. 355.

24 L. W. Labaree, *Royal Government in America*, pp. 247–54.

25 These devices included appointing commissioners to carry out legislative statutes, legislating with respect to the qualifications for officers, and utilizing the legislative power of the purse to exert their will. See for instance Keir, *The Constitutional History*, p. 355.

26 Madden, 'Not for Export', p. 16.

27 Keir, *The Constitutional History*, p. 356.

28 Keir, *The Constitutional History*, p. 357.

29 Greene, *The Quest for Power*, p. 453.

30 Amplification of these phases can be found in Greene, *The Quest for Power*.

31 One of the best treatments of the constitutional battle is Charles Howard McIlwain, *The American Revolution: A Constitutional Interpretation* (Ithaca, NY: Cornell University Press, 1968), originally published by Macmillan Company, 1923. A British refutation of this theory is given by Robert Livingston Schuyler, *Parliament and the British Empire* (New York: Columbia University Press, 1929), esp. chap. 1.

32 Schuyler, *Parliament and the British Empire*, p. v.

33 From Galliard Hung (ed.), *Writings of James Madison*, Vol. VI, p. 373; as quoted in Schuyler, *Parliament and the British Empire*, p. 196.

34 For a comprehensive explanation, see Frederick Madden and David Fieldhouse (eds.), *The Classical Period of the British Empire* (Westport, CT: Greenwood Press, 1985), pp. 549–50.

35 For amplification of the anti-taxation sentiments, see Madden and Fieldhouse, *The Classical Period*, pp. 564–91.

36 Wight, *The Development of the Legislative Council*, p. 40.

37 Keir, *The Constitutional History*, p. 442.

38 Madden, 'Not for Export', p. 18.

39 This review does not cover the rise of the dominions, but rather emphasizes the evolution of the dependent colonies under the Crown Colony system.

40 Most settled colonies graduated to dominion status. The demarcation from old to dominion status is seen in the Durham Report, which introduced the concept of responsible government in which cabinet members were selected from popularly elected members of the legislature. See Sir C. P. Lucas (ed.), *Lord Durham's Report on the Affairs of British North America*, 3 vols. (Oxford: Clarendon Press, 1913), especially Vol. 2, pp. 279–80. The Quebec Act is as important in the history of the non-self-governing empire as the Durham Report is in the history of the dominions because it became the chief model for the Crown Colony system. The act concentrated power in the governor, with legislative power vested in a nominated council, operating under the consent of the governor.

41 Paraphrased from Wight, *The Development of the Legislative Council*, p. 47.

42 See Martin Wight, *British Colonial Constitutions*, pp. 40–67, and T. O. Elias, *British Colonial Law* (London: Stevens and Sons, Ltd., 1962), p. 49.

43 Fred D. Schneider, 'The Study of Parliamentary Government in the Commonwealth,' *Parliamentary Affairs*, 4 (1960–1): 467.

44 Schneider, 'The Study of Parliamentary Government in the Commonwealth'.

45 Wight, *The Development of the Legislative Council*, p. 144.

46 Colonial Regulation 105, as cited in Wight, *The Development of the Legislative Council*, p. 145.

47 Lord Bryce, *The American Commonwealth* (New York, Macmillan: 1914), p. 39.

48 Wight, *The Development of the Legislative Council*, p. 144.

49 The Ceylon Interpretation Ordinance, No. 21 (1901); also found in *Legislative Enactments of Ceylon*, 1938, i, II.

50 Until revision of Colonial Regulations in 1934, the normal term of a governor was six years.

51 Keith, *The Constitution of the Empire*, p. 208.

52 Actual command of the regular forces of the colony is usually given to a military officer.

53 Except private bills.

54 In addition, there is a whole class of bills which a governor shall not assent to unless given approval by the Secretary of State, including bills for divorce, grants of land or money to himself, currency, differential duties, and so on.

55 An Order in Council is issued only by the Queen. The governor-in-council may, however, issue subsidiary legislation (regulations, rules, notices, orders) provided that they are authorized by the appropriate ordinance.

56 Keith, *The Constitution of the Empire*, p. 273.

57 Except in those cases where he believes the consultation would prejudice the results, or in cases too unimportant to require the council's advice, or by contrast, in those cases where urgency is imperative. In the latter type of exception, the governor must communicate to the council the actions he has taken and the rationale underlying his activities.

58 Keith, *The Constitution of the Empire,* p. 271.

59 Wight, *The Development of the Legislative Council,* p. 127.

60 *The Nyasaland Royal Commission Report* (Rhodesia, 1939), CMD. 5949, para. 446.

61 Duke of Buckingham, as quoted in *The Nyasaland Royal Commission Report*, p. 101, from a Circular dispatch of 17 August 1868.

62 Richard Sisson and Leo M. Snowiss, 'Legislative Viability and Political Development', in Joel Smith and Lloyd D. Musolf (eds.), *Legislatures in Development* (Durham, NC: Duke University Press, 1979), p. 51.

63 Sisson and Snowiss, 'Legislative Viability', p. 8.

64 Further, there is usually little or no change in what is presented as those who propose estimates (officials) are in the majority.

65 The governor is also directed to reserve special types of bills for Her Majesty's pleasure. See K. Roberts-Wray, *Colonial and Commonwealth Law* (London: Stevens and Sons, 1966), pp. 225–6.

66 Certification, called the Governor's Reserve Power, is normally inserted into the Letters Patent when the Legislative Council obtains an unofficial majority for the first time and the governor can no longer be certain of passing any legislation he wishes by the votes of the officials. See fuller explanation in Wight, *The Development of the Legislative Council,* p. 105.

67 Wight, *The Development of the Legislative Council,* p. 229. Alternative means of control and improved methods of communication between governors and the Secretary of State have reduced disallowance to rare occasions.

68 Keith, *The Constitution of the Empire,* p. 27.

69 Colonial laws shall be void only when repugnant to any act of Parliament relating to the colony, not when it is held that the colonial law is repugnant to English law in general. Parliament typically limits its legislative authority over colonies to one of three instances: where legislation is beyond the power of the local legislature; where the subject is one of concern to more than one country and uniformity is desired; and where the subject is an important one to the United Kingdom, e.g. related to defence, treaties, and nationalities.

70 Repugnancy was clarified in the Colonial Laws Validity Act of 1865, which designated those laws which were to be made by the British Parliament and those which were to be made by the local colonial legislature. This act provided that any colonial enactment contrary to an act of the British Parliament extending to the colony is void. The act also clarified that if a colonial legislature was a *representative*

legislature it shall have full power to make laws respecting the constitutions, powers, and procedure of the legislature. This provision was later to provoke fears from mainland China that the Legislative Council would be able to write the territory's constitution once a majority of its members were elected. For background regarding the law, see T. O. Elias, *British Colonial Law,* p. 51.

71 Keith, *The Constitution of the Empire,* p. 18. This limitation effectively hampered the creation of colonial navies and can be seen as the dividing line between a colony and a dominion.

72 Though it may alter its constitution. Quote from Keith, *The Constitution of the Empire,* p. 21.

73 Robert A. Packenham, 'Legislatures and Political Development', in Allan Kornberg and Lloyd D. Musolf (eds.), *Legislatures in Development Perspective* (Durham, NC: Duke University Press, 1970), pp. 527–8.

74 Wight, *The Development of the Legislative Council,* p. 70.

75 Barry Munslow, 'Why has the Westminster Model failed in Africa?', *Parliamentary Affairs,* 36, 2 (Spring 1983): 224.

76 B. Schaeffer, 'The Concept of Preparation', *World Politics* , 18 (October 1965): 53.

77 Raymond Hopkins, *Political Roles in a New State: Tanzania's First Decade* (New Haven: Yale University Press, 1971), p. 28.

78 Wight, *The Development of the Legislative Council,* pp. 116–17.

79 Hearnshaw, *Democracy and the British Empire,* p. 149.

80 Austin, 'History of the Gold Coast', p. 7.

81 Jean Grossholtz, 'Integrative Factors in the Malaysian and Philippine Legislatures', *Comparative Politics,* 3 (1970): 94.

82 For additional information on mobilization, see Michael Mezey, 'Third World Legislatures', in Gerhard Loewenberg, Samuel C. Patterson, and Malcolm E. Jewell (eds.), *Handbook of Legislative Research* (Cambridge, MA: Harvard University Press, 1985), pp. 733–72. Raymond Hopkins also found this was perceived as a major role to be performed by Tanzanian legislators. See Hopkins, 'The Role of the MP in Tanzania', *American Political Science Review,* 64 (1970): 754–71.

83 F. J. C. Hearnshaw, *Democracy and the British Empire* (London: Constable and Company Ltd., 1920), p. 105.

84 Dennis Austin, 'Institutional History of the Gold Coast-Ghana', in *What are the Problems of Parliamentary Government in Africa?* (London: Hansard Society, 1958), p. 7.

85 W. M. Macmillan, *Africa Emergent* (London: 1938), p. 354.

86 Wight, *The Development of the Legislative Council,* p. 109.

87 Officials are expected to vote with the government; should they be unable to do so, it is expected that they will resign their seat as well as their office in the government. This view was established by the Duke of Buckingham in a circular despatch in 1868. This position was further clarified and amended in 1882 in an additional despatch by Lord Kimberley that determined that it was a well-understood principle that officials should vote together on all questions on which the government's policy was decided, unless they were expressly granted freedom to vote according to their personal views. However, in 1930 the question of official voting was again reconsidered and it was determined that the governor could provide whatever latitude he saw fit depending on the particular situation. See Wight, *The Development of the Legislative Council,* pp. 109–12.

88 Wight, *The Development of the Legislative Council,* p. 112.

89 Alan Burns, 'The History of Commonwealth Parliaments', in Alan Burns (ed.), *Parliament as an Export* (London: Allen and Unwin, Ltd., 1966), p. 19.

90 Wight, *The Development of the Legislative Council,* p. 113.

91 Quote from the Duke of Buckingham's circular despatch of 1868 as quoted in Wight, *The Development of the Legislative Council*, p. 112.

92 Wight, *The Development of the Legislative Council*, p. 113.

93 Wight, *The Development of the Legislative Council*, p. 113.

94 As quoted in Schaeffer, *Concept of Preparation*, p. 51. For additional information about changes in the Gold Coast, see Martin Wight, *The Gold Coast Legislative Council* (London: Faber and Faber, 1947).

95 A. F. Pollard, *Evolution of Parliament* (London: Longmans, Green & Company, 1920), p. 3.

96 Munslow, '*Why has the Westminster Model Failed*', p. 224.

97 Abdo I. Baaklini, 'Legislatures in New Nations: Towards a New Perspective', *Polity*, 8, 4 (Summer 1976): 572.

98 Wight, *The Development of the Legislative Council*, p. 98.

99 N. J. Miners, *The Government and Politics of Hong Kong*, 3rd edn. (Hong Kong: Oxford University Press, 1981), p. 3. See also Hilary Blood, 'Parliaments in Small Territories', in Burns, *Parliament as an Export*, pp. 247–62. Burns notes that Hong Kong is a remarkable exception to the general rule of British colonial constitutional development.

100 Miners, *The Government and Politics of Hong Kong*, p. 3.

Notes to Chapter 3

1 See Peter Wesley-Smith, 'Legislative Competence', *Hong Kong Law Review*, 2, 1 (1981): 3–31.

2 For an excellent understanding of the early history of Hong Kong, see G. B. Endacott, *A History of Hong Kong*, 3rd edn. (Hong Kong: Oxford University Press, 1964). Endacott makes a convincing argument that all Hong Kong history is economic history and, further, that its history has been most influenced by events outside as well as beyond its control.

3 British trade with China had previously been centred in Canton where the British were confined to the factory area and allowed to remain only for the trading season after which they were made to return with their families to the nearby Portuguese colony of Macau. The traders were distressed by the arbitrariness of shipping dues and continued to trade in opium, even after the Chinese government made such trade illegal. These restrictions, which they found to be 'vexing and humiliating' resulted in hostilities between the British and Chinese governments which eventually led to the Convention of Chuanbi, of 20 January 1841, which ceded Hong Kong Island to the British. This was formally recognized by both governments in the Treaty of Nanking, which provided for compensation to British traders for opium destroyed in the Co-Hongs as well as cession in perpetuity of the island of Hong Kong. See G. B. Endacott, *Government and People of Hong Kong* (Hong Kong: Hong Kong University Press, 1964), chap. 1, as well as Endacott, *A History of Hong Kong*, especially p. 14, which lists the seven underlying causes of the Opium War.

4 Endacott, *History of Hong Kong*, p. 22. Another historian simply stated that Hong Kong was needed 'to secure a land base from which [British traders] could conduct their business of purveying to China the illegal import opium.' See Nigel Cameron, *An Illustrated History of Hong Kong* (Hong Kong: Oxford University Press, 1991), p. 4.

5 British Secretary of State for War and the Colonies, 1841–5.

6 Endacott, *Government and People*, p. 20.

7 Norman Miners, *The Government and Politics of Hong Kong*, 3rd edn. (Hong Kong: Oxford University Press, 1981), p. 66.

8 Sir Henry Pottinger, who served as Governor until 1844. Pottinger legislated so much on his own authority that he was referred to as 'Sir Henry Notification.' See J. W. Norton Kyshe, *The History of the Laws and Courts of Hong Kong* (Hong Kong: 1898). He was also seen as a better plenipotentiary than governor, in that 'the deserved fame of the plenipotentiary has been seriously tarnished by the acts of the Governor.' See E. J. Eitel, *Europe in China* (London: 1895).

9 Letter of Lord Aberdeen to Sir Henry Pottinger, 4 January 1843, no. 16, CO 129/3.

10 Endacott, *Government and People*, p. 23.

11 Miners, *Government and Politics*, p. xv.

12 For additional discussion, see Endacott, *Government and People*, pp. 25–36.

13 Endacott, *Government and People*, p. 25.

14 Cameron, *History of Hong Kong*, p. 41.

15 Disallowance in this first instance came because an Act of Parliament already dealt with the subject. Disallowance typically occurred when the acts were *ultra vires* on the grounds of extra-territoriality, contrary to principles of English law or repugnant to an Act of Parliament. See N. J. Miners, 'Disallowance and the Administrative Review of Hong Kong Legislation by the Colonial Office, 1844–1947', *Hong Kong Law Review*, 18, 2: 218–48.

16 Pottinger complained to the British Secretary of State Lord Stanley that 'I have stood alone . . . [acting with] unassisted judgment.' Endacott concludes that 'he was alone in upholding the public interest in the infant colony. . . . ' See Endacott, *A History of Hong Kong*, p. 49.

17 Sir John Davis, Governor of Hong Kong, 1844–8.

18 Sir John Davis to Lord Stanley, 13 May 1844, No. 4, CO 129/6, as quoted in Endacott, *Government and People*, p. 52.

19 Endacott, *A History of Hong Kong*, p. 42.

20 The Governor proposed to tax imported wines and spirits in an attempt to make the Colony more financially self-sufficient. The members of the Legislative Council voiced their opposition to this measure as the tax would be contrary to the proclamation that Hong Kong was a free port. The Secretary of State, Gladstone, ruled that it was impossible to go against the unanimous wish of the Legislative Council. For additional discussion, see Endacott, *Government and People*, p. 42ff.

21 Governor of Hong Kong, 1848–54.

22 Sir John Davis attempted to raise revenue by creating monopolies and farms, levying rates on property for police and other local services. As a result, land values plummeted, and many landholders renounced their claims. The merchants then presented a memorial to the Secretary of State condemning as unconstitutional an ordinance to impose rates, and asked for some form of municipal self-government. In so doing, they were echoing the earlier American colonial demand of 'no taxation without representation.'

23 This sentiment ran contrary to efforts in Parliament to reduce imperial expenditure for Hong Kong, and as such proved to be impractical.

24 Endacott, *Government and People*, p. 44.

25 The delay can be attributed in part to a change in Governors as well as the fact that the new Governor, Sir George Bonham, was preoccupied with effecting retrenchment in the civil service.

26 The Justices of the Peace were local agents of government with administrative as well as purely judicial responsibilities. At that time they consisted of 16 members. Bonham had insisted upon this type of selection when he found he

was unable to make a choice for unofficial membership. The next Governor, Sir John Bowring, believed that the election by the justices was an established precedent. Eventually, this form of election was dropped in 1857 but revived again in 1884.

27 Sir James Stephen of the Colonial Office quoted in a communication by Sir John Davis to Lord Stanley, 20 August 1845, No. 114, CO 129/13.

28 Governor from 1854–9.

29 As quoted in Endacott, *Government and People*, p. 47.

30 The Blue Book was an annual report on the state of the Colony sent to the Colonial Office in London giving detailed statistics and information on all aspects of the Colony's administration. Bowring was propounding the constitutional doctrine that 'where a Crown Colony was financially self-supporting, it should be allowed free discretion in the allocation and control of its funds.' See Endacott, *Government and People*, p. 50. But he was a little hasty in proclaiming the financial independence of the Colony. While in 1855 Bowring announced that no imperial subvention would be needed, war against China in 1857 necessitated a request for Home Government financial assistance.

31 The electorate at that time totalled 69 British, 42 Chinese, and 30 other foreigners. As a matter of comparison, those paying police rates of 10 pound sterling or more totalled 1,999 of whom 1,637 were Chinese, 186 British, and 176 other foreigners. Endacott, *Government and People*, p. 51.

32 Endacott, *Government and People*, p. 50

33 Endacott, *Government and People*, pp. 51–2.

34 Endacott, *Government and People*, p. 52.

35 See Endacott, *Government and People*, p. 58.

36 Endacott, *Government and People*, p. 59.

37 Governor of Hong Kong, 1859–65.

38 In addition, nine Chinese ports were opened to foreign trade and British subjects were given permission to travel in China.

39 Governor of Hong Kong, 1866–72.

40 CO 381/35 as quoted in Endacott, *Government and People*, p. 82. These instructions reduced the power of the Governor, as he alone had been able to choose official and unofficial members, subject to the nominal assent of the Colonial Secretary. Now official membership was to occur by virtue of office rather than personality.

41 For the next 20 years, the four unofficial members consisted of one government official and three members of the community. This make-up continued a tradition established by Sir Hercules Robinson in December 1858 when he recommended that the proportion of officials to non-officials should be two to one, excluding the Governor.

42 Although occasionally Governors may excuse them from this requirement and allow them total discretion, such as occurred with respect to legislation to repeal an ordinance forbidding the sale of drinks at hotel bars except for ready cash (1923), a bill imposing rent control (1923), and legalization of abortion (1968). In addition, they have been instructed to abstain from voting in the face of unanimous opposition of Legislative Council unofficials. This has only been put into effect three times in recent years: in 1949, regarding opposition to an elected Municipal Council; in 1960, with respect to legalized gambling; and in 1984, regarding a taxi license fee increase.

43 Endacott suggests that the Chinese were acting upon the Governor's suggestion. See Endacott, *Government and People*, p. 93.

44 See Colonial Office minutes on Hennessy's dispatch to Sir Michael Hicks Beach, 20 January 1880, No. 9, CO 129/187. Summarized in Endacott, *Government and People*, p. 94.

45 His predecessor, Sir John Pope Hennessy, began the practice of giving British

nationality by private ordinance to local Chinese, however, stipulating that this nationality was valid only in the Colony.

46 Endacott, *Government and People*, p. 98.

47 At the time of his survey of the Legislative Council (May 1883), not one but two members of the Legislative Council were paid officials.

48 Endacott, *Government and People*, p. 100.

49 Secretary of State for the Colonies, 1882–5. Significantly, he negated the idea of excluding from appointment unofficials who were not paid government servants, concluding that the practice of nominating officials to unofficial seats was designated to select the best-qualified individual for membership in the Council.

50 Endacott, *Government and People*, p. 101.

51 The Registrar General was given the obligation to insure that Chinese customs and usages were respected. The Chinese also had alternative representation through the Directors of the Tung Wah, a Chinese organization established to care for the sick, aged, and homeless, and later occurred through the District Watchmen Committee, which superintended the operations of the District Watch Force, a body of constables paid for by the Chinese merchants. It is of interest that a Chinese unofficial on the legislature, Wei Yuk, proposed the formation of the District Watch Committee, which was instituted in 1893 with the Registrar General (Protector of Chinese) as chairman. This committee was composed of the 'elite of the Chinese community,' who used the committee as a forum for communication to the government regarding a variety of matters. See Norman Miners, *Hong Kong Under Imperial Rule 1912–1941* (Hong Kong: Oxford University Press, 1987), p. 54.

52 Co-optation of the Chinese eventually was even more effective through the creation of the District Watch Committee which 'provided the government with its principal means of exercising control and influence over the Chinese population by co-opting its natural leaders.' See Miners, *Hong Kong Under Imperial Rule*, p. 62.

53 Endacott notes that 'the Bowen reforms did not therefore impair the influence of the leading commercial houses and helped to continue the representation of property and commercial interests but not of the people or communities as such.' See *Government and People,* p. 104.

54 Actually established in 1872.

55 Bulkeley Johnson, quoted in the *Hong Kong Telegraph*, 15 March 1883, as quoted in Ian Scott, *Political Change and the Crisis of Legitimacy in Hong Kong* (Hong Kong: Oxford University Press, 1989), p. 58.

56 Sir Kai Ho Kai, qualified as a doctor and educated in England. Unlike his predecessor, Wong Shing, who was content to adopt a cooperative attitude, Dr. Ho Kai more closely identified himself with the 'minority opposition' of unofficials. See Endacott, *Government and People*, pp. 110–14.

57 Quoted in G. H. Choa, *The Life and Times of Sir Kai Ho Kai* (Hong Kong: The Chinese University Press, 1981), p. 112.

58 Sir George William Des Voeux, Governor of Hong Kong, 1887–91.

59 The Marquis of Ripon, Secretary of State for the Colonies. Quoted in Endacott, *Government and People,* p. 118.

60 Endacott, *Government and People,* p. 118.

61 Endacott, *Government and People*, p. 110. The Colonial Office noted that there were forms of representative government in Jamaica, Honduras, and Mauritius, providing a basis for the assumption that the negro was more capable of participating in representative institutions 'whereas it is common ground between us and Mr Whitehead that an ordinary Chinaman is not.' Endacott, *Government and People*, p. 120.

62 Europeans and Americans numbered 8500; only 4,200 of these were civilians, and of these only 1,450 were British, of whom only 800 were male adults, who alone were given the suffrage.

63 Endacott, *Government and People*, p. 121.

64 Endacott, *Government and People*, p. 135.

65 Peter Wesley-Smith, *Unequal Treaty 1898–1997* (Hong Kong: Oxford University Press, 1980), p. 29.

66 Wesley-Smith, *Unequal Treaty*, p. 44. The author earlier notes that 'to Great Britain it was primarily a matter of preserving her predominance in the Chinese market and framing a suitable policy to prevent, if possible, dismemberment of the Chinese empire.' See p. 22.

67 See views of Major MacDonald, the colonial negotiator in Wesley-Smith, *Unequal Treaty*, p. 41.

68 Sir Henry Blake, Governor of Hong Kong, 1898–1903.

69 No legal distinction was made between the leased territory and the original area of the Colony, and hence all laws and ordinances in effect were made applicable to the New Territories upon securement.

70 The Secretary for the New Territories was eventually to sit in the legislature. It was this individual rather than the unofficial members of the legislature who prior to 1985 performed the traditional legislative functions of representation and systems maintenance in the New Territories. See Miners, *Government and Politics*, p. 194. Additionally, the people of the New Territories were represented locally in the Heung Yee Kuk (Rural Consultative Committee) established in 1926. Eventually, in 1977, the New Territories achieved unofficial representation on the Legislative Council with the appointment of Mr Yeung Siu-cho, who was a member of the Heung Yee Kuk.

71 Particularly Sir Cecil Clementi, Governor of Hong Kong, 1925–30.

72 Wesley-Smith argues that treaties not concluded on the basis of mutual recognition of the equality and sovereignty of the contracting states, and which do not contain the crucial element of reciprocity of rights and obligations, are 'unequal'. Hence Chinese claims for the return of the New Territories from 1919 onwards could be given legitimacy as China clearly derived no benefit from the treaty, as there was not even a rent payment discussed. While classification of a treaty as unequal does not necessarily mean it is invalid under international law, eventually this classification was to weaken Britain's hand in future negotiations. See Wesley-Smith, *Unequal Treaty*, pp. 3, 184.

73 Pollock suggested that the electoral body for European unofficials consist of the Justices of the Peace and the Chamber of Commerce.

74 The petition was sent to A. Bonar Law (Colonial Secretary, 1914–16) and signed by 566 persons, all British except for approximately one dozen. The first 28 signatures were those of representatives of the most important shipping, commercial, and financial institutions in the Colony.

75 Actually it was envisioned that there would eventually be a total of 12 unofficials, as Pollock suggested that two more appointed Chinese members be added to preserve the proportion of Chinese members. The petition noted that unofficial majorities had already been obtained in the colonies of Cyprus and British Honduras.

76 Endacott, *Government and People*, p. 138.

77 Sir Francis Henry May, Governor of Hong Kong from 1912–19. The Secretary of State rejected the petition by simply noting that he was in agreement with his predecessors in refusing to amend the constitution.

78 Endacott, *Government and People*, p. 140.

79 Quoted in Miners, *Imperial Rule*, p. 134.

80 For a fuller discussion, see Miners, *Imperial Rule*, pp. 136–7.

81 See Miners, *Imperial Rule*, p. 138.

82 The first manifestation of the anti-colonial movement occurred on 4 May 1919 when thousands of students demonstrated against foreign militarism and oppression

in China. Hong Kong as an embodiment of the unequal treaties was a focal point of the anti-imperial movement.

83 Miners, *Imperial Rule*, p. 146.

84 The basis of the 1922 strike was the demand by the Chinese Seamen's Union for a wage increase. When the shipping companies refused, the seamen went on strike, and they were soon followed by most of the work-force. The 1925 strike came in protest to the shooting of several Chinese demonstrators on 30 May 1925 by British policemen assigned to the International Settlements in Shanghai. For more details see Miners, *Imperial Rule*, pp. 14–19.

85 Ng, the first Chinese unofficial, became secretary and legal adviser to Viceroy Lit Hung-change. Sir Kai Ho Kai, who served in the Legislative Council from 1890 to 1914, took part in early abortive attempts to overthrow the Manchu government. Following the 1911 Revolution he not only raised money for the new regime but secured appointments for his relatives and, more fundamentally, assisted in drafting the constitution. His colleague, Wei Yuk, who served in Legislative Council from 1896 to 1914, also raised money for the Chinese government and eventually was recognized as the 'unofficial liaison officer' between the Hong Kong and Manchu governments. In 1921 senior Chinese unofficial Lau Chu-pak raised money to support General Chen Chiungming, in the hope that he would defeat Sun Yat-sen and unite forces with the government in Peking. In 1938, Sir Shouson Chow, the first Chinese member of the Executive Council (and a member of the Legislative Council, 1921–31), was active in the sale of Chinese bonds. Finally, following the Japanese invasion of China, the Chinese unofficial members requested that the government offer financial relief to Chinese war victims. These actions reinforced the impression that Hong Kong, even for such well-established figures, was a temporary home, with China remaining the focus of their loyalty. See T. C. Cheng, 'Chinese Unofficial Members of the Legislative and Executive Councils in Hong Kong up to 1941,' *Journal of Royal Asiatic Society*, 9 (1969): 7–27.

86 See a similar conclusion in Miners, *Imperial Rule,* p. 59.

87 Miners, *Imperial Rule,* p. 61.

88 Miners, *Imperial Rule,* p. 61. An important exception to this pattern occurred when Lo Man-kam joined the Council in 1935. In the next four years, he asked more questions than the rest of the Council put together, many of which were focused on cases of discrimination against the Chinese.

89 Miners, *Imperial Rule,* p. 72.

90 Sir Mark Young, Governor in 1941, prisoner-of-war, 1941–5, resumed governorship, 1946–7.

91 Quoted in the *South China Morning Post*, 2 May 1946. As demonstrated first in 1847, this was not the first initiative to create a more municipally based government. The most promising move in this constitutional direction occurred when the Sanitary Board was created in 1883, as it was quickly composed of both official and unofficial members, some of whom were elected by ratepayers whose names were on special and jury lists. Although it was at one time anticipated that the Sanitary Board might evolve into a municipal council, colonial authorities later deemed that a municipality for Hong Kong was not practical, as it was impossible to draw the line between colonial and municipal matters. The Sanitary Board evolved into the Urban Council in 1936.

92 *Treaty between the United States and China for the Relinquishment of Extraterritorial Rights in China and the Regulation of Related Matters* (signed in Washington, 11 January 1943).

93 For a more complete summary of the intentions of China, Britain, and the United States towards Hong Kong during this time period, see Chan Lau Kit-Ching, 'The Hong Kong Question during the Pacific War 1941–45', *The Journal of Imperial and Commonwealth History*, 2, 1 (1973–4): 56–78.

94 Endacott, *Government and People,* p. 186.

95 The Municipal Corporation Bill, the Municipal Electors Bill, and the Corrupt and Illegal Practices Bill. These bills provided for a municipal council consisting of a mayor and 30 councillors, half of whom were to represent the Chinese community, the other half the non-Chinese population. Functionally, the Council would begin with control of functions exercised by the existing Urban Council with the addition of the fire brigade, parks, gardens, and recreation grounds. Eventually it was to control education, social welfare, and town planning.

96 Hong Kong *Hansard*, 1949, p. 91.

97 Hong Kong *Hansard*, 1949, p. 137.

98 Only one member, Sir Chau Sik-nin, argued against the restriction of the vote to British subjects, with the remainder of the unofficials supportive.

99 Yet this would not appear to be the case, at least with respect to 142 Chinese organizations, collectively representing a membership of 141,800 Chinese, who presented the Governor with a petition requiring a more comprehensive and progressive reform of the Legislative Council, as well as creation of a municipal council. This petition asked that the Legislative Council be composed of elected not nominated unofficials, and that the electorate should consist of all taxpayers, regardless of race. For a more complete discussion of the debate, seen Endacott, *Government and People*, pp. 182–95.

100 Secretary of State Olive Lyttleton's conclusion in 1952 as quoted in Endacott, *Government and People*, p. 195.

101 Endacott, *Government and People*, p. 189.

102 Miners, *Government and Politics*, p. 238.

103 See Scott, *Political Change*, p. 79.

104 The attitude of the colonial officials may be attributed to the desire of Britain to further economic relations with China. Britain was the first Western power to formally recognize the new People's Republic of China shortly after the revolution, recognition which was made as 'a matter of convenience.' See David C. Wolf, '"To Secure a Convenience" Britain Recognizes China—1950', *Journal of Contemporary History*, 18, 2 (April 1983): 299–326.

105 Miners, *Government and Politics*, p. 237.

106 From an estimated 500,000 inhabitants at the end of the Second World War, the population grew by the end of 1946 to 1.6 million and by 1950 to 2.36 million.

107 The new economic focus became manufacturing, first of garments and later of light industrial products.

108 The cause of the riots the first year was unacceptable social conditions brought about by the resettlement of Chinese refugees from the mainland following the Chinese revolution; the 1967 disturbances were fueled by the Cultural Revolution in China with its anti-colonial stance. See for instance Scott, *Political Change*, pp. 81–106.

109 See Scott, *Political Change*, pp. 78–80.

110 It is significant to note the Legislative Council itself did not even discuss the riots except in connection to their cost to the taxpayers.

111 An investigation after the riots suggested that the causes of the riots lay in the 'economic and social conditions which were, in turn, a product of the colonial regime's political and class structure.' The investigatory commission also found that the complaints about the system of government were based not so much on a desire to change it as to provide readier access. See *Kowloon Disturbances, 1966: Report of Commission of Inquiry* (Hong Kong: Government Printer, 1967), p. 127; as quoted in Scott, *Political Change*, pp. 92–3.

112 By the end of 1969, 10 city district officers had been appointed to liaise with Chinese organizations and assess the impact of, as well as explain, government policies. See Brian Hook, 'The Government of Hong Kong: Change within Tradition', *The China Quarterly*, 95 (September 1983): 501.

113 Personal interview, Respondent No. 6, 14 May 1987.

114 See H. A. Turner, *The Last Colony: But Whose?* (Cambridge: Cambridge University Press, 1980), p. 11.

115 S. K. Lau, *Society and Politics in Hong Kong* (Hong Kong: The Chinese University Press, 1982), p. 157.

116 Lau, *Society and Politics*, p. 187.

117 The notion of preparation connotes the laying of the foundations, before independence, for the working of a Western model (Westminster or whatever) which will then be transferred. See B. B. Schaffer, 'The Concept of Preparation', *World Politics*, 18, 1 (October 1965): 42–67.

Notes to Chapter 4

1 The transfer of Hong Kong's sovereignty from the British to the Chinese has spurred a 'cottage industry' of various treatises on the subject. See for instance: Peter Wesley-Smith and Albert Chen, *The Basic Law and Hong Kong's Future* (Hong Kong: Butterworth & Co., Ltd, 1988); Kathleen Cheek-Milby and Miron Mushkat (eds.), *Hong Kong: The Challenge of Transformation* (Hong Kong: Centre of Asian Studies, 1989); Ian Scott, *Political Change and the Crisis of Legitimacy in Hong Kong* (Hong Kong: Oxford University Press, 1989); Ming K. Chan and David J. Clark (eds.), *The Hong Kong Basic Law: Blueprint for 'Stability and Prosperity' under Chinese Sovereignty?* (Hong Kong: Hong Kong University Press, 1991); William McGurn, *Perfidious Albion: The Abandonment of Hong Kong 1997* (Washington, DC: Ethics and Public Policy Center, 1992); Robert Cottrell, *The End of Hong Kong: The Secret Diplomacy of Imperial Retreat* (London: John Murray, 1993).

2 As seen in Chapter 3, China had been stating that it wanted to re-establish sovereignty since the beginning of the twentieth century. From China's perspective, the treaties of 1842, 1860, and 1898 were all 'unequal' and hence invalid. Its position was that the status of Hong Kong should be settled peacefully through negotiations with the British government when the 'time was ripe'. When China was admitted to the United Nations in 1972 it asked that Hong Kong be removed from the list of territories that came under the purview of the UN Committee on Colonialism, as they believed that Hong Kong's future was a Chinese rather than UN responsibility. In the late 1970s concern about the future of Hong Kong was manifested both within the territory as well as among foreign investors, particularly with respect to the granting of land leases which were to expire by 1997. It was clear that the shortening span of the leases and the inability of the Hong Kong government to grant new ones extending beyond 1997 was beginning to damage confidence and stability in the territory. Hong Kong's Governor, Sir Murray MacLehose, visited China in 1979, at which time he found out that China intended to recover sovereignty over Hong Kong. He informed the British Foreign Office of this but not the people of Hong Kong. Formal Sino-British talks on the future of Hong Kong commenced after British Prime Minister Margaret Thatcher visited Beijing in September 1982. The negotiations ran over a two-year period and produced the Joint Declaration.

3 Consultation was with the unofficials who were members of the Executive Council. However, due to the overlap of five of the unofficials who were also members of the legislature, the Legislative Council was at least indirectly represented in consultations. Unofficials visited London to discuss negotiations in July 1983, and in January, April, May, September, and December 1984. Subsequent events were to demonstrate that even the British government did not totally accept

the Legislative Council's views or status as legitimate. In addition, three unofficials also visited Beijing in June 1984, where they were received individually. For a different perspective as to the value of unofficial consultations, see Lydia Dunn, 'The role of Members of the Executive and Legislative Councils', in Cheek-Milby and Mushkat, *The Challenge of Transformation*, pp. 77–90.

4 See Chalmers Johnson, 'The Mouse-trapping of Hong Kong: A Game in which nobody wins', *Asian Survey* 24, 9 (September 1984). Deng Xiaoping had argued that any Chinese government which failed to recover Hong Kong would also fall from power and would be condemned by history and the nation.

5 Earlier, Prime Minister Thatcher voiced the belief that negotiations should occur on the basis of a three-legged stool, with Britain, China, and Hong Kong each comprising one leg; if any one of the legs was missing, the stool (agreement) would collapse. However, China was adamant that the matter was between the two sovereign governments. When Hong Kong's Governor Youde joined the negotiating team in July 1983, he stated that he would be representing the people of Hong Kong. China was quick to point out that he was a member of the British negotiating team and not representing Hong Kong; Youde did not attempt to refute this.

6 Margaret Ng, 'Now we stand alone', *South China Morning Post*, 28 March 1984, p. 2.

7 The members decided to have the debate in the form of a motion. Questions could be ruled out of order by the Governor and an adjournment debate would have restricted the debate to just 30 minutes, 10 of which would be reserved for the government's response. A motion allows for every councillor to have his say without time limit and adds a touch of legality to the proceedings.

8 See 'Leftists slam Lobo motion', *South China Morning Post*, 27 February 1984, p. 2.

9 Hong Kong *Hansard*, 14 March 1984, p. 703.

10 Comments of Mr Stephen Cheong, Hong Kong *Hansard*, 14 March 1984, p. 730.

11 Five unofficials called for an end to confidentiality. See 'Rebels demand an end to secrecy', *South China Morning Post*, 15 March 1984, p. 1.

12 Comments of Mr Alex Wu, Hong Kong *Hansard*, 14 March 1984, p. 708.

13 Comments of Mr Allen Lee, Hong Kong *Hansard*, 14 March 1984, p. 716.

14 Comments of Ms Selina Chow, Hong Kong *Hansard*, 14 March 1984, pp. 738–41.

15 Comments of Mr David Ford, Hong Kong *Hansard*, 14 March 1984, p. 757.

16 Throughout 1983 China reiterated its intention to regain sovereignty over the territory. Formal British recognition of this claim and an indication that their attempt to retain administration over the territory had failed came during a news conference by Sir Geoffrey Howe on 20 April 1984.

17 Comments by senior unofficial Ms Lydia Dunn before the Foreign Correspondents Club. See 'Election call wins support', *South China Morning Post,* 8 January 1984, p. 1. Two weeks later the Financial Secretary, Sir John Bremridge, was quoted as stating that direct elections for the councils was just 'a matter of time.' See 'Legislative Council elections a matter of time—Bremridge' in the *Hong Kong Standard*, 23 January 1984.

18 The position paper stated that the acceptability of the agreement depended on it containing full details of the post-1997 administrative, legal, social, and economic systems; that adequate and workable assurances be made to honour the terms of the agreement; that provisions of the Basic Law be incorporated into the agreement; and that the rights of British nationals be safeguarded. See *UMELCO 1984 Annual Report*, Appendix IV.

19 See 'A solid "Yes" vote for Umelco', *South China Morning Post*, 25 May 1984, p. 1.

20 During the London visit, Former Governor MacLehose attacked the UMELCO position paper as being both 'ill-considered and badly-timed' and noted that members should 'give leadership at home rather than seeking it from the British Government.' See 'Umelco's clash with MacLehose', *South China Morning Post,* 14 May 1984, p. 2. Later, when three unofficials visited Beijing, Deng Xiaoping informed them that their views did not represent the interests of Hong Kong and he would only see them on an 'individual basis', as China refused to recognize that the Executive and Legislative councils were anything other than advisory bodies to the Governor.

21 Comments of Mr Peter C. Wong, Hong Kong *Hansard,* 8 August 1984, p. 422.

22 The Joint Declaration was formally entered into force on 27 May 1985 when instruments of ratification were exchanged in Beijing between the two governments. It was registered at the United Nations by the two governments simultaneously on 12 June 1985. In April 1985, the Hong Kong Act 1985 was passed by the British Parliament, which formally recognized the end of British sovereignty over Hong Kong as of 1 July 1997. A few days later the National People's Congress of the People's Republic of China ratified the Joint Declaration.

23 Except in foreign and defence affairs, which were to be the responsibilities of China.

24 The concept of 'one country–two systems' originated in 1978 when Deng Xiaoping addressed the Standing Committee of the Fifth National People's Congress and urged compatriots in Taiwan to rejoin China. This concept was applied to Hong Kong to persuade both the British government and the people of Hong Kong to accept reassertion of Chinese sovereignty over the territory.

25 For instance, a survey conducted by the Survey Research Hong Kong Ltd. taken at the time indicated that 82 per cent of the people believed that the draft agreement was good for Hong Kong. Furthermore, when faced with the choice between the draft agreement and no agreement, 90 per cent opted for the draft agreement. See Hong Kong *Hansard,* 15 October 1984, p. 63. Yet because no referendum was held on the subject, it is difficult to determine the extent of public approval. Rather, the lack of vocal disapproval was taken, by both the British and Chinese governments, as acquiescence if not support for the agreement.

26 *Joint Declaration,* p. 199.

27 Rather than come under the direction of the Chief Executive, who, as noted in Chapter 3, was president of the Council.

28 As noted in Chapter 3, estimates could only be decreased, not increased by the legislators. In addition, the Legislative Council had no authority over government revenue.

29 The requirements were first publicized in May and reiterated at a press conference with Sir S. Y. Chung, senior unofficial of the Executive Council, on 28 September 1984. They specified that the agreement must contain full details of the administrative, legal, social, and economic system after 1997; that workable assurances must be provided that the terms will be honoured; that provisions of the Basic Law must incorporate the provisions of the agreement; and that the inputs of British nationals must be safeguarded. Nonetheless, some members expressed disappointment that the future political system was left to be specified in a Basic Law rather than written into the agreement.

30 Derek Davies, 'Initialed, sealed and delivered', *Far Eastern Economic Review,* 4 October 1984, p. 16.

31 The Chinese government had originally wanted to state a 12-point proposal, which it issued during negotiations in 1983. The British were able to convince them that Hong Kong's future stability and prosperity required more comprehensive guarantees of future freedoms.

32 Comments of Kwok-wing So, Hong Kong *Hansard,* 15 October 1984, p. 94.

33 Comments of Ms Lydia Dunn, Hong Kong *Hansard*, 15 October 1984, pp. 71–2.

34 Comments of Mr J. J. Swaine, Hong Kong *Hansard*, 15 October 1984, pp. 105–6; he abstained from voting as did Mr K. C. Chan.

35 Comments of Mr Roger Lobo, Hong Kong *Hansard*, 18 October 1984, pp. 175–6.

36 Comprised of a senior representative and four other members from both countries, the Joint Liaison Group is to discuss matters relating to the smooth transfer of government in 1997 and to exchange information and enter into consultations on whatever issues both sides determine are appropriate to discuss.

37 Comments of Ms Lydia Dunn, Hong Kong *Hansard*, 18 October 1984, p. 73.

38 The first initiative to broaden political participation in government can be traced to 1982 when the District Boards with consultative functions were established with a partially elected membership. The expansion of the elective element of the District Boards, the increase in the elective element of the Urban Council, and the establishment of the Regional Council can be seen as a continuation of this trend. This chapter will highlight the more significant reforms aimed at the legislature since the 1984 Sino-British Agreement.

39 'Hong Kong People Ruling Hong Kong' was a popular phrase often used during the drafting process in an attempt to quell the fears of the Hong Kong people over their political future. It was first voiced by China (as *gangren zigang*) although no details were provided for its implementation. 'One country–two systems' related to the fact that while incorporated into a socialist regime, Hong Kong's capitalist system would remain unchanged for 50 years.

40 *Green Paper: The Further Development of Representative Government in Hong Kong* (Hong Kong: Government Printer, 1984), p. 4.

41 1984 *Green Paper*, p. 8. While geographical constituencies had previously been recognized in elections to the Urban Council, Heung Yee Kuk, rural committees, and District Boards, the only formally denoted functional constituencies for the legislature were the Justices of the Peace and the General Chamber of Commerce, who, as highlighted in Chapter 3, had the right to nominate one Legislative Council member for appointment by the Governor. The Green Paper argued that informally the Governor's choice of unofficials for the Executive and Legislative councils had always been based on both geographical and functional considerations. According to the Secretary for Home Affairs, Mr Denis Bray, 'The change from appointed system is that the constituency will be defined in law not by the Governor'. See 'Proposed LEGCO elections by Functional Constituencies Explained', *Government Information Services Bulletin (GIS)*, 22 August 1984, p. 1.

42 Both elected and appointed members of these bodies would be able to elect a representative for the legislature.

43 1984 *Green Paper*, p. 9.

44 Comments of Mr Peter Wong, Hong Kong *Hansard*, 2 August 1984, p. 1359.

45 Wong Po Yan noted that in the March 1982 elections, the New Territories only witnessed a 14 per cent turnout of eligible voters, the urban areas having a lower 12 per cent turnout, and the 1983 Urban Council election only witnessing a miniscule 6 per cent turnout of eligible voters. See his comments in the Hong Kong *Hansard*, 2 August 1984, p. 1370.

46 Comments of Mr Alex Wu, Hong Kong *Hansard*, 2 August 1984, p. 1354.

47 Comments of Ms Lydia Dunn, Hong Kong *Hansard*, 2 August 1984, p. 1357. See also comments of Stephen Cheong and Selina Chow, both of whom supported a ministerial style of government.

48 Comments of Mr Allen Lee, Hong Kong *Hansard*, 9 January 1985, p. 484–5.

49 Norman Miners, 'Alternative Governmental Structures for a Future Self-Governing Hong Kong', in Y. C. Jao, Leung Chi-Keung, Peter Wesley-Smith, and

Wong Siu-Lun (eds.), *Hong Kong and 1997: Strategies for the Future* (Hong Kong: Centre of Asian Studies, 1985), p. 15.

50 S. K. Lau, 'Political Reform and Political Development', in Jao et al., eds., *Hong Kong and 1997*, p. 37.

51 Scott, *Crisis of Legitimacy*, p. 276, for analysis of the membership of the 1985 legislature. Also see Norman Miners, *Government and Politics*, 4th edn., p. 122.

52 See summary by Norman Miners, 'Moves Towards Representative Government, 1984–1988', in Cheek–Milby and Mushkat, eds., *The Challenge of Transformation*, p. 21.

53 *White Paper: The Further Development of Representative Government in Hong Kong* (Hong Kong: Government Printer, November 1984), chap. III, sect. j.

54 Only Selina Chow abstained from voting as she believed the White Paper left too many questions unanswered. See her comments, Hong Kong *Hansard*, 10 January 1985, pp. 555–7.

55 For instance, 89 political groups staged a mass rally demanding this form of election.

56 Comments of Stephen Cheong, Hong Kong *Hansard*, 10 January 1985, pp. 511–12.

57 See comments of Mr S .L. Chen, Mr Wong Po-Yan, and Mr Cheung Yan-Lung, Hong Kong *Hansard*, 10 January 1985.

58 See his comments, Hong Kong *Hansard*, 10 January 1985, pp. 562–7.

59 One unofficial, Peter Wong, likened Hong Kong's process of evolution to that of Ceylon from 1920 to independence in 1947. In Ceylon, unofficials were both appointed and elected under two different methods: territory-wide and community. While the original suffrage was restricted to 4 per cent of the population, it gradually was enlarged to incorporate universal suffrage and ministerial government prior to actual independence. See his comments as well as a table regarding Ceylon's political development in Hong Kong *Hansard*, 2 August 1984, pp. 1361–2.

60 See comments of Stephen Cheong, Hong Kong *Hansard*, 2 August 1984, p. 1377.

61 Miners, 'Alternative Government Structures,' p. 13.

62 The Hong Kong electorate had been characterized as 'minimally-integrated' and apathetic in earlier writings. However, by the mid–1980s, the rapid economic growth, expanded educational opportunities, and the decline of traditional institutions and social customs in Chinese society generated a more highly politicized political culture with an institutionalized set of participatory norms. See S. K. Lau, 'The Changing Political Culture of the Hong Kong Chinese', in Joseph Cheng (ed.), *Hong Kong in Transition* (Hong Kong: Oxford University Press, 1986), pp. 26–66.

63 Scott, *Crisis of Legitimacy*, p. 277.

64 Reasons given against the election of Executive Council members by the unofficials of the Legislative Council was that it would encompass too many changes at once, would require full-time politicians, and that unofficials already possessed policy-making power through their membership on the Executive Council.

65 S. K. Lau, 'Political Reform and Political Development', p. 25. In this vein it is notable that discussion of the reform was occurring coincident to the British Parliament's discussion of Hong Kong's future.

66 Miners, 'Alternative Structures,' p. 11.

67 Lau, 'Political Reform and Development,' p. 38.

68 Lau, 'Political Reform and Development,' p. 38.

69 Points raised by Maria Tam, p. 518; by Dr Henrietta Ip, p. 521; by Rita Fan, p. 534; by Keith Lam, p. 552; and by Selina Chow, p. 556; all in Hong Kong *Hansard*, 10 January 1985.

70 Comments of Chief Secretary David Ford, during debate on the 1985 White Paper, Hong Kong *Hansard*, 9 January 1985, p. 463.

71 Comments of Mr Helmut Sohmen, Hong Kong *Hansard*, 16 July 1987, p. 2151.

72 Comments of Ms Maria Tam, Hong Kong *Hansard*, 16 July 1987, p. 2166.

73 For a good critique of the government's strategy in this Green Paper, see Ming K. Chan, 'Democracy Derailed: Realpolitik in the Making of the Hong Kong Basic Law, 1985–1991', in Chan and Clark (eds.), *The Hong Kong Basic Law*, pp. 3–35, esp. p. 10. Also see Norman Miners, 'Towards Representative Government', pp. 27–32.

74 After publication of the 1984 initiatives, China stated it was under no obligation to honour the proposed reforms after 1997. For a discussion of the Chinese viewpoint, see Miners, 'Towards Representative Government', p. 21.

75 The most direct statement of China's view came through Li Hou, deputy director of China's State Council's Hong Kong and Macau Affairs Office and secretary general of the Basic Law Drafting Committee, who claimed that direct elections in 1988 would not only fail to converge with the Basic Law but were contrary to the 'spirit' of the Joint Declaration. He went on to argue that direct elections would only sharpen contradictions between different classes and segments in Hong Kong society, leading to political, economic, and social instability, harmful to the 1997 transfer of power. *Liaowang* (overseas edition) 45 (22 June 1987): 20. British acquiescence to China's pressure for convergence was first apparent from remarks of Timothy Renton, the British minister with responsibility for Hong Kong, who spoke of the need for convergence in November 1985 and reiterated this goal again in January 1986. See 'Wrenching words of woe', *Far Eastern Economic Review*, 6 February 1986, p. 18. Renton also stated that Britain was under no 'moral obligation' to introduce the Westminster system to Hong Kong. See *Hong Kong Standard*, 22 January 1986. Even earlier, a high-ranking Hong Kong official had laid the groundwork for the retreat by saying that the future political system must be compatible with the desires of China. See comments by David Akers-Jones, Secretary for District Administration, 'Be compatible with China: Akers-Jones', *South China Morning Post*, August 13, 1984, p. 1.

76 Comments of Mr Martin Lee, Hong Kong *Hansard*, 16 July 1987, p. 2133.

77 Comments of Ms Maria Tam, Hong Kong *Hansard*, 16 July 1987, p. 2166–7.

78 The 1984 White Paper promised a 'small number of directly elected members in 1988 . . . building up to a significant number . . . by 1997.' See *White Paper: The Further Development of Representative Government* (Hong Kong: Government Printer, 1984), p. 8.

79 Comments of Mr Martin Lee, Hong Kong *Hansard*, 16 July 1984, p. 2133.

80 Comments of Dr Lam, Hong Kong *Hansard*, 16 July 1984, p. 2125.

81 The 1985 elections had involved less than 0.5 per cent of the territory's people; this small electorate returned individuals who were acceptable to the government as they were mostly businessmen or professionals. Nonetheless, the 24 indirectly elected members were to herald changes in the legislature as it moved from its old consensus style to something approaching democratic politics.

82 Comments of Mr Clydesdale, Hong Kong *Hansard*, 16 July 1984, p. 2116.

83 Comments of Mr Wong Po-Yan, Hong Kong *Hansard*, 15 July 1987, p. 2063.

84 Comments of S. L. Chen, Hong Kong *Hansard*, 15 July 1987, p. 2050.

85 Comments of Mr Helmut Sohmen, Hong Kong *Hansard*, 16 July 1987, p. 2153.

86 Comments of Dr Ho, Hong Kong *Hansard*, 15 July 1987, p. 2055.

87 Comments of Ms Chow, Hong Kong *Hansard*, 15 July 1987, p. 2077.

88 Comments of Dr Ho, Hong Kong *Hansard*, 15 July 1987, p. 2055.

89 Comments of Dr Ho, Hong Kong *Hansard*, 15 July 1987, p. 2156.

90 Hong Kong Observers, 'Choice: A basic right', *South China Morning Post*, 30 July 1987.

91 Comments of Mr Martin Lee, Hong Kong *Hansard*, 15 July 1987, p. 2131.

92 Comments of Mr Szeto Wah, Hong Kong *Hansard*, 15 July 1987, p. 2159.

93 Comments of Mr Szeto Wah, Hong Kong *Hansard*, 15 July 1987, p. 2159.

94 Comments by Dr. Chiu, Hong Kong *Hansard*, 15 July 1987, p. 2109.

95 The significance of direct elections from the liberal perspective is also ably summarized in Scott, *Crisis of Legitimacy*, p. 278.

96 See comments of Chief Secretary, Hong Kong *Hansard*, 16 March 1988, p. 914.

97 Comments of Mr Sohmen, Hong Kong *Hansard*, 16 July 1987, p. 2151.

98 See 'Omelco report is a failure', *South China Morning Post*, 5 March 1987, p. 3.

99 See Chief Secretary's comments, Hong Kong *Hansard*, 4 November 1987, pp. 185–9.

100 Survey Research Hong Kong Ltd., Marketing Decision Research Co. Ltd., and Frank Small & Associates had surveys taken during the same time period. Further, a consultant brought in by the *Far Eastern Economic Review*, Norman Webb, President, Gallup International, determined that if a referendum had been held on the subject, Hong Kong people would have been 2 to 1 in favour. See comments of Mr Martin Lee, Hong Kong *Hansard*, 17 March 1988, p. 1019.

101 Comments of Mr Desmond Lee, Hong Kong *Hansard*, 18 November 1987, p. 461.

102 Comments of Mr Chan Kam-Chuen, Hong Kong *Hansard*, 18 November 1987, p. 421.

103 This allowed for the creation of an accountancy functional constituency as well as a second one for health-care professionals.

104 For instance, see Ming Chan, 'Democracy Derailed', and Norman Miners, 'Towards Representative Government 1984–1988'.

105 Mr Martin Lee offered an amendment which attempted to attach the wording 'but regrets the Government's decision not to introduce partial direct elections to the Legislative Council in 1988.' Only seven members voted in favor of the amendment. Mr Szeto Wah then offered an amendment regretting 'The Government's decision to introduce only 10 directly elected members . . . in 1991', but this in turn was defeated by voice vote. See Hong Kong *Hansard*, 17 March 1988, pp. 1022 and 1057, respectively.

106 Comments of Mr Martin Lee, Hong Kong *Hansard*, 17 March 1988, p. 1013.

107 Comments of Mr Desmond Lee, Hong Kong *Hansard*, 17 March 1988, p. 1047.

108 Comments of Mr Jackie Chan, Hong Kong *Hansard*, 16 March 1988, p. 955.

109 See comments of Mr Ngai, Hong Kong *Hansard*, 16 March 1988, p. 1051 and Ms. Chow, Hong Kong *Hansard*, 16 March 1988, p. 937.

110 Comments of Ms Dunn, Hong Kong *Hansard*, 16 March 1988, p. 919.

111 Comments of Professor Poon, Hong Kong *Hansard*, 17 March 1988, p. 1057.

112 The Basic Law is referred to as a mini-constitution for Hong Kong. It is actually a subordinate statute of the Chinese Constitution. Nonetheless, since the Basic Law provides for the structures and powers of government in the future special administrative region, it will be referred to here as Hong Kong's Constitution.

113 This commentary on the Basic Law is from the perspective of how that document shapes legislative power under the future special administrative region. For a broader perspective on the Basic Law, see *Journal of Chinese Law*, 2, 1 (Spring, 1988); *Journal of International Law* 2, 1 (Winter 1988); Martin Lee and Szeto Wah, *The Basic Law: Some Basic Flaws* (Hong Kong: Kasper Printing Press, June 1988); William McGurn (ed.), *Basic Law, Basic Questions: The Debate Continues* (Hong Kong: Review Publishing Co., 1988); Peter Wesley-Smith and Albert Chen, eds., *The Basic Law and Hong Kong's Future* (Hong Kong: Butterworth, 1988); and Ming K. Chan and David J. Clark (eds.), *The Hong Kong Basic Law: Blueprint for Stability and Prosperity under Chinese Sovereignty?* (Hong Kong: Hong Kong University Press, 1991).

114 Former Legislative Council members T. K. Ann and Rayson Ruang served as Basic Law Drafting Committee chairs, as did current member David Li (elected

member representing the banking industry). In addition, Legislative Council members Wong Po-Yan, Martin Tam, Szeto Wah, and Martin Lee served on the Basic Law Drafting Committee. See statements of Lu Ping, Director of the Hongkong and Macau Affairs Office of the People's Republic of China, 'Law "will be based on people's views" ', *South China Morning Post*, 24 January 1986, p. 20.

115 The Basic Law Consultative Committee proved itself to be a focus of controversy when its executive committee was established by 'consultation', which the Chinese stated was a form of 'election', providing a foreboding of disputes yet to arise over the future selection of legislators. The heavy-handed appointment technique in establishing the executive committee was made to look more legitimate with an eventual 'election' of the new leaders, but there was only one election slate.

116 Conservative Hong Kong businessmen had joined in alliance with the Chinese to oppose local democratic initiatives. They appeared to believe that the development of democratic politics was a greater threat to Hong Kong's prosperity and stability than its takeover by communist China. See 'Power to the people', *South China Morning Post*, 8 May 1988, p. 2. One important Hong Kong figure, Lord Kadoorie, who served on the executive committee of the Basic Law Consultative Committee, called for Hong Kong to be governed by a small select group of wealthy individuals. He believed that 'All Hong Kong is one big business and it must have a good management and a well-chosen board of directors'. See 'Kadoorie backs "right of the few to rule" ', *South China Morning Post*, 6 January 1986, p. 1.

117 The first and second drafts of the Basic Law can be found in Chan and Clark, *The Hong Kong Basic Law*.

118 A second option simply forbade members from introducing any bill concerning public expenditures or public policy.

119 Peter Wesley-Smith, 'The Legal System and Constitutional Issues', in Chan and Clark, *The Hong Kong Basic Law*, p. 178.

120 The Basic Law simply specified that members of the Executive Council be chosen from among the legislature, executive authorities, and other public figures. It envisioned it as merely consultative, an advisory body for the Chief Executive. There was no provision for its members to acquire executive responsibility as present in cabinets.

121 The Basic Law stipulates that the Chief Executive 'shall be accountable to the Central People's Government and the Hong Kong special administrative region'. There is no specific requirement that he or she be accountable to the legislature, as was stated in the Joint Declaration.

122 This was the conception put forward earlier by Chinese leader Deng Xiaoping to the Basic Law Drafting Committee. See Scott, *Crisis of Legitimacy*, pp. 288–9, 304. It was also concluded that 'China has simply not yet established constitutionalism whereby justice may prevail over political authority'. See Kuan Hsin-Chi, 'Chinese Constitutional Practice', in Wesley-Smith and Chen, *The Basic Law and Hong Kong's Future*, p. 61.

123 Comments of Ms Lydia Dunn, Hong Kong *Hansard*, 13 July 1988, p. 1829.

124 Comments of Mr Andrew Wong, Hong Kong *Hansard*, 13 July 1988, p. 1834.

125 See comments of Professor Poon and Mr Martin Lee for opposing views in Hong Kong *Hansard*, 14 July 1988, p. 1912 and p. 1896, respectively.

126 For opposing views, see comments of Mr Szeto Wah and Ms Selina Chow, Hong Kong *Hansard*, 14 July 1988, p. 1914–15 and 13 July 1988, p. 1852, respectively.

127 Comments of Mr Martin Lee, *Hong Kong Hansard*, 14 July 1988, p. 1895. Lee argued that the electoral college idea was really just an appointment system which could be easily manipulated.

128 Composed of representatives of business and financial circles, professional bodies, labour, grass roots, religious organizations, and district organizations. Variations on this idea were offered.

129 See comments of Mr Andrew Wong, Hong Kong *Hansard*, 14 July 1988, p. 1839, as well as comments of Ms Chow, p. 1853.

130 Comments of Dr Ho, Hong Kong *Hansard*, 14 July 1988, p. 1841.

131 Comments of Dr Ho, Hong Kong *Hansard*, 14 July 1988, p. 1841.

132 See comments of Mr Desmond Lee, Hong Kong *Hansard*, 14 July 1988, p. 1898.

133 The draft Basic Law suggested only that members of Legislative Council be one of three sources of appointment for the Chief Executive to consider. See comments of Mr Cheong-Leen, Hong Kong *Hansard*, 14 July 1988, p. 1863.

134 Comments of Mr Cheong-Leen, Hong Kong *Hansard*, 14 July 1988, p. 1863.

135 See comments of Mr Cheung, Hong Kong *Hansard*, 13 July 1988, p. 1849, and Mr Hui Yin-Fat, Hong Kong *Hansard*, 14 July 1988, p. 1882.

136 See comments of Ms Dunn, Hong Kong *Hansard*, 13 July 1988, p. 1830–31; also comments of Mr Pang, Hong Kong *Hansard*, 14 July 1988, p. 1908.

137 Additional points raised during debate concerned the interpretation and amendment of the Basic Law, the possible erosion of the judicial power of the special administrative region's courts, and the application and enforcement of the two international covenants on civil rights.

138 Ming K. Chan, 'Democracy Derailed', p. 14.

139 A survey conducted in May 1988 reflected that 24 per cent of the respondents wanted to emigrate, rising to 45.5 per cent of those with a tertiary education. See *Ming Pao,* 18 May 1988.

140 According to a poll taken that spring, 70 per cent of the people believed that the Chief Executive should be elected by universal suffrage, 60 per cent wanted direct elections to the legislature, and 55 per cent did not believe that China would keep its, 'one country, two systems' promise. See Chan, 'Democracy Derailed', p. 21.

141 See a similar conclusion by Byron S. J. Weng, 'The Hong Kong Model of "One Country, Two Systems" Promises and Problems' in Wesley-Smith and Chen, *The Basic Law and Hong Kong's Future*, pp. 73–89, esp. p. 77.

142 *OMELCO Annual Report 1989*, appendix 2, p. 78.

143 Ming K. Chan, 'Democracy Devailed', p. 17.

144 *South China Morning Post,* 4 June 1989.

145 See for instance McGurn, *Perfidious Albion*.

146 Wording first used by Ming K. Chan to describe the change in attitude during this period. See Chan, 'Democracy Derailed', p. 13.

147 On 20 December 1989 the British government announced a package granting full British citizenship, without requirement of residence in Britain, to 50,000 Hong Kong people and their families. After a stormy debate, the scheme was enacted into law by the British Parliament on 26 July 1990.

148 They met with Foreign Secretary Douglas Hurd on 15 January 1990, and a delegation visited London later that month prior to promulgation of the Basic Law. In light of the increased time spent in London to urge acceptance of the Hong Kong-based initiative, OMELCO established a London office in April 1990 to monitor events and provide support services for those members visiting Britain.

149 Legislative composition adopted by the Basic Law was approved by the 10 mainland members of the Basic Law Drafting Committee's political subgroup, against the objections of all six Hong Kong members. See Bretigne Shaffer, 'Beijing, the West and the approaching sack of Hong Kong', *Orbis* (Summer 1991): 329–45.

150 Comments of Mr McGregor, Hong Kong *Hansard*, 4 April 1990, p. 1225.

151 Among the more divisive issues was the stationing of People's Liberation Army troops in the territory and provision for a declaration of emergency if deemed appropriate by Chinese authorities.

152 Comments of Mr Martin Lee, Hong Kong *Hansard*, 4 April 1990, p. 1196.

153 Comments of Dr Leong, Hong Kong *Hansard*, 4 April 1990, p. 1221.

154 Mr Martin Lee noted that 'after taking so much time and trouble to consult the people of Hong Kong while drafting it, it is difficult to find any justification for not having to consult them through their properly constituted Legislative Council on any changes to the Basic Law in future'. See Hong Kong *Hansard*, 4 April 1990, p. 1197. In an article published in the *Beijing Review* it was noted that 110 changes had been made since publication of the first draft; eight of these were substantive and the remainder simply wording changes. Of the substantive changes, 250 were in direct response to Basic Law Consultative Committee opinions. See Chan and Clark, *The Hong Kong Basic Law*, p. 237.

155 Comments of Mr Hui Yin-fat, Hong Kong *Hansard*, 4 April 1990, p. 1204.

156 Eight of the abstentions were officials.

157 The correspondence was published in the *South China Morning Post*, 29 October 1992.

158 The Prime Minister, John Major, met with leaders of the United Democrats in London that spring; later, while in Hong Kong, the British Minister of State for the territory, Alastair Goodlad, suggested that if the political will existed, it would be possible to amend the Basic Law to accelerate the pace of democratization.

159 One new idea suggested by China was to allow local delegates of the National People's Congress to stand for election in the 1995 electoral polls. Since the Basic Law specified that these delegates formed part of the election committee and preparatory committee for the special administrative region in 1996, Lu Ping, Director of the State Council's Hong Kong and Macau Affairs Office, suggested that they should participate 'in order to ensure a smooth transition'. Under present regulations, they are barred from taking part in the polls because they hold office in another country's legislature. See 'Legco convergence main issue for talks', *South China Morning Post*, 2 September, 1992. China also suggested that the Election Committee could be determined by having Hong Kong and China each appoint half of the committee. See 'Secretary confident reforms will proceed', *South China Morning Post*, 10 October 1992.

160 'Shaken and stirred: Governor Patten unveils new political programme', *Far Eastern Economic Review*, 5 October 1992, p. 13.

161 He also suggested that in 1994 all District Board members be directly elected.

162 In the 1991 election, the liberal United Democrats won an overwhelming majority of seats. Yet the United Democrats were not acceptable to China due to their push for local democracy. The previous governor, David Wilson, had decided to withhold appointment of United Democrats to the Executive Council in order not to antagonize China. Patten believed that ignoring their popular mandate was ill-conceived, hence he overrode the issue by not appointing any Legislative Council members onto the Executive Council.

163 Beijing had been briefed on Patten's speech in advance when British Foreign Secretary Douglas Hurd met his Chinese counterpart, Foreign Minister Qian Qichen, in New York in late September. Patten had also sent a letter to Lu Ping on 26 September via the British Ambassador to China. Lu Ping sent a letter dated 3 October to Patten objecting in particular to the creation of the government–Legislative Council committee. Lu was particularly incensed that Patten planned to make public his proposals before coming to Beijing.

164 'Throwing down the gauntlet', *South China Morning Post*, 10 October 1992.

165 Voiced in the left-wing media, *Wen Wei Pao*, as quoted in 'China imposes Patten deadline for "backdown"', *South China Morning Post*, 26 October 1992. Patten dismissed China's personal attacks on him as 'exotic and mildly demeaning'.

166 'Beijing accuses Patten of acting like a petty thief', *Japan Times*, 20 March 1993.

167 Characterization by Chinese Premier Li Peng during the annual meeting of the Chinese National People's Congress, 17 March 1993.

168 'Governor attacked for behaving like "saviour"', *South China Morning Post*, 13 October 1992.

169 Patten was a different kind of Governor, possessing a background in politics rather than diplomacy. His argument that the 'secret diplomacy of the past' had done little for Hong Kong's future found a receptive audience in Hong Kong. See 'Governor dismisses "secret diplomacy"', *South China Morning Post*, 7 January 1993.

170 See 'China protests are based on little substance', *Hong Kong Standard*, 28 October 1992.

171 Article 55 concerns the formation of the Executive Council and notes that members can be appointed 'from among' various groupings, including legislators—but it does not say that they must be included. Article 62 sets out the powers and functions of the government of the special administrative region; the Chinese were concerned that the new committee would lead to greater legislative power than allowed in the Basic Law. Article 74 relates to the tabling of bills by legislators; the Chinese stated that there was no provision in this article for this committee.

172 In that these elections should be through more narrowly defined sectors via indirect elections. Further, China argued that functional constituencies comprise functional constituencies, not functional sectors. The Chinese cited Appendix II of the Basic Law in which functional constituency elections were to be 'indirect through "authorised groupings" rather than direct elections from the different walks of life'. See 'Battle lines drawn as Patten, Lu stand firm', *Hong Kong Standard*, 24 October 1992.

173 'Why Patten proposals are complete breach of faith', *South China Morning Post*, 11 April 1993.

174 'Why Patten proposals are complete breach of faith', *South China Morning Post*, 11 April 1993.

175 'Patten proposals a "diplomatic fraud"', *South China Morning Post*, 22 December 1992.

176 Lu Ping revealed there were secret agreements between China and Britain on arrangements for the 1995 elections. He claimed that British Foreign Secretary Mr Douglas Hurd and his Chinese counterpart, Mr Qian Qichen, had reached agreement that the election committee for the 10 Legislative Council seats in 1995 was to be modeled on Annex I of the Basic Law which related to the selection of the Chief Executive. Moreover, Lu charged that Qian and Hurd had exchanged correspondence which categorically pointed out that functional constituency elections were to be indirect. Britain later released the correspondence, which showed that while discussion had taken place, no definitive decisions had been reached.

177 'Beijing in threat over rule for '97', *South China Morning Post*, 24 October 1992.

178 See 'Governor dares Beijing to point out "violations"', *South China Morning Post*, 10 October 1992.

179 'Governor dares Beijing to point out "violations"', *South China Morning Post*, 10 October 1992.

180 'Legco to vet Patten rivals', *South China Morning Post*, 20 December 1992.

181 The new airport at Chek Lap Kok had been a long-standing source of acrimony between the British, Chinese, and Hong Kong governments. The Chinese were initially against the project, as it committed funding beyond 1997. They also expressed the desire for better use of Chinese airports, particularly that at Shenzhen, rather than construction of a new, and competitive, one in Hong Kong. The lack of progress in the Sino-British talks prompted a visit by British Prime Minister John Major to China in 1991, where an agreement was reached, yet the haggling continues.

182 'Now we know exactly where we stand: Alone', *Hong Kong Standard*, 24 October 1992.

183 Best example of this tactic was when China criticized Jardines for their support of Patten by charging that it was a British hong which had amassed its fortunes by selling opium in China and that it was continuing to collude with London in frustrating Hong Kong's smooth transition to sovereignty. Eventually, pro-China forces were successful in removing Jardine's representative on the executive committee of the General Chamber of Commerce. This individual was also an appointed member of the Legislative Council. See 'Attack a bid to undermine confidence', *Hong Kong Standard*, 19 December 1992.

184 This threat was first aimed at the Container Terminal No. 9; later the Chinese government alleged that any contracts, leases, and agreements signed and ratified by the Hong Kong government which were not approved by China would be invalid after 1997. This was China's most explicit threat that it wanted veto power over any project spanning the handover of the colony to China. See 'How Beijing has put rule of law at risk', *South China Morning Post*, 23 December 1992.

185 See conclusion of the Bar Council of the Hong Kong Bar Association, 'How Beijing has put rule of law at risk', *South China Morning Post*, 23 December 1992.

186 'Beijing in threat over rule for '97', *South China Morning Post*, 24 October 1992.

187 Establishing a 'second kitchen' relates to the Chinese custom of a married son setting up a second kitchen in his father's household. In April 1993, China appointed 49 locally based 'Hong Kong Affairs Advisers'.

188 'Patten "votes for all" plan', *South China Morning Post*, 8 October 1992.

189 Patten was particularly critical of allowing members of the National People's Congress and Chinese People's Consultative Committee to be candidates for the legislature, as he believed they were not elected in an acceptable manner. For additional information, see 'China bid to silence Governor', *South China Morning Post*, 11 October 1992.

190 'Legco to vet Patten rivals', *South China Morning Post*, 20 December 1992.

191 See 'Patten treading on dangerous territory,' *Hong Kong Standard*, 18 January 1993. The 1995 election, for instance, occurs just 20 months before the transfer of sovereignty.

192 The British House of Lords held a debate on the proposals on 10 December 1992. Baroness Dunn, who is also the senior non-civil servant in the Executive Council, asked 'why the people of Hong Kong are faced yet again with paying the price for a dispute which is not of their making.' See summary of her speech before the House of Lords in 'Hong Kong pays price for dispute it did not create', *South China Morning Post*, 10 December 1992. Lord MacLehose added that he was concerned that there were 'elements in those proposals that appear in breach at least of the spirit of the 1990 [Basic Law] agreement'. His criticism was shared by Lords Sharp and Sharcross. See summary in *Window*, 25 December 1992.

193 'A tonking in Hong Kong', *Guardian Weekly*, 7 February 1993.

194 It could be constitutionally possible to implement any agreement reached in the Sino-British negotiations by prerogative legislation, that is, by an Order in Council. But this would be politically impossible after the Governor assured the legislators that they would have the final say.

195 Christopher Patten, 'Who believes in one country, two systems', *Ming Pao Monthly*, December 1992. While initially there were calls for a referendum, this mechanism was not favoured by either the Chinese or Patten, the former for fear of having to acknowledge a strong mandate for more democracy, the latter because this would undermine the legitimacy of both the Governor and the legislature to provide leadership.

196 See 'Plea to China on Legislative Council vote', *South China Morning Post*, 5 January 1993. China was not alone in opposing the Legislative Council's ability to have the final say over political reform. One conservative legislator charged that allowing the Legislative Council the ability to amend the Governor's reform was a violation of the executive-led governmental tradition, as well as burdening legislators with 'massive amendment work' even though they don't have the professional expertise to handle the job. Comments of Selina Chow, 'Changing reforms "not Legco's role" ', *South China Morning Post*, 12 February 1993.

197 'Beijing trip was doomed before the plane landed', *South China Morning Post*, 24 October 1992.

198 'Why Hong Kong must back Patten', *South China Morning Post*, 11 October 1992.

199 'Patten in warning to legislators', *South China Morning Post*, 31 October 1992.

200 Conservatives called for a three-month hiatus over the reforms, hoping that Britain and China would 'cut a deal' which would allow the Legislative Council the more traditional role of simply agreeing to decisions made elsewhere. The call for delay was initiated by members of the conservative Cooperative Resources Centre, which was soon renamed the Liberal Party. This suggestion immediately drew the ire of liberals who charged that delay would set a dangerous precedent where bills are deferred for political rather than technical reasons.

201 'Lu hits Basic Law "breaches" ', *South China Morning Post*, 24 October 1992.

202 'Lu hits Basic Law "breaches" ', *South China Morning Post*, 24 October 1992.

203 Moved by Mr McGregor. Quote from Hong Kong *Hansard*, 14 October 1992, pp. 114–15. Note: because the *Hansard* was not collated and bound by the time of this writing, the page numbers from here on only reflect those of a rough transcript of the 1992–93 proceedings.

204 Moved by Ms Loh. Quote from Hong Kong *Hansard*, 11 November 1992, p. 60.

205 Amendment moved by Mr McGregor and approved by a vote of 27 to 22. Multi-seat districts would be larger and hence more disadvantageous to independent candidates. Quote from Hong Kong *Hansard*, 15 July 1992, p. 215. There was also an amendment offered by Mr Fung which asked for the establishment of an independent committee to study the fairness of the functional constituency system. See Hong Kong *Hansard*, 16 July 1992, p. 7.

206 First suggested by the Select Committee on Legislative Council Elections, whose report was debated 15 July 1992.

207 The commission is a statutory body responsible for making recommendations to the Governor on electoral boundaries but will not decide on policy matters such as the number of constituencies or the number of seats per constituency.

208 Mr McGregor originally intended to pose an amendment to the motion to determine the degree of support for individual proposals. Lacking support for this, however, he withdrew his amendment from consideration.

209 See comments of Philip Wong in 'Why Legco should not be sent the Patten package', *South China Morning Post*, 10 January 1993.

210 Views issued during the debate are summarized in 'Resounding vote for Governor's reform plan', *South China Morning Post*, 14 January 1993.

211 Comments of Mr Martin Lee, 'Massive rejection of bid to block reform', *South China Morning Post*, 14 January 1993.

212 Hong Kong was allowed to send two delegates but only as support for the British representative. China insisted that they be labelled 'experts and advisers'. Britain insisted they be full members of the negotiating team; both sides ended up agreeing to differ and hence no mention was made of them in a joint communiqué announcing the talks.

213 Establishing a precedent for the Legislative Council to act as a better check on the executive, providing greater accountability after 1997. See 'New medicine for Hong Kong', *The Economist*, 20 February 1993, p. 31.

Notes to Chapter 5

1 UMELCO Annual Reports 1984 and 1985. The actual number of staff employed in October of both years was 68 and 109, respectively.

2 See for instance Norman Miners, *The Government and Politics of Hong Kong*, 3rd edn. (Hong Kong: Oxford University Press, 1986), pp. 157–64; Peter Harris, *Hong Kong: A Study in Bureaucratic Politics* (Hong Kong: Heinemann Asia, 1978), pp. 89–90; and especially Ian Scott, 'Hong Kong', in Gerald E. Caiden (ed.), *International Handbook of the Ombudsman: Country Surveys* (Westport, CT: Greenwood Press, 1983), pp. 113–21.

3 See conclusions in Malcolm E. Jewell and Samuel C. Patterson, *The Legislative Process in the United States* (New York: Random House, 1966), p. 249; and John F. Manley, 'Congressional Staff and Public Policymaking: The Joint Committee on Internal Revenue Taxation', in Nelson W. Polsby (ed.), *Congressional Behavior* (New York: Random House, 1971), pp. 42–58.

4 For a comprehensive summary of legislative staff literature, see Susan Webb Hammond, 'Legislative Staffs', in Gerhard Loewenberg, Samuel C. Patterson, and Malcolm Jewell (eds.), *Handbook of Legislative Research* (Cambridge, MA: Harvard University Press, 1985), pp. 273–319.

5 Nelson Polsby, 'The Institutionalization of the U.S. House of Representatives', *American Political Science Review* 62 (March 1968): 1–44. See also Samuel P. Huntington, 'Political Development and Political Decay', in Claude E. Welch Jr. (ed.), *Political Modernization* (Belmont, CA: Wadsworth Publishing Co., 1967), pp. 215–23.

6 Samuel C. Patterson, 'The Professional Staffs of Congressional Committees', *Administrative Science Quarterly*, 15 (1970): 22–37.

7 See, for instance, Manindra Kumar Mohapatra, 'The Ombudsmanic Role of Legislators in an Indian State', *Legislative Studies Quarterly*, 1 (1976): 295–314.

8 Harold L. Wolman and Dianne M. Wolman, 'The Role of the U.S. Senate Staff in the Opinion Linkage Process: Population Policy', *Legislative Studies Quarterly*, 2 (1977): 281–93.

9 See David E. Price, 'Professionals and 'Entrepreneurs'': Staff Orientations and Policy-making on Three Senate Committees', *Journal of Politics*, 33: 316–36.

10 Patterson, 'Professional Staff'; and Manley 'Congressional Staff', especially pp. 49–52.

11 See, for instance, Lawrence C. Dodd and Richard L. Schott, *Congress and the Administrative State* (New York: John Wiley and Sons, 1979), pp. 83ff.

12 See Manley, 'Congressional Staff', p. 49.

13 See Jewell and Patterson, *Legislative Process*, p. 263; Manley, 'Congressional Staff', p. 45; Patterson, 'Professional Staff', p. 29; and Randall B. Ripley, *Congress: Process and Policy* (New York: W.W. Norton & Co., Inc., 1975), p. 161.

14 Hammond, 'Legislative Staffs', p. 271.

15 See Abdo I. Baaklini, 'Legislative Staffing Patterns in Developing Countries', in James J. Heaphey and Alan P. Balutis (eds.), *Legislative Staffing: A Comparative Perspective* (New York: John P. Wiley & Sons, 1975); and Abdo I. Baaklini and James J. Heaphey, *Legislative Institution Building in Brazil, Costa Rica, and*

Lebanon (Beverly Hills, CA: Sage Professional Papers in Administrative and Policy Studies, no. 03-27, 1974).

16 James Robinson, 'Legislative Staffing', in Allan Kornberg and Lloyd D. Musolf (eds.), *Legislatures in Developmental Perspective* (Durham, NC: Duke University Press, 1970).

17 Norman Meller, 'Legislative Staff in Oceania as a Focus for Research', in Allan Kornberg (ed.), *Legislatures in Comparative Perspective* (New York: McKay, 1973), pp. 314–34.

18 Meller, 'Legislative Staff', p. 328.

19 Michael T. Ryle, 'Legislative Staff of the British House of Commons', *Legislative Studies Quarterly*, 6 (1981): 497–520; Stanley Campbell and Jean La Porte, 'The Staff of the Parliamentary Assemblies in France', *Legislative Studies Quarterly*, 6 (1981): 521–32; Werner Blischke, 'Parliamentary Staffs in the German Bundestag', *Legislative Studies Quarterly*, 6 (1981): 533–58.

20 See Hammond, 'Legislative Staffs', p. 296, for further legislative research questions.

21 For additional information on Hong Kong's political culture, see Lau Siu-kai, *Society and Politics in Hong Kong* (Hong Kong: The Chinese University Press, 1984).

22 *Umelco Annual Report 1970–71*, p. 8.

23 *Umelco Annual Report 1970–71*, p. 8.

24 *Umelco Annual Report 1970–71*, p. 8.

25 Interview with Complaints Division staff, 22 February 1993.

26 Personal Interview with Secretary General, 8 January 1988.

27 The standing orders of the Legislative Council forbid discussion of individual cases in the chamber. See Standing Order No. 18.

28 *Omelco Annual Report, 1987*, p. 28.

29 However, the increase in the number of cases has not been steady. For instance, in the late 1970s OMELCO investigations of police complaints was largely taken over by CAPO (Complaints Against Police Officers), which is within the jurisdiction of the Royal Hong Kong Police; in addition, the ICAC (Independent Commission Against Corruption) began to function fully during this period. Both of these initiatives led to a decrease in the number of complaints received by OMELCO. More recent drops in complaint cases may be attributed to an increase in complaints received by other government entities, such as the District Boards and the Urban Council. This has led to a drop of approximately 100 cases a month, according to a telephone interview with Press Officer Alex Choi, 24 May 1988. In addition, complaints alleging maladministration may be referred by the members to the Commission for Administrative Complaints.

30 Information obtained from Secretary General's office, 11 May 1993.

31 In 1984, for instance, the Complaints Division had the most staff in OMELCO, consisting at that time of 12 staff members, whereas the Members Division, forerunner of the Committees' Division, consisted of five staff; by 1993 the Complaints Division had increased to 24 staff members but the Committees Division was now staffed by 39 individuals.

32 Interview with the Secretary General, 8 January 1988.

33 Interview with Committees Division staff, 24 February 1993.

34 The panels, of which there are currently 16, monitor government policy. The Bills Committees are established to investigate bills being examined by the Legislative Council. There are four standing committees: Finance, Public Accounts, House, and Members' Interests. The panels and committees will be the subject of more extensive analysis in Chapter 6.

35 The Secretariat consists of deputy and assistant secretaries general of OMELCO.

36 Members Interests' Committee was created in 1991 and the House Committee in 1992.

37 Interview with Secretary General, 8 January 1988.

38 Interview with Committees Division staff, 23 February 1993.

39 Interview with Committees Division staff, 23 February 1993.

40 Norms revealed in interviews with senior administrative officers. Interviews conducted 14 December 1987 and 8 January 1988.

41 Interview with Committees Division staff, 23 February 1993.

42 Most of the information concerning the activities of the press section was provided in interviews with the Press Secretary (Chief Information Officer), OMELCO, 13 January 1988 and 17 November 1992.

43 Information provided by Secretary General's office, 1988.

44 Information about this post was provided by the public relations adviser in an interview on 14 January 1987.

45 Interview with the Public Relations Adviser, 14 January 1987.

46 Interview with the Public Relations Adviser, 14 January 1987.

47 A regular meeting of members held each Friday afternoon during the session. At this meeting the order of business for the next chamber meeting is discussed, as well as other internal matters of importance to the membership. This committee became a standing committee and was renamed the House Committee in 1992.

48 Interview with Public Relations Adviser, 14 January 1987.

49 Information elicited from formal job description of Legal Adviser as well as discussions with the Legal Adviser on 14 November 1987 and 25 February 1993.

50 Interview with the Legal Adviser, 14 November 1987.

51 Interview with the Legal Adviser, 14 November 1987.

52 Description of the work of the Clerk-of-Council's Office is based on an interview with the Clerk of Council, 25 February 1993.

53 It is not known when the account of Council and committee proceedings was first published, but copies exist from 1890 onwards and are noted on the title page as being 'Reprinted from the Hong Kong Daily Press, revised by Members'; this continued until 1928 when it became an official publication. See Endacott, *Government and People,* p. 111.

54 The Members' allowances were to be raised to HK$73,000 (May 1993), but this increase had not yet gone into effect at the time of this writing. The salary remains HK$39,400 per month.

55 Interviews were conducted in 1987–8 and 1992–3. Some of the tables in this chapter will refer solely to the most recent data (1992–3) collected. In addition, since not all members answered each question, there will be variations in totals and percentages.

56 Interview with a personal staff member, 24 February 1993.

57 Interview with a personal staff member, 12 January 1988.

58 Interview with a personal staff member, 23 February 1993.

59 There was no direct question put to all members about about an increase in staff, but rather several voiced this need during the interview discussion.

60 But some members, due to a high profile on a particular issue, nonetheless receive a significant number of complaints and representations.

61 Interview with personal staff, 18 June 1987.

62 See for instance Alan J. Wyner, 'Legislative Reform and Politics in California: What Happened, Why? and So What', in James A. Robinson (ed.), *State Legislative Innovation* (New York: Praeger, 1973).

63 The remainder of the OMELCO secretariat, particularly the Complaints Division, was seen to have less significance in providing for legislative independence.

64 Interview with Members Division staff, 8 January 1988.
65 Interview with Members Division staff, 31 December 1987.
66 Interview with Members Division staff, 8 January 1988.
67 Interview with Members Division staff, 8 January 1988.
68 Interview with an Appointed Member, 3 August 1987.
69 See Baaklini, 'Legislative Staffing Patterns'.
70 Baaklini, 'Legislative Staffing Patterns', p. 236.
71 Interview with OMELCO staff, 22 April 1992.
72 Interview with OMELCO staff, 21 April 1992.
73 Interview with OMELCO staff, 27 May 1992.
74 Interview with OMELCO staff, 2 November 1992.
75 Interview with OMELCO staff, 21 April 1992.
76 Based on interviews conducted during 1992–3, 43 members responding. While 100 per cent of the directly elected member favored independence, less than 75 per cent of appointed and functional members favoured this move.
77 Interview with personal staff member, 24 February 1993.
78 The electoral connection is promoted by providing services for constituents, who will then vote for the member in the next election. This phenomena of services for votes has been uncovered in many previous political studies of Western democracies, most prominently by David R. Mayhew, *Congress: The Electoral Connection* (New Haven: Yale University Press, 1974).

Notes to Chapter 6

1 See Jean Blondel, *Comparative Legislatures* (Englewood Cliffs, NJ: Prentice Hall, Inc., 1973); Michael Mezey, *Comparative Legislatures* (Durham, NC: Duke University Press, 1979); Gerhard Loewenberg and Samuel C. Patterson, *Comparing Legislatures* (Lanham, MD: University Press of America, 1979); Inter-Parliamentary Union, *Parliaments of the World: A Comparative Reference Compendium,* 2nd edn. (Hants, UK: Gower Publishing Co., 1986).
2 Clause 24 of the Royal Instructions, incorporated into Legislative Council Standing Order 23. Since almost any change in law requires the expenditure of monies, at the very least for administrative costs, this restriction has precluded non-government members from introducing any legislation other than private bills, typically for the incorporation of a charity.
3 Yet the government was always careful to promote consensus with the unofficials, and since the Second World War only twice used its official majority to override the unanimous opposition of non-government members. See Miners, *Government and Politics*, 3rd edn., p. 130.
4 Although there were instances when unofficials opposed government policy, typically these divisions ended with the government view prevailing. Exceptions occurred when officials were given permission to abstain from voting, such as on the Young proposals (1949) and an attempt to legalize betting on football pools (1960). Since 1968 a revision in the Legislative Council's standing orders allowing the Governor to determine when divisions could be recorded resulted in no further divisions until quite recently. See Miners, *Government and Politics,* appendix 6 (f), pp. 359–63.
5 In 1987, the government re-enacted an old law making it an offence for a newspaper to publish false news that would disturb the public order. See Hong Kong *Hansard*, 1987, pp. 1016–84. Twenty-one months later, a bill repealing this

clause was introduced. On both occasions, in spite of the inconsistency, the appointed members supported the government.

6 The accident at the Chernobyl nuclear power plant in April 1986 aroused widespread public concern over the proposed construction of a nuclear power plant at Daya Bay in China, only 50 kilometres (30 miles) from Hong Kong. The legislature was active in monitoring this development through the use of panel meetings, adjournment debates, and fact-finding tours. Yet even with widespread doubts about the safety and feasibility of the project, the Chinese and Hong Kong governments, with support of appointed members and conservative functional constituency members, were able to commence construction. Movement to hold another debate was declined for fear of offending China. This decision came with the support of all 24 appointed members but only 9 of the 22 elected members.

7 Such as the successful opposition to a 1992–3 budget proposal for a tax-rate increase. Conservatives and liberals demanded a higher personal tax allowance and wider tax base and opposed any rise in the rates. The Financial Secretary was later to claim that an unexpected surplus allowed him to revise plans so that the rate increase would not go into effect.

8 An exception to this was legislation initiated by Mr Martin Lee, directly elected, to amend the Electoral Provisions Ordinance so that all geographical constituencies were approximately equal in terms of population. This was the first instance in Hong Kong's history of a public bill being introduced by an unofficial. Yet because of the prohibition on unofficial bills that impose a financial obligation, the future will see no change in the custom of bureaucratic initiated legislation.

9 The government has always prided itself as based on 'consultation and consent' and by the 1990s had established almost 400 boards and committees that were to advise the various executive departments.

10 In 1984 the Executive Council was composed of six officials and eleven unofficials, five of whom were also unofficial members of the legislature. By 1991, six of the nine unofficials on the Executive Council were also legislators. But in 1992 Governor Patten separated the Executive Council from the Legislative Council, mandating no membership overlap.

11 Though many of their conclusions are legally subject to ratification by the Legislative Council and its Finance Committee, 'in practice this is normally achieved without much difficulty.' See Miners, *Government and Politics*, p. 83.

12 While before 1985 most policy branch secretaries were formally official members of the Legislative Council, the number has been gradually decreased so that now the current officials (three) must cover a broad range of policy areas. In 1995 there will be no officials sitting on the legislature, but it is expected they will be present at meetings to assist in the passage of legislation.

13 The Legal Unit is more comprehensively discussed in Chapter 5.

14 A new Bills Committee structure was created in 1992 to consider legislation. From the early 1970s bills were considered in *ad hoc* groups; before that time, deliberation was more informal and cursory. Each Bills Committee is formed anew for a particular piece of legislation and then goes out of existence once the legislation has been passed back up to the House Committee. Bills Committees are composed of at least three members, although any member may join. The House Committee holds an election and determines members of the Bills Committee; then the president of the Legislative Council is notified and he in turn formally nominates them. The members elect a chairman, who is given a casting vote in the case of a tie. Their deliberations are held in public, unless the chairman deems that the subject necessitates a closed proceeding. Bills Committees have the power to call any person to attend their sessions and provide evidence or documents, although the exercise of this power requires approval by the full House Committee.

15 The report typically explains what amendments are recommended and attaches draft amendments to the bill. But these amendments are not binding on the House Committee or the full chamber.

16 The House Committee does not carry out an executive function, like the Rules Committee of the US House of Representatives, which determines what rule (open or closed) will govern chamber deliberations. Rather, the House Committee reviews the bill to allow members informally to consider its merits prior to formal deliberation in chamber.

17 If a bill has been particularly controversial, the second reading debate is adjourned a second time in order that the bill may be reconsidered by the governor-in-council (Executive Council).

18 This was always the case until 1985, when five unofficials spoke to defend the amended Legislative Council (Powers and Privileges) Bill.

19 Prior to 1992, on rare occasions a select committee was formed to scrutinize legislation. One such committee is the Select Committee on the Complex Commercial Crimes Bill, which was formed in 1986. The committee met for six months and recommended fundamental changes to the legislation. An *ad hoc* panel was formed after publication of the White Paper on the Complex Commercial Crimes Bill in December 1987. Members of the panel raised a number of objections to the bill, arguing that the legislation departed from the recommendations of the select committee. The administration eventually accommodated many of these suggestions, resulting in passage of the legislation in July 1988. While the history of this legislation demonstrates significant deliberative power on the part of legislators, it is important to emphasize that this process was a critical exception to the typical pattern of legislative involvement.

20 Although the panels remained the same as those of 1984 numerically, there was some change in titles.

21 And this does not measure the actual time spent at the meetings. While accurate statistics are unavailable, it can be hypothesized that the length of meetings has also increased tremendously.

22 Twenty-eight members attacked the government's record over a myriad of policies ranging from inflation to property speculation and constitutional developments. See 'New-era legislators demand greater say', *South China Morning Post*, 31 October 1991.

23 Of the 47 members present, 34 voted in favour of the 'vote of thanks', two against, eleven abstained, and one 'forgot to vote'. The two negatives and most of the abstentions were from directly elected members.

24 The Finance Committee was created in 1872. See Chapter 3 for additional details.

25 Except for confidential matters, for which meetings are closed to the public upon a consensus agreement of the members.

26 Instituted in 1961, the Establishment Subcommittee consists of 28 members along with the Secretary for Civil Service and the Secretary for the Treasury. The Public Works Subcommittee, created in the late nineteenth century, consists of 31 members, along with the Secretary for Planning, Environment, and Lands and the Secretary for Works.

27 At least every fortnight while the Council is in session to examine proposals for supplementary expenditures and new financial commitments.

28 Established in 1978. See Chapter 3 for additional details.

29 Latest statistics on membership were from the *OMELCO Annual Report* 1992. The members are nominated by the president of the Legislative Council.

30 But starting in 1979 accountability was strengthened when the Financial Secretary formally reported to the legislature on actions taken to correct problems uncovered in that year's report. This has now become a customary procedure.

31 A series of Public Accounts Committee hearings were held over the misman-agement of the construction of a new science and technology university when its cost rose to HK$3.4 million from an estimate of HK$1.9 million.

32 *OMELCO Annual Report* 1991, p. 48. Motions must relate to specific policies. A 12-day notice is required; if amendments are to be offered to the motion, notifi-cation of them must occur five days prior to debate. Two motions are allowed per sitting, or a motion and an adjournment debate. The mover may speak up to 15 minutes, but the president can limit speaking time upon recommendation of the House Committee. Other speakers have seven minutes in which to speak and there is no time limit on the government's response. There is also no limit on the number of speakers.

33 Adjournment debates require a seven-day notice and are limited to one hour; 45 minutes are allotted for members' speeches and 15 minutes allotted for the official reply.

34 Questions must be short, precise, and factual and appear in either written or oral form for chamber consideration. The questioner has to be prepared to substan-tiate any query to ensure that it is based on a real case rather than a hypothetical situation. After the official response, the questioner, and others who care to join it, can ask supplementary questions. The administration requires seven days' notice prior to the submission of each question. The number of questions is limited to two per member, of those one must be written; an additional question may be allowed if it is deemed important. A total of 20 questions are allowed per sitting: 14 written and 6 oral. Finally, the nature and wording of the questions is stringently controlled: a question can not refer to debates or answers to questions in the current session or attempt to elicit any opinions; nor can they contain any arguments, inferences, opinions, imputations, or offensive expressions.

35 The subject matter is determined by the Governor. The first few sessions were almost exclusively devoted to matters arising under the Governor's constitutional proposals of 1992.

36 The Governor has, however, restricted the questions asked at times to just the subject addressed by him in his opening comments. He further restricts questions by controlling the time spent on his speech versus that allowed for questions, and by designating which questioner may speak. With the advent of the new president of Council, his ability to control this time may decline.

37 Background rationale provided by C. M. Leung, deputy assistant secretary, Constitutional Affairs Branch, 22 February 1993.

38 Once to defeat a motion of censure demanding that the government should 'modify its present unfair and repressive policy with regard to the renewal of the seventy-five year Crown Leases,' and second, on a resolution to amend the royalty to be paid by the Yaumatei Ferry Company so as to bring it into line with that levied by the Star Ferry Company.

39 Miners, *Government and Politics*, 3d edn., p. 129. The appearance of unanim-ity was heightened with the adoption of a new standing order in 1968 that allowed the president (up to 1992, the Governor) to refuse a division if, in his opinion, the division is unnecessarily claimed after a voice vote.

40 K. C. Wheare, *Government by Committee* (Oxford: Oxford University Press, 1955), p. 69.

41 Miners, *Government and Politics*, 3d edn., p. 180.

42 Peter Wesley-Smith, *Constitutional and Administrative Law in Hong Kong* (Hong Kong: China and Hong Kong Law Studies, 1987), Vol. 1, p. 163.

43 Lucian W. Pye, *Asian Power and Politics: The Cultural Dimensions of Author-ity* (Cambridge, MA: Harvard University Press, 1985), p. 22.

44 Quoted in J. S. Hoadley, 'Hong Kong is the Lifeboat: Notes on Political Culture and Socialization', *Journal of Oriental Studies* 8 (1970): 211.

45 Unofficial Li Fook-shu, Hong Kong *Hansard*, 1967, pp. 153–4, as quoted in Miners, *Government and Politics*, 3d edn., p. 255.

46 S. K. Lau, *Society and Politics in Hong Kong* (Hong Kong: The Chinese University Press, 1984), p. 129.

47 With the exception of the 1878 memorial to the Governor for 'increased participation in the management of public affairs.' But, as Endacott notes, this was probably due to the instigation of the Governor himself rather than from the Chinese élite. See Endacott, *Government and People*, pp. 92–3.

48 Though it is appropriate to take note of the activities of Lo Man-kam, who used questions to prod the government to act on a variety of measures. Yet he never used his vote to express his rejection of government policy. See Chapter 3, note 88.

49 See, for instance, David R. Mayhew, *Congress: The Electoral Connection* (New Haven: Yale University Press, 1974).

50 See Seymour Scher, 'Conditions for Legislative Control', *Journal of Politics,* 25 (August 1963): 526–640; and Robert Stauffer, 'The Philippine Congress: Causes of Structural Change', *Sage Research Papers in Social Science*, No. 90-024 (Beverly Hills, CA: Sage Publications, 1975).

51 Lau, *Society and Politics*, p. 129.

52 P. B. Harris, 'Government and Politics', *1951–1976: A Quarter-Century of Hong Kong, Chung Chi College Anniversary Symposium* (Hong Kong: The Chinese University Press, 1977), p. 72.

53 The difficulty of legislative generalists deliberating on executive proposals that require expertise has been a dilemma uncovered in many comparative studies. See, for instance, Gerhard Loewenberg, Samuel C. Patterson, and Malcolm E. Jewell, *Handbook of Legislative Research* (Cambridge, MA: Harvard University Press, 1985).

54 Miners, *Government and Politics,* 3d edn., p. 134.

55 It has traditionally been assumed that appointed members want to please the Governor so that they can secure their re-appointment to the legislature. With the stipulation that all members be elected in 1995, this rationale is no longer appropriate in characterizing their actions in Council. Additionally, since 1992 the support of appointed members has been further diminished with the change of Governors. All but three of these members had been appointed by the previous Governor. With the advent of a new Governor, let alone one with more liberal views which are incompatible with the conservative inclination of most appointees, the lack of support has become more marked. If anything, the directly elected members have become more pro-government, with the appointed members and conservative functional constituencies taking on the role of the opposition.

56 Such as determination of when to call divisions, which allowed him to stifle dissent in the chamber as well as camouflage any lack of consensus. Since 1991, members may call for a division.

57 Institutionalization connotes the gaining of organizational autonomy, internal specialization that takes shape in greater complexity, and the evolution of standardized procedures and universalistic criteria for ordering affairs. For further discussion, see Samuel C. Huntington, *Political Order in Changing Societies* (New Haven: Yale University Press, 1968).

58 In July 1991, for instance, a motion was passed which incorporated a total of 47 amendments to the standing orders covering the use of questions, length of speeches, sponsorship for motion and adjournment debates, establishment of a Committee on Members' Interests, and electronic voting. The Committee on Members' Interests examines the arrangements for the compilation, maintenance, and accessibility of the Register of Members' Interests. It considers any matter of ethics relating to the conduct of members and gives advice and guidelines on ethical

matters. It consists of a chair and six other members, all of whom are appointed by the president of the Legislative Council.

59 The possibility of the Legislative Council having a committee system was first raised by the Chief Secretary in 1985. At that time it was believed that stronger committees were needed because 'the Legislative Council members would be more closely involved in the formulation of government policy in coming years'. See 'The Legislative Council may have committee system', *South China Morning Post*, 9 October 1985.

60 In addition, revamping the committee system was coupled with an attempt to prevent appointed Executive Council unofficials from also serving on the committees. These individuals had dominated the panels in the past, since they were typically chosen as chairmen due to their seniority. The liberals argued that they lacked legitimacy, as none of them were directly elected; further, Governors typically appointed conservatives who operated by the informal rules of confidentiality and collective responsibility and could be expected always to support the Governor and hence not allow the panels to be used as oppositional platforms. The issue of unofficial Executive Council participation in committee proceedings was effectively resolved when Governor Patten separated the two bodies in October 1992. It is significant to note that China did not want any standing committees to be created, as they feared this would lead to a stronger exercise of legislative powers. The liberals consequently charged that the conservatives were more interested in pleasing China than in fulfilling their legislative responsibilities. See for instance, 'Chinese worried by introduction of committees', *South China Morning Post*, 6 December 1991.

61 See *Ming Pao*, 17 December 1991, p. 6.

62 *Report by the Working Group on Matters Arising from the Winding up of OMELCO* (5 February 1993). The paper noted that the function of panels would be to monitor government policies and to examine new policies. As there were bound to be grey areas as to whether a bill contains any policy implications, it was suggested that new policy in blue bills would be examined first by panels and then by Bills Committees. This report was awaiting the endorsement of the House Committee at the time of this writing.

63 Gained from a revamp of the *Legislative Council (Powers and Privileges) Ordinance of 1984*.

64 Even more so now, since as of 1992 no legislator sits on the Executive Council.

65 The concern over this bill was so great that a select committee was established to study it in 1985. After six months, the committee's report, containing recommendations for fundamental changes in the prosecution and trial of complex cases, was tabled in the Legislative Council. The committee also rejected the proposal to replace the judge and jury system in certain cases with a tribunal consisting of a judge and three commercial adjudicators. The bill was eventually enacted in 1988, after substantial amendments had occurred.

66 See note 6 above.

67 Provided for the establishment of a three-tiered classification of films. The *ad hoc* group set up to scrutinize the draft bill held 37 meetings over a 14-month period; its deliberations resulted in a large number of amendments to the first draft. The most contentious issue concerned a provision allowing the censorship authority to ban or excise films which might be seriously prejudicial to Hong Kong's good relations with other territories. During the second reading, a proposal was offered requiring the censor to 'take into account' Article 19 of the International Covenant on Civil and Political Rights, as a way to prohibit infringement on the rights and freedoms of individuals. While this was adopted, liberals in the Council remained dissatisfied with the breadth of censorship allowable under the law.

68 Comments of Secretary for the Treasury Yeung Kai-yin, 'Buck stops with Yeung', *Hong Kong Standard*, 8 May 1993.

69 The amendments were offered by Mr Martin Lee and Mr Kingsley Sit, respectively. Because they did not raise, but rather lowered, a charge on revenue, they were initially deemed appropriate. However, a later opinion established that the amendments should not have been offered without the approval of the Governor since they lowered tax income and hence reduced the territory's revenue. See 'Budget proposal a "legal hiccup"', *South China Morning Post*, 25 March 1992.

70 See 'Officials bombarded with blitz of Budget queries', *South China Morning Post*, 11 March 1992.

71 Comments of Financial Secretary Mr Hamish McCleod, Hong Kong *Hansard*, 1 April 1992, pp. 47 and 49, respectively. In subsequent debate, members' speeches focused as much on revenue measures as on the Appropriations Bill, with special attention given to a salaries tax proposal, personal allowances, and tax bands.

72 The rejected papers were wide ranging: they concerned the creation of a post in the Government Information Services, a University and Polytechnic Grants Committee (UPGC) recommendation, a study for redevelopment of the airport, a study to examine the need for a science park, and an increase in allowance for jurors.

73 The motion was moved by functional constituency legal representative Mr Simon Li.

74 See his comments in 'The Legislative Council says no to final court deal', *South China Morning Post*, 5 December 1991.

75 Comments of Mr Martin Lee in 'The Legislative Council says no to final court deal', *South China Morning Post*, 5 December 1991.

76 'The Legislative Council shows newfound assertiveness,' *Financial Times*, 4 May 1993.

77 For instance, by the end of 1991, only four bills were passed, compared to 21 passed the previous year. The former senior unofficial, an appointed member, charged that the new directly elected members were 'crippling the efficient operation of the council.' See 'Elected legislators cripple council: Lee', *Hong Kong Standard*, 31 December 1991.

78 A sitting is a session of the legislature, held either bi-monthly (as in the past) or weekly (as is contemporary practice). The longest sitting of the Legislative Council occurred from 15 to 16 June 1992, lasting a total of eighteen hours and thirteen minutes.

79 Membership increased from 48 (1984) to 60 (from 1988).

80 Concern over passage of bills has been frequently expressed and has even led to a proposal that the Legislative Council extend its meetings to twice a week when needed. This was the suggestion of the Ad Hoc Group on Legislative Procedures; see 'Two-day sittings likely', *South China Morning Post*, 22 January 1992.

81 With the exception of 1988, during which the appointed members asked more questions than the functional constituency but fewer than the electoral college members.

82 John Adams, 'Letter to John Penn', *Works* (Boston: Little Brown and Company, 1852), Vol. IV, p. 203.

83 See for instance Carl T. Smith, 'Chinese Elite in Hong Kong', *Journal of the Hong Kong Branch of the Royal Asiatic Society*, 11 (1971): 74–115. The author observes that the Legislative Council members were regarded as 'the elite of the elite' (p. 113).

84 Ambrose King, 'Administrative absorption of politics in Hong Kong: emphasis on the grass roots level', *Asian Survey*, 15, 5 (May 1975): 426.

85 Aline Wong, 'Apathy and the Political Systems in Hong Kong', *United College Journal*, 8 (1970–71): 15–16.

86 Scott, *Political Change,* p. 61.

87 As portrayed in Chapters 3 and 4, although the members were for the promotion of economic interests, they were not as concerned about the promotion of political rights, particularly should that in any way exact cost or threaten their economic gains. See discussion of merchant petition for municipal government in the late 1840s, their lack of support for the institution of the Sanitary Board, forerunner of the Urban Council; the 1894 petition, shown to be motivated for prevention of taxation rather than promotion of representation; their opposition to the Young reforms; and their mixed views on constitutional reform since 1984, with the majority supporting the government's retreat from more democratic initiatives as evident in the 1988 White Paper as well as their back-down from their own OMELCO consensus model in a later vote.

88 Sectors included commerce, industry, labour, finance, social services, education, and the legal, medical, and engineering professions.

89 There were ten geographical constituencies and two special constituencies for the urban areas and the New Territories. Each of the ten districts was composed of roughly 500,000 people; each district had between one and four District Boards, depending on population size. Electors consisted of both elected and appointed members of the District Boards and the two councils; the ratio between elected and appointed district members was 2 to 3; in the councils it was 1 to 1.

90 The 1988 election is not seen as significant as the electoral contours (electoral college, functional constituency) remained the same, although two more functional constituencies were added to the membership.

91 The constituencies were of unequal size, with the largest comprising a population of 794,900—more than double the size of the smallest, which had a population of 392,400. See Rowena Y. F. Kwok, 'Government and the Electoral Process: The Need for Review', in Rowena Kwok, Joan Leung, and Ian Scott, *Votes Without Power: The Hong Kong Legislative Council Elections 1991* (Hong Kong: Hong Kong University Press, 1991), pp. 187–210.

92 Financial services and real estate/construction, respectively. See Clarence Leung, 'Politics and 1991 Elections in Hong Kong', *The Foundation* (March 1992): 12–13. The functional constituency electorate, which was composed of both individuals and corporate groups, ranged from 181 in one electorate (social services) to 38,678 in another (teaching).

93 See editorial, *South China Morning Post*, 17 September 1991.

94 See Donald McMillen and Michael Degoyler, 'Government Administration of the 1991 Elections: A Public Opinion Analysis', paper presented to An International Conference on Hong Kong Public Administration in Transition: A Regional Perspective, Hong Kong Polytechnic, 10–12 December 1992. The authors argue that no provision was made for absentee voters; registration rolls were not purged nor validated prior to the election, hence many did not receive voter instructions; finally, a number of registered voters were confused over voting procedures and therefore did not vote.

95 For this election was about 'votes without power', in that the voter could only elect a small portion of legislators to a body which was not responsible for governing. For elaboration of this idea, see *Votes Without Power*, especially chapter 1.

96 See Ian Scott, 'An Overview of the Hong Kong Legislative Elections of 1991', in Kwok, Leung, and Scott, *Votes Without Power*, p. 4. Scott goes on to argue that a survey revealed that the non-voters held similar beliefs to those that voted (p. 7).

97 Scott, 'An Overview', p. 12.

98 Scott, 'An Overview', p. 17.

99 See 'Liberals still not in lead', *Hong Kong Standard,* 14 September 1991.

100 Although the 1984 Green Paper argued that Governors had always selected their Legislative Council appointees on the basis of occupation, the functional

system was the first explicit statement of the need for occupational representation in the legislature.

101 But from a sexual classification, the post-1985 legislature has become less representative. While 20 per cent of the legislature was female in 1984 under the old appointed system, this percentage shrank to 15 per cent in 1985, increasing slightly to 19 per cent in 1988 before shrinking to 12.5 per cent in 1991.

102 Discussed in Chapter 3. One scholar notes that the committee 'had become the Chinese executive council'. See Lennox A. Mills, *British Rule in Eastern Asia* (Oxford: Oxford University Press, 1942), p. 398.

103 A philanthropic association. See also discussion in Chapter 3.

104 Miners, *Imperial Rule*, p. 62.

105 Mezey, *Comparative Legislatures*, p. 255.

106 B. B. Schaffer, 'The Concept of Preparation', *World Politics*, 18, 1 (October 1965): 53.

107 Jean Grossholtz, 'Integrative Factors in the Malaysian and Philippine Legislatures', *Comparative Politics*, 3 (October 1970): 94.

108 Lau, *Society and Politics*, p. 122.

109 Lau, *Society and Politics*, p. 122.

110 J. Stephen Hoadley, ' "Hong Kong is the Lifeboat": Notes on Political Culture and Socialization', *Journal of Oriental Studies*, 8 (1970): 212.

111 Lau, *Society and Politics*, p. 118.

112 'Few know about role of Legco', *Hong Kong Standard*, 31 March 1984.

113 Mezey, *Comparative Legislatures*, p. 270.

114 King, 'Administrative Absorption', p. 126.

115 Editorial, 'New Breed infusing life into Legco', *Hong Kong Standard*, 4 November 1991.

116 Editorial, 'New Breed infusing life into Legco', *Hong Kong Standard*, 4 November 1991.

117 Particularly as seen in the dispute over the 1992 Patten proposals.

118 Hong Kong *Hansard*, 6 November 1991, p. 394.

119 Hong Kong *Hansard*, 6 November 1991, p. 393.

120 Except for Elsie Elliott Tu, an elected member of the Urban Council. Ms Tu is currently the functional representative of the Urban Council.

121 See, for instance, 'Hong Kong hails tough new Legco', *South China Morning Post*, 29 December 1991; and 'Public Mood Swings Lessen', *Hong Kong Standard*, 17 February 1993.

122 'Hongkong hails tough new Legco', *South China Morning Post,* 29 December 1991; and 'Beijing Row Hits Patten Popularity', *Hong Kong Standard*, 24 December 1992.

123 'Elsie Tu tops popularity polls', *South China Morning Post*, 1 January 1993.

124 Although it has been argued that the Hong Kong government itself has brought upon its own crisis of legitimacy. See Scott, *Crisis of Legitimacy*.

125 Mezey, *Comparative Legislatures*, p. 140.

126 Mezey, *Comparative Legislatures*, p. 281.

127 'Let member ride through '97—poll', *South China Morning Post*, 13 September 1992.

128 See 'Public Mood Swings Lessen', *Hong Kong Standard*, 17 February 1993.

129 'Eve of election opinion poll', *South China Morning Post*, 15 September, 1991.

130 'Governor urged to give way', *South China Morning Post*, 4 April 1993.

131 *Personal Interview,* 18 May 1992.

132 Mezey, *Comparative Legislatures*, p. 121.

133 Mezey, *Comparative Legislatures*, p. 121.

134 Currently no legislation can be offered which imposes a charge on the revenue. Under the Basic Law, members cannot introduce bills which relate to public

expenditure or political structure or the operation of government. Further, the written consent of the Chief Executive is required before bills relating to government policies can be introduced. These restrictions on legislative activity make amendments of any kind difficult to secure.

135 Mezey, *Comparative Legislatures*, p. 127.

136 According to Article 50 of the Basic Law, the Chief Executive may dissolve the Legislative Council if it refuses to pass a budget or any other important bill introduced by the government.

137 See Lau, *Society and Politics*; Lau Siu-Kai, 'The Political Values of the Hong Kong Chinese', in Wesley-Smith and Chen, *The Basic Law*, pp. 19–42.

138 With the exception of some surveys taken in conjunction with Governor Patten's 1992 reforms. Even then, questions about the legislature lacked a broad basis and depth.

139 Specific support relates to satisfaction with the performance of the legislature; diffuse support is based upon a general allegiance to the legislative body. While specific support can fluctuate depending on the popularity of issues deliberated upon, diffuse support persists over time, even through periods of unpopular or unsuccessful policies. For elaboration of the concept, see David Easton, *A Systems Analysis of Political Life* (New York: Wiley & Sons, Inc., 1965), pp. 367–74. For application of the concept to the legislatures, see Mezey, *Comparative Legislatures*, pp. 30–6.

140 The extent of executive co-optation during the deliberative phase is an exaggeration of what occurs in Hong Kong. See Mezey, *Comparative Legislatures*, p. 116. The past two years indicate that the Legislative Council is beginning to exercise more financial oversight than most marginal legislatures. Finally, the extent of intimidation exercised by executive élites in marginal legislatures is not applicable to Hong Kong, although the future remains unclear. See Mezey, *Comparative Legislatures*, pp. 116, 127, and 130, respectively, for elaboration of these details.

141 Mezey, *Comparative Legislatures*, p. 283.

Notes to Chapter 7

1 The dispute centres on the composition of the Election Committee, which will choose 10 members in 1995, and the basis for additional functional constituencies. See Chapter 4 for details.

2 The tables depicting these roles reflect data obtained by questioning 52 members of the legislature in 1987–8 and 1992–3. The percentages in the tables will vary as not all respondents answered all questions. Additional information about the research design can be found in the Appendix.

3 The Electoral College response here is puzzling but may be explained by the fact that one-fifth want to 'serve the public', which would involve knowing what the public desires and acting upon it, the basic requirements of representation. The directly elected members' desire to promote democracy can also be interpreted in representative terms, as representative democracy is the basis of most legislative systems in which legislators perceive they are chosen to make choices for the public.

4 This question was not asked in 1993.

5 Gerhard Loewenberg and Samuel C. Patterson, *Comparing Legislatures* (New York: University Press of America, 1979), p. 167.

6 Edmund Burke, who in the 1770s represented the city of Bristol in the British House of Commons, gave a classic description of the conflicting forces under which

legislators must determine their appropriate focus of representation. He contrasted the territorially defined district versus the larger interests of the nation and noted that 'Parliament is not a congress of ambassadors from different and hostile interests . . . [but] a deliberative assembly of one nation, one interest.' See Edmund Burke, *Works* (London: C. and J. Ribington, 1826), p. 18.

7 This represents the 1993 responses; 50 per cent agreed in 1988.

8 As seen in Chapter 4, 12 of the 21 functional constituency seats were uncontested but all of the directly elected member seats were contested in the 1991 election.

9 For further elaboration, see the discussion in Wahlke, Eulau, Buchanan, and Ferguson, *The Legislative System*, p. 276.

10 And even then, as seen in Chapter 4, they simply ratified decisions taken by the executive branch.

11 See for instance, S. K. Lau, *Society and Politics in Hong Kong* (Hong Kong: The Chinese University Press, 1984).

12 See Miners, *The Government and Politics of Hong Kong*, 4th edn., chapter 13.

13 See similar conception in Wahlke, Eulau, Buchanan, and Ferguson, *The Legislative System*, p. 311. For rationale of the merits of pressure groups in the political system, see Norman J. Ornstein and Shirley Elder, *Interest Groups, Lobbying and Policymaking* (Washington, DC: Congressional Quarterly Press, 1978); and M. Von Nordheim and R. W. Taylor, 'The Significance of Lobbyist-Legislator Interaction in German State Parliaments', *Legislative Studies Quarterly*, 1 (1976): 511–31.

14 For a good review of the literature on interest group impact on the legislative process, see Keith E. Hamm, 'Legislative Committees, Executive Agencies, and Interest Groups', in Loewenberg, Patterson, and Jewell, *Handbook of Legislative Research*, pp. 573–620.

15 For additional questions, see Wahlke, Eulau, Buchanan, and Ferguson, *The Legislative System*, p. 313.

16 For appointed members, 94 per cent favoured their personal convictions over those of an interest group, but only 38 per cent favoured 'their constituency' over views of an interest group, reinforcing the previous conclusion that who they represent in the legislature remains ill-defined. Most of the appointed members responded that 'it depends' on the issue in determining their vote when views of their constituency, however defined, conflicted with the views of a major interest group.

17 The reader should be aware that these are simplified generalizations; there are important exceptions to each of the descriptions.

18 The electoral college member has been left out of this summary since this position no longer exists.

19 Appointed members are the most senior, with some of them serving the longest tenure in the legislature. For additional comments on the role of the ritualist, see Roger H. Davidson, *The Role of the Congressman* (New York: Pegasus Publishing Company, 1969), p. 180.

20 Yet the overall conservative nature of appointed members is a characterization which has some notable exceptions, particularly those recent appointees of Governor Patten.

21 And it should be noted that the Broker orientation was only held by a few of those functional constituency members from the larger constituencies; many of the functional constituencies are fairly monolithic in terms of point of view.

22 See summary of this role in Davidson, *The Role of the Congressman*, p. 180.

23 See Miners, *Government and Politics*, p. 186. While the government has made it a policy to encourage the proliferation of interest groups, lately group activity has constrained the government's traditional unilateral policy making as the interest groups have become more independent of, and often more critical of, the govern-

ment. Consequently, it can be expected that officials may have less favorable views of interest group activities in the future.

24 This role had a forerunner in the form of the deputy president, appointed by the Governor in 1991 to assist him in administering Legislative Council meetings in his absence. The Governor never officiated the chamber meetings once this post was created.

25 This position is found in clause XXI of the Royal Instructions. The only time the casting vote has been used was in the case of an amendment to a motion regarding the appointment of the Governor. The deputy president voted in this case to preserve the status quo by not supporting an amendment to the motion. See Hong Kong *Hansard*, 22 January 1992, pp. 1456–7.

26 The need for impartiality was specified in an interview with the incumbent on 22 May 1992 and from analysis of a question asked to members in 1992–3 in which 92 per cent listed impartiality as the prime requirement for the job.

27 Interview with deputy speaker, 22 May 1992.

28 Studies in a number of countries have found roles to be a useful concept in comparing legislators but caution should be used in interpreting similarities and differences due to variations in conceptualization, definitions, and measurements. See discussion in Malcolm E. Jewell, 'Representative Process', in Gerhard Loewenberg, Samuel C. Patterson, and Malcolm E. Jewell, *Handbook of Legislative Research* (Cambridge, MA: Harvard University Press, 1985), p. 104.

29 Jewell, 'Representative Process', p. 110.

30 Because classification by purposive role categories has not been employed to any great degree outside of the United States, only gross functional responses will be evaluated.

31 See Roger H. Davidson, *The Role of the Congressman*; and Wahlke, Eulau, Buchanan, and Ferguson, *The Legislative System*.

32 Chong Lim Kim, Joel D. Barkan, Ilter Turan, and Malcolm E. Jewell, *The Legislative Connection: The Politics of Representation in Kenya, Korea, and Turkey* (Durham, NC: Duke University Press, 1984).

33 Several international surveys have revealed that while few legislators in developing countries note representation as the prime function or as a 'purposive role', nonetheless an increasing number of legislators are spending more of their time in constituency services. See Jewell, 'Representative Process', p. 111.

34 See for instance Wahlke, Eulau, Buchanan, and Ferguson, *The Legislative System*, chapter 15; Frank J. Sorauf, *Party and Representation* (New York: Atherton Press, 1963); Haruhiro Fuku, *Party in Power* (Berkeley: University of California Press, 1970); Giuseppe DiPalma, *Surviving without Governing: The Italian Parties in Parliament* (Berkeley: University of California Press, 1977); Aage Clausen and Soren Holmberg, 'Legislative Voting Analysis in Disciplined Multi-Party Systems: The Swedish Case', in William O. Aydelotte (ed.), *The History of Parliamentary Behavior* (Princeton: Princeton University Press, 1977).

35 See for instance Wahlke, Eulau, Buchanan, and Ferguson, *The Legislative System*, chapter 14; Malcolm E. Jewell, 'Representative Process', p. 107; Malcolm E. Jewell and Samuel C. Patterson, *The Legislative Process in the United States*, 3rd edn. (New York: Random House Inc., 1973), chapter 16.

36 See Charles G. Bell and Charles M. Price, *The First Term: A Study of Legislative Socialization* (Beverly Hills, CA: Sage Publications, 1975). A good summary of studies is provided in Jewell and Loewenberg, *The Legislative Process in the United States*.

37 S. E. Franzich, *A Comparative Study of Legislative Roles and Behavior*, Ph.D. dissertation, University of Minneapolis, 1971.

38 R. M. Brown, 'Indian State Legislative Behavior: The Uttar Pradesh Legislative Assembly, 1952–1968', Ph.D. dissertation, The American University, Washington, DC, 1971.

39 R. D. Morey, 'Representational Role Perceptions in the Japanese Diet: The Wahlke-Eulau Framework Reexamined', Prepared for delivery at the Annual Meeting of the American Political Science Association, Chicago, Illinois, 1971.

40 Chong, Barkan, Turan, and Jewell, *The Legislative Connection*.

41 See Wahlke, Eulau, Buchanan, and Ferguson, *The Legislative System*, chapter 12; Frank J. Sorauf, *Party and Representation* (New York: Atherton Press, 1963); Robert S. Friedman and Sybil L. Stokes, 'The Role of the Constitution-Maker as Representative', *Midwest Journal of Political Science*, 9 (1965): 413–17; Allan Kornberg, *Canadian Legislative Behavior* (New York: Holt, Rinehart, Winston, 1967); Kenneth Prewitt, Heinz Eulau, and Betty H. Sisk, 'Political Socialization and Political Roles', *Public Opinion Quarterly*, 30 (1966–7): 569–82.

42 Wahlke, Eulau, Buchanan, and Ferguson, *The Legislative System*, p. 280.

43 Most research on legislative roles has simply classified legislators according to their role orientations. Few efforts have been made to identify variables that may explain role orientations, let alone behavioural consequences of role orientations. See Jewell, 'Representative Process', p. 104.

44 Data from 1993 interviews which actually revealed that 31 per cent of the directly elected members and 33 per cent of the functional constituency members adhere to the inventor role.

45 The 1993 data revealed that 52 per cent of Legislative Council members (and 87 per cent of directly elected members) agreed; 1988 and 1993 compiled data revealed that 72 per cent of the officials disagreed, with only 28 per cent agreeing.

46 Particularly with the demise of the position of senior unofficial. See Chapter 6 for details.

47 It should be noted that there are some disparities between individual roles and the role of the Legislative Council. For instance, while most elected members evidenced their orientation towards representational activities, particularly the directly elected members (27 per cent), the majority of elected members interpreted the Legislative Council's role in terms of policy making rather than representation. It would appear that many elected members are concerned with representation, but they perceive that this can be fulfilled through the policy-making function.

48 This may appear inconsistent with the original coding of responses which depicted more functional constituency members had a purposive role of Inventor (in 1993, 33 per cent of the functional constituency members versus 31 per cent of the directly elected members). Yet when subjected to more direct questioning, it was clear that directly elected members were much more supportive of an active policy-making role for the legislature than were their functional constituency counterparts.

49 Norms relate to the shared side of group members about how the membership should, ought, or is expected to behave. See George C. Homans, *Social Behavior: Its Elementary Forms* (New York: Harcourt Brace and World), p. 123.

50 Previous research has found that the rules of the game exist in all legislative institutions: 'No study, regardless of the cultural setting or the unit of government, failed to identify rules of the game.' Ronald D. Hedlund, 'Organizational Attributes of Legislative Institutions: Structure, Rule, Norms, Resources', in Loewenberg, Patterson, and Jewell, *Handbook of Legislative Research* , p. 336.

51 Barbara Hinckley, *Stability and Change in Congress*, 2nd edn. (New York: Harper & Row, 1978).

52 Wahlke, Eulau, Buchanan, and Ferguson, *The Legislative System*, pp. 155–65.

53 See Chapter 6 for discussion of the development of new committees and the refinement of regulations guiding legislative activity.

Notes to Chapter 8

1 R. Coupland, ed., *The Durham Report, An abridged version with an introduction and notes* (Oxford: Oxford University Press, 1945), vol. 2, p. 73.

2 But this is not to imply that Hong Kong's prosperity came about because of a conservative, undemocratic Legislative Council, but that the Legislative Council's role was minimal if not irrelevant in this development.

3 While there were parliamentary settings for the Joint Declaration and Basic Law, these were in the context of China's National People's Congress and Britain's Parliament.

4 Because most Legislative Council members have served fewer than two terms and are just beginning to develop their legislative orientations, it is important to emphasize that investigation of Legislative Council members' roles is exploratory rather than definitive.

5 This consensus will be particularly important as the Basic Law limits legislative power by requiring that motions, bills, or amendments to government bills introduced by members require a majority vote of each membership type in the legislature. This restriction is found in Annex II of the Basic Law.

6 As of this writing, 12 of the 18 directly elected members members belong to the liberal United Democrats; of the largest block of partisan functional constituency members, as of 1993, 8 of the 21 functional constituency members belong to the conservative Liberal Party.

7 The interviews witnessed, however, some inconsistencies. Although functional constituency members had the highest percentage of Inventors, direct questions about the role of the legislature itself, as well as forced choice questions regarding the role of the legislature vis-à-vis the executive branch, revealed that functional constituency members were less inclined to support Legislative Council policy-making activities than were the directly elected members.

8 Emphasis on policy formulation can only occur through an amendment to the Basic Law or the institution of a ministerial system in which members of the legislature are given policy portfolios. The recommendation for greater emphasis on oversight is made under the assumption that neither of these developments will occur.

9 Executive and legislative relations are further exacerbated by the disinclination of the members to perform a legitimizing role for government. As one directly elected member noted in an interview, 'No one wants to support the government now—not even the conservatives. You don't want to be stigmatized as a "loyalist" to a group of people who will soon no longer be in power.' This oppositional stance may be heightened with the Chinese-appointed Chief Executive in the future.

10 Total from combined 1988 and 1993 surveys.

11 Although some liberals argue that in their eagerness to please China, the conservatives are co-opted rather than simply cooperative.

12 For a more balanced discussion of this issue, see Flora Lewis, 'China, the Next Superpower? Where the Giant Stands', *International Herald Tribune*, 21 May 1993. China has already been ranked, by the International Monetary Fund, as the world's third-biggest economy. See 'Beijing Dispute IMF's Economy Ranking', *International Herald Tribune*, 25 May 1993. Additionally, 'Greater China', consisting of China, Taiwan, and Hong Kong, is becoming 'the fourth growth pole of the global economy', according to a recent World Bank report. See 'The Next Economic Giant? Watch "Greater China"', *International Herald Tribune*, 27 April 1993.

13 This has led some to suggest that the anti-centrifugal forces could lead to

a breakup of the nation. See report entitled 'Strategic Survey 1992–93', by the International Institute for Strategic Studies. A summary appeared in 'China growth could force breakup', *The Japan Times*, 21 May 1993.

14 Dick Wilson, 'The future mat for China's open door', *South China Morning Post*, 7 October 1984.

15 On a recently compiled scale of 'economic freedoms' of the world's major economies, Hong Kong rated at the top of the list (at 95.6 per cent) and China at the bottom (13.1 per cent). Simon Ogus, 'How to Add to the Wealth of Nations', *The Asian Wall Street Journal*, 8 June 1992.

16 The Hong Kong and Chinese economies, including that of Guangdong province, are becoming increasingly intertwined. More than 60 per cent of China's trade passes through the port of Hong Kong, and it holds half of its foreign reserves in the territory. Further, China now controls companies listed on the Hong Kong Stock Exchange with an aggregate market value of nearly HK$70 billion; it also owns at least 3 per cent of the territory's property market, estimated at HK$50 billion. On the other side, Hong Kong's investment in Guangdong is considerable. Hong Kong businessmen employ three million persons in Guangdong, and their investment has done much to fuel the expansion in the Chinese economy. See Simon Holberton, 'A revealing tale of three cities', *Financial Times*, 4 May 1993, section 3, p. 1. See also, Yun-Wing Sung, 'The Economic Integration of Hong Kong with China in the 1990s: The Impact on Hong Kong,' Research Paper No. 1 (Toronto: Joint Centre for Asia Pacific Studies, 1992), pp. 7–35.

17 See comments of Goh Chok Tong, Prime Minister of Singapore, who gave the keynote address, 'Geo-Politics in Asia', before the Asia Society conference in Tokyo, 13 May 1993.

18 Holberton, 'A revealing tale'.

19 Ian Scott, 'The Political Transformation of Hong Kong: From Colony to Colony,' in Aluin So and Reg Kwok, eds., *The Hong Kong–Guangdong Nexus* (forthcoming).

20 See remarks of Winston Lord, former United States Ambassador to China and current Assistant Secretary of State for East Asian and Pacific Affairs, as quoted in 'Why it is China's crisis and not the Governor's', *South China Morning Post*, 14 December 1992.

21 Lord, quoted in 'Why it is China's crisis', p. 5.

22 The conspiracy theory was given wide coverage particularly when it was detailed by Singapore's senior statesman Lee Kuan Yew in a December 1992 television interview. See 'Patten "just lead actor" in a pre-written plot: Lee Kuan Yew', *Window*, 25 December 1993.

23 Comments of Singapore Minister Lee Kuan Yew, 'Hongkong is China's battleground—Lee', *South China Morning Post*, 16 December 1992.

24 'Conspiracy theory gains credibility', *South China Morning Post*, 17 December 1992.

25 This point is made with great clarity by Gerald Segal, 'The Struggle Over Hong Kong Is about China Itself', *International Herald Tribune*, 8 December 1992. The internationalizing of the issue has particularly occurred in America, where in 1990 immigration laws were changed to allow for more Hong Kong immigrants. In 1992 a U.S.–Hong Kong Policy Act reaffirmed the promises in the Joint Declaration and provided for America to treat Hong Kong as a non-sovereign entity distinct from China. For further details, see William McGurn, *Perfidious Albion: The Abandonment of Hong Kong 1997* (Washington, DC: Ethics and Public Policy Center, 1992), pp. 119–27.

26 McGurn, *Perfidious Albion,* and editorial, 'Hong Kong Needs Clinton', *International Herald Tribune*, 23 December 1992.

27 China warned that playing the 'international card' would fail. See 'Patten

"playing" international card', *Hong Kong Standard*, 14 December 1992.

28 It is important to emphasize that Patten's proposals would not bring democracy to Hong Kong. Under both the Joint Declaration and the Basic Law, the Chief Executive of the Hong Kong special administrative region will not be democratically elected. The proposals focus on democratizing the legislature.

29 See a similar viewpoint expressed by former Urban Councillor Walter Sulke in 'Our chance to take charge of Hongkong's destiny', *Hong Kong Standard*, 15 January 1993. Also, some argue that Hong Kong's 'subjugation' to China has occurred since 1984, particularly in promotion of 'convergence'. See Chapter 4 for details. Also see argument presented by Ross Munro, 'Who lost Hong Kong?' *Commentary* (December 1990): 33–8.

30 This view is developed in 'Patten plays St George', *The Economist*, 20 March 1993, pp. 29–30.

31 See interview with Governor Patten, 'Putting up the Panes of Glass', *Time*, 14 March 1994, p. 20.

32 'Patten plays St George', p. 30.

33 Gerald Segal, 'The Struggle Over Hong Kong Is About China Itself.'

34 'Trying times ahead', editorial, *South China Morning Post*, 25 January 1993.

35 Kevin J. O'Brien, *Reform without Liberalization: China's National People's Congress and the Politics of Institutional Change* (Cambridge: Cambridge University Press, 1990). O'Brien notes this rubber stamp role for the Chinese legislature occurring from 1978 to 1989, when it was found that 'institutionalized legislative legitimacy was designed to supplement legitimacy based on performance and ideology'. See p. 173.

36 Spokesman from Xinhua news agency, Beijing's *de facto* embassy in Hong Kong. See 'China hits Hong Kong body for backing Patten', *Japan Times*, 13 November 1992.

37 This point made in 'Patten plays St George', *The Economist*, 20 March 1993, pp. 29–30.

38 Bowring, 'Why the Patten Revolution has Beijing Up in Arms.'

39 Particularly when the Governor argued in his October speech that 'democracy provides a well-tried system for a mature and sophisticated people to have a say in how their community is run.' See Chapter 4 for more details.

40 Additionally for Locke an emphasis on the importance, if not the superiority, of the legislature in the governmental structure.

41 Arguments along these lines are identified by George Hicks, 'Hong Kong should seize a democracy opportunity', *International Herald Tribune*, 30 October 1992.

42 Democracy is a term which connotes a multitude of often confusing meanings. Hence, to evaluate democracy in Asia in general, and its prospects in Hong Kong in particular, it is necessary to define its genesis. Schumpter, in his book *Capitalism, Socialism and Democracy,* provides the most useful definition by stating that it relates to how those in power are selected and given the power to rule. Rulers in non-democratic countries claim power based on birth, appointment, examination, wealth, or coercion. By contrast, in democracies, rulers are selected through voting under fair, honest, periodic elections in which there is a choice amongst candidates and in which virtually all of the adult population can participate. In this context, elections are the essence of democracy. A second component of democracy involves the ability to exert influence and demand accountability upon those who are elected to govern. This is often accomplished through periodic elections; in addition, executive branch accountability is enhanced by the checking of its activities by a legislature.

43 India and Pakistan have been governed by democratic practices and institutions since 1947, Indonesia since 1949, Japan since 1952, Malaysia since 1957, and

Singapore since 1965.

44 See Samuel Huntington, *Political Order in Changing Societies* (New Haven: Yale University Press, 1968).

45 Democracy has been categorized as a Western phenomenon until recently, going through three waves of development. See Samuel P. Huntington, *The Third Wave: Democratization in the Late Twentieth Century* (Norman: University of Oklahoma Press, 1991). During this last period of development many Asian countries have become classified as democracies, including Japan, South Korea, the Philippines, India, Singapore, Malaysia, Pakistan, Thailand, Indonesia, Taiwan, and South Korea.

46 Samuel Huntington, 'Democracy: Its Evolution and Implementation', paper presented to the Asia Society conference, Asian and American Perspectives on Capitalism and Democracy, Singapore, 28–30 January 1993. Huntington adds that with respect to most Asian countries 'virtually no tradition of human rights against the state exists. . . . [T]o the extent that individual rights are recognized, they are viewed as rights created by the state. Harmony and cooperation are preferred over disagreement and competition. The maintenance of order and respect for hierarchy are viewed as central values.'

47 Comment by Singapore's Lee Kuan Yew, in 'Who Needs Democracy', *Newsweek*, 22 November 1993, p. 25.

48 Huntington, 'Democracy: Its Evolution and Implementation'.

49 For further elaboration, see Chan Heng Chee, 'Asian and American Perspectives on Capitalism and Democracy', paper presented to the Asia Society's conference, Asian and American perspectives on Capitalism and Democracy, Singapore, 28–30 January 1993.

50 See Gerald Segal, 'The Struggle Over Hong Kong Is about China Itself', *International Herald Tribune*, 8 December 1992.

51 Richard Baum, ed., *Reform and Reaction in Post-Mao China* (New York: Routledge, 1991).

52 See Andrew J. Nathan, *Chinese Democracy* (Berkeley: University of California Press, 1985); also Jia Qing-Guo, 'The Dilemma of Power: The Choice of the People's Republic of China', in J. Barton Staff (ed.), *The United States Constitution: Its Birth, Growth and Influence in Asia* (Hong Kong: Hong Kong University Press, 1988), pp. 201–16.

53 'As communist ideology withers away in the consciousness of the Chinese people and leadership, and the economy becomes more complex, a looser and more differentiated political system may well develop. ' See Baum, *Reform and Reaction*, p. 4.

54 George Hicks, 'For Hong Kong There Is No Return to Square One', *International Herald Tribune*, 3 December 1992.

55 See statement of Baroness Lydia Dunn before the House of Lords, 10 December 1992. She lamented that 'history and politics deny us the control over our own destiny for which we are so amply qualified'. Her speech was reviewed in 'Hongkong pays price for dispute it did not create', *South China Morning Post*, 10 December 1992.

56 Statement of Martin Lee, leader of the United Democrats, who won 12 of the 18 seats in the 1991 election. See his comments in 'Hong Kong winners demand freer rein', *Japan Times*, 17 September 1992. The conservatives' response to the electoral return has been to form a political party which also advocates a democratic government. In a statement of the party's platform, the chairman, Mr Allen Lee, noted they 'try to enhance liberty and advance [Hong Kong's] democracy to suit its circumstances.' See 'Why we are the true liberals of Hongkong', *South China Morning Post*, 4 April 1993.

57 Martin Lee notes that legislators will either have to 'shut up or shout

about' people's rights. See 'Fighter for A Paper Door', *Time*, 27 May 1991, p. 21.

58 See plea of Margaret Ng, 'Lee would have Hongkong on its knees before Beijing', *South China Morning Post*, 22 December 1992.

59 Philip Bowring, 'Follow the politics of the poisoned shrimp', *South China Morning Post*, 14 October 1992.

60 'China "doesn't know how Hongkong ticks"', *South China Morning Post*, 11 August 1985.

61 Already it is developing some political characteristics which are distinct from its neighbors; witness the rise of two strong, and several weaker, political parties.

62 Citi Hung Ching-Tin, 'Great communicator must talk', *South China Morning Post*, 17 January 1993.

63 Article 68 of the Basic Law notes that 'the ultimate aim is the election of all members of the Legislative Council by universal suffrage'. Annex II provides for the electoral format of the first three terms (up to the year 2007); the third term provides for 30 directly elected and 30 functionally elected members.

64 Comments of Mr Martin Lee, 'What I would have said to Lu Ping . . .', *South China Morning Post*, 12 January 1992.

65 See Brett Free, 'Mood of depression signals a ragged retreat from stability', *Hong Kong Standard*, 24 December 1992.

Notes to the Epilogue

1 See Charles S. Maier, 'Democracy and Its Discontents', *Foreign Affairs* 73, 4, July/August 1994: 48–64.

2 See Kishore Mahbubani, 'The Dangers of Decadence: What the Rest Can Teach the West', *Foreign Affairs*, 72, 5, November/December 1993: 10–14. See also Fareed Zakaria, 'A Conversation with Lee Kuan Yew', *Foreign Affairs*, 73, 2, March/April 1994: 109–126.

3 Samuel P. Huntington, 'The Clash of Civilizations?', *Foreign Affairs*, 72, 2, Summer 1993: 22–49. Huntington argues that the fundamental source of conflict in the post-cold war world is neither ideological or economic, but rather cultural, with cleavages amongst the eight major civilizations of the world.

4 See Kim Dae Jung, 'Is Culture Destiny? The Myths of Asia's Anti-Democratic Values', *Foreign Affairs*, 73, 6, November/December 1994: 189–194.

5 See 'Democracy Works Best', *The Economist*, 27 August 1994: 9.

6 See Edward Neilan, 'Democracy on a Winning Streak in Asia', *The Japan Times*, 25 November, 1994.

7 'Asian Values', *The Economist*, 38 May 1994: 9.

8 A concept given most prominence in Singapore and Malaysia where Western soft-headedness is derided, and the undemocratic Asian alternative is celebrated. See 'Year in Review '94, Free Trade: Key Asian Value', *Far Eastern Economic Review*, 29 December 1994: 26–32.

9 See, for instance, 'Slippery Succession,' *Far Eastern Economic Review*, 4 August 1994: 22–23.

10 The succession crisis in China was seen as frustrating the resolution of many of the remaining political issues in Hong Kong, particularly those relating to future autonomy. See 'Year in Review '94, Free Trade: Key Asian Value, *Far Eastern Economic Review*, 29 December 1994: 26–32.

11 Comments by Allen Lee, leader of the Liberal Party, as quoted in 'Legco's

Bumpy Sitting', *Hong Kong Standard*, 10 July 1994.

12 The Financial Secretary noted that 420,000 workers would not pay any tax and that 1.1 million workers would see a reduction in their tax bills this fiscal year. He also predicted that the territory's fiscal reserves would reach $120 billion by 31 March 1997. See 'Officials Blitzed on Estimates', *South China Morning Post*, 9 March 1994.

13 In this instance, the amendment passed the second reading of the bill but was defeated by one vote in the third reading when absent legislators returned to the chamber. Government officials joined in defeating the amendment. See 'Liberals, UDHK in Battle over Bill', *South China Morning Post*, 7 July 1994.

14 The government attempted to forestall the bill by changing the administrative code to guide civil servants in determining what information should be made public, with a further provision that the Commissioner for Administrative Complaints be given enforcement powers over the code. Yet sponsors of the legislation remained dissatisfied, believing that the power of law rather than administrative guidelines was necessary to allow public access to information in the future. See Simon Ip, 'British Should Understand that Taxation Means Representation' *Hong Kong Standard*, 4 June 1994. None the less, it is expected that the bill, sponsored by appointed member Christine Loh, will be introduced as a private member's bill during the 1994–95 session.

15 The Equal Opportunities legislation was drafted by Anna Wu, an experienced lawyer, who was assisted by two law lecturers at the University of Hong Kong, and a barrister who translated the provisions into Chinese. The Access to Information legislation was drafted by a different law lecturer at the University of Hong Kong. Notably, both were drafted without the help of the Legal Unit, as their present duties do not include the drafting of legislation offered by legislators. This points to a deficiency which needs to be addressed in the future to enable the legislature to assume a more active policy-making role.

16 It is significant to note that the Equal Opportunities Bill was offered by an appointed rather than an elected member. This member, Patten-appointee Anna Wu, noted that she was able to offer such comprehensive legislation because she had more time than her elected colleagues, whose time was taken up attending to constituency matters. See her comments in 'Legislators Take Law into Their Own Hands', *South China Morning Post*, 15 April 1994. While this example would seem to contradict the findings in Chapters 6 and 7—namely that elected rather than appointed members were more active in policy-making activities—it could be argued that Anna Wu is an exception to the more passive policy-making orientation of most appointed members.

17 Words of appointed member Anna Wu, quoted in 'Legislators Take Law into Their Own Hands', *South China Morning Post*, 15 April 1994. The administration replied that the growing use of private member's bills was undermining their legislative programme. See comments of Chief Secretary Anson Chan Fang On-sang in 'Legislators Warned off Private Bills', *South China Morning Post*, 9 July 1994.

18 According to the subsequent British White Paper released after the talks broke down, the British decided to break off discussions when China reneged on an agreement to abolish appointed seats to the district and municipal bodies. In late October, 1993, China stated that it would restore appointed membership after 1997, regardless of the views of the new SAR government. See 'About-Face Led to Breakdown', *South China Morning Post*, 25 February 1994: 9. China, however, countered that it was the British insistence that the 'single-seat, single-vote' system be part of an interim agreement which led to the breakdown of the talks.

19 The Chinese preferred the 'multi-seat, single vote' method in which pro-China candidates would stand a better chance of getting elected.

20 Patten had proposed that for the twenty-one existing functional constituen-

cies, all forms of corporate voting should be replaced with voting by individuals, in order to make the elections more open and fair, and less liable to be tainted by corruption. For the nine new functional constituencies, the Governor had proposed to define them in a way which would include the entire working population. The Chinese wanted the composition and voting method for the existing twenty-one constituencies to remain the same (with the retention of corporate voting) and proposed that the nine new functional constituencies be given to the Hong Kong Chinese Enterprises Association; an extra seat for the Labour Functional Constituency; seats for agriculture and fisheries; textiles and garments; Importers and Exporters Association; Kai Fong Welfare Associations; insurance; maritime; and sports. These would add about 20,000 votes to the existing functional franchise of 110,000.

21 Although the size of the Committee was to be about 600 people, not 800 as stipulated in Annex 1.

22 Britain charged that China's ambiguous language concerning the determination of anti-Government activities left it unclear if the rules would be applied retrospectively. See 'Importance of Through-Train Largely Ignored', *South China Morning Post*, 25 February 1994: 8.

23 Britain noted that the ambiguity of tense for the clause on anti-government activities made it fear that these rules would be applied retroactively. China's requirements for determining if legislators were sufficiently loyal included the stipulations that they would have to love Hong Kong and China; that they would not oppose the Basic Law; that they would not participate in activities aimed at overthrowing Chinese rule; and that they would not undermine China's socialist system. The Chinese also stipulated that the legislators should be dedicated to bringing a smooth transition and transfer of power while upholding the resumption of Chinese sovereignty over Hong Kong. Also essential was full support of the principle of 'one country, two systems'. While the British negotiators noted that these points were already covered in the Basic Law, their adamance that these criteria be forward-looking rather than based on past political views or actions was never given sufficient assurance.

24 Term from article of that title in the *Far Eastern Economic Review*, 10 March 1994.

25 Governor Patten retorted that to some Chinese officials, sincerity means that 'everybody else in the world must agree with us, otherwise they're not sincere'. See 'Patten Gazettes Democracy Plan', the *Japan Times*, 11 December 1993, p. 4.

26 The bill was titled 'Electoral Provisions (Miscellaneous Amendments)'. In addition, the legislation prohibited local members of the Chinese National People's Congress from standing for election for the local legislature.

27 Comments by Mark Hughes in his article 'Elsie's Star Act Earns Brickbats and Bouquets,' *South China Morning Post*, 24 February 1994: 1.

28 At the age of 80, Mrs Tu is one of Hong Kong's longest battling pro-democracy advocates. But she believed that reconciliation with China at this time was of paramount importance to the future stability of Hong Kong. For analysis, see 'Elsie's Star Act Earns Brickbats and Bouquets,' *South China Morning Post*, 24 February 1994: 1.

29 Remarks of directly elected members Martin Lee and Emily Lau respectively. See 'Reform Debate Focus on Tu,' *South China Morning Post*, 24 February 1994: 6.

30 See her comments in unbound *Hansard*, 23 February 1994, pp. 71–2.

31 Remarks of Dr Leong Che-Hung, unbound *Hansard*, 23 February 1994, p. 85.

32 Remarks of Mr Jimmy McGregor, unbound *Hansard*, 23 February 1994, p. 68.

33 Supporters of her motion included the fifteen conservative appointed and

functional members of the new Liberal Party and seven pro-China legislators and independents. It was ironic that supporters of her motion were typically those who had opposed her many pro-democracy actions of the past, namely, conservative businessmen.

34 Appointed legislator Eric Li sought to restore appointed seats to the district and municipal boards; his action was supported by only eight members, with forty-one members opposed. Appointed member Allen Lee moved to delay action on the 'single-seat, single-vote' electoral system, but this motion, after an additional three hours of debate, was rejected by 35 to 15. A third motion was offered by directly elected member Martin Lee to scrap the ex-officio seats given to rural leaders on the Regional Council and District boards; and was defeated by the combined forces of the conservative appointed and elected members, as well as official members. A final motion, offered by directly elected member Andrew Wong, to correct some technical details of the bill was approved by voice vote.

35 With two abstentions.

36 If the Liberal Party initiative had succeeded, the legislature would have given the Chinese a package more acceptable than the British were willing to give them during negotiations. Additionally, if a later initiative for a fully directly elected legislature in 1995 passed, the Governor would have been in the uncomfortable position of possibly vetoing a measure which was more democratic than his initiatives. If either would have passed, the Chinese would have had to acknowledge that the legislature was not merely a tool of the Governor. Therefore for the British, Hong Kong and Chinese governments, the passage by the legislature of the original Patten proposals presented the ideal alternative. See Frank Ching, 'Patten Reforms Prevail' *Far Eastern Economic Review*, 21 July 1994.

37 Emily Lau originally wanted her initiative to come in the form of an amendment, but this manoeuvre was denied by the President of the Council.

38 Margaret Ng, 'Don't Waste Chances Offered by Reforms', *South China Morning Post*, 5 July 1994.

39 Simon Holberston writing in the *Financial Times* under the title 'Two Stones in China's Path' as reproduced in the *Japan Times*, 27 February 1994: 17.

40 See 'Legco Stands Up,' *Asian Wall Street Journal*, 25 February 1994: 10.

41 See 'Patten's Sidestep,' *Far Eastern Economic Review*, 13 October 1993: 13.

42 Margaret Ng, 'Patten Unrepentant,' *South China Morning Post*, 9 July 1994.

43 Margaret Ng, 'Patten Unrepentant,' *South China Morning Post*, 9 July 1994.

44 Hong Kong legislators later raised additional pertinent issues—the reluctance of Britain to endorse a human rights commission for Hong Kong and its refusal to grant full British citizenship to 3.5 million Hong Kong nationals. See 'Hurd Fails to Allay Hong Kong Lawmakers' Fears,' *International Herald Tribune*, 17–18 September 1994.

45 One commentator charges that the 'betrayal' started even earlier—even before the Sino-British Declaration had been endorsed. See Frank Ching, 'The Betrayal of Hong Kong,' *The Far Eastern Economic Review*, 19 May 1994.

46 See comments of directly elected member Szeto Wah in 'Hong Kong Lawmakers Accuse London, Beijing of Betrayal,' the *Japan Times*, 7 May 1994: 4. The main complaints against China were that it was interferring with Hong Kong's promised freedoms by resisting Patten's reforms; that it was trying to weaken the powers of the Court of Final Appeal which would oversee the future legal system; and that it had already established a 'shadow government' in the territory. The British in turn were accused of acquiescing in these moves.

47 Patten based his decision on the Royal Instructions stricture which disallows any move by unofficials to offer legislation imposing a charge on the territory's revenues. The rejected amendment would have reduced the revenues by not allowing an increase in tax rates to go into effect.

48 This was, of course, the cry of American colonists on the eve of their Indep-

endence from Great Britain. See similar conception by legislator Simon Ip in 'British Should Understand that Taxation Means Representation', *Hong Kong Standard*, 4 June 1994.

49 Motion was offered by directly elected member Szeto Wah. The vote, of 21 to 11, was along party lines, with most liberals supportive, and conservatives abstaining 'because the motion's wording is too strong'. See 'Crisis Looms over Censure of Governor,' *South China Morning Post*, 5 June 1994.

50 A similar conclusion was recently reached by Nihal Jayawickrama, a lecturer in law at the University of Hong Kong. See his comments in 'Legco, Governor Rows "Will Grow" ', *Eastern Express*, 15 June 1994.

51 See comments of legislator Elsie Tu in 'Legco Gets Set to Stand Alone', *South China Morning Post*, 31 March 1994.

52 See comments of legislator Emily Lau and Yeung Sum, 'Legco Gets Set to Stand Alone,' *South China Morning Post*, 31 March 1994.

53 See 'China Vows to Terminate All Hong Kong Councils', *International Herald Tribune*, 25 February 1994: 1. Even before the vote on the second part of the reform, a Chinese official stated that Hong Kong would dismantle the 1995 legislature in 1997 regardless of how the legislature voted on the reform—an action in total disregard not only of the Hong Kong government, but also the National People's Congress which issued a decision on 4 April 1990 about the first post-1997 legislature. See Frank Ching, 'The Betrayal of Hong Kong', *Far Eastern Economic Review*, 19 May 1994: 36.

54 China charged that the recently passed electoral reforms violated the Joint Declaration, the Basic Law and previous decisions by the National People's Congress. See 'China to Abolish Hong Kong's Legislature', *International Herald Tribune*, 1 September 1994: 1.

55 See 'Beijing Plans Colony Council', *International Herald Tribune*, 8 September 1994: 8. The *China Daily* noted that it would oversee major areas of policy, have the ability to write new bills before and after 1997 and declare invalid those believed to be counter to the Basic Law. It will also be given the power to nominate the chief justice of Hong Kong's Court of Final Appeal, as well as the chief judge of Hong Kong's High Court.

56 See Frank Ching, 'China Calls a Deer a Horse', *Far Eastern Economic Review*, 8 December 1994: 32. The main functions of this temporary legislature would be to establish electoral laws and make domestic laws consistent with the Basic Law. It will also exercise financial powers in the passing of budgets, as well as appointment power in the selection of judges.

57 For additional queries, see 'Derailed: Beijing Kills Hopes for Post-1997 Political "Through-Train" ', *Far Eastern Economic Review*, 22 September 1994: 36.

58 'Derailed: Beijing Kills Hopes for Post-1997 Political "Through-Train" ', *Far Eastern Economic Review*, 22 September 1994: 36.

59 Established 7 July 1993, the PWC is composed of 57 members, 30 of whom are from Hong Kong, all of whom were chosen by Beijing.

60 See 'China Derails the Through-Train Concept for Hong Kong', the *Japan Times*, 8 September 1994: 17. If China's views prevail, it will lead to the disenfranchisement of the 2.7 million workers voting in the new functional constituencies arrangement.

61 A poll taken by the Sing Pao showed that Hong Kong people continue to distrust China. See 'The *Next* Vote: Hong Kong is Up For Grabs,' *Far Eastern Economic Review*, 6 October 1994: 5.

62 These fears were aggravated with the announcement that China will not guarantee that the British-appointed judges on the Court of Final Appeal will be retained. See 'No Appeal: China Rules Against Hong Kong', *Far Eastern Economic Review*, 22 December 1994: 5.

Notes to the Appendix

1 David Easton, *A Framework for Political Analysis* (Englewood Cliffs, NJ: Prentice Hall, 1965), pp. 39–57; Talcott Parsons, *The Social System* (Glencoe, IL: The Free Press, 1951) pp. 25–40; Robert K. Merton, *Social Theory and Social Structure* (Glencoe, IL: The Free Press, 1957), chaps. 8 and 9; Gabriel A. Almond and G. Bingham Powell, Jr., *Comparative Politics: A Developmental Approach* (Boston: Little, Brown and Company, 1966), p. 21.

2 A person's role is a pattern of social behaviour which seems appropriate in terms of the demands and expectations of those in his group, has ingredients of cultural, personal, and situational determinants, but none of these alone is the whole determinant. See for instance, Neal Gross, Ward S. Mason, and Alexander W. McEachern, *Explorations in Role Analysis* (New York: John Wiley and Sons, 1958), p. 13ff.

3 For further information about the concept of institutionalization and stability, see Samuel P. Huntington, *Political Order in Changing Societies* (New Haven: Yale University Press, 1968).

4 John C. Wahlke, Heinz Eulau, William Buchanan, and LeRoy C. Ferguson, *The Legislative System: Explorations in Legislative Behavior* (New York: John Wiley and Sons, Inc., 1962).

5 Chong Lim Kim, Joel D. Barkan, Ilter Turan, and Malcolm E. Jewell, *The Legislative Connection: The Politics of Representation in Kenya, Korea, and Turkey* (Durham, NC: Duke University Press, 1984). This study was chosen as a model of replication as it is the most comprehensive study of developing legislatures. It was also believed that a broad base of comparative material would be available from investigating the study, as the three countries have many variations: located at different corners of the developing world (Africa, Middle East, and East Asia), with distinct cultures, histories, and political milieux.

Index

ADAMS, JOHN, 168–9

Ad hoc groups, 149, 217, 289 n14

Adjournment debates, 149, 154, 162, 167, 291 n33

Advisory Committees, *see* 'Consultation and Consensus', Ordinances

Amendments, 166

American Revolution, impact upon development of Legislative Council, 21–3, 229, 262 n30, n31

Alliance in Support of the Patriotic Democratic Movement in China, 94

Anglo-French War, 24

Appointed members of Legislative Council, 4; and Sino-British Negotiations of 1984, 65–7; and staff allowance, 132; and Young Plan, 58; conservative ideology, 178; contribution to the legislature, 226; distinctions from officials, 45; in Executive Council 27; interest group roles, 213–15, 298 n16; introduced in Hong Kong, 41–3; purposive roles, 186–94; relationship to Governor, 33–4, 223, 292 n55; representational roles, 196–211; role summary, 215; views towards direct elections to the legislature, 82; White Paper of 1988, 85

Appropriation Bill, *see* Ordinances

Arena, *see* Policy making

Assent, *see* Ordinances

Assessment Office, *see* Public opinion

Asian democracy, 236–7, 239, 241–2, 250

Attorney General, 149

Autonomy, 3, 185

BASIC LAW: drafts, 70, 86–97, 278 n112; drafting procedure, 86–7, 91–2, 281 n154; and future chief executive, 87–9, 90–1, 279 n121; and future legislature, 4, 87–91, 95–7, 182, 184–5, 280 n149; Legislative Council debates, 70–2, 89–90, 92, 95–7; *see also* Sino-British Agreement, Sino-British negotiations

Basic Law Consultative Committee, 87, 90–1, 94, 279 n115

Basic Law Drafting Committee, 86–7, 91, 94, 96, 258 n11

Bill of Rights, 94

Bills, 166, 243, 294 n77; *see also* Ordinances

Bills Committee, 148–9, 161–2, 181, 217, 289 n14

Black, Hugo, 249

Blake, Sir Henry, 53

Blischke, Werner, 114, 286, n19

Blondel, J., 8

Blue Book, 42, 267 n30

Bonham, Sir George, 41–2

Boundary and Election Commission, 105

Bowen, Sir George Ferguson, 47–8

Bowring, Sir John, 42–3, 47

Boynton, G.R., 8, 259 n31

British Dependent Territories passports, 94

British Empire, First, 17–21; Second, 24–34

British government; and founding of Hong Kong, 37–9; and early political reforms in Hong Kong, 41–3, 46, 49–52, 55, 63; and lease of New Territories, 52–4. 63–4, 269 n66; and nationality to Hong Kong citizens, 267 n45, 280 n147; and Young Plan, 58, 60; pre–1984 relations with China, 47, 53, 55, 60, 271 n104; Legislative Council rebuke, 246–7; *see also* Patten Proposals, Sino-British Agreement, Sino-British Negotiations